The Roman

A historical dictionar

The Romani World

A historical dictionary of the Gypsies

DONALD KENRICK

Research assistant: Clare Paul

UNIVERSITY OF HERTFORDSHIRE PRESS

This edition first published in Great Britain in 2004 by
University of Hertfordshire Press
Learning and Information Services
University of Hertfordshire
College Lane
Hatfield
Hertfordshire AL10 9AB

*This is a completely revised edition of Historical Dictionary of the Gypsies (Romanies)
published in 1998 by Scarecrow Press*

British Library Cataloguing in Publication Data
A catalogue record for this book is available from the British Library

ISBN 1-902806-26-3

Design by Geoff Green Book Design, CB4 5RA
Cover design by John Robertshaw, AL5 2JB
Printed in Great Britain by Antony Rowe Ltd, SN14 6LH

Contents

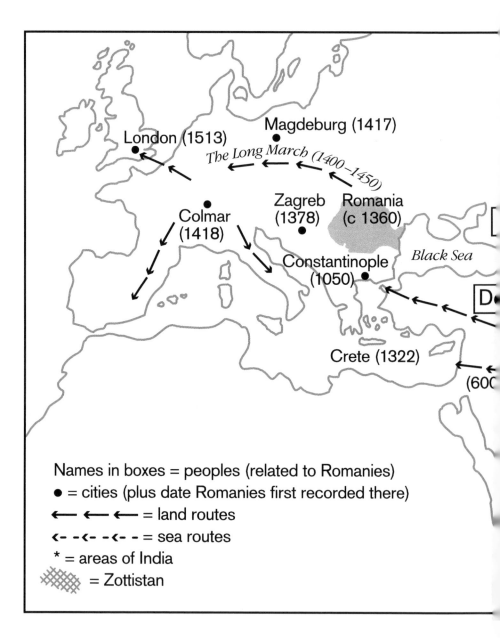

Magdeburg (1417)
●

London (1513)
●

The Long March (1400–1450)

Colmar
(1418)
●

Zagreb
(1378)
●

Romania
(c 1360)

Constantinople
(1050)
●

Black Sea

Crete (1322)

[D●

(600

Names in boxes = peoples (related to Romanies)
● = cities (plus date Romanies first recorded there)
← ← ← = land routes
<- -<- -<- - = sea routes
* = areas of India
▨▨▨ = Zottistan

The map shows, first, the areas in India from where the ancestors of the Romanies came – Punjab, Rajasthan and Sindh. From here many travelled along the coastal route into Iran where some then lived and worked in Baghdad. The Vaghri are a clan with a similar lifestyle who migrated south rather than west.

Others sailed as merchants or were taken by force by the Arabs across the sea to what is now southern Iraq, between the Tigris and the Euphrates. There they set up a short-lived republic (Zottistan) which was crushed by the new Arab rulers of the area who sent many of their captives to Khaneikin. From Arab-dominated Iran some

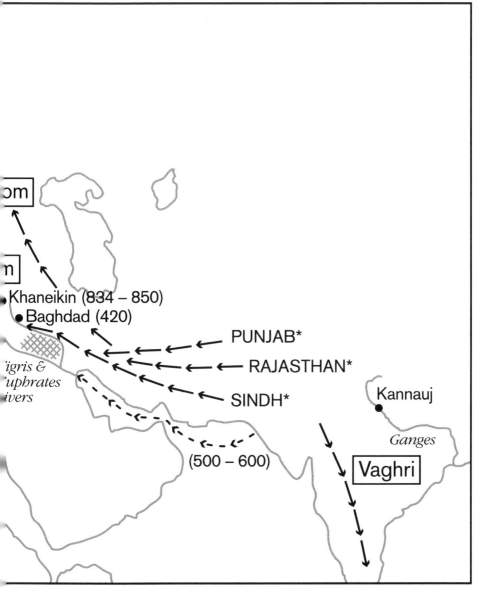

om

n

Khaneikin (834 – 850)
● Baghdad (420)

PUNJAB*

RAJASTHAN*

SINDH*

Tigris &
Euphrates
Rivers

(500 – 600)

Kannauj

Ganges

Vaghri

moved north to Armenia (the Lom) and others stayed in the Middle East (the Dom), while Khaneikin was perhaps the focal point for the Romanies to gather before moving on – to Byzantium and towards Constantinople.

After their arrival in Europe we find Romanies treated as slaves in Romania but a large company preferred to set off on the Long March to the west. The map shows two of the earliest towns they reached (Colmar and Magdeburg). There were forays into Italy and Spain while one adventurous family crossed the Channel from Calais to England.

Preface

This publication is designed to be a tool for all those working in civil rights, culture, education, immigration and politics who need more information concerning a name, date or event related to the past and current history of the Romani and other Gypsy people. But it will also be of interest to the general reader.

For reasons of space alone, this handbook cannot fulfil the role of a complete Who's Who, a discography or a directory of organisations, The Internet sites listed will be the best way to trace the current contact details for organisations. There are entries for those Gypsies who have become historically significant in their field, many of whom have excelled in music and entertainment and the representatives of international organisations. Regrettably few scientists appear, as professional people have often hidden their Gypsy origin. Conversely entertainers proclaim their Romani grandmother with enthusiasm.

This is not an encyclopaedia of Gypsy life. There are no entries for *bori* (daughter-in-law) or 'bellows', for instance, though these and many other potential keywords would shed an interesting light on the way of life of the Gypsies.

This was originally a volume in a series devoted to Europe. Additional entries have been added for several countries on the road the Romanies took from India to Europe. What I hope the reader will find is a concise, yet informative, companion that is accessible and promotes an understanding of the history of the Romani people and other Gypsy groups. Major organisations and museum resources have been listed as an entry into the subject for those who wish to go deeper. Finally, there is a small selection of the current addresses of the main journals and websites (at the end of the bibliography) to help readers get in touch with the vast network available to them.

As the Romani proverb says: 'It is easy to begin but hard to finish.' I welcome corrections and suggestions for inclusion in any future edition.

DONALD KENRICK

Acknowledgments

We have drawn heavily on the published literature and websites listed in the bibliography as well as on the knowledge of experts in different fields. The following have been particularly helpful. The final form of the entries remains, however, the responsibility of the author.

Alev Adil
Antonio Gómez Alfaro
Angus Fraser
Victor Friedman
Reimar Gilsenbach
Milena Hübschmannová
Valdemar Kalinin
Jakub Krcik
Bernard Leblon
Jean-Pierre Liégeois
Gunilla Lundgren
Elena Marushiakova and Veselin Popov
Michaela Mudure
Diana Tong
Etudes Tsiganes
European Race Audit
Folk Roots Magazine
Interface
Journal of the Gypsy Lore Society (now *Romani Studies*)
Lacio Drom
Romano Centro (Vienna)
Romnet
Rough Guide to World Music
Tocher
US Government Country Reports

Christopher Gwyn and Lucy Kaye have assisted in compiling the A–Z section.

Notes on Spelling and Terminology

For typographical reasons and the convenience of the general reader, Romani words cited are spelled in the Latin alphabet as commonly used. We have not employed the International Phonetic Alphabet nor that adopted by the fourth World Romani Congress. (See the entry ALPHABET).

č = *ch* pronounced as in *church*
š = *sh* as in *ship*
ž = *zh* as in *leisure*
x as in *loch* or German *doch*
rr (where it occurs, for example, in names of organisations, represents a guttural or retroflex *r* (as opposed to trilled or flapped *r*), depending on the dialect. (See the entry for RR).

It has regrettably not been possible to reproduce in one font all the accents used in personal names, periodicals and organisations in all the languages using the Latin alphabet. Cyrillic and Devenagari alphabets have been transcribed in accordance with common usage. Geographical names are generally spelt as in Philip's *World Atlas*.

Gypsy and *Traveller* have been capitalised and spelt thus—except in citations and book titles. This volume uses the spelling *Romani*, rather than *Romany*, for the Gypsy language and for the people (except when citing the name in use by an organisation). *Gypsy*, *Rom* and *Traveller* are used as explained in the relevant entries.

The definition of who is a Gypsy is much discussed. This dictionary includes as Gypsies those who are accepted as such by the community or who proclaim themselves to be Gypsies. A number of non-Gypsies whose life or works are relevant to Gypsy history have been included in the dictionary. They are identified by the headword for the entry being in italics.

The country first cited in personal entries is normally the place of birth as it was called at that time, e.g. Russia rather than USSR.

Cross-references in the text are in bold type. The terms *Gypsy*, *Rom* and *Romani* are, however, never printed in bold, nor are the various countries where they live.

Abbreviations and Acronyms

CDCC	Council for Cultural Co-operation
CDMG	European Committee on Migration
CIS	Commonwealth of Independent States (previously USSR)
CIT	Comité International Tzigane
CJPOA	Criminal Justice and Public Order Act
CLRAE	Congress of Local and Regional Authorities of Europe
CMERI	Centre Missionaire Evangelique Rom Internationale
CoE	Council of Europe
CPRSI	Contact Point on Roma and Sinti Issues
CRT	Centre de Recherches Tsiganes
CSCE	Conference on Security and Co-operation in Europe
ECRE	European Committee on Romani Emancipation
FCNM	Framework Convention for the Protection of National Minorities
GLS	Gypsy Lore Society
GT-ROMS	Groupe de Travail – See EUROPEAN ROMA FORUM
hCa	Helsinki Citizens Assembly
IRU	International Romani Union
JGLS	*Journal of the Gypsy Lore Society*
MBE	Medal of the British Empire
MG-S-ROM	Specialist Group on Roma, Gypsies and Travellers of the Council of Europe
MP	Member of Parliament
MRG	Minority rights group
NATT	National Association of Teachers of Travellers
NGO	Non-governmental organisation
ECOSOC	Economic and Social Council (of the United Nations)
ODIHR	Office for Democratic and Human Rights
OSCE	Organisation for Security and Co-operation in Europe
PER	Project on Ethnic Relations
ROI	Romani Civic Initiative
SS	*Schutzstaffel* (Storm Troopers)
STAG	Scottish Travellers' Action Group
STAG	Southwark Travellers' Action Group
T-LAST	Telephone Legal Advice Service for Travellers
UK	United Kingdom
UNESCO	United Nations Economic and Social Organisation
UNICEF	United Nations Children's Fund
UN	United Nations

UNHCR	United Nations High Commissioner for Refugees
US	United States of America
USSR	Union of Soviet Socialist Republics
WRC	World Romani Congress

Introduction

Describing the early history of the Gypsies is like putting together a jigsaw puzzle when some of the pieces are missing and parts of another puzzle have been put into the box. They suddenly appear in Europe speaking an Indian language yet there is no sure trace of their passage across the Middle East. But their language is the key to the route of their travels as they borrowed words from the various peoples they met as they journeyed west.

The Gypsies or Romanies are, in fact, an ethnic group who arrived in Europe around the fourteenth century. Scholars argue about when and how they left India but it is generally accepted that they emigrated from northern India sometime between the sixth and eleventh centuries, then crossed the Middle East and came into Europe. Some stayed in the Middle East and the Nawwar in particular are mentioned in the dictionary. Their language (closely related to European Romani) also belongs to the north Indian group alongside Hindi and Punjabi.

The word 'Gypsy' is an abbreviation of 'Egyptian', the name by which the Romani immigrants were first called in western Europe because it was believed they came from Egypt. The French word *gitan* and Spanish *gitano* come from this etymology. The German word *Zigeuner* and Slav *tsigan* or *cigan* have a different etymology. They come from the Greek word *athinganos*, meaning a 'heathen.' This term was originally used of a heretical sect in Byzantium and, because the Gypsies who arrived in Europe were not Christians, they were given the name of this sect.

The Gypsies' name for themselves is 'Rom' (with a plural 'Roma' in most dialects). This is generally considered to be cognate with the Indian word *dom,* whose original meaning was 'man.' Even groups (such as the Sinti) who do not call themselves Rom still preserve this word in their dialect in the sense of 'husband.'

Some six million Gypsies or Romanies live in Europe and they form a substantial minority in many countries. The vast majority have been settled for generations. Most still speak the Romani language. As the Romanies are an ethnic group and not a class, individuals pursue various professions; some are rich and others poor. It is only in western Europe that Gypsies are seen as a nomadic people and that the term 'Gypsy' is loosely used for nomadic Travellers who are not of Indian origin.

History

The ancestors of the Gypsies of Europe began to leave India from the sixth century AD onward. Some left voluntarily to serve the rich courts of the Persian and later Arab dynasties in the Middle East. Others were brought as captives. A third, smaller group, who were nomadic and found that their way back to India, had been cut off by conflict and instead moved westward.

The first Gypsy migration into Europe during the fourteenth and fifteenth centuries included farmworkers, blacksmiths and mercenary soldiers, as well as musicians, fortune-tellers and entertainers. They were generally welcome at first as an interesting diversion in the dull everyday life of that period. Soon, however, they attracted the antagonism of the three powers of the time: the state, the church and the guilds. The civil authorities wanted everyone to settle legally at a permanent address, to have a fixed name and to pay taxes. The church was worried about the heresy of fortune-telling, while the guilds did not like to see their prices undercut by these newcomers who worked at all hours of the day and night, with wives and children helping, trading from tents or carts.

Other factors also led to feelings of mistrust toward the newcomers. They were dark-skinned, itself a negative feature in Europe, and they were suspected in some countries of being spies for the Turks because they too had come from the east. Some problems were also caused by small groups of Gypsies who claimed – with some justification – to be Christians fleeing from Muslim invaders from Turkey and lived mainly by asking for alms.

It was not long before these feelings of antagonism and mistrust led to a reaction. As early as 1482 the assembly of the Holy Roman Empire passed laws to banish the Gypsies from its territory. Spain introduced similar legislation ten years later and other countries soon followed. The punishment for remaining was often death. There was some migration to Poland mirroring that of the Jews. The policy of expulsion failed in most cases, however, as the countries to which they were deported often returned them quietly over the borders. Only the Scandinavian countries and the Netherlands managed to efface all visible trace of Gypsies for over two centuries. Most governments finally had to try a new policy – enforced integration or assimilation.

In Spain in 1499 and in Hungary in 1758 new laws required Gypsies to settle down or leave the country. They had to become land workers or be apprenticed to learn a craft. But they also had to be assimilated into the native population. Everywhere laws forbade Gypsies to wear their distinctive colourful clothes, to speak their language, to marry other Gypsies or to ply their traditional trades. As a result of these policies, today large populations of long-settled Gypsies can be found in Spain and Hungary, while in Romania Gypsy land workers and craftspeople were reduced to a status below that of serfs, to virtual slavery.

The latter part of the nineteenth century saw a new migration westward as Romania released its Gypsies from bondage. Many thousands emigrated, some as far as America, Australia and South Africa. Well over a million Gypsies live in North and South America today, with the Kalderash clan forming the majority.

The nomadic Gypsies, however, have survived as a distinctive group until the present day. The reason for this was partly the inefficiency of local constabularies but also because the Gypsies developed as a fine art the practice of living on the border of two countries or districts and slipping over the border when the forces of law and order approached. Also, the nobility and large landowners throughout Europe protected the Gypsies. They encouraged semi-nomadic families to stay on their land and were able to employ the men as seasonal labourers. The women could serve in the house or sing and dance when guests came.

In the nineteenth and twentieth centuries in western Europe, Gypsies encountered problems finding stopping places. Camping on the side of the main roads was made difficult by laws such as the UK *Highways Act* of 1835. Large shanty-town settlements developed on wasteland, but then the authorities stepped in and evicted the families. Such incidents occurred in England, starting with the Epping Forest eviction of 1894 and continuing until the 1960s. In this way many families who would have settled down were forced back into nomadism.

Discriminatory laws (on language and dress) fell into abeyance, but laws against nomadism remained a threat in both western and eastern Europe, to those Gypsies practising traditional crafts. Studies from all over the world have shown that sedentary peoples have an inherent fear of the nomad, even when the latter performs useful services. The policy of banning nomadism without helping the nomads to settle proved a failure through-out Europe, and Gypsy nomadism continued unchecked until the Second World War.

The Holocaust

When the Nationalist Socialist Party came to power in Germany in 1933, the nomadic Gypsies were already subject to restrictions. But the Nazis regard-ed Gypsies as a race and made both nomads and sedentaries subject to the Nuremberg Laws of 1935. These forbade marriages between Gypsies and 'Aryan' Germans. Adolf Hitler's Germany saw the Gypsies as no less a danger to the purity of the German race than the Jews and set about their isolation and eventually their destruction.

This policy of exclusion was a contrast to the assimilationist policies practised in the past. Gypsies were now not allowed to practise music as a profession and boxers were similarly barred from competition. Next, Gypsy children were excluded from school. Camps were set up for nomads on the edge of towns. They were guarded and the inmates were not allowed to practise their traditional trades but were put into labour gangs. Even seden-tary Gypsies were removed from their houses and placed in these intern-ment camps.

In 1939 it was decided to send all the 30,000 Gypsies from Germany and Austria to Poland. In May 1940 the first steps in this programme were taken with the expulsion of over 3,000. The deportations were stopped largely because of a shortage of transport. In 1942 Heinrich Himmler (head of the SS) signed the so-called Auschwitz Decree, and in the following year some 10,000 German Gypsies were sent to Auschwitz. A sterilisation campaign was undertaken both within and outside the camps. The slave labour of the Gypsies was needed, for example, in the underground factories where the V1 and V2 rockets were made, but they were not to be permitted to reproduce.

In the occupied countries of eastern Europe, the Task Forces – *Einsatz-gruppen* – massacred Gypsies in the woods outside the towns where they lived. Then extermination camps were opened, the four largest being Belzec, Chelmno, Sobibor and Treblinka. Gypsies were brought to these camps – sometimes in their own caravans – and shot or gassed, alongside

Jews. It is estimated that between a quarter and a half million Gypsies were killed during the Nazi period.

After 1945

In the first years following the end of the Nazi domination of Europe, the Gypsy community was in disarray. The small educational and cultural organisations that had existed before l939 had been destroyed. The family structure was broken with the death of the older people – the guardians of tradition. While in the camps the Gypsies had been unable to keep up their customs – the *Romanía* – concerning the preparation of food and the washing of clothes. They solved the psychological problems this presented by not speaking about the time in the camps. Only a small number of Gypsies could read or write and so they could not tell their own story. But also they were unwilling to tell their stories to others, and few non-Gypsies were interested anyway. In the many books written describing the Nazi period and the persecution of the Jews, Gypsies usually appear as a footnote or an appendix.

It was hard for the Gypsies to come to terms with the Holocaust for a persecution on this scale had never occurred before. There had been executions of smaller numbers, but nothing like this. A group of survivors in Munich began collecting evidence of the Gypsy genocide but it was not until twenty years after the downfall of Hitler that Jewish writers such as Miriam Novitch, Ben Sijes and Sylvia Steinmetz made available to the public a documentation of the fate of the Gypsies under the Nazis. No global reparations were made and not many individuals received restitution. Eventually, those Gypsies who held German citizenship did receive compensation for their suffering. In recent years Swiss banks and other international funds have helped individual ageing survivors.

After 1945 in both eastern and western Europe, a return to nomadism was discouraged if not suppressed although many Yugoslav Romanies came west as migrant workers. In western Europe the supply of empty land for caravans had diminished. The increasing speed of motor traffic made living on the side of the road, whether in a horse-drawn wagon or a lorry-drawn caravan, too dangerous. Gypsies were largely seen as a social problem to be integrated into the wider community. A term often used was 'resettlement' although most of the nomads concerned had never been settled. Pressure from central governments to set up campsites was largely ignored by the local authorities, the Netherlands being an exception.

In the east they were one more minority likely to cause trouble to the monocultural states created by communism. Here, where several million Gypsies lived under totalitarian rule, they were not allowed to form organisations and their language was again suppressed. In most countries of eastern Europe, the Gypsy population was very large and policies were evolved to meet the challenge of this large unassimilated minority. In the case of the Soviet Union, Stalin had decided that the Gypsies had no land base and therefore could not be a nation and their earlier status as a nationality was abolished. Assimilated Gypsies were encouraged to change the 'nationality' in their passports to that of the majority and answer the census questions, for example, as Serbs or Russians. The few activists were sent into internal exile or imprisoned, such as the parliamentarian Shakir Pashov in Bulgaria.

In eastern Europe, too, the small numbers of nomads were forcibly prevented from travelling by laws and by measures such as shooting or confiscating their horses and removing the wheels from their caravans. Here and there, however, Gypsy national sentiment was still alive. In Czechoslovakia organisations were formed and began to demand their rights – a demand temporarily squashed after Soviet troops entered Prague in 1968.

In the west after the end of the Second World War, the communities were smaller in number and largely continued or returned to being nomadic. But it was in the west that the foundations of an international Gypsy organisation could be formed. The real beginning was the committee known as the Comité International Tzigane, set up in Paris by Vanko Rouda. This body organised the first World Romani Congress and since then further international congresses have been held by the International Romani Union. The fourth Congress in Warsaw in 1990 – as the political changes in eastern Europe began – saw the attendance for the first time of delegations or individuals from Romania, the Soviet Union and even Albania. The fifth Congress was held in Prague with considerable support from the Czech government and international organisations. The emergence of a rival organisation – the Romani National Congress – has, however, not helped the Gypsies to present a united front for their aspirations.

The idea of Romanestan, a homeland for the Gypsies, emerged in Poland in the 1930s, clearly influenced by the Zionist movement. Since 1945 this has not been seriously considered though many intellectuals are fostering the link with the 'Motherland' of India. Two festivals have been held in Chandigarh (Punjab) to which Gypsy intellectuals and musicians were invited from Europe. Some Gypsy writers have introduced Hindi and Sanskrit words into their poetry.

With the fall of the totalitarian regimes in eastern Europe came a new freedom to form organisations. The new opportunities for travel both from and to eastern Europe have enabled the holding of international Gypsy festivals such as those in Bratislava and Gorzow, in addition to formal conferences. Newspapers opened as fast as pavement cafés. The Gypsies who had never completely forgotten how to trade privately were the first to set up small businesses. Their ability to survive the changes better than their compatriots led to jealousy and an outbreak of anti-Gypsy violence in Poland. The road to capitalism was not as smooth as had been expected, and with no Jews to act as scapegoats, the population of eastern Europe in general turned to the Gypsies as the reason for their real or imagined troubles.

Freedom also meant freedom for right-wing racists to organise, and this movement was facilitated by a falling away of the control previously exercised by the police. As early as January 1990, a crowd of 700 Romanians and ethnic Hungarians attacked the Gypsy quarter in Turu Lung in Romania. Thirty-six of the forty-two houses belonging to Romanies were set on fire and destroyed. Two similar incidents took place that year in Romania, resulting in the death of four Gypsies. In September 1990, skinheads attacked Romani houses in Eger and Miskolc in Hungary. The following year saw a pogrom in Mlawa, Poland, where nine houses were destroyed, and in Bohemia (Czechoslovakia), a Gypsy was killed during an attack by skinheads on a Romani club. Between January 1990 and August 1991 eighty-eight racist attacks were reported in eastern Europe during which twenty Romanies were killed. Police have often stood by during these attacks and are sometimes themselves aggressive towards the Gypsies. In Rostock in eastern Germany, a refugee centre inhabited by Romanies (among others) was burned down by right-wing rioters. These attacks have continued to the present day, and a selection is listed under each country entry and in the chronology. It is estimated that more than 200 Romanies have been killed in racial incidents in eastern Europe.

In the former Czechoslovakia, Hungary, Macedonia and Romania, Gypsy political parties have stood in the elections, alone or alongside established parties and Romanies have been elected to Parliament partly by the votes of their own people. In Bulgaria 'ethnic' parties are theoretically banned while the surviving population in Poland is too small to have any political influence, though there are musical groups and cultural centres.

Many Romanies, particularly those from Poland and Romania, have sought asylum in the west since 1990 because of the harassment they are suffering but very few have been granted refugee status. At the end of 1996, the German government announced plans to repatriate 30,000 Gypsies to Romania from where they had fled to avoid the racist attacks during which many houses had been burned. Less has been heard about an earlier repatriation programme from Germany to the ex-Yugoslav republic of Macedonia while individual families have been less publicly returned from Britain and France.

The comparatively smaller Gypsy populations in most western countries saw a revival of national feeling as they came into contact with the Romani-speaking communities of the east. These had retained their traditions and under the new regimes found it easier to travel and to invite other Gypsies to their festivals and competitions. The Romani language is being revived in the west by the influx of immigrant and refugee families for whom it is still the dominant community language.

The European Union and the Council of Europe began to take an interest in the Gypsies by inviting their organisations to send representatives to meetings and passing resolutions calling on central governments to work towards improving the living conditions of Gypsies. The overall effect was that Gypsy people have been recognised by cross-national bodies as a minority in their own right and measures have been introduced, if not implemented, in most countries toward improving their situation. The pages of the Dictionary will reveal a plethora of meetings and ad hoc organisations that have been trying to exert pressure on national governments to ameliorate the living conditions of the Romanies of eastern Europe in particular. Nicolae Gheorghe – advisor to ODIHR – recently said, "There is a growing gap between an almost restless activism on the international stage and the situation on the ground where we are not seeing as much tangible progress as we would like."

The sedentary Gypsies of eastern Europe have quite different needs from the nomadic Gypsies of many western countries. The children of the former had not managed to acquire many new skills or paper qualifications as the years of compulsory education had often been spent in segregated schools or classes. They were the first to go in the new capitalist climate in the east when factories began to downsize and shed surplus labour. They have found it the hardest to obtain new jobs because of discrimination. The nomads of the west are self-employed and primarily seek secure stopping places for their caravans.

Several eastern European counties entered the European Union in May

2004. It would be hazardous to predict whether this will lead in the long run to a massive new migration to the west. It is noteworthy that the large Spanish Gypsy population has not felt any great desire to migrate – at least no farther than the south of France. Under Franco, they were treated as second-class citizens and the end of official discrimination merely brought a new unofficial discrimination. The Spanish Gypsies or *gitanos* are still at the bottom of the ladder for housing and jobs. Their children are not easily accepted into schools. However, even the accession of Spain to the European Union did not cause any noticeable new emigration of Gypsies from Spain.

In the west some young Gypsies are coming out of houses and taking to the caravan life again. In eastern Europe the Romani language is beginning to be taught in schools and intellectuals of Gypsy origin are finding their roots and reaffirming their identity. Writers have been, pessimistically or optimistically, predicting the disappearance of the Gypsies each generation since they came to Europe at the beginning of the second millennium, but they have survived as an ethnic group and will do so into the foreseeable future.

Chronology of Gypsy History

224–41	Persia. In the reign of Shah Ardashir, Gypsies first come from India to work.
420–438	Persia. Bahram Gur, shah of Persia, brings Gypsy musicians from India.
661	Arab Empire. Indians (*Zott*) brought from India to Mesopotamia.
669–70	Arab Empire. Caliph Muawiya deports Gypsies from Basra to Antioch on the Mediterranean coast.
c. 710	Arab Empire. Caliph Walid resettles Zott from Mesopotamia to Antioch.
720	Arab Empire. Caliph Yazid II sends still more Zott to Antioch.
803–904	Byzantium. 'Atsingani' are settled around Plovdiv (Thrace).
820	Arab Empire. Independent Zott state established in Mesopotamia.
834	Arab Empire. Zott defeated by Arabs and many of them resettled in border town of Ainzarba.
855	Arab Empire. Battle of Ainzarba: Greeks defeat the Arabs and take Zott soldiers and their families as prisoners to Byzantium.
c.1050	Byzantium. Acrobats and animal doctors (called *athinganí*) in Constantinople.
1192	India. Battle of Terain. Last Gypsies leave for the west.
1290	Greece. Shoemakers (possibly Gypsies) on Mount Athos.
1322	Crete. Nomads reported on the island.
1347	Byzantium. Black Death reaches Constantinople. Some Gypsies move west again.
1348	Serbia. Shoemakers (possibly Gypsies) in Prizren.
1362	Croatia. Gypsies in Dubrovnik.
1373	Corfu. Gypsies reported on the island.
1384	Greece. Gypsy shoemakers in Modon.
1385	Romania. First recorded transaction of Gypsy slaves.
1399	Bohemia. The first Gypsy is mentioned in a chronicle.
1407	Germany. Gypsies visit Hildesheim.
1416	Germany. Gypsies expelled from Meissen region.
1417	Holy Roman Empire. King Sigismund issues a safe conduct to Gypsies at Lindau.
1418	France. First Gypsies reported, in Colmar.

1418	Switzerland. First Gypsies arrive.
1419	Belgium. First Gypsies reported in Antwerp.
1420	Holland. First Gypsies reported in Deventer
1422	Italy. Gypsies come to Bologna.
1423	Italy. Andrew, Duke of Little Egypt, and his followers set off to visit Pope Martin V in Rome.
	Slovakia. Gypsies in Spissky.
1425	Spain. Gypsies in Zaragoza.
1447	Catalonia. First report of Gypsies.
1453	Turks capture Constantinople. Flight of some Gypsies westward.
	Slovenia. A Gypsy smith reported in the country.
1468	Cyprus. First report of Gypsies.
1471	Switzerland. Parliament meeting in Lucerne banishes Gypsies.
1472	Rhine Palatinate. Duke Friedrich asks his people to help the Gypsy pilgrims.
1485	Sicily. First reports of Gypsies.
1489	Hungary. Gypsy musicians play on Czepel Island.
1492	Spain. First draft of the forthcoming law of 1499.
1493	Italy. Gypsies expelled from Milan.
1498	Germany (Holy Roman Empire). Expulsion of Gypsies ordered.
1499	Spain. Expulsion of the Gypsies ordered (Pragmatica of the Catholic Kings).
1500	Russia. First record of Gypsies.
1501	Belarus and Lithuania. Vasil appointed to be chief of Gypsies.
1504	France. Expulsion of Gypsies ordered.
1505	Denmark. Two groups of Gypsies enter the country.
	Scotland. Gypsy pilgrims arrive, probably from Spain.
1510	Switzerland. Death penalty introduced for Gypsies found in the country.
1512	Catalonia. Gypsies expelled.
	Sweden. First Gypsies arrive.
1514	England. First mention of a Gypsy in the country.
1515	Germany. Bavaria closes its borders to Gypsies.
1516	Portugal. Gypsies mentioned in literature.
1525	Portugal. Gypsies banned from Portugal.
	Sweden. Gypsies ordered to leave country.
1526	Holland. Transit of Gypsies across country banned.
1530	England and Wales. Expulsion of Gypsies ordered.
1534	Slovakia. Gypsies executed in Levoca.
1536	Denmark. Gypsies ordered to leave country.
1538	Portugal. Deportation of Gypsies to colonies begins.
1539	Spain. Any males found nomadising to be sent to galleys.
1540	Scotland. Gypsies allowed to live under own laws.
1541	Czech lands. Gypsies accused of starting a fire in Prague.
1544	England. Gypsies deported to Norway.
1547	England. Boorde publishes specimens of Romani.

1549	Bohemia. Gypsies declared outlaws and to be expelled.
1553	Estonia. First Gypsies in the country.
1554	England. The death penalty is imposed for any Gypsies not leaving the country within a month.
1557	Poland and Lithuania. Expulsion of Gypsies ordered.
1559	Finland. Gypsies on the island of Åland.
1562	England. Provisions of previous acts widened to include people who live and travel like Gypsies.
1563	Italy. Council of Trent affirms that Gypsies cannot be priests.
1564	Lithuania. Nomadic Gypsies to be expelled.
1569	Lithuania and Poland. Nomadic Gypsies to be expelled.
1573	Scotland. Gypsies to either settle down or leave the country.
1574	Ottoman Empire. Selim II legislates for Gypsy miners in Bosnia.
1579	Portugal. Wearing of Gypsy dress banned.
	Wales. First record of Gypsies.
1580	Finland. First Gypsies on the mainland.
1584	Denmark and Norway. Expulsion of Gypsies ordered.
1586	Belarus. Nomadic Gypsies expelled.
1589	Denmark. Death penalty imposed for Gypsies not leaving the country.
1595	Romania. Stefan Razvan, the son of a slave, becomes ruler of Moldavia.
1611	Scotland. Three Gypsies hanged (under 1554 law).
1633	Spain. Pragmatica of Felipe IV. Expulsion.
1637	Sweden. Death penalty for Gypsies not leaving the country.
1692	Austria. Gypsies in Villach.
1714	Scotland. Two female Gypsies executed.
1715	Scotland. Ten Gypsies deported to Virginia.
1728	Holland. Last Gypsy hunt.
c.1730	Wales. Arrival of Abraham, founder of the Wood clan.
1746	Spain. Gypsies to live in named towns.
1748	Sweden. Foreign Gypsies expelled.
1749	Spain. Round-up and imprisonment of all Gypsies ordered.
1758	Austro-Hungarian Empire. Maria Theresa begins assimilation programme.
1759	Russia. Gypsies banned from Saint Petersburg.
1763	Holland. Pastor Valyi is the first to discover the Indian origin of Romani.
1765	Austro-Hungarian Empire. Joseph II continues assimilation program.
1776	Austria. First published article on the Indian origin of the Romani language.
1782	Hungary. Two hundred Gypsies charged with cannibalism.
1783	Germany. Heinrich Grellmann publishes the first academic work establishing the Indian origin of the Romani people.
	Russia. Settlement of nomads encouraged.

	Spain. Gypsy language and dress banned.
	United Kingdom. Most legislation against Gypsies repealed.
1791	Poland. *Settlement Law.*
1802	France. Gypsies in Basque province rounded up and imprisoned.
1812	Finland. Order to confine nomadic Gypsies in workhouses.
1822	United Kingdom. Gypsies camping on the roadside will be fined.
1830	Germany. Authorities in Nordhausen remove children from their families for fostering with non-Gypsies
1835	Denmark. Hunt for Travellers in Jutland.
	United Kingdom. *Highways Act* strengthens the provisions of the 1822 *Turnpike Act.*
1837	Spain. George Borrow translates St. Luke's gospel into Romani.
1848	Transylvania. Emancipation of serfs (including Gypsies).
1849	Denmark. Gypsies allowed into the country again.
1855	Romania. Emancipation of Gypsy slaves in Moldavia.
1856	Romania. Emancipation of Gypsy slaves in Wallachia.
1860	Sweden. Immigration restrictions *eased.*
1865	Scotland. *Trespass (Scotland) Act.*
1868	Holland. New immigration of Gypsies.
1872	Belgium. Foreign Gypsies expelled.
1874	Ottoman Empire. Muslim Gypsies given equal rights with other Muslims.
1875	Denmark. Gypsies barred from the country once more.
1879	Hungary. National conference of Gypsies in Kisfalu.
	Serbia. Nomadism banned.
1884	Sweden. Sonya Kavalevsky appointed professor of mathematics at Stockholm University.
1886	Bulgaria. Nomadism forbidden.
	Germany. Bismarck recommends expulsion of foreign Gypsies.
1888	United Kingdom. Gypsy Lore Society established.
1899	Germany. Police Gypsy Information Service set up in Munich by Alfred Dillmann.
1904	Germany. Prussian Parliament unanimously adopts proposal to regulate Gypsy movement and work.
1905	Germany. A census of all Gypsies in Bavaria is taken. Dillmann publishes his *Zigeunerbuch.*
	Bulgaria. Sofia conference, demanding voting rights for Gypsies.
1906	Germany. The Prussian minister issues special instructions to the police to "combat the Gypsy nuisance."
	France. Identity card introduced for nomads.
	Finland. Mission to the Gypsies set up.
1907	Germany. Many Gypsies leave for other countries in western Europe.
1914	Norway. Some thirty Gypsies are given Norwegian nationality.

Sweden. Deportation Act also makes immigration of Gypsies difficult.

1918   Holland. *Caravan and House Boat Law* introduces controls.

1922   Germany. In Baden all Gypsies are to be photographed and fingerprinted.

1924   Slovakia. A group of Gypsies tried for cannibalism. They are found to be innocent.

1925   USSR. All-Russian Union of Gypsies established.

1926   Germany. Bavarian state parliament brings in a new law "to combat Gypsy nomads and idlers."
Switzerland. Pro Juventute starts a program of forced removal of Gypsy children from their families for fostering.
USSR. First moves to settle nomadic Gypsies.

1927   Germany. Legislation requiring the photographing and fingerprinting of Gypsies instituted in Prussia.
Germany. Bavaria institutes laws forbidding Gypsies to travel in large groups or to own firearms.
Norway. *The Aliens Act* bars foreign Gypsies from the country.
Russia. Journal *Romani Zorya* (*Romany Dawn*) founded.

1928   Germany. Nomadic Gypsies in Germany are to be placed under permanent police surveillance.
Germany. Professor Hans F. Günther writes that it was the Gypsies who introduced foreign blood into Europe.
Slovakia. Pogrom in Pobedim.

1929   USSR. Nikolai Pankov's Romani book *Buti i Džinaiben* (*Work and Knowledge*) published.
USSR. Journal *Romani Zorya* (*Romany Dawn*) starts publication.

1930   Norway. A Norwegian doctor recommends that all Travellers be sterilised.
USSR. The first issue of the journal *Nevo Drom* (*New Way*) appears.

1931   USSR. Teatr Romen opens in Moscow.

1933   Austria. Officials in Burgenland call for the withdrawal of all civil rights for Gypsies.
Bulgaria. Journal *Terbie* (*Education*) starts publication.
Germany. The National Socialist Party comes to power. Measures against Jews and Gypsies begin.
Germany. Gypsy musicians barred from State Cultural Chamber.
Germany. Sinto boxer Johann Trollmann was stripped of his title as light-heavyweight champion for "racial reasons".
Germany. *Act for the Prevention of Hereditarily Ill Offspring*, known as the Sterilisation Act.
Germany. 'Beggars' Week'. Many Gypsies arrested.
Latvia. St John's Gospel translated into Romani.
Romania. General Association of the Gypsies of Romania

	founded. National conference held.
	Romania. Journals *Neamul Tiganesc* (*Gypsy Nation*) and *Timpul* (*The Time*) founded.
	USSR. Teatr Romen performs the opera *Carmen*.
1934	Germany. Gypsies who cannot prove German nationality expelled.
	Romania. Bucharest 'international' Congress.
1935	Germany. Marriages between Gypsies and Germans banned.
	Yugoslavia. Journal *Romano Lil* published.
1936	Germany. The right to vote removed from Gypsies.
	Germany. Opening of internment camp at Marzahn in June.
	Germany. General Decree for Fighting the Gypsy Menace.
	Germany. Racial Hygiene and Population Biological Research Unit of the Health Office begins its work.
	Germany. The Minister of War orders that Gypsies should not be called up for active military service.
1937	Poland. Janusz Kwiek elected King of the Gypsies.
1938	
April	Germany. Decree on the Preventative Fight against Crime. All Gypsies classed as antisocial.
	Germany. Many Gypsies arrested to be forced labour for the building of concentration camps.
June	Germany. Second wave of arrests to provide labour to build the camps.
Autumn	Germany. Racial Hygiene Research Centre begins to set up an archive of Gypsy tribes.
October	Germany. National Centre for Fighting the Gypsy Menace established.
December	Germany. Order for the "Fight against the Gypsy Menace."
	USSR. Joseph Stalin bans Romani language and culture.
1939	
September	Germany. Deportation of 30,000 Gypsies planned.
October	Germany. Settlement Decree. Gypsies cannot travel.
October	Poland. Special identity cards for Gypsies.
November	Germany. Gypsy fortune-tellers arrested and sent to Ravensbrück concentration camp.
November	(German occupied) Czech lands. Nomadism forbidden.
1940	
April	France. French government opens internment camps for nomads.
April	Germany. Heinrich Himmler orders the resettlement of Gypsies in the General Government of Poland.
August	Austria. Internment camp built at Maxglan, Salzburg.
August	Czech lands. Labour camps set up in Lety and Hodonín.
October	Austria. Order for the internment of the Gypsies in Burgenland.
November	Austria. Internment camp for Gypsies is set up in Lackenbach.

1941

March   Germany. Exclusion of Gypsy children from school begins.

April   Slovakia. Decree on the Organisation of the Living Conditions
            of the Gypsies. They are to be separated from the majority
            population.

May   Serbia. German military commander's order states that
            Gypsies will be treated as Jews.

June   USSR. SS Task Forces move into the occupied areas of the
            Soviet Union and systematically kill Jews and Romanies.

July   Germany. Reinhard Heydrich, SS Chief Himmler's deputy,
            brings the Gypsies into the plans for a "Final Solution to the
            Jewish problem".

August   Croatia. Jasenovac concentration camp opened.
            USSR. All the Sinti Gypsy families who lived in the Volga
            Republic are deported to Kazakhstan.

September   USSR. SS Task Forces carry out mass executions of Jews and
            Romanies in the Baby Yar valley.

October   Yugoslavia. German army executes 2,100 Jewish and Gypsy
            hostages (as reprisal for soldiers killed by partisans).

October   Czech lands. Decision that Gypsies from the so-called
            Protectorate are to be sent to a concentration camp.

November   Serbia. German military command orders the immediate
            arrest of all Jews and Gypsies, to be held as hostages.

October   Poland. A Gypsy camp is set up in the Jewish ghetto of Lodz for
            5,000 inmates.

December   USSR. Task Force C murders 824 Gypsies in Simferopol.

December   Latvia. All 101 Gypsies in the town of Libau are executed.

December   Baltic States. State Governor Hinrich Lohse orders that Gypsies
            should be given the same treatment as Jews.

1942

January   Poland. All Sinti and Romanies still in the Lodz ghetto are
            transported and gassed at Chelmno.

March   Germany. A special additional income tax is levied on Gypsies.

April   Poland. Romanies are brought into the Warsaw ghetto and kept
            in the prison in Gesia Street.

May   Croatia. The government and the Ustasha issue the order to
            arrest all Gypsies and deport them to the extermination camp
            in Jasenovac.

May   Poland. All Gypsies in the Warsaw district are to be interned in
            Jewish ghettoes.

Spring and summer
            Romania. Some 20,000 Romanies are deported to
            Transdnistria.

July   Poland. Several hundred Polish Romanies killed at Treblinka
            extermination camp.

July   Germany. A decree of the general staff of the army orders that
            German Gypsies are not to be taken for active military service.

August	Czech lands. 6,500 Gypsies registered by the police on one day. Bulgaria. Compulsory labour for Gypsies introduced.
August	Serbia. Harald Turner, head of the German military administration, announces that "the Gypsy question has been fully solved."
September	Germany. Himmler and Justice Minister Otto Thierack agree to transfer any Gypsies in prison to concentration camps.
December	Germany. Himmler issues the order to deport the Gypsies in Greater Germany to the concentration camp of Auschwitz-Birkenau.

1943

January	Poland. Gypsies from Warsaw ghetto transferred to the extermination camp at Treblinka.
February	Poland. First transports of Sinti and Romanies from Germany are delivered to the new Gypsy Section in Auschwitz-Birkenau.
March	Poland. In Auschwitz the SS gas some 1,700 men, women and children.
May	Poland. In Auschwitz the SS gas some 1,030 men, women and children.
	Poland. SS Major Dr Josef Mengele is transferred at his own request to Auschwitz-Birkenau concentration camp.
July	Poland. Himmler visits the Gypsy Section in Auschwitz and orders the remaining Gypsies to be killed.
September	Germany. Several hundred Gypsy prisoners start work on the production of the V1 and V2 weapons in underground work shops in the Kohnstein Hills.
November	USSR. Minister for the Occupied Eastern Territories orders all nomadic Gypsies in the territories are to be "treated as Jews".

1944

January	Belgium. A transport of 351 Romanies and Sinti from Belgium is despatched to the Auschwitz-Birkenau concentration camp.
May 16	Poland. The prisoners in the Auschwitz Gypsy Camp resist an attempt to take them to the gas chambers.
May 21	Holland. A transport of 245 Romanies and Sinti arrives at Auschwitz concentration camp.
August 2	Poland. 1,400 Gypsy prisoners are sent from Auschwitz to other concentration camps. The remaining 2,900 Gypsies are killed in the gas chamber.
Autumn	Slovakia. Romanies join the fight of partisans in the Slovak National Uprising.

1945

January 27	Auschwitz. At 3pm the first Soviet soldiers reach the main camp and find one Romani among the survivors.
May	Second World War ends in Europe. All surviving Gypsies freed from concentration camps.
	Bulgaria. Gypsy Organisation for the Fight against Fascism and Racism set up.

	Germany. Nuremburg Trials of Nazi leaders begin. Crimes against Gypsies are included in the charges.
1946	France. Matéo Maximoff's novel *The Ursitory* published. Poland. Roma Ensemble founded.
1947	Bulgaria. Teatr Roma established in Sofia.
1951	Bulgaria. Teatr Roma in Sofia closed.
1952	France. The Pentecostal movement among Gypsies starts.
1953	Denmark. Gypsies re-admitted to the country.
1958	Bulgaria. Nomadism banned.
1958	Czechoslovakia. Nomadism banned. Hungary. Gypsy organisation established.
1960	England and Wales. *Caravan Sites Act* reduces provision of caravan sites. France. Communauté Mondiale Gitane established.
1962	German Federal Republic. Courts rule that Gypsies were persecuted for racial reasons. Norway. Government Gypsy Committee set up.
1963	Ireland. Report of the Commission on Itinerancy published. Italy. Opera Nomadi education scheme set up.
1963	Yugoslavia. Gypsies move to Shuto Orizari after Skopje earthquake.
1964	Ireland. Itinerant Action Group set up.
1965	France, Communauté Mondiale Gitane banned. Comité International Tzigane set up.
Italy.	Pope Paul VI addresses some 2,000 Gypsies at Pomezia.
1966	Britain. Gypsy Council set up.
1967	Finland. Gypsy Association established.
1968	Council of Europe. Rudolf Karway leads Zigeunermission deputation to the Human Rights Commission in Strasbourg. England and Wales. *Caravan Sites Act*. Councils to build sites. Holland. All districts must build caravan sites.
1969	Bulgaria. Segregated schools are set up for Gypsies. Council of Europe. Assembly passes a positive resolution on Gypsies. Yugoslavia. Macedonia. Faik Abdi elected as MP for Parliament.
1970	Norway. Report published on proposed work with the Gypsies. United Kingdom. National Gypsy Education Council established.
1971	England. First World Romani Congress held near London. Scotland. Advisory Committee on the Travelling People starts work.
1972	Czechoslovakia. Sterilisation programme for Gypsies begins. England. Romany Guild founded. France. Band known as Los Reyes (later Gypsy Kings) is founded. Sweden. Stockholm's Finska Zigenarförening founded.

1973	German Federal Republic. Three Gypsies shot by farmer in Pfaffenhofen.
	Scandinavia. Nordiska Zigenarrådet to link organisations.
	Yugoslavia. Macedonia. Radio broadcasts in Romani start from Tetovo.
1975	Council of Europe. Committee of Ministers passes a positive resolution on nomads.
	Hungary. The first issues of the magazine *Rom som* (I am a Romani) appear.
1977	England and Wales. Cripps Report on Gypsies published.
	Holland. Integration of 500 'illegal' Gypsy immigrants.
	United Nations. Sub-commission resolution on protection of Gypsies.
1978	Switzerland. Second World Romani Congress in Geneva.
1979	Hungary. National Gypsy Council formed.
	Hungary. First national exhibition of self-taught Gypsy artists.
	Norway. ABC Romani primer produced for mother tongue teaching.
	Romania. Underground publication of St John's Gospel in Romani.
	United Nations. Romani Union recognised by ECOSOC.
1980	Yugoslavia. Grammar in Romani published in Skopje.
1981	Council of Europe. CLRAE resolution on helping nomads.
	German Federal Republic. Third World Romani Congress in Göttingen.
	Poland. Pogrom in Oswiecim.
	Yugoslavia. Gypsies granted national status on an equal footing with other minorities.
1982	France. New Mitterand government promises to help nomads.
1983	Council of Europe. Council of Ministers passes a resolution on stateless nomads.
	England. First national Pentecostal convention.
	Italy. Gypsy caravans removed from Rome at the start of the *Annus Sanctus*.
	Northern Ireland. Belfast Traveller Education Development Group established.
	Yugoslavia. Romani teaching begins in one school in Kosovo.
1984	European Parliament passes a resolution on aiding Gypsies.
	India. Chandigarh Festival.
1985	England. Bradford's attempts to make it illegal for nomadic Gypsies to come within city limits overthrown by the courts.
	France. First International Exhibition (Mondiale) of Gypsy Art in Paris.
	Ireland. Report of the Travelling People Review Body published.
	Sweden. Attack on Gypsy family in Kumla with stones and a fire bomb.

1986	France. International Gypsy conference in Paris.
	Spain. Gypsy houses set on fire in Martos.
	Yugoslavia. International Romani seminar in Sarajevo.
1988	Hungary. Organisation Phralipe founded.
1989	European Community Council. Resolution on promoting school provision for Gypsy and Traveller children.
	Germany. Government initiates the deportation of several thousand foreign Gypsies from the country.
	Germany. Gypsies demonstrate in the ex-concentration camp at Neuengamme against the deportation of asylum seekers.
	Hungary. Roma Parliament set up.
	Poland. First Romane Divesa Festival.
	Romania. Border guards shoot party of Gypsies.
	Spain. Gypsy houses attacked in Andalusia.
1990	Macedonia. Egyptians Association set up.
	Poland. Permanent exhibition on Romanies opens in Tarnow.
	Poland. Fourth World Romani Congress held near Warsaw.
	Poland. Standard alphabet for Romani adopted by World Romani Congress.
	Poland. Journal *Rrom p-o Drom* (Romanies on the Road) founded.
	Romania. Miners attack Romani quarter in Bucharest.
	Yugoslavia. Kosovo. Egyptians Association set up.
1991	Czech Republic. Romani teaching starts at Prague University.
	Italy. Ostia international conference.
	Macedonia. Romanies have equal rights in new republic.
	Poland. Pogrom in Mlawa.
	Slovakia. Government gives Romanies nationality status and equal rights.
	Ukraine. Police attack on settlement of Velikie Beryezni.
1992	Hungary. Arson attack on Gypsies in Kétegyháza.
	Poland. Attack on remaining Gypsies in Oswiecim.
	Slovakia. Romathan Theater established in Košice.
	Ukraine. Mob attacks Gypsy houses in Tatarbunary.
	United Nations. Commission on Human Rights passes resolution on protection of Gypsies. Gypsies recognised as an ethnic group.
1993	Bulgaria. A crowd of Bulgarians attacks the Gypsy quarter in Malorad, killing one Romani man.
	Council of Europe. CLRAE Resolution on Gypsies.
	Council of Europe Assembly. Resolution on Gypsies.
	Czech Republic. Tibor Danihel drowns running away from skinhead gang.
	Czech Republic. Seven Romanies deported from Uští nad Labem to Slovakia.
	Hungary. International Conference in Budapest.

Macedonia. Official introduction of Romani language in schools.

Romania. Three Gypsies killed in pogrom in Hadareni.

Scotland. Scottish Gypsy/Traveller Association set up.

Slovakia. Cyril Dunka beaten up by police after a parking incident.

United Nations. [International] Romani Union upgraded to Category II consultative status.

1994 Britain. *Criminal Justice Act*. Nomadism criminalised.

Hungary. Budapest OSCE meeting sets up Contact Point for Roma and Sinti Issues, based initially in Warsaw.

Hungary. Gypsies vote for their local 'minority' councils.

Poland. ODIHR organises Warsaw seminar on Romanies.

Poland. Gypsy boy beaten up and houses inhabited by Romanies attacked in Debica.

Spain. European Congress in Seville

France. At a meeting in Strasbourg the Standing Conference of Romani Associations is formed.

1995 Austria. Four Gypsies killed by a bomb in Oberwart, Burgenland.

Bulgaria. One Gypsy died following an arson attack on a block of flats in Sofia.

Bulgaria. Angel Angelov shot by police in Nova Zagora.

Czech Republic. Tibor Berki killed by skinheads in Zdár nad Sázavou.

France. Council of Europe in Strasbourg sets up specialist advice group on Romanies.

Hungary. Second International Exhibition (Mondiale) of Gypsy Art.

Poland. Gypsy couple murdered in Pabianice.

Poland. Grota Bridge settlement of Romanian Gypsies in Warsaw dispersed by police. Residents deported across the border to Ukraine.

Slovakia. Mario Goral burnt to death by skinheads in Ziar nad Hronom.

1996 Albania. Fatmir Haxhiu dies of burns after a racist attack.

Bulgaria. Kuncho Anguelov and Kiril Perkov, deserters from the army, shot and killed by military police.

Bulgaria. Petra Stoyanova shot dead by police in Rakovski.

European Court of Human Rights. The Court rejects the appeal by Mrs Buckley against the refusal of planning permission in England for her caravan.

France. Second Meeting of the Standing Committee of Gypsy Organisations and first meeting of the Committee of Experts of the Council of Europe in Strasbourg.

Greece. Police officer shoots Anastasios Mouratis in Boetia.

Hungary. European Roma Rights Centre set up in Budapest.

Republic of Ireland. National Strategy on Traveller Accommodation proposed.

Poland. Houses occupied by Romanies attacked in Wiebodzice.

Romania. Twenty-one Romani houses burned down in Curtea de Arges.

Romania. Mircea-Muresul Mosor shot and killed by the chief of police in Valcele.

Slovakia. An eighteen-year-old Romani youth was beaten to death by skinheads in Poprad.

Slovakia. Jozef Miklos died when his house was set on fire in Zalistie.

Ukraine. Mrs H. raped by police in Mukacevo.

1997

January	Hungary. Fine increased on appeal for the owner of an inn in Pecs who had discriminated against Romanies.
	Hungary. Symposium on the Legal Defence of the Rights of Romanies held in Budapest.
	Romania. Mob attacks Gypsy houses in Tanganu village.
	Turkey. Mob attack Gypsies in Sulukule district of Istanbul.
	Ukraine. Gypsies beaten by police in four separate incidents in Uzhorod.
February	Bulgaria. Killing of three Gypsies by police reported. Police attack the Gypsy quarter in Pazardzhik.
	Hungary. Gypsies beaten up in police station in Szombathely and in a police car in Mandatany in a separate incident.
March	France. Jose Ménager and Manolito Meuche shot dead by police in Nantes.
	Germany. President Roman Herzog visits the Romani Holocaust Exhibition in Heidelberg.
	Czech Republic. Four skinheads sentenced to prison in connection with the death of Tibor Danihel (see 1993).
	Romania. Conference in Bucharest on the Prevention of Violence and Discrimination against Romanies in Europe.
April	Greece. Eviction of 100 families from Ano Liosia. Partial resettlement in a guarded camp.
June	Poland. Romanies attacked in Wiebodzice.
June 27–28	Croatia. Seminar on Roma in Croatia today.
August	Czech Republic. Several hundred Romanies fly to Canada to seek asylum.
	Czech Republic. Monument erected at Hodonin to concentration camp victims.
Nov 6–9	Barcelona, Spain. European Congress
Nov 17–30	Bulgaria. International conference. Gypsy children and their education.
November	United Kingdom. National Front demonstrates in Dover against asylum seekers from the Czech and Slovak Republics.

1998	USA. New Jersey Governor Christine Whitman signs Assembly Bill 2654 which rescinds the last anti-Gypsy law of any US state.
May 16	UK. Music festival in London with Czech and Polish Gypsy bands composed of asylum seekers.
Sept 4–6	Czechia, Prague. International Romany cultural festival RESPECT
October 19	Wales. Cardiff County Council organises a Gypsy and Traveller Awareness Day.
October	UK Home Secretary Jack Straw introduces visas for Slovak citizens to keep out asylum seekers.
November	Bulgaria. British Prince Charles visits Stolipino, Romani quarter of Plovdiv.
November	England. Romani Ball organised in London by Czech and Slovak asylum seekers.
December	USA. International Romani Union delegation, led by Rajko Djurić, attends Nazi Gold conference on Holocaust assets in Washington.
December.	Czechia. International Conference on the Roma at Castle Stirin.
1999	France. Loi Besson encourages the provision of council-run caravan sites.
January	Czechia. Over 100 prominent persons sign protest to government over siting of pig farm on site of Lety concentration camp.
February	Greece. Local authority sets fire to five Roma houses in Aspropyrgos to construct Olympic sports facilities.
June	Bulgaria. Sofia Conference on Peace and Security for Roma in the Balkans
September	Macedonia. Government admits 500 refugees from Kosovo held for a week at the border.
November	Turkey. OSCE Istanbul Conference welcomes the development of the Romani civil rights movement.
December	Romania, Bucharest. International Conference on Public Policies and Romani Women.
2000	Finland. Publication of St Luke's Gospel in Romani. Poland. IRU and RNC sign a joint declaration in Warsaw.
January	Doctors of the World colloquium on Gypsies in Europe.
March	Pope John Paul II asks for forgiveness for the mistreatment by Catholics of Gypsies.
May	Germany, Stuttgart. Conference Die unerwünschte Deutschen (The unwanted Germans).
July	Czechia. Fifth World Romani Congress in Prague.
September	UK. 1,000 police block the traditional Horsmonden Fair.
2001	South Africa. Roma attend the Durban World Conference against Racism.
January	Macedonia. *Roma Times* begins publication.

April	India. International Romani Union leaders visit the Romano Kher (Nehru House) in Chandigarh.
July	Serbia. Anti-Roma graffiti appear in Panchevo and Surdulica.
July	Russia, Volgograd. Thirty skinheads attack a Gypsy camp setting it on fire and killing two men.
August	Poland. Permanent Romani Holocaust exhibition opened at Auschwitz.
November	Italy. 200 members of the National Alliance march to protest against new Roma housing in Rome.
November	Germany, Cologne. Romani writers meet and agree to set up an international association.
2002	Finland. *Drabibosko liin* published. The first ABC reader for Gypsies in Finland.
March	Irish Republic. *Housing Act* criminalises trespass by caravans.
May	Poland. RNC organise International Romani Congress in Lodz.
June	Hungary. A Rom, Laszlo Teleki, appointed as the State Secretary for Roma Affairs.
July	Irish Republic. Traveller Movement pickets the Dáil (Parliament) opposing the new *Housing Act*.
July	Finland, Helsinki. International Romani Writers Association founded.
September	Croatia, Drzimurec-Strelec. One hundred Croat parents prevent Romani children from entering a newly integrated school in the village.
October	France, Paris. Delegation representing a dozen Gypsy organisations meets Home Secretary to discuss slow process of caravan site provision.
November	Exhibition of Gypsy children's photos at the Victoria and Albert Museum.
2003	Irish Republic. Internal Security Bill proposes fines of 3,750 euros for Travellers who trespass.
May	UK, Liverpool. Fifteen-year-old Johnny Delaney killed in a racist attack.
June	Hungary, Budapest. World Bank sponsors International conference on Roma in Eastern Europe.
August	British Gypsies protest against UK policy at UN Conference in Geneva.
October.	Croatia. Ms Mukić, Deputy Ombudsman, attacked for condemning segregation in schools.
November	UK. Villagers in Sussex burn caravan and effigies of Gypsies.

The Dictionary

A

ABAD, Marina (La Canillas). Spain. Contemporary singer. She stars with the **flamenco**-rock band Ojos de Brujo.

ABDI, Faik. Macedonia. Contemporary political activist. In 1948 he was a founding member of **Phralipe**. This was the first Romani cultural association permitted by the post-war communist authorities in Macedonia which acted as a covert forum of Romani national aspirations. Son of a blacksmith, Faik Abdi was one of only a handful of Roma of his generation in the former Yugoslavia to obtain a university degree. He attended the first **World Romani Congress** in London while serving as an MP in the Macedonian Parliament (1969–74). He later formed the Roma Emancipation Party but later suffered from a campaign by the Government to undermine his authority through various allegations. He was deprived of his passport for four years to prevent his participation in international meetings.

ACKOVIĆ, Dragoljub 1952–. Yugoslavia, Serbia. Journalist and broadcaster. He studied at Belgrade University. From his youth, he took part in the drive for the advancement of the Gypsies and participated in international gatherings. He has published many articles and two books – one on the history of the Gypsies in Yugoslavia and the other on the **Jasenovac** concentration camp. Dragoljub Acković currently works as a journalist and has been responsible for broadcasts in Romani. He is also president of the **Romano Kulturako Klubi** in Belgrade.

ACTON, *Thomas* 1948–. England. Sociologist and author. Professor of Romani Studies at Greenwich University. He has been active in the **Gypsy Council**, the **National Gypsy Education Council** and other bodies.

ADAM, Gejza. Slovakia. Twentieth-century teacher and political activist. The president of the **Únia Rómskej Obcanskej Iniciatívy** (Romani Union Citizens' Initiative). He is currently teaching music in **Košice**.

ADELSBURGER, Sidone. 1933–43. Austria. Schoolgirl who died in **Auschwitz** and whose story was retold as fiction by Erich Hackl in his book *Abschied von Sidonie* (Farewell to Sidonie).

ADJAM, Tikno. France. A mythical Resistance fighter and poet during the Second World War. He was apparently invented by a French priest as a vehicle for poems (later printed in *Etudes Tsiganes*) to raise the spirits of Gypsies in the internment camps.

ADVISORY COUNCIL FOR THE EDUCATION OF ROMANIES AND OTHER TRAVELLERS (ACERT). UK. Chair: David Cannon. In 1988 the **National Gypsy Education Council** split, with some of the committee forming ACERT. The committee has widened its mission from education to include planning for caravan sites.

ADVISORY COMMITTEE ON TRAVELLERS. Scotland. Est. 1971. A committee set up to advise the Secretary of State for Scotland, mainly on the provision of camping sites for **Travellers**. Members include the Traveller **Charles Douglas**. It has published a series of reports with recommendations.

AFGHANISTAN. Estimated Gypsy population 7,000. Afghanistan is the first country to the west of India and Pakistan where we can identify industrial nomads who do not speak any of the local languages but a dialect from north India, in this case Inku. Aparna Rao has identified four clans – Jalali, Pikraj, Shadibaz and Vangawala – who fall into this definition of 'Gypsy'. The locals call them 'Jat' which is used in a pejorative way. They will say of a child or a teenage girl of whose behaviour they do not approve: *misle Jat asti* (they are like a Jat).

The Jalali have performing monkeys, sell fruit and are professional musicians while the Pikraj trade in donkeys and horses. The Shadibaz also train monkeys while the Vangawala, as their name indicates, sell bangles. They live on the edge of Afghan society.

ALBAICÍN, Joaquin 1965–. Spain. Author. He has written a history of the Romani people as well as short stories and a novel.

ALBAICÍN, Maria. Spain. Twentieth-century actress. She was a film star in Spain in the 1920s whose films included *La Fuente Mágica*, *Los Pianos Mecánicos* and *Cafe de Chinitas*.

ALBAICÍN, Miguel. Spain. Twentieth-century actor. He appeared in the film *El Amor Brujo*, directed by Antonio Roman.

ALBAICÍN, Rafael. Spain. Twentieth-century bullfighter and actor. He appeared in several films including *La Fiesta Sigue*, *Maria Antonia* and *La Caramba*.

ALBANIA. Estimated Gypsy population: 100,000 in addition to a small number of so-called **Egyptians**. The first Gypsies probably arrived in Albania during the fourteenth century though the first record is from 1523. From 1468 to 1912, the country was part of the **Ottoman Empire**. Music and craftwork were common occupations of the Romanies in the area. Around 1920 a law stopped Gypsies from dancing in public for money. From 1934 – the previous regulation having failed to stop the practice – dancers had to pay a special fee to license their performances. During the Second World War, the Italians who were mainly in control seem to have ignored the Gypsy population, as did the post-war Communist government. Music re-emerged as an important occupation.

The fall of communism, as elsewhere in Eastern Europe, led to the emergence of latent anti-Gypsy sentiments. Early in 1996 stories appeared in the Albanian press of Gypsies killing their children to sell their organs for transplants. These reports seem to have followed a court case where some Romanies in Durres were accused of selling their children for adoption. In July 1996 Fatir Haxhiu, a fifteen-year-old boy, died as a result of being burned during a racist attack.

The Gypsies of Albania are mainly Muslim and speak Balkan dialects of Romani. A branch of the cultural association **Romani Baxt** has been formed and Albanians have taken part in the Romani Summer Schools.

ALIEV, Mustafa (Manush Romanov) 1927–. Bulgaria. Playwright and politician. He was director of the **Teatr Roma** in Sofia until 1951 when the theatre was closed after which he worked in a Turkish theatre. Mustafa Aliev became an MP on the list of the Union of Democratic Forces in the first post-Communist parliament (1990). However, at the next election he was not re-elected. A booklet has been published in Poland containing some of the songs he collected.

ALL-PARLIAMENTARY GROUP ON ROMA AFFAIRS. UK. Est. 2003. Spokesperson: Paul Stinchcombe. The Group was set up in 2003 to alert the UK Government to the Third World living conditions of Roma Gypsies in the EU accession countries of central and Eastern Europe. Their report, *Roma Rights in Stage One Accession Countries*, outlines the situation of Roma in four CEE countries: Hungary, the Czech Republic, Poland and the Slovak Republic. The Group was a joint initiative of Paul Stinchcombe, the Labour MP for Wellingborough and Rushden, and **European Dialogue**. The stated purpose of the Group is to raise the profile of Roma human rights issues within the states of central and Eastern Europe that are acceding to the EU. All-parliamentary groups by definition have to have at least one member from at least three parties.

ALL-PARTY PARLIAMENTARY GROUP ON TRAVELLER LAW REFORM. UK. Est. 2001. Chairperson: Kevin McNamara.

The Group, in accordance with House of Commons rules, is composed of MPs from the Labour, Conservative and Liberal parties. Its stated purpose is to effect the social inclusion of the Gypsy and **Traveller** community and improve relations between the settled and Traveller communities. The Group have been active in debates in Parliament.

ALPHABET. It seems probable that the Gypsies did not bring any writing system with them when they came to Europe. The alphabet given in Jean-Paul Clébert's book, *The Gypsies,* is spurious. Publications in Romani in the twentieth century have used the Latin or Cyrillic alphabets. The first **World Romani Congress** recommended a broad phonetic alphabet based on Latin letters and most literature produced since then has been in the Latin alphabet.

The alphabet of the first World Romani Congress was as follows: a b č čh d e f g h ȟ i j k kh l m n o p p ph r s š t th u v z ž

At the second Congress ȟ was replaced by x.

At the fourth **World Romani Congress** in Warsaw in 1990 a writing system elaborated by the linguist **Marcel Cortiade** was adopted. Its purpose was to enable speakers of different dialects to use the same spelling system to represent different dialect pronunciations. The presidium of the **International Romani Union** approved the alphabet on 7 April 1990. Later, a meeting of the Language Commission of the Union, held during the Helsinki **Summer School**, recommended that no change be made in the alphabet for a period of ten years. It has been adopted in the Netherlands and Romania for educational purposes and has been used in a number of publications.

The alphabet accepted at the fourth Congress was as follows: a b ć ç čh d e f g h i j k kh l m n o p p ph r ś t th θ u v x z ž ӡ

The letters ç and q are used morphophonemically, that is, they always represent the same grammatical form but are pronounced differently. So, in raklesqe (to the boy) and raklenqe (to the boys), q is pronounced 't' in the former word and 'd' in the latter.

The letters ćh and ӡ are pronounced differently according to the dialect. Most speakers of **Vlah** dialects would read them as /shy/ and /zhy/ (approximately the sound in English 'treasure') while speakers of Balkan dialects would read them as aspirated 'tch' and (English) 'j.'

AMADOR, Raimundo 1960–. Spain. Musician. A **flamenco** guitarist. In the 1980s together with his brother Rafael he fused flamenco with blues to produce "a fast witty sound" (as Giles Tremlett described it in *The Guardian*). He has recorded with BB King.

AMARO DROM (our road).(i) See INTERNATIONAL UNION OF THE ROMA OF THE BALTIC STATES AND THE CIS.

(ii) A name used for their periodicals by several organisations including the **Roma Parliament** (Hungary).

AMAYA, Carmen 1913–63. Spain. Dancer. She emigrated to the US at the time of the Spanish Civil War. Her metallic, harsh voice and powerful dancing gained her success in the New York nightclub scene. She appeared in over thirty films. A biography, *A Gypsy Dancer*, was published in 1942.

AMAYA, Lorenza Flores (La Chunguita). Spain. Contemporary dancer. A **flamenco** performer in Spain whose career started in 1965. The younger sister of Micaela Amaya.

AMAYA, Micaela (La Chunga) 1938–. Spain. **Flamenco** dancer. The elder sister of **Lorenza Flores Amaya**.

AMAYA, Pepe. Spain. **Flamenco** dancer. He took part in the Paris Exhibition of 1900.

AMENZA KETANE (We together). Music group from Austria whose latest music contains traditional **Lovari** songs together with more modern songs from the pen of Hojda and **Ceija Stojka**.

AMERICA. Estimated population is over two million, the majority being descendants of the **Kalderash** and other **Vlah** immigrants. English Romanies and **Irish Travellers** are found in North America and descendants of Spanish Gypsies in Central and South America. Some writers give a figure as high as four million with one million in Brazil alone.

It is thought that Romanies began to arrive in the Americas during the late fifteenth/early sixteenth century, from Europe. Many came during the period of colonisation, with deportations to the new colonies bringing Portuguese Gypsies to Brazil and those from Spain to countries newly colonised by the Spanish. Aside from the forced deportations, many Romani families decided to come to the New World in order to seek new horizons and escape the persecution they were facing in their countries.

At the beginning of the twentieth century many European Rom began to emigrate voluntarily to various destinations in Central and South America. These groups included Kalderash, **Machvaya**, **Bayash**, **Sinti** and the Spanish and Portuguese **Calos**. More recently, due to the political events in Eastern Europe and the continued poverty and racism, many Rumanian, Serbian and Bosnian Roma have also arrived in Latin America. Jose Bernal from Argentina is a poet and well-known figure at international conferences

In 1908 the Machvano Adams family founded the National Gypsy Association of America and in 1928 the Kalderash Steve Kaslov set up the Red Dress Gypsies' Association. Attempts to set up a national organisation in the US have been hampered by the vast geographical distances between centres. However, more recently the American Romani Alliance was established by **Ian Hancock** and John Nickels. Amongst its activities is a family counselling centre in New York for newly arrived Roma.

Vlah families have been coming to Canada from the nineteenth century while recent years have seen several thousand asylum seekers from Eastern Europe, many of whom have been have

given refugee status. The Romany Community and Advocacy Centre was set up in Toronto in 1998 and the magazine *Romano Lil* started publication that same year. See also LEE, Ronald; BERNAL, Jorge and QUITO COMFERENCE.

AMICO ROM. Italy. Est. 1994. An international competition for Romani literature and the arts.

ANDO DROM. Hungarian band, founded by **Jeno Zsigo**, that plays **Vlah** music in a popular style and is currently one of the most successful of Hungary's professional Romany ensembles. CD: *Kaj phirel o Del* (Where God walks) and *Phari Mamo* (It's hard, mother).

ANGLO-ROMANI. See POGADI CHIB.

ANTHEM. See NATIONAL ANTHEM

ANTI-SOCIAL BEHAVIOUR ACT 2003. UK. This Act introduced stronger powers against unauthorised caravan sites than the ***Criminal Justice and Public Order Act of 1994.***

APPLEBY FAIR. A traditional horse fair in the north of England dating back to 1685, attended nowadays mainly by Gypsies and tourists. Attempts were made by local people to ban it in the 1960s and the Boswells – a respected Romani family – set up a defence committee to save the fair. In 2001 the fair was suspended because of foot and mouth disease. It takes place from the second Wednesday in June and moving the popular **Derby** horse race from midweek to the same weekend to suit TV has produced a clash of interests. Most Gypsies seem to have opted for Appleby and in 2003 some 10,000 Gypsies and other Travellers attended.

ARCADE FOUNDATION. Sweden. Based in Sweden, the Arcade Foundation is an internationally run Roma organisation dedicated to developing and supporting Roma related projects around the world.

ARLIA. See ERLIA.

ARMENIA. Estimated Gypsy population: 10,000. The Romanies came into contact with Armenian speakers on their way from India to Europe as they passed through the Caucasus and what is now north-eastern Turkey. A number of Armenian words were borrowed by Romani at this time such as bokoli (a type of cake or bread). Some Gypsies remained in Armenia and other parts of what is now the CIS and Turkey, and they are known as **Bosha** or **Lom**.

ARPAD, Toni. Hungary. Contemporary musician. A **cimbalom** player, he has played with *Muszikas* and other folk bands.

ART. Since 1945 a number of Gypsy artists have emerged. In Austria **Karl Stojka** and his sister, **Ceija Stojka**, have become well known. Karl's paintings have been exhibited widely outside Austria. In the Czech Republic Rudolf Djurko paints on glass. Another painter in the Czech Republic is Mirka Preussova. Unschooled artists have emerged, particularly in Hungary where there have been two national exhibitions of work by self-taught Gypsy artists. The first exhibition was held in 1979 and the second in 1989. Seventeen artists showed their work at the second exhibition, including **János Balázs**.

ASHKALI. The Ashkali are an ethnic group in Kosovo who are related to the Romanies but do not speak the language now although it is likely that they did once speak it. Alternatively, they could be the descendants of a nomadic group of local origin such as the many **Travellers** in Europe who are not of Indian origin. Similar groups in Albania and Macedonia are called *evgit* or *gupt* (as opposed to the Romany Gypsies who are called *medjup*) to the extent that the majority population do not distinguish between the groups. All three names appear to be derived from the term '**Egyptian**'.

The largest number live in Ferizaj. Many Ashkali are educated and have professional qualifications. They have taken the lead in wanting to be called Egyptians, rather than Ashkali, and claim descent from Egyptians who came to the Balkans many centuries ago. There have also been Ashkali political associations some of which survived the recent conflict. The pro-Albanian Democratic Party of the Ashkali of Kosovo was set up in Ferizaj in 2000.

During the hostilities Ashkali were attacked first by Serbs and then by Albanians and many fled to neighbouring Macedonia and Montenegro. The situation at the time of writing is that it is still not safe for Ashkali in many parts of Kosovo.

ASOCIACIÓN SECRETARIADO GENERAL GITANA. Spain. A Catholic-oriented organisation operating from Madrid. It works for improvements in the educational and employment prospects for Gypsies. The Association publishes the bulletin *La Senda* devoted to training and employment.

ASSOCIATION INTERNATIONALE DES ECRIVAINS TZIGANES. France. Est. 1964. This group is no longer active.

ASSOCIATION OF GYPSIES / ROMANI INTERNATIONAL. US. Est. 1995. President: Harold Lush. A Christian non-profit making association set up with the intention of assisting the Gypsy population.

ASSOCIATION OF GYPSY ORGANISATIONS. UK. Est. 1977. Secretary: Roy Wells. Formed by ex-members of the **Gypsy Council**, it linked a number of Gypsy and Gypsy support organisations. Its activities ceased around 1981, except for a small number of projects now run by the independent **Gypsy Sites Management** and Welfare Committees.

ASSOCIATION OF ROMA COMMUNITIES OF THE BALTIC COUNTRIES AND THE COMMONWEALTH OF INDEPENDENT STATES (ARBCIS)). See INTERNATIONAL UNION OF THE ROMA OF THE BALTIC STATES AND THE CIS.

AŠUNEN ROMALEN (Listen, Romanies). A radio programme broadcast from Belgrade (1981–7).

ATHINGANI. Czechia. An organisation for the education of Romani youth.

ATSINGANI (ATHINGANI) ('ungodly'). Heretical Christian sect that flourished in the **Byzantine Empire** during the eighth and ninth centuries. The term was used pejoratively and two Byzantine Emperors (Michael II and Nikephorus I) were referred to by their enemies as athingani. When the Gypsies arrived from the East, they did not practise Christianity but were probably still following Hinduism or Zoroastrianism. As a result, they too were called atsingani. The 'Atsingani' who settled in Thrace (near the modern town of Plovdiv in Bulgaria from 803 may well have been Gypsies. The term has survived in the names given to the Gypsies in many countries, including *cingene* (Turkey), *tsigan* (most Slav-speaking countries), the German word *Zigeuner* and French *tsigane*.

ATKINS REPORT. UK. The report on the working of the ***Caravan Sites Act of 1968*** prepared for the government in 1991 by a firm of private consultants W.S. Atkins Planning and Management Consultancy. The researchers were G. Clark and D. Todd. The report accepts that the Caravan Sites Act was intended to enable Gypsies to continue their traditional way of life while using official caravan sites and criticises local councils for not carrying out the provisions of the Act (which has since been repealed). The report also accepted the idea of 'designation' by which Gypsies were barred from certain areas of England and Wales.

AUSCHWITZ. A Nazi concentration camp in Poland. Auschwitz (Oswiecim) was opened in 1940 and Gypsies were among the first prisoners. Several transports of Czech Gypsies arrived in the camp in 1942. A satellite camp was opened nearby at Auschwitz-Birkenau, and in March 1943 a Gypsy Family Section was created within the barbed wire wires of the larger camp. Between March 1943 and August 1944, over 20,000 Romanies were brought to Auschwitz and held in poor conditions. The death rate from disease and malnutrition was high, especially among the children. On 16 May 1944 the SS attempted to take the Gypsies to the gas chambers but were frustrated by resistance with improvised weapons. Following this all the adult internees were sent to other camps to work and the remaining prisoners, some 2,800 women, children and elderly men, were gassed on the night of 2–3 August 1944. The memorial to the several million people killed in Auschwitz has an inscription in Romani. See also HOLOCAUST.

AUSCHWITZ DECREE (Auschwitz-Erlass). In December 1942, Heinrich Himmler, head of the German police, issued an order that Gypsies from Germany and a number of other, mainly Western European, countries should be sent to the new **Auschwitz**-Birkenau Camp. Certain categories of Gypsies were to be exempted, for example, those who had served in the German forces and those **Sinti** who were considered to be of pure Gypsy blood and capable of forming a small company of nomads that would be preserved as a form of living museum. When the instructions to the police were published early in 1943, these exemptions were mostly ignored so that when the time finally came to arrest the Gypsies and deport them to the concentration camp, few exceptions were made.

AUSTRALIA. Many Gypsies were deported from England as petty criminals from 1787. The main clans to be found today are English Romanies (descendants of the earlier deportees and newer arrivals), **Kalderash** (who came from the late nineteenth century) and immigrants from Eastern Europe after 1945. Organisations include the Romani Association of Australia (founded 1990) and Romani International Australia. There is an annual gathering at Bendigo every November.

Notables among the Romani community include Kenneth Lee, a university lecturer, the poets Lee Fuhler and Henry Lawson, together with Brian Hungerford, musician and playwright.

AUSTRIA. Estimated Gypsy population: 25,000. Gypsies probably first reached

Austria in the fifteenth century. From 1758 **Maria Theresa** began a policy of settling nomads and assimilating them. She prohibited Gypsies from living in tents, wandering, dealing in horses, speaking in Romani and marrying other Gypsies. All of these decrees were ignored by the Gypsies, or 'New Hungarians' as she wished them to be called. By the twentieth century, however, the majority of the Gypsies were at least semi-settled, travelling only in the summer.

In 1924 a Gypsy primary school opened in Stegensbach (**Burgenland**) and seems to have operated successfully after a difficult start. No provision was made in the school programme for classes in Romani, German being the only language used. But it did include special subjects like the violin and Gypsy history, as well as a topic entitled *Die Zigeuner als Landplage* (The Gypsies as a National Menace). The Nazis closed the school in 1938.

Austria was annexed to Hitler's Germany in 1938 and the measures already operating against Gypsies in Germany were applied to Austria. Gypsies were fingerprinted and forbidden to leave the country. In June 1938 sporadic arrests began of Romani men who were sent to Dachau concentration camp. In autumn 1939 several hundred women were arrested and sent to Ravensbrück camp. An internment camp was then set up at Salzburg (Maxglan) to hold Gypsies in readiness for a planned deportation to Poland that in the event was not to happen until much later. In November 1940 a forced labour camp was opened at Lackenbach. The families were permitted to live together but conditions in many ways resembled a concentration camp. The highest total of inmates was 2,300 in November 1941. Many died in the early years from the poor conditions and were buried in the nearby Jewish cemetery. In 1941 transports containing 2,000 persons were sent from Lackenbach to the Jewish **Lodz Ghetto**, mainly women and children. Few survived. A further 2,600 Gypsies were sent from Austria to Auschwitz, including many from the Salzburg camp, which was closed.

One bright chapter in this sad story was the action of Baron Rochunozy, who was determined that none of the families who worked for him should fall into the Nazis' hands. He helped them to escape across the frontier to Hungary and was later forced to flee himself. Toward the end of the war conditions were improved in Lackenbach camp as the prisoners were put to work helping the German war effort and many were able to survive. Two-thirds of the some 11,000 Austrian Romanies and **Sinti** are estimated to have perished during the Nazi period.

After 1945, those Gypsies who had been imprisoned in Lackenbach or Salzburg did not get any compensation until 1961. It was not until 1988 that they were put on the same basis as those who had been in the concentration camp at Auschwitz.

The small number of Austrian Romanies and Sinti surviving the **Holocaust** has been augmented by immigrants coming to work, in particular from Yugoslavia, and more recently by refugees from Eastern Europe. Considerable anti-Gypsy feeling persists among the Austrian population at large. This sentiment surfaced in 1995 when a sign appeared near the Romani settlement of Oberwart in Burgenland reading (in German) 'Romanies back to India'. When four Gypsies tried to remove it, a bomb blew up, killing all four. The Austrian playwright Elfrieda Jeleneck wrote a play on the subject but, because of the racist attacks on her, decided the play should have its performances in Hamburg and not in Vienna. The probable perpetrator was to commit suicide in prison.

The first Gypsy organisation in Austria, Verein Roma, was founded in 1989 in Oberwart and was followed by other groups. In 1993 some Gypsies were given recognition as a *Volksgruppe* (ethnic group) – a status shared, for example, by the Hungarians and Croats. The 5,000 or so Gypsies recognised as the ethnic group are those who belong to families who have been in Austria for three generations. They have some legal rights as a result of this status. There is now a Romani advisory council (which includes non-Romani representatives) that advises the prime minister.

The unrecognised Gypsies are in a precarious situation as they are affected by a number of laws for aliens (*Asylum Law of 1992*, *Aliens* and *Residence Laws of 1993*). Neither the police nor the authorities have been particularly helpful to these Gypsies. In 1996, Nicola Jevremovic, and his wife were beaten by police after a traffic incident. Their complaint ended with their being given suspended prison sentences for 'resisting arrest'

The **Romano Centro**, Vienna, acts as a cultural and advice centre for many Romanies. Other associations, including the Kulturverein Österreichischer Roma (Cultural Association of Austrian Roma) are also in Vienna. Recently workers at the University of Graz have developed an extensive collection of reading materials in the Burgenland dialect of Romani.

AUTONOMIA FOUNDATION. Hungary. Est. 1990. Founder: Andras Biro. A voluntary organisation that includes work with Romanies among its activities. In the past it has supported income-generating projects in co-operation with registered local Romani organisations.

AVEN AMENTZA FOUNDATION (Come with us) (also known as Romanathon). Romania. Est. 1990. President: Vasile Ionescu. The main aim of Aven Amentza is to aid the institutional building and development of Roma communities. This is achieved through policies for asserting ethnic identity such as multicultural education.

B

BAGLAENKO, Valentin 1938–88. USSR, Crimea. Singer. He first performed with a Gypsy Circus and finally in 1967 joined the **Teatr Roma**. He has toured in Europe with the Kharkov Operetta, performed as a horse rider and dancer, as well as making several recordings.

BAIRD, Reverend John 1799–1861. Scotland. Cleric. The leader of a mission to reform Gypsies and **Travellers** in Scotland in the nineteenth century.

BAJRAMOVIĆ, Šaban 1936–. Serbia. Singer and composer. He has performed in the films of Emir Kusturica and has often sung on radio. He has also recorded his songs.

BAKO, Maria. Hungary. Contemporary actress. She is the star of the Italian film *Un' anima divisa in due* by the director Silvio Soldini. She was invited to the Venice Festival of 1993 but was refused entry by the immigration authorities at Milan airport, who suspected her of being an illegal immigrant.

BALAZS, Gustav. Hungary. Contemporary musicologist and dance instructor. He has studied the Gypsy form of the **czardas** in Hungary and Transylvania and teaches a dance summer school each year in Hungary. He is currently resident in Holland.

BALAZS, Janos 1905–77. Hungary. Artist. Self-taught, he began to draw as a child but was discouraged by his parents. He took up painting again in 1968. His first solo show was in 1977 at Salgotarjan and his work has been exhibited since in Hungary and abroad. He said that his paintings show distorted figures because they stem from our own distorted world.

BALIARDO, Manero 1940–. France. Singer.

Born in Montpellier, where he still lives. He is a cousin of **Ricardo Baliardo**. He works as a builder and sings largely for his own entertainment.

BALIARDO, Ricardo (Manitas de Plata) 1940–. France. Musician. His stage name literally means 'Little hands of Silver'. Born in Arles, he learned to play the guitar from his father, who was a horse dealer. Ricardo Baliardo has made many recordings and has toured widely. He is father to three of the **Gypsy Kings** and uncle to the other four.

BALIĆ, Sait. Serbia. Twentieth century engineer and political activist. He was a member of the Serbian Parliament and was elected president at the third **World Romani Congress**.

BALKANROM. Sofia. Est. 2000. A Romani federation founded in Sofia on 28 January 2000 with representatives from ten Balkan states.

BALOGH, Attila 1956–. Hungary. Writer. His poems and essays are mainly written in Hungarian. He is Director of the From the Danube to the Ganges Foundation which aims at reconstructing the origins of Europe's Gypsies.

BALOGH, Kalman 1959–. Hungary. Musician. A **cimbalom** player from Miskolc, he was taught by his uncle Elemér, also famous in his time, and then studied classical music at the Ferenc Liszt Academy of Music in Budapest. Possessing a wide repertoire, he has played with many bands such as Teka and Muszikas and has recorded as a soloist. He has made a number of tours throughout the world, including three in North America. Kalman Balogh also teaches the cimbalom.

BALT-SLAVIC ROMANI. A name given by some scholars to a cluster of Romani dialects spoken in Belarus, Lithuania, Poland and Russia by over 800,000 persons.

BALTIC STATES. See Estonia, Latvia and Lithuania

BALTZAR, Veijo 1942–. Finland. Author. As a child he shared a tiny cottage with his horse-dealer father, mother and nine

sisters and brothers. He describes Gypsy life and culture from inside his own group in his first novel *Polttava Tie* (Burning Road), published in 1968. This work was translated into Swedish. The second novel *Verikihlat* (The Blood Engagement) published the following year, describes the consequences of a vendetta while the third *Mari*, published in 1973, is the story of a woman's role in Gypsy society. He is also a talented painter.

Veijo Baltzar was the prime mover in the setting up in 2002 of the **International Union of Romani Writers**.

BAMBERGER, Jakob. Germany. Twentieth century boxer. A runner-up in the German national flyweight championships. He was a member of the Olympic team in 1936. In 1940 he was arrested in Prague and sent to the Flossenburg and later Dachau concentration camps.

BANAT. Province in the Balkans bordering Romania that has at different times been under Hungarian (c. 850 – c.1550) **Ottoman** (c.1550–1718) and Austrian (1718–1920) rule. Records exist of Gypsies in the eighteenth century engaged in charcoal burning, gold washing, bear leading, horse trading and coppersmithing. They performed services for the villagers, the value of which was recognised in an edict of 1757 to stop tax collectors from driving Gypsies out of the villages by extortionate taxation. In 1763 a census recorded some 5,000 Gypsies. The historian Angus Fraser has suggested, on linguistic grounds, that the **Kalderash** coming into Western Europe in the nineteenth century had emigrated from the Banat and not from Wallachia and Moldavia, as others maintain. In 1920 the Banat was divided between Hungary and Yugoslavia. During the Second World War, the Yugoslav Banat was under direct German military rule, and persecution of the Gypsy minority began towards the end of the war.

BANGA, Dezider 1939–. Slovakia. Poet. He writes in both in Slovak and Romani. A collection of his works in Slovak – *Piesen Nad Vetrom* (Songs of the Wind) – was published in 1964. He has also collected and published folk tales and songs. Dezider Banga set up the organisation Romani Kultura.

BANJARA. A tribe found throughout India who live a similar life to that of the nomadic Gypsies of Europe. They are also known as Lambadi and their language is called Gor-Boli. In 1953 the first congress was held of the All-India Banjara Seva-Sangh. A Banjara delegation attended the second **World Romani Congress.**

Dr Shyamala Devi was one of the first of the tribe to go through university and she has visited Europe many times and made a video about the Banjara-Romani connection.

BARGOENS. A variety of Dutch spoken by **Travellers** in Belgium and Holland (the *Woonwagenbewoners*). Some of the vocabulary is of Romani origin e.g.lobie (money).

BARI, Karoly 1952–. Hungary. Poet and dramatist. He was imprisoned in the 1970 because of his 'political' poems. He spent sixteen years collecting and publishing Gypsy tales and songs from Hungary, where he lives, and Transylvania. Nevertheless, Karoly Bari writes mainly in Hungarian and regards himself as a Hungarian rather than a Gypsy author.

BARRETT, Frank (Francie) 1977–. Ireland. Boxer. An **Irish Traveller** and the amateur light welterweight champion of Ireland. He carried the Irish flag and took part in the 1996 Olympic Games.

BAXT(Good fortune). Cultural festival held in Trondheim, Norway, April 2000.

BAYASH, BEYASH, BOYASH. Gypsy clan living in east Hungary and Transylvania. They do not speak Romani but an archaic form of Romanian. A start has been made on developing a written language.

BELA, Osztojkan 1948–. Hungary. Poet. He is the chief editor of *Phralipe*, a monthly Romani literary magazine and the president of The Phralipe – Free Organisation of Gypsies, a Hungarian Roma Rights group. His publications include a book of poems, a collection of short stories titled *Nincs itton az isten* (God isn't home) and a novel *Atyin Joskanak nincs, aki megfizesse* (Nobody will pay for Atyin Joska).

BELARUS. Estimated Gypsy population: 17,500. The census in 2000 counted 11,500. The main groups are Belarussian Roma and **Haladitka**. The first document referring to Gypsies on the territory of present-day Belarus dates from 1501 when Earl Alexander of Lithuania gave the Gypsies a certain autonomy under their chief Vasil, in Belarus, Lithuania and Poland. In 1586, however, the Parliament of Lithuania-Poland issued a decree expelling all Gypsies who refused to settle down. This applied to Belarus. There was still some measure of self-government, as in 1778 when Jan Marcinkiewicz was appointed the chief of the Gypsies in the area around Mir, and he continued in this role until 1790. At that time there was a famous academy where bear trainers were educated at Smorjan. In 1780 the Polish king, Stanislaw II, authorised a non-Gypsy, Jakob Zniemarowski, to be king over the Romani people in Belarus (as well as Lithuania, Ukraine and Poland). He continued to rule until 1795 when Belarus was annexed by the Russian Empire. From then until 1991, the history of Gypsies in Belarus followed that of Russia and the Union of Soviet Socialist Republics.

During the German occupation (1941–4), half of all the Gypsies in Belarus were killed by the Task Forces (**Einsatzgruppen**) and army units in concentration camps, such as Polask and Trastiniets, as well as in the woods near their homes. Others, including Admiral Kotslowski, served in the Soviet armed forces or the partisans.

After the end of the Second World War in 1945, little cultural activity took place, although from 1987 to 1989 **Valdemar Kalinin** ran the folk group Belvelitko (Evening Party). The major dialect (**Balt-Slavic**) is similar to that of northern Russia and had been used during the 1930s for literacy purposes. Since the break-up of the Soviet Union, there have been some isolated racist incidents, including a pogrom at Sitlagorsk. Nevertheless, there has been a new wave of immigration from the Baltic countries following nationalist attacks there.

The **Belarussian Association of Romanies** campaigns against discrimination in particular in the fields of housing and education. **Oleg Kozlovsky** is the Chairperson of the Cultural Association of Roma. There is also a cultural group in Mogilev headed by A. Kasimirov.

BELARUSSIAN ASSOCIATION OF ROMANIES. Belarus. President: Vladimir Mateev. The main activities of the Association are campaigning against discrimination, in particular in the fields of housing and education, as well as reparations for the **Holocaust.**

BELGIUM. Estimated Gypsy population: 30,000 (excluding **Travellers**). The territory of present-day Belgium saw its first Gypsies possibly as early as 1400, but certainly in 1419 in Antwerp and again in 1420, with the arrival of Duke Andrew of **Little Egypt**, in Brussels. In 1421 they came to Bruges. Duke Andrew said he and his followers had been expelled from their homes by the Turks, and he was given money and food. Later opinion turned against these 'pilgrims.' In 1504 the bailiff of Rouen was told by King Louis XII of France to chase any 'Egyptians' across the frontiers and out of the country. A period likely followed when very few Gypsies were in the country. Decrees in 1856 and 1900 said that foreign nomads should not be included in the population registers. In 1872 foreign nomads were to be stopped from entering the country and those already there, expelled. In 1933 the Foreigners Police was set up, and one of its tasks was to issue special passes for nomads. In 1941 the occupying German forces withdrew these passes and introduced the nomad's card (*zigeunerkaart*), which

was not abolished until 1975.

At the outbreak of the Second World War perhaps only twenty extended families were living permanently in Belgium together with others who had been trapped there by the outbreak of war. Nomadic Gypsies were arrested under the orders of the Germans from October 1943 in both Belgium and northern France, which was administered from Brussels. The encampments were surrounded and everyone taken. No serious effort was made to seek out housedwelling Gypsies. The nomads were held in local prisons and gradually transferred to Malines. On 15 January 1944, a party of 351 Romanies of mixed nationality were handed one piece of bread and loaded into cattle trucks for the journey to **Auschwitz**. Some 300 died or were killed in that camp. The remainder were transferred to other camps, and twelve of these survived until the end of the war.

There are four groups; (1) **Manouche** and **Sinti** who have travelled for several centuries in Belgium, France and Germany; (2) **Vlah** Roma who came to Western Europe from Romania in the nineteenth century and the beginning of the twentieth; (3) Roma who came from Eastern Europe (especially Yugoslavia) after 1945; and (4) some 7,000 non-Romani Travellers (known as *Woonwagenbewoners* or *Voyageurs*), some of whom speak **Bargoens**.

Many Romanies of the second and third groups still travel, whereas the Manouche, Sinti and Travellers mostly live on caravan sites. Many are moving into houses. In Flanders and Brussels some thirty official camping sites are available for about 400 families. It is estimated that fifty more permanent or transit sites are needed for a similar number who park their caravans on private sites, usually without planning permission. In Wallonia a few illegal sites are tolerated. Only one could be regarded as more or less official. Most of the nomads live from recycling or house-to-house sales of craftwork. There has been no long-term Gypsy organisation in Belgium, although individual lawyers and others have helped with casework. The Vlaams Centrum Woonwagenwerk was founded in 1977 but the Association des Roms de Belgique no longer functions. Romano Dzuvdipe and Opre Roma are two recently established Romani organisations recognised by the authorities, representing over 70 per cent of the Roma community in Belgium, with more than 30,000 members.

BELUGINS, Aleksandr Aledzunz (Leksa Manuš) 1941–97. Latvia. Librarian, poet and translator. A graduate of the Latvian State University, he was later Research Librarian at the Institute of Scientific Information in Moscow. Following his long military service in Kazakhstan he wrote a story *Where are you Roma?* His writings include a translation (published in the journal *Roma*) of the Indian classic *The Ramayana*. He was competent in many Romani dialects and several of his poems have been published in *Roma* and – in translation – in various periodicals. He was also the editor of an anthology of Gypsy poetry and of a Romani ABC for both Russian and Latvian Romani.

BENG. The Romani word for the Devil. It is likely that it was already used by the Romanies for reptiles inhabiting the Hindu version of Hell and transferred to the dragon-like Devil they saw being killed by St George in **Byzantine** icons.

BERBERSKI, Slobodan 1919–89. Belgrade. Poet. He was elected president of the **World Romani Congress** at the first congress in 1971. He served until the second congress. In 1972 He became the editor of the Romani newspaper *Krlo e Rromengo* (The voice of the Roma; nine issues in Roma and Serbian language from 1972 to 1973). His poetry is inspired by Roma symbols, traditions and images of everyday life.

BERGITKA ROMA. The so-called mountain Gypsies of Poland. They are later arrivals and speak a different dialect from the lowland Gypsies.

BERNAL, Jorge (Lolo) 1968–. Argentina. Political activist. **Kalderash** Rom from Buenos Aires. He is President of the Romani Organisation for Latin America and is actively involved in collecting Romani fairy tales from his homeland.

BESSARABIA. Territory belonging to Russia (1812–1917) and Romania (1917–40). After 1945 it was retained by the USSR and divided between the Moldavian and Ukrainian republics.

BETTER FUTURE. Croatia. Secretary: Ramiza Mehmedi. A Roma women's organisation based in Zagreb. It aims to raise the status of Roma women in Croatian society and improve their health and literacy.

BEWLEY, Victor 1914–99. Ireland. Social reformer and philanthropist. Victor Brewley was an energetic man who aided **Irish Travellers** in the 1960s and 1970s by raising the issue of their needs. He founded the Dublin Committee for Travelling People that pressed for accommodation in housing and 'halting sites' for the city and country Travellers. He advised the Minister for Local Government on a programme of settlement and was the chairperson of the National Council for Travelling People.

BIBLE TRANSLATIONS. The first time a complete gospel was translated into Romani was in 1837, by **George Borrow**. Verses 30–37 of St Luke, Chapter 10, had been translated into Czech Romani by Anton Puchmayer in 1821 and published in his book *Romani Chib*.

A list of post-1945 translations can be found in the bibliography (in the section Literature in Romani).

BIELENBERG, Raya. USSR. Contemporary singer. It is recounted how, when the Moscow **Teatr Romen** came to play in her town, she jumped on the stage and joined in the singing. The director was so impressed he hired her on the spot. Later, she married a Norwegian journalist and since then has lived in Norway and Paris. She has made several records of traditional songs. Currently she plays in the group Raya and her Gypsy Legacy with members of her family.

BIENNALE KLEINERE SPRACHEN. See ZIGEUNERLEBEN.

BIHARI, János 1764–1827. Hungary. Musician. He composed Verbunkos music and led his own band. In 1808 he wrote the piece Krönungs-Nota for the coronation of Empress Maria Louisa and collaborated in the composition of the *Rakoczy March*, later to become the Hungarian national anthem. He was one of the Gypsy musicians who influenced **Franz Liszt**.

BILA, Vera 1954–. Czechoslovakia. Singer. From **Rokycany**, Vera Bila's repertoire includes songs with contemporary themes. With her group Kale, she has made two recordings and toured much of Europe and USA. She was also the main focus of the documentary *Ziganska Musica*, made by Joachin Kreck in Germany, 1988 CD: *Kale Kaloré*.

BISMARCK, Otto von 1815–98. Germany. Politician. In 1886, as newly appointed Chancellor of the Second German Empire, Bismarck sent a letter to all the states comprising the empire to unify, at least in practice, the various valid decrees against Gypsies. Bismarck recommended the expulsion of all foreign Gypsies to free the territory of the country completely and permanently from this 'plague.'

BITTEL, May 1953–. Switzerland. Pastor and civil rights activist. He has for more than twenty-five years been an activist for the Gypsy cause, in Switzerland as well as abroad and is the symbol of the fight for recognition of the Swiss Gypsies' rights. May Bittel is a member of the Swiss Foundation Assurer l'avenir des Gens du Voyage and the Swiss Commission against Racism,

BITTOVA, Iva. Slovakia. Contemporary musician and composer. A violinist and composer who comes from a musical family, she creates pieces merging Gypsy, folk and jazz idioms. CD: *Iva Bittova With the Skampa Quartet* and *Bilé*

Inferno.

BLACK VIRGIN. A number of churches where there is a statue of a Black Virgin have been the object of pilgrimages by Gypsies. In 1471 the Gypsy chief, 'Duke Paul of Egypt', went to visit the statue of Our Lady the Black Virgin of Guadalupe at Compostela in Spain. Some scholars believe that the Gypsies see in the Black Virgin a reminder of the Indian goddess Kali.

BLAIRGOWRIE. Village in Scotland famous for its berries and music. In season many **Travellers** and townspeople come to help in the picking, and informal music-making sessions take place in the evenings after the picking is over. An annual music festival is also held. **Belle Stewart** and her family are closely associated with Blairgowrie and she wrote the song *The Berryfields o'Blair* as long ago as the 1920s.

BLOCH, Jules 1880–1953. France. Academic and author. He was an expert on Indian studies. In 1953 his book *Les Tsiganes* was published in the series *Que sais-je?* This book has been superseded in the collection by a new book with the same title written by N. Martinez.

BLOCK, Martin. Germany. Academic and author. A professor of linguistics at Marburg University, he wrote in 1936 the book *Die Zigeuner: ihr Leben und ihre Seele* (The Gypsies: their Life and their Soul) which summarised what knowledge there was at the time among outsiders of the Gypsies' life and beliefs.

BLYTHE, James. Scotland. Historical figure. Ancestor of a clan of **Scottish Travellers** in the south of the country.

BLYTH, William Jefferson. See CLINTON, William Jefferson (Bill) .

BODY SHOP HUMAN RIGHTS AWARDS. Launched in 2000, these awards demonstrate a continuing commitment to ethical consumerism by this global cosmetics brand. In 2002 the focus of the awards was the right to housing and the **Romani Baxt** foundation in Sofia, Bulgaria, was selected as a winner from fifty nominees.

BOGDAN, Janos. Died 1999. Hungary. Teacher. A **Beyash** Romani, he studied at the universities of Szeged and Budapest before starting a teaching career. He helped to set up and became the first headmaster in 1994 of the **Gandhi School** in Pecs. He was killed in a car crash.

BOJAXHIU, Agnes (Blessed Mother Teresa). 1910–1997 Macedonia, Skopje. An **Ashkali**, she became a Catholic and emigrated to India where she ran an order based in Calcutta to help the poor.

BOORDE, Andrew 1490–1549. England. Author. He compiled an encyclopedia entitled *The Fyrst Boke of the Introduction of Knowledge* (1547). It had a chapter on Romani, which includes some of the earliest specimens of the language, probably collected in Calais.

BORROW, George 1803–81. England. Author and linguist. He lived with Gypsies in England and visited Spain to learn the language of the Gypsies there. He translated St Luke's Gospel into Spanish **Caló**. George Borrow also wrote several works on the Gypsies, in particular *The Bible in Spain* (1843), *Lavengro* (1851) and *The Romani Rye* (1857).

BOSHA (POSHA). See LOM.

BOSNIA-HERZEGOVINA. Estimated Gypsy population before the recent conflict: 80,000. An unknown number of Bosnian Romanies have sought refuge in other countries since 1992. The 1991 census recorded 8,000 Romanies.

Before 1428 the Gypsy population of Bosnia probably consisted of only a handful of families but no records from that time exist. Then in the period 1428-1875 Bosnia was under the rule of the Turkish **Ottoman Empire** and Gypsies followed the conquerors into the area. Under Turkish rule the Gypsies were treated as any other minority ethnic group, with some discouragement of nomadism, largely because of the difficulty of raising taxes from nomads. In 1574 Sultan Salim II decreed that the Gypsies who worked in the Bosnian mines were to be exempted from certain taxes and had to choose a headman for each group of fifty adults.

From 1875 to 1918 the country was under the rule of the Austro-Hungarian Empire. In 1918 it became part of the newly established Yugoslavia and then in 1941 was incorporated into the puppet fascist state of Croatia.

In the federal state of Yugoslavia which was re-established after 1945, the Romanies were recognised as a national minority in the Republic of Bosnia and Herzegovina. They were allowed to run their own organisations and use the Romani language. In 1986 the **Sarajevo Conference** was held, which was a landmark in the development of Romani culture for the whole of Europe. Delegates came from many countries – though not from the local community – and Romani was used by many of the speakers as well as in the final conference report.

During the armed conflict in Bosnia (1992–5) Gypsy men were conscripted for military service by all three warring parties (Bosniaks, Croats and Serbs). Men from Zavidovici formed an all-Romani unit called Garavi Vod that fought alongside the Bosnian government forces. It is thought that some eighty Romanies were killed in the Serbian-run concentration camp at Manjaca. At least 500 were killed during the fighting in Bihac, Sarajevo and Zvornik. There was no functioning Romani organisation in Bosnia during the war period except in Sarajevo.

At the end of hostilities in 1995, there were still sizable Romani populations in Tuzla and Sarajevo and other towns although though many had fled to western Europe

Some 300–400 Gypsies are living in what was the Serbian district of Ilidza in Sarajevo, and others are in Gorica. The Gypsy population of all Sarajevo is between 1,000 and 2,000, with a high proportion of children. Some six active organizations operate in Bosnia. Braca Romi (Romani Brethren) functions locally in Sarajevo, as do other bodies in

Kiseljak (See Roma), Visoko and Zenica. However, several deputations visiting Tuzla and other towns found that the Romanies were at the bottom of the list for receiving humanitarian help from outside agencies. The German-based **Gesellschaft für bedrohte Völker** helped set up the All-Bosnian Romani Union which held its first conference in 1997.

At the time of writing several thousand Romani refugees from Bosnia are still in Germany and smaller numbers live in other western countries. Some are being sent back to Bosnia, though the new constitution does not allow all the Gypsies who once lived in Bosnia to become citizens of the new federation as they may not all be able to establish residence. A fact-finding mission under the auspices of the **Council of Europe** visited Bosnia in May 1996. It recommended that both parts of the Republic (Bosnia-Croatia and Republika Srpska) recognise Romanies as a nationality. The granting of equal rights to other minorities – Muslim Bosniaks, Serbs and Croats has meant squeezing the Roma out from participation in politics at the higher levels.

Many examples have been reported of police abuse and racist attacks by Bosniaks and Serbs. In 2000 the Bosniak villagers of Meskovici verbally abused Roma passing along the main road on their way to their own nearby settlement and for a short time set up barricades. In 2002 Mr Mehic from Sapna was accused of robbery and beaten with sticks in the police station. He was then thrown out of a police car near his house, sustaining severe injuries. See also REPUBLIKA SRPSKA.

BOSWELL MUSEUM. A privately run museum of caravans and other traditional items in Lincolnshire, England.

BOSWELL, Sylvester Gordon C19th–20th. England. Soldier and author. He was born in the large Gypsy camp on the North Shore in Blackpool, the eleventh son of Trafalgar Boswell. He served in the First World War in the Royal Veteri-nary Corps. He then married and travelled across the British Isles, later settling in Lincolnshire, near Spalding. Boswell was a close friend of members of the **Gypsy Lore Society**. He succeeded in saving and expanding the threatened **Appleby Fair**. In 1970 *The Book of Boswell*, his autobiography, was published from a transcript of a tape recording made by him. It contains a lively account of his life in the army and on the roads.

BRATINKA REPORT. In October 1997 the Czech government adopted the Report by Pavel Bratinka, Minister without Portfolio, *On the Situation of the Romani Community in the Czech Republic*. It addressed a number of issues including discrimination and education. In particular, it proposed amending the *Citizenship Law of 1992* to enable more Gypsies of Slovak origin living in the Czech Republic to obtain Czech citizenship.

BRATSCH. France. Founded in 1979, a popular non-Gypsy band that sings in Romani as well as Yiddish, Kurdish and other languages. Their CD, somewhat misleadingly entitled *Gypsy Music from the Heart of Europe*, contains three Gypsy songs.

BREGOVIC, Goran 1950–. Yugoslavia. Composer and performer. He wrote the music for the film *The Time of the Gypsies*. In his live performances he incorporates Romani musicians.

BRIAVAL, Coco. France. Contemporary musician. He is a musician in the **Django Reinhardt** style. His music has been recorded with the title *Musique Manouche*.

BRITAIN. See separate entries for ENGLAND, NORTHERN IRELAND, SCOTLAND and WALES. Legislation passed in the London Parliament will generally apply in Wales.

BRITISH COMMITTEE ON ROMANI EMANCIPATION. Chairman Len Smith. See EUROPEAN COMMITTEE ON ROMANI EMANCIPATION.

BRITISH ROMMANI UNION. UK. Est.

1990s. President: the poet Tom Odley. It has had a strong Romani nationalist position.

BRNO MUSEUM. The town of Brno in the Czech Republic is the home of the Museum of Romani Culture founded in 1991. The Museum now has its own building. It publishes a journal and books as well as offering public lectures. The director is Ilona Laznickova.

BROTHERTON COLLECTION. Part of the Leeds University Library. It is one of the largest collections of books on Gypsy subjects. The original collection was donated by Mrs McGrigor Phillips in 1950 and an endowment enables its continued progress.

BRUSSELS DECLARATION 1996. A round table on the Roma/Gypsies was held in the European Parliament in Brussels on 12 July, attended by representatives from the major Romani organisations and those working with Gypsies. The declaration adopted by the participants called for recognition for the Romani language and way of life in the school system. It also asked for special attention to be paid to creating employment possibilities for Gypsies as well as healthcare. The Gypsy organisations said they needed support and asked for the international bodies in Europe to each appoint someone as an official representative of the Romani people.

BRYNNER, Yul 1920–85. Japan, Sakhalin. Actor and film star whose trademark was his shaved head. He played the King of Siam in the Broadway (1951) and film version (1956) of Roger's and Hammerstein's *The King and I*. He also gained critical acclaim for his role as leader of the *Magnificent Seven* in the film of the same name in 1956. In a June 1978 interview published by the *New York Times* he said it was uplifting to hear the call Upre, Roma! (Arise, Romanies!) at the second **World Romani Congress**, of which he was patron, and announced that he intended to go to the forthcoming **Chandigarh Festival**. However, his claim to have Romani ancestry is thrown into doubt by his son Rock's biography (*The Man Who Would Be King*) which states that his father was brought up with Gypsies but was not one himself. He appears on a Mantitor LP, produced in New York, singing in Russian and Romani with Aliosha Dimitrievitch.

BUCHAREST CONFERENCE. 1934. This conference was organised by **Lazarescu Lazurica** and the Uniunea Generala a Romilor din Romania (General Union of the Gypsies of Romania). There were a number of invitees from abroad though it is uncertain whether any attended. A number of resolutions were passed and the final declaration asked for equal civil rights for Gypsies and help with education and employment. There was little if any change. It has been considered as the first international meeting of Gypsies.

BUFFALO (*Bubalus bubalis*). The Asian buffalo played an important part in the migration of the Romanies from India to Europe. Many of the latter were brought by the Arabs as captives from India to serve as herdsmen in Mesopotamia and from there to the coast of the Mediterranean. Gypsies were photographed and painted with buffalo in the nineteenth century in 'Rumelia' and Transylvania. It is likely that they had accompanied herds of buffalo from Turkey into the Balkans under the **Ottoman Empire**.

BULGARIA. Estimated Gypsy population: 800,000. The 2001 Census gave the number as number 370,908. Many Roma tended to identify themselves to the authorities as ethnic Turks or Bulgarians. The town of Sliven has a Gypsy population of around 20,000.

The '**Atsingani**' who came to Bulgaria in the ninth century may well have been the first Roma in the country. By 1396 Bulgaria had become part of the **Ottoman Empire** and the Empire's tax records in 1430 mention Gypsies (Cingene) for the first time. The Gypsies were treated generally as other ethnic minorities by the Ottomans, provided they paid their taxes. There were many craftsmen and farm workers. Some of the Bulgarian Gypsies converted to Islam while other Muslim Gypsies arrived with the Turkish conquerors.

In 1878 Bulgaria was liberated from the Ottoman Empire. In 1886 the new government instituted a decree forbidding nomadism and the *Frontier Law* could be used to prevent the immigration of Gypsies. Neither of these measures was enforced. As a result of economic (rather than legal) pressure many Gypsies took jobs in the newly opened factories, such as textile factories in Sliven, for example. Others continued to nomadise until well after the Second World War.

The central government wished to prevent nomadic and Muslim Gypsies from voting under the new constitution. A conference of Gypsies in Sofia in 1905 was organised to protest against this law and a Bulgarian lawyer Marko Markoff helped the Gypsies in their campaign. A committee was formed and a manifesto drawn up. In 1919 voting was extended and made compulsory for the whole population,

Between the two World Wars, Christian missionaries were active among the Gypsies in Bulgaria. In the 1930s the Scripture Gift Mission published brochures in two dialects of Romani and A. Atanasakiev translated two of the gospels. In Sliven, however, the Gypsies were working in factories and turning toward socialism. Romani trade unionists in Sliven were to take a lead in 1927 in organising a petition to the US government against the execution of the two anarchists, Nicola Sacco and Bartolomeo Vanzetti. Gypsies had also taken part in the largely peasant uprisings against the government in 1923.

The Gypsy periodical *Terbie* (Education), which was the organ of the Muslim National Cultural Organisation, appeared in 1933 but closed in 1934 when opposition political organisations were banned.

During the Second World War some Gypsies from the towns were rounded up and sent to work in labour camps. Others, however, served in the army, and yet others joined the partisans. Dimiter Nemtsov from Sliven, who was serving with the Bulgarian army of occupation in Yugoslavia, deserted and joined the local resistance movement. In May 1942 a decree was issued providing for Gypsies to be directed to compulsory employment. A year later some Gypsies from Sofia had been sent to a labour camps in Dupnitsa and elsewhere. Those who remained had only limited access to the centre of town and the trams.

After 1944 the Gypsies were at first encouraged by the Communist government to develop their own ethnicity. A newspaper was set up under the aegis of the Communist Party, and a theatre **Teatr Roma** was established in Sofia in 1947. The newspaper was at first given the Romani name *Romano Esi* (Romany Voice). The name was changed three times and finally given a Bulgarian title *Nov Put* (New Way). The first editor was **Shakir Pashov**. It proclaimed integration into socialist society as the desirable aim for the Gypsies and was to cease publication with the fall of the Communist regime. In 1945 the Gypsy-led Organization Ekhipe (Unity) was founded with the aim of raising the cultural and educational level of the Gypsies. Shakir Pashov was its head. It was soon closed and absorbed into the Otechestven Front (Fatherland Front), a mass organisation allied to the Communist party. The Romani theatre in Sofia was closed in 1951 and its director, **Mustafa Aliev** (Manush Romanov) left to work in a Turkish theatre. Shakir Pashov himself was interned in a labour camp on the island of Belen.

The government was determined to end nomadism and it was banned in 1958. A circular in the following year referred to 14,000 travelling Gypsies and also stressed the need to get the Gypsies to integrate to the Bulgarian majority and not align themselves with the Turkish minority. The government opened many boarding schools for Gypsy children from poor families and seasonal workers. From the 1950s, Muslim Gypsies were pressurised to adopt Bulgarian names. Gypsies accused of nationalist deviation during this period were sent into internal exile.

When the Communist party fell from power in 1989, Gypsies were allowed once more to have their own journals and organisations. Four acknowledged Gypsies were elected to the first democratic Parliament.

The collapse of the Communist regime, on the other hand, led to a rise in anti-Gypsy articles in the press and racist attacks. Skinheads attacked Gypsies in Pleven at the end of 1995. Others have attacked homeless children who sleep in the Sofia railway station. In March 1995 one Rom died when an apartment block was set on fire in Sofia. In April 2002, five or six people armed with bats and chains attacked a group of fifteen Roma who were on their way home from a **Pentecostal** Church meeting in Pazardzhik. Five Roma were hospitalised as a result. Two fatal attacks on Roma were carried out by private security guards: in May 2002, nineteen-year-old Miroslav Zankov was killed at the abandoned military airport in Gabrovnitsa, near Montana, and in August of the same year, twenty-one-year-old Pavel Y. was shot and killed in Sofia. In August of the following year, twenty-one-year-old Gunal Taliat was murdered at a disco in Silistra, sparking off a fierce demonstration outside the local police station.

Serious violence against Roma in Bulgaria continues: in May 2003, thirteen-year-old Assen Todorov was beaten by his teacher whilst studying at a Romani school in the northern Bulgarian village of Bukovlak. A complaint was filed with the Pleven local court but at the time of writing there had been no response to this from the Regional Prosecutor's Office. Also in March 2003, a guard from the Marcy company shot an eight-year-old Romani boy in the arm, in the town of Burgas, on the coast of the Black Sea. The boy had been attempting to collect scrap wood for heating. Although the boy was hospitalised as a result of his injuries, his mother refused to file a complaint with the police as she and her son live beside the company building and she was afraid of possible repercussions. Three Romani men sustained gunshot wounds and several others were brutally beaten by ten police officers and rangers whilst collecting wood for heating in the forest near Lukovit in northern Bulgaria in March 2003. One of the three Romani men was ordered to dig two graves and another of the men was tortured with electric prods. The local prosecutor refused to initiate legal action on the men's behalf.

There have been other reports of police brutality. Five Romanies, including Angel Angelov, died in custody during 1995 and 1996. No action has been taken against the police regarding these deaths. The investigation into the 2001 police shooting of a thirty-year-old Rom, Slavi Velev, concluded with no results. In other cases, however, action has been taken in respect of persons beaten up by police. In June 1992 Kiril Yosifov from Pazardzhik was beaten. In December 1995 the regional court ordered the Ministry of the Interior to pay compensation. In March 1996 police officers from Pleven were given a suspended sentence of eight months in prison for beating two boys in Vidin. In 2001 a police sergeant was sentenced to pay compensation to Mitko Naidenov after he had beaten him so badly that the victim was hopitalised for twelve days. Heavy-handed police raids took place in March 1996 in Russe and in April in Barkach. A Roma woman was physically abused by police officers while collecting scrap metal from in a gully in March 2003. During the incident, which took place in the Odesos region near Varna on the coast of the Black Sea, she was hit in the stomach with the handle of a mattock. In October 2002, two seventeen-year-old Romani youths were undressed and abused with a truncheon while in police custody in Sofia.

In 2002 the Ministry of the Interior initiated programmes to improve its relations with the Roma and formed a special group to attract them to work in the Ministry, using the Romani language in training. Since the end of 2001 the Ministry had reserved places in the Police Academy for minority candidates to address their under-representation in the police. The Government reported that the number of Romani police officers rose from fifty-nine to 158 during the year, including four officers, eighty-nine sergeants and fifty-five constables. A special Officer for Roma Training Programmes was appointed and bilingual training manuals were published.

The Framework Programme was created by the **Human Rights Project** in 1998 and supported by more than seventy-five organisations throughout the country. In April 1999 it was approved by the then Government. Much of the money allocated for the implementation of the Action Plan was not exclusively earmarked for Roma but for disadvantaged groups, including the Roma, and many of the proposals contained in earlier drafts of the Action Plan were missing from the final version, for example, the plan to create a fund to help towards the process of desegregation of the Roma schools. In October 2003 the Bulgarian Government approved an Action Plan for Implementation of the Framework Programme for Equal Integration of Roma.

There have been a number of projects which have attempted to improve economic opportunities for Roma, including the Ethnic Integration and Conflict Resolution project which was launched in Lom in 2000. The project includes providing limited funds to small enterprises which employ Roma,

undertaking activities to reduce drop-out rates from school and provide tutoring for university enrolment exams, as well as training for leaders where young Roma can develop leadership and conciliation skills. Similar projects have also been developed by other organisations. The Government and the European Bank for Reconstruction and Development funded the construction of new apartments in Sofia for Roma families relocated from the Abyssinia Gypsy quarter.

More than 400 Romani NGOs have been set up and over ten political parties in spite of a theoretical ban on ethnic parties. On 18 November 2002 in Sofia the National Movement for Social Development: Roma was founded by fifty organisations under the leadership of the MP Alexander Filipov. The goal of the Movement is to work for the improvement of the living standards of the Romani population.

There are two Roma members of parliament in the 240-seat National Assembly elected in 2001: Alexander Filipov and Toma Tomov. In 2002 the EuroRoma party (a predominantly ethnic Roma political formation) was technically a member of the governing coalition although it had no representatives in the Cabinet or the National Assembly.

Roma are gaining a higher profile in local politics; in the local elections held in October 2003, the number of Roma municipal councillors elected on the lists of Roma parties rose to 162, as compared with around 100 elected on the lists of Roma parties in the 1999 elections. Others were elected on the lists of other parties. However, the increased political participation of Roma in the election campaign has stirred up anti-Romani sentiment in some parts of the Country.

In February 2003 over 3,000 Roma from the Stolipinovo neighbourhood in Plovdiv took part in a demonstration. They were protesting against the local electricity company's decision to cut off power to the whole neighbourhood after some people omitted to pay their bills.

In December 1991 circular 232 of the Council of Ministers permitted Romani to be taught up to four hours a week on a voluntary basis, and an alphabet book was produced. Then, from 1997, an experimental programme of Romani culture has been on offer in some schools to all children. Figures collected in 2002 showed that less than 8 per cent of Romani children had completed secondary education. Many Romani children starting school have problems from the outset as a large number are not prepared for school and some are not proficient in Bulgarian. Romani and ethnic Bulgarian children usually attend separate schools although integration programmes, including bussing, have been set up in several localities including Vidin. The recognition that poverty has prevented many Romani children from accessing education has also led to the Government and Romani NGO's providing free lunches and subsidising textbook and tuition costs. In March 2002 a project in the Silistra region started providing weekend classes for Romani children under the age of fifteen who did not attend school. Experiments in desegregated schooling are helping to raise educational standards amongst the Roma. In July 2002 the **Romani Baxt** foundation started to implement the desegregation programme for Roma schools in Sofia with the support of Open Society. In 2003 the University of Veliko Tarnovo opened a special department headed by **Hristo Kyuchukov** where teachers of Romani are being trained.

The Gypsy population of Bulgaria today is mixed, Christian and Muslim. The recently settled nomads speak a variety of Romani dialects, both **Vlah** and non-Vlah, while the established sedentary communities speak mainly **Erlia**, Turkish or Romanian as their first language. Thanks mainly to compulsory education in the Communist period, Gypsies are found at all levels of society, from surgeons to labourers. Music is a popular profession.

BUNYAN, John 1628–88. England. Baptist preacher and author. His major work was *Pilgrim's Progress* (1678). He said he came from a **tinker** family but there is no evidence that he was an ethnic Romani. The surname, with the spelling Bonyan, however, was recorded as used by Gypsies in the 1590s in England.

BURGENLAND. Province in the east of Austria. Many Gypsies were settled there by **Maria Theresa**. During the 1930s their economic position as casual farm workers was becoming difficult and friction arose with local Austrians competing for work. They were among the first to be interned by the National Socialists after Germany annexed Austria in 1938. Most perished in **Auschwitz**, Buchenwald, Chelmno and Ravensbrück. There is a small surviving population but few of the children speak Romani. A cultural centre was set up in recent years. Attempts are being made with the help of the University of Graz to preserve the dialect (known as **Roman**) as a written language.

BURHAN, Rahim 1949–. Macedonia. Theatre director and actor. He founded the **Pralipe** theatre company in 1970. He was a joint winner of the 2002 **Hiroshima Foundation** Award.

BURTON, Richard 1821–90. England. Writer, voyager and linguist. One of his books was *The Jew, the Gypsy and El Islam* (1898). In spite of his being probably partly of Romani descent, he painted a bad picture of Gypsies in this work.

BUTTLER, Liljana 1944–. Yugoslavia. Singer. Born in Belgrade, she later left Yugoslavia and stopped singing for several years. She has recently performed with the Bosnian band Mostar Sevdah Reunion.

BUZYLOV, Lyona. Russia. Contemporary singer. As a child she sang in the film

The Gypsy tribe goes to in Heaven. Now she and the family form the Ensemble Buzylov.

BYZANTINE EMPIRE/BYZANTIUM. The name given to the Greek Empire, which covered modern Greece and what is now Turkey. The first Gypsies are recorded in Byzantium in 1054 in Constantinople (present-day Istanbul). They were magicians, fortune-tellers and veterinary surgeons. It is thought these Gypsies entered mainland Europe across the Bosphorus. Others crossed the Mediterranean to the Greek islands and mainland.

C

CABRERA, Maria C16th. Spain. The first Romani woman in Europe to be publicly renowned for her beauty.

CAINE, Michael 1933–. England. Actor. Born in Rotherhithe, Michael Caine has a Romani heritage. His father, Maurice Joseph Micklewhite, was part Romani and his parents and grandparents spent much time at the old horse repository at the Elephant and Castle in London.

CALCUTTA ASIATIC SOCIETY. UK. Est. 1784. Founder: Sir William Jones. It was established at a time when scholars found a link between Latin and Sanskrit, and European interest in Indian languages grew. This was to lead to the recognition of the Indian origin of the Romani language and the Gypsies.

CALDARAS, Hans 1948–. Sweden. Singer and composer. He has recorded mainly traditional music in Swedish and Romani. His autobiography: *I betrakterens ögon* (In the eye of the beholder) was published in 2002. CD: *Caldaras and Stefan Bucur Ensemble.*

CALDARAS, Monica 1943–. Sweden. Teacher, writer and musician. A member of the music group **Gypsy Brothers**.

CALÓ. (i) A variety of Spanish with many Romani words. It replaced Romani as the language of Spanish Gypsies. **George Borrow**'s translation of the Bible is in Caló. (ii) Sometimes used instead of **Gitano** to describe a Spanish or Portuguese Gypsy. It is a Romani word meaning 'black.' See also KALO.

CAMARON DE LA ISLA. See CRUZ, Jose Monja.

CAMMINANTI. Non-Romani **Travellers** in Sicily. Their speech is a variety of the Sicilian dialect of Italian, with many words disguised by inserting a meaningless syllable.

CANNSTADT CONFERENCE. In 1871 during the Wurtemberg Annual Festival, the editor of a Stuttgart paper played a trick announcing that a Gypsy parliament would be held. Many curious people went to see this event. The trains coming to Cannstadt were apparently packed. In January 1872 *The Times* published a notice about the Parliament as did *The Evening Standard* a month later. From this joke the conference has slipped into some books about Gypsies.

CANT. The term used for the language used by **Irish** and **Scottish Travellers**. These are two distinct varieties of English. The syntax and grammar are English but the vocabulary comes from many sources, including the medieval vocabularies known as **Shelta** and **Gammon**. The vocabulary is taught from birth alongside the English equivalent and as the children grow up they learn which words are used by their community and which are the general English words. There is some overlap between Irish and Scottish Travellers' cant. Most Travellers know some 400 words. These words are used within the community to give a sense of identity and sometimes so that the Travellers can speak without being understood by outsiders. In the Scottish Highlands and Islands a third variety of language is found: again a special vocabulary but in this case with the syntax and grammar of Scottish Gaelic.

Examples of cant:Irish Travellers: Bug muilsha gather skai. [Give me a drink of water].Lowland Scottish Travellers: I slummed the pottach in the gowl and then I bing'd avree. [I hit the boy in the stomach and then I went out].Highland and Islands Scottish Travellers: S'deis sium a meartsacha air a charan. [We are going on the sea].

CANTEA, GEORGI. See KANTEA, GEORGI.

CARAVAN. The horse-drawn living caravan was not invented by the Gypsies but rapidly adopted by them in the nineteenth century. It first appeared in France and northern Europe about 1800. The earliest picture of a caravan in England dates from 1804. In 1817 Van Gogh painted Gypsy caravans in France. There are a number of different types such as the Reading wagon. The horse-drawn caravan is called a vardo in the Romani language, a word earlier used for a more primitive type of cart.

CARAVAN SITES ACT 1960. UK. This Act introduced new planning controls on caravan sites in England and Wales. As a result, it became difficult to open new sites and many existing sites were closed if they had not been operating long before 1960. The Act gave local authorities the power to build sites for Gypsies but very few did so.

CARAVAN SITES ACT 1968. UK. This Act placed a duty on county councils in particular to build sites for Gypsies 'residing in and resorting to their area.' At the same time, new powers were introduced to make parking a caravan in an area illegal when the area was 'designated' as having provided enough caravan pitches or when the government judged it was not 'expedient' for the area to do so. Progress under the Act was slow and by 1994 only some 30 per cent of Gypsies were housed on official caravan sites. Others had obtained permission for private sites in accordance with a number of circulars that followed the passing of the 1968 Caravan Sites Act. The section of the Act relating to Gypsies was repealed in 1994 by the *Criminal Justice and Public Order Act*.

CARI, Olimpio. Italy. Contemporary painter. He exhibited at the second **Mondiale of Gypsy Art** in Budapest (1995).

CARINTHIA. Now a province of Austria, previously (1276–1918) part of the Austro-Hungarian Empire. Gypsies are mentioned in the area for the first time in 1692 at Villach. There was a small Gypsy population of Romanies and **Sinti** in the period up to the Second World War. Many of them were transported to Lackenbach internment camp and others put on a train heading in the direction of Tschenstochau. It is possible that they never reached Tschenstochau as the route passed near **Auschwitz**. Plans are under way to erect a memorial in Villach to the victims of the Nazi regime.

CARMEN. *Carmen*, the fictitious story of a Spanish Gypsy, was written by Prosper Merimée (1846) after visiting a Spanish cigarette factory and turned into an opera by Bizet (1875). It is said that Merimée wrote the story in just eight days. The story of a love triangle (or quadrilateral, if we count Carmen's husband) has been filmed by, amongst others, Jean-Luc Godard, Cecil B. De Mille, Francesco Rosi and Carlos Saura. It has recently been turned into a flamenco opera (by **Antonio Gades**) and an ice-show – the latter with a sequence of Irish step-dancing on skates which has no parallel in the original story or opera. It was adapted to be the musical *Carmen Jones* – with a black heroine – in 1943 (and later filmed). In 1997 James Robinson produced a play at the Court Theater in Chicago based on Merimée's original novel with moderate success. The story carries the essentially misogynistic message that female sexual liberation is ultimately punishable by death but this has not served to diminish its enduring appeal.

CARRASCO, Manuela 1958–. Spain. Dancer. After her first public performance at the age of ten she has performed at many festivals in Spain and abroad.

CASH, Johnny 1932–2003. US. Singer and musician. In his last biography, Johnny Cash said that he was part Gypsy. There is a famous family of **Irish Traveller** musicians known as the Cashs.

CATALONIA. In 1447 the first Gypsies were recorded in Catalonia. In 1512 they were ordered to leave the region. Catalonia became administratively part of Spain later in the sixteenth century.

CEDIME-SE. The Centre for Documentation and Information on Minorities in Europe – South East. Based in Greece, it has reported on the situation of Roma and other minorities in central and south-east Europe.

CENTRE FOR CENTRAL AND EASTERN EUROPEAN ROMA. The offices of the organisation are in Brno, Czech Republic, and the director is Karel Holomek.

CENTRAL EUROPEAN UNIVERSITY. Hungary, Budapest. The University runs an academic summer school with a programme on the Roma community.

CENTRE DE RECHERCHES TSIGANES. France, Paris. The centre held a database of organisations, books and articles and up till recently published the journal *Interface*. At its peak, three research and action groups were managed by the centre – on history, education and language leading to the **Interface** book collection. The director was the sociologist and writer **Jean-Pierre Liégeois**. The Centre ceased operation in 2003 due to the ending of its funding.

CENTRE MISSIONAIRE EVANGELIQUE ROM INTERNATIONALE (CMERI) France. Est. 1995. President: Loulou Demeter. A **Pentecostal** group, mainly **Kalderash**, that split from the original Vie et Lumière group in 1995 and formed its own association. They have a central church in Bondy (France) and some sixty-five churches, mainly in Germany and Sweden. They use the Romani language in services. The Roma congregation in London belong to CMERI.

CENTRO STUDI ZINGARI. Italy. Est. 1966. Director: Mirella Karpati. An Italian cultural and educational organisation founded in 1966. It published the journal *Lacio Drom* and has organised several international meetings, including the **Ostia Conference**. The centre ceased activity around 2000.

CERIFINO, Jiménez Malla (El Pele) 1861–1936. Spain. Cattle dealer. In 1926 he became a brother in the Third Order of the Holy Friars. At the outbreak of the Civil War, he defended an imprisoned priest and was thrown into prison. He refused the offer of freedom and was shot in August with other brothers of the order. His beatification took place in 1997.

CHACHIPE. Spain. Contemporary dancer. He began his career performing for tourists. At the age of eight he went to Paris and by the time he was fifteen he had danced in the major cities of Spain and throughout South America.

CHANDIGARH FESTIVALS. The Indian scholar **W. R. Rishi** organised two festivals so that European Romanies could come to their original homeland India and meet their long-lost cousins. Receiving the European delegates to the 1984 festival was one of the last public engagements of Indira Gandhi before her assassination.

CHAPLIN, Charles 1889–1977. England. Film star. His hits included *The Great Dictator* and *Limelight*. In his autobiography he wrote that his mother was half-Gypsy and that his grandmother's maiden name was Smith. According to other sources, she was called Mary Ann Terry. A further possibility is that his maternal grandfather Charles Frederick Hill, a shoemaker, was an **Irish Traveller**. Charlie Chaplin's biographer, Joyce Milton, felt that he was well aware of his heritage and that his tramp character recalled the image of the eternal Romani wanderer.

CHERENKOV, Lev 1936–. USSR. Civil rights activist and writer. For many years after the Second World War he corresponded with western scholars and through them contributed to learned journals on the subject of Romani.

CHERGASHI or CHERHARI (tent dweller). The name given to a number of Gypsy clans: (i) The Chergashi of Bosnia who speak a Balkan dialect of Romani. Many emigrated to Western Europe after 1966. On their visits to London, flower-selling was a major source of income. (ii) The Cherhari of East Hungary who speak a **Vlah** dialect.

CHINCHIRI, Hassan 1932–94. Bulgaria. Band leader, singer and composer. He started performing after 1945 and made several recordings before the clampdown on Romani culture.

CHOCOLATE, EL. See MONTEYA, Antonio.

CHUHNI. Dialect of Romani, spoken in Latvia. Some speakers of Chuhni have recently emigrated to Lithuania. The total number of speakers is perhaps 10,000. A translation of St John's Gospel into the dialect was made as early as 1933.

CHUNGA, La. See AMAYA. Micaela.

CHUNGUITA, La. See AMAYA, Lorenza Flores.

CHURARI. A Gypsy clan that evolved in Romania. Later many emigrated after the end of serfdom in the nineteenth century. The term is considered by some to be derived from the Romani word churi (knife) but this is disputed.

CIBULA, Jan 1932–. Slovakia. Political activist and medical doctor. He currently resides in Switzerland. He served as president of the **World Romani Congress/International Romani Union** from 1978 to 1981.

CICA, Dzintars 1993–. Latvia. Student and singer. He represented Latvia in the Junior Eurovision Song Contest held in Copenhagen 2003 with his own composition *You are summer* and was placed ninth. Dzintars Cica sings in a children's choir in the town of Talsi and has performed with several Romani groups. CD. *Come and Sing.* 2003

CIMBALOM. It is thought that the cimbalom was brought to Europe by the Gypsies. It is a stringed instrument played with sticks and is related to the Indian *santur*. In the nineteenth century it was enlarged and provided with legs, which is the way it is played in Hungary today, though elsewhere in the Balkans it is still hung from the neck.

CIOABA, Florin. Romania. Contemporary political activist. He was elected King of all the Gypsies in 1997 to succeed his father, **Ioan Cioaba**. The marriage of his twelve-year-old daughter in 2003 aroused great public interest.

CIOABA, Ioan 1935–97. Romania. Political activist. An elder of the **Kalderash** clan, he kept in contact with the **Comité International Tzigane** and agitated for Gypsy rights during the Communist period. In 1986 he was jailed under a trumped-up charge of cheating the Government on a copper contract. After the fall of Nicolae Ceausescu, he was a member of the Provisional National Council. He and his son **Florin Cioaba** ran for the senate in 1995 but were not elected. In September 1992 in Romania he was proclaimed King of All the Gypsies. His authority as king was limited to the Kalderash clan but many other Romanian Gypsies saw him as their spokesman. His daughter Lucia is married to the son of Emperor Iulian of All the Gypsies who was crowned in August 1993, while a second daughter **Luminita Mihai Cioaba** is a well-known writer.

CIOABA, Luminita Mihai 1957–. Romania. Poet and journalist. Daughter of **Ioan Cioaba**, she won first prize for poetry in the second **Amico Rom** contest. Her poetry includes the Romeo and Juliet-style ballad *Mara thai Bakro* and the poetry collection *Die Wurzel der Erde* (The Roots of the Earth – published in Romani, Romanian, German and English).

CIULLI, Roberto. Germany. Contemporary theatre director. Director of the Theater an der Ruhr in Mühlheim which was for several years used as a base by the **Pralipe** Company. His support for this company over many years earned him a share of the 2002 **Hiroshima Foundation Award**.

CIVIC UNION OF ROMA. Czech Republic. An umbrella organisation of groups in Hodonin and other towns in the Czech Republic. Its programme includes pre-school activities and a music festival.

CLAN. (i) This term is used in the dictionary in preference to 'tribe' as a collective noun for groupings of Gypsies sharing a cultural and linguistic heritage. These include the **Sinti** and the **Romani chal**, who do not use the word Rom as a self-ascription as well as for those groups that in addition to the general word Rom call themselves by names related to their traditional trade, for example **Kalderash** (coppersmiths) or **Sepedji** (basket-makers). Some clans have a geographic name, e.g. Istriani Sinti.(ii) In Spanish the word '*clan*' is used, by the press in particular, to describe extended families of Gypsies.

CLINTON, William Jefferson (Bill) 1946–. US. Politician. He is the former President of the United States of America, elected in 1993, and descended from Scottish Gypsies. William Clinton was originally called William Jefferson Blyth. Charles Blyth, who held the title of Charles I of the Gypsies, was crowned at Kirk Yetholm in 1847. He is Clinton's great-great-great-great-uncle. Charles's brother Andrew settled in the American south and his son Andrew Jefferson Blyth was born in 1801 in South Carolina. He is the great-great-grandfather of Bill Clinton.

COHEN, Emil. Bulgaria. Contemporary political activist. President of the **Minority Rights Group** in Bulgaria.

COLOCCI, Adriano. Italy. Author. An Italian Gypsylorist. He met Gypsies during a visit to the Balkans and in 1889 wrote a book about them *Gli Zingari: storia di un popolo errante* (Gypsies: The Story of a Wandering People). He was later elected as president of the **Gypsy Lore Society.** He was not just an amateur student of Gypsy lore for he also took up the defence of the Gypsies in 1911 at the First Ethnographic Congress in Rome where he denounced intolerance against Gypsies. He also opposed a proposal in the Italian Parliament to ban the immigration of Gypsies.

COLOGNE CONFERENCE. February 1989. Conference and arts festival attended by more than 450 persons, mainly Romanies, from towns in Germany and elsewhere. A manifesto was issued at the end of the conference – the Cologne Appeal for the Implementation of Human Rights for Sinti and Roma.

COLUMBUS, Christopher 1451–1506. Spain. Explorer. On his third voyage to the Americas (1498) it is said that he was accompanied by four Gypsies.

COMBAYS. Trio from Zaragoza playing rumbas. They made one record in Spain and were the support for the **Gypsy Kings** at the Nimes Festival in 1989. The trio no longer plays together.

COMITÉ INTERNATIONAL ROM. See COMITÉ INTERNATIONAL TZIGANE.

COMITÉ INTERNATIONAL TZIGANE (CIT: International Gypsy Committee). France. Est. 1965. President: Vanko Rouda. This committee sought to overcome religious and **clan** differences amongst the Romani community to create a united body. Muslim, Catholic, Orthodox and Protestant all worked together. The CIT formed several branches in other countries and adopted non-Gypsy strategies, such as demonstrations, to gain publicity for its aims. These aims included preserving Gypsy culture and language and promoting the right of Gypsies to nomadise. It launched the first **World Romani Congress** held near London in 1971. It later changed its name to Comité International Rom (CIR). The CIR's international role was gradually taken over by the World Romani Congress and the **International Romani Union**. The CIR continues to operate on a small scale in Paris.

COMMITTEE FOR THE DEFENCE OF MINORITY RIGHTS. Bulgaria. The

Bulgarian partner in a current project under the auspices of the UK **Minority Rights Group**. Amongst other activities, the committee set up three curriculum working groups to create educational materials about the Romanies' history, literature and music. The Bulgarian Ministry of Education has recently agreed that some of these materials can be used in schools.

COMMUNAUTÉ MONDIALE GITANE (CMG). France. Est. Early 1960s. Founder: **Vaida Voevod III**. An international organisation, it was banned by the French government in 1965 and most of its work taken over by the **Comité International Tzigane**. The CMG nevertheless continued to operate unofficially until 1984 at least under the presidency of M. Stefanovic.

CONFEDERATION OF INDEPENDENT STATES (CIS). A loose confederation of former states of the USSR. There are separate entries for the member countries of the CIS in Europe and neighbouring territories

CONFERENCE ON SECURITY AND CO-OPERATION IN EUROPE (CSCE). Established in 1975 at a meeting of world leaders in Helsinki. One of its aims was to increase democracy in Europe and a development of this has been the protection of minority rights. Both the participating states and the associated non-governmental organisations have taken on board the Gypsy issue. At the CSCE follow-up meeting in Helsinki in 1992 and the CSCE Council meeting in Rome in 1993, it was proposed and confirmed that the **Office for Democratic Institutions and Human Rights** (ODIHR) – an institution of the CSCE – would organise a number of specialised meetings. The seventh of these seminars dealt with Gypsies in the CSCE region and took place in Warsaw in September 1994. A consolidated summary of the discussions was published by the CSCE. In 1994 it the CSCE became the **Organisation for Security and Co-operation in Europe** (OSCE).

CONGRESS. See **World Romani Congress** and **Lodz Congress.**

CONGRESS OF LOCAL AND REGIONAL AUTHORITIES OF EUROPE (CLRAE). The CLRAE works as part of the **Council of Europe**. It was among the first international bodies to concern itself with Gypsies though recently it has done little. In 1979 its Cultural Committee organised a hearing on the subject of the problems of populations of nomadic origin (Roma and Sami).

In 1981 a Resolution on the Role and Responsibility of Local and Regional Authorities in regard to the Cultural and Social Problems of Populations of Nomadic Origin (Resolution 125) contained a number of recommendations mainly directed at the Council of Europe and other bodies. They included the recognition by countries of the Romanies and the Sami as an ethnic minority and the provision of camping and housing facilities.

In July 1991 a second hearing was held in Strasbourg with representatives of Gypsy communities from twelve countries. One of the results of this hearing was the setting up of the **Standing Conference for Co-operation and Coordination of Romani Associations in Europe**.

In 1993 the CLRAE passed a resolution specifically on the Gypsies. This was Resolution 249 on Gypsies in Europe, concerning the role and responsibility of local and regional authorities. It called on various authorities to integrate Gypsies into their local communities by providing camping sites and housing, and consider the possibility of launching a European Gypsy Route as part of the European Cultural Routes programme.

In October 2003 CLRAE discussed the Romanies at its meeting in Rome. An earlier proposal to establish a network of municipalities with Gypsy populations was re-launched.

CONNORS, Johnny (POPS). Ireland. Contemporary civil rights activist and songwriter. After moving to England, he was active in the early days of the **Gypsy Council**. His songs and fragments of his autobiography (*Seven Weeks of Childhood*) have been published in Jeremy Sandford's *Rokkering to the Gorgio* and various ephemera.

CONTACT POINT FOR ROMA AND SINTI ISSUES (CPRSI). Hungary. Est. 1994. The Contact Point was set up at the Budapest meeting of the **Organization for Security and Co-operation in Europe (OSCE)** in 1994. The first coordinator was Jacek Paliszewski, followed by **Nicolae Gheorghe** in 1999. The CPRSI logs all reported instances of violence against Romanies and Sinti and informs the national authorities in the respective countries. In January 1996 the CPRSI organised a Workshop on Violence against Roma in Warsaw attended by representatives of thirty-five Romani and **Sinti** organisations and non-governmental organisations. On 21 November 1996, alongside the **Council of Europe**, they held a meeting, again in Budapest, with representatives of governments and Romani organisations to discuss minority rights and the legal situation of Romanies. This meeting appears to have taken place simultaneously with one of the **Standing Conference for Co-operation and Co-ordination of Romany Associations in Europe** in Vienna. The CPRSI has also prepared a special report on violence against Gypsies for the OSCE Permanent Council and published a newsletter for OSCE's **Office for Democratic Institutions and Human Rights (ODIHR.**

COOK, Albert David (David Essex) 1947–. England. Singer and film actor. He is a singer and actor who took the part of Jesus in *Godspell* (1971) and Che Guevara in *Evita* (1978). David Essex assisted at the official opening of the office in Essex of the **Gypsy Council for Education, Culture, Welfare and Civil Rights** (of which he is patron) in 1995. He has recorded the poems of **Charles Smith** and is the presenter on **Jeremy Sandford**'s video, *Spirit of the Gypsies*.

CD: *Forever* .

CORFU. In the fourteenth century Gypsies were already living on Corfu under the leadership of one of their own **clan**.

CORSICA. Gypsies were first recorded in the latter half of the fifteenth century.

CORTES, Joaquín 1969–. Spain, Cordoba. Dancer and choreographer. His passion for dance was inspired by his uncle, Cristobel Reyes, who performed **flamenco** in local bars and persuaded his nephew to study ballet. His grandfather was the flamenco singer **Antonio Reyes**. Cortes joined the Spanish National Ballet at fifteen and soon became the principal dancer but left five years later to pursue a solo career. In 1992 he established his own company and began to develop his individual style. Combining ballet and flamenco, he caused an instant sensation in the Spanish national press but was also criticised for diluting Gypsy culture. He has appeared in two major films: *The Flower of My Secret* and *Flamenco*. His first show as producer and choreographer was *Cibayi*, followed by *Pasión Gitana* which went on a world tour during 1995–7. Joaquín Cortes insists that his style is in fact a combination of "precision and passion, symbolising the pride of a marginalised tribe, and that just as the younger generation of Gypsies is now adapting to white culture and wants to be absorbed, so Gypsy culture is adapting too."

CORTES, Luis. Spain. Contemporary sculptor. He is currently living and working in Italy.

CORTIADE (COURTHIADE), Marcel 1948–. France. Linguist, lecturer and translator. He has served as vice president of the **International Romani Union**. He has been active in promoting a standard **alphabet** and a common language for literary purposes and organises annual language **summer schools**.

COUNCIL FOR CULTURAL CO-OPERATION (CDCC). France. Est. 1983. The CDCC organised a series of training courses and seminars for teachers on schooling for Gypsy and **Traveller** children. It commissioned, from **Jean-Pierre Liégeois**, an expanded edition of a **Council of Europe** publication on the Gypsies of Europe, which has now appeared under the title *Roma, Gypsies and Travellers* (with a number of translations).

COUNCIL OF EUROPE. Based in France, Strasbourg and including the majority of European countries. The Council first took an interest in Gypsies in 1969 when the Consultative Assembly adopted Recommendation 563 on the Situation of Gypsies and other Travellers in Europe. It recommended to the Committee of Ministers (of the Council) that it urge member governments to stop discrimination, provide a sufficient number of equipped caravan sites and houses, set up special classes where necessary, support the creation of national bodies with Gypsy representation and ensure that Gypsies and other travellers have the same rights as the settled population.

Six years later, in 1975, the Committee of Ministers adopted Resolution 13 containing recommendations on the Social Situation of Nomads in Europe. This again stressed the need to avoid discrimination, provide caravan sites, education and training for adults, and ensure nomads could benefit from welfare and health services.

In 1983 the Committee of Ministers adopted Recommendation R1 on Stateless Nomads and Nomads of Undetermined Nationality, recommending the linking of such nomads with a particular state.

In 1993 the Parliamentary Assembly adopted Recommendation 1203 on Gypsies in Europe. It again proceeded by making recommendations to the Committee of Ministers. Recognition was given to the existence of large settled Gypsy populations in many countries. These recommendations were far-reaching, covering the teaching of music and the Romani language, training of teachers, the participation of Gypsies in processes concerning them, the

appointment of a mediator and programs to improve the housing and educational position of Gypsies.

A first reply was given by the Committee of Ministers to the Assembly in January 1994. The Committee then instructed the European Committee on Migration to conduct an in-depth study of the situation of Gypsies in Europe. Further, in September 1995 the Committee of Ministers replied again to Recommendation 1203 adopted in 1993. The report of the study was declassified and made available to the assembly. The Committee of Ministers has transmitted the Committee on Migration's report to the European Commission against Racism and Intolerance and other bodies.

In 1996 the Council of Europe set up a Specialist Group on Roma/Gypsies, chosen from nominees by the different member states. The first meeting was held in March in Strasbourg. The council appointed a co-ordinator of activities on Roma/Gypsies, John Murray who was based in Strasbourg. He has been succeeded by Henry Scicluna. The co-ordinator visited Romani settlements in several countries during 2003 including Albania,

Regular meetings are organised by the Council. In October 2002, for example, a seminar was held on Roma Political participation: A Way Forward. A newsletter (*Activities on Roma, Gypsies and Travellers*) is published regularly giving an account of the council's work in respect of Gypsies. Issue no.25 appeared in November 2003. See also CONGRESS OF LOCAL AND REGIONAL AUTHORITIES OF EUROPE.

COUNCIL OF SLOVAK ROMA (RRS). Slovakia. Est. 2003. Chairperson: Frantisek Gulas. The Council held its first conference in **Košice** in January 2003, and has over 15,000 members. Through co-operation with other Romani organisations they aim to work with the Slovak government to improve the situation for the country's Roma population. At the time of writing, the RRS envisage an Office for Romany Affairs in Košice to be set up in 2004, where they will, among other things, train social workers and run fundraising projects and activities.

COUNTESS MARITZA. Operetta by the Hungarian composer Emmerich Kalman (1882–1953). The heroine in the aria *Höre ich Zigeunergeigen* (When I hear Gypsy violins) praises the spirit of Gypsy music where one can fulfil all one's romantic desires.

CRABB, JAMES 1872–1940. England. Cleric. He set up a number of educational projects for Gypsies, including a centre for Gypsies in Southampton and tried to promote Christianity among them.

CRETE. Gypsies were recorded in Crete in 1322, living in black tents. It is likely that they returned to the coast of present-day Lebanon. Others came later, and the presence of Gypsies, living in poverty, was noted again in 1528.

CRIMEA. See UKRAINE.

CRIMINAL JUSTICE AND PUBLIC ORDER ACT 1994. UK. This Act repealed the provisions relating to Gypsies in the *Caravan Sites Act of 1968* and introduced new penalties for camping on private land without the permission of the owner.

CRIPPS REPORT. The Labour Government in the United Kingdom in 1977 commissioned John Cripps (later to be Sir John Cripps) to write a report on the working of the *Caravan Sites Act of 1968*. He wrote a detailed report with many recommendations. Some of these were incorporated in a new Caravan Sites Bill that, however, was never passed due to the fall of the Labour government in 1979.

CRIS. See KRIS.

CRISS. See RROMANI CRISS.

CROATIA. Estimated Gypsy population: 100,000. Official census figures were 313 Gypsies in 1961, rising to 1,257 in 1971, 3,858 in 1981, and 6,695 in 1991.

The first written record of Gypsies on the territory of present-day Croatia dates from 1362 and refers to two Gypsies in Dubrovnik. Other early arrivals noted in the next century were a trumpeter and a lute player.

Until 1918 Croatia was associated with the Austro-Hungarian Empire. It then became part of Yugoslavia. During the Second World War, after the German occupation of Yugoslavia, a puppet state was set up covering Croatia and Bosnia-Hercegovina under the control of the fascist Ustashe movement and Andre Paveli. The Ustashe considered all Gypsies, Jews and Orthodox Serbs as the enemy. Muslim Gypsies had a certain amount of protection from the Muslim authorities because Germany wanted the friendship of Muslim leaders in the Middle East.

Under Decree No. 13-542 of the Ministry of the Interior, all Gypsies had to register with the police in July 1941. They were forbidden to use parks and cafés. By 1943 most of Croatia's Gypsies were put in the Ustashe-run concentration camps: **Jasenovac**, Stara Gradiška, Strug and Tenje. At the time of the creation of the Independent State of Croatia, there had been over 30,000 Gypsies, either nominally Orthodox or Moslem. At least 26,000 perished between 1941 and 1945.

Croatia became part of Yugoslavia from 1944 to 1991. At the end of the war very few Gypsies survived in Croatia itself but there was a steady immigration from other parts of Yugoslavia.

Croatia became independent in 1991. During the 1991–5 war in Yugoslavia, many Romanies who did not manage to escape from Baranja (in western Slavonia) were killed by the Serbian occupiers. On 31 November 1991, Serbian irregular units burnt down the Gypsy quarter of the village of Torjanici and killed the remaining eleven inhabitants. Because the Gypsies were Catholics, they were accused of collaborating with the Croats. In 1993 Romanies were driven out of Dubac, a suburb of Zagreb, by Croats returning from fighting the Serbs and have had to resettle elsewhere in Croatia. Several attacks have taken place in Zagreb. In February 2003 Safet Muratovič was attacked by ten youths while searching for scrap metal. They set his van on fire with a Molotov cocktail. Alen Secić was shot and killed in the hamlet of Poljica in southern Croatia. His killer, who was drunk at the time, claimed he targeted Mr Secić because he was selling carpets door to door on Good Friday.

Segregation in education is common. In September 2002 around 100 ethnic Croatian parents prevented Romani children from entering a school in the village of Drzimurec-Strelec in north-western Croatia in protest at the formation of integrated classes. Meanwhile, Romani parents in Cakovec filed a lawsuit against the Education Ministry alleging that their children are racially segregated.

The Cidinipe Romano (Romani Society) was founded in 1991 with its headquarters in Virovitica and as president Vid Bogdan. In 1994 the bulletin Romano *Akharipe /Glas Roma* (Romani Voice) was established and this was followed by *Romengo Čačipe* in 1997, the organ of the first Romani poitical party Stranak Roma Hrvatske(The Croatian Romani Party). In 1997 the Party elected Cana Kasum as its president and he stood for parliament, but unsuccessfully. In 1994 the first summer school was organised in Zagreb for Romani children and a youth organisation was established in 1998. There are other Romani associations in Rijeka, Zagreb (Zajednica Roma Grada Zagreba and Cidinipe Roma ani Zagreb) and other towns.

CRUZ, Jose Monje (Camarón de la Isla) 1950–92. Spain. Singer. Jose Cruz began to sing **flamenco** music at the age of eight and made his first album in 1969. In 1979 he began to expand his repertoire importing influences from rock, jazz and oriental traditions. His first gold album (*Soy Gitano*) came out in 1989. *Alma y corazon flamencos* is a three-CD compilation of his music.

CSARDAS (czardas). A popular couple dance in Hungary and Romania. The Gypsy csardas is traditionally danced with the man and woman not holding hands. The dance may go on for some time with a new man or woman taking over the role of one of the partners.

CYPRUS. Estimated Gypsy population: 4,000 (in both parts of the island). The first recorded presence of Gypsies on the island is from 1468 but it is thought that they were there some years earlier. In 1549 a report described them earning their living from making and selling nails and belts. In this century they trade in jewellery and meat skewers, tell fortunes and sell donkeys. They also travel to different parts of the island to help with the harvest. Many villages and towns allocated sites where the nomadic Gypsies could stop.

In 1974 Cyprus was divided into two parts. In that year Muslim Gypsies fled to the Turkish-held part of the island and Christian Gypsies to the Greek part, whereas previously both groups had circulated freely throughout Cyprus. Shortly after Turkish troops entered Cyprus rumours circulated that the Turkish Government was bringing in large numbers of Gypsies. This proved to be false – the new immigrants were Laz (a Turkic group). The traditional circuit for harvest work in the west of the island for carob and olives and then to the east for grapes has been stopped by partition.

All reports suggest that the small Gypsy population in Greek Cyprus lives in comparative harmony with the Greek-speaking population, although there is little social mixing. In Greek they are known by two names: Yieftos (**Egyptians**) and Tsignos (from **athingani**).

Asylum seekers in the UK from Turkish Cyprus stated that the situation of several thousand Gypsies, known as Gurbet (or Çingan) there, is not as good as in the Greek part. There is a great deal of racism and discrimination in employment. Many tried to seek asylum in Britain to join relatives who came legally as citizens of Cyprus when it was a British colony. In 1994 over 350 Gypsies sought asylum on one day and all were refused. In 1994, too, some Turkish airline companies refused to sell tickets to Romanies, saying they gave Turkey a bad name by seeking asylum in the West. A well-known personage in the community is the painter Asik Mene. The majority of the Gypsies in Turkish Cyprus live in the town of Guzelyurt, in the centre of the olive-growing area.

CZECH REPUBLIC (Czechia). The Czech Republic was established in 1993 when Czechoslovakia became two separate states. Estimated Gypsy population: 200,000. The 1991 census (taken before Czechoslovakia was divided) only recorded 33,000 Romanies. The 2001 census recorded 72,000 with Romani as their mother tongue but only 11,000 declared themselves as belonging to the ethnic group (narodnost).

Most of the families in Czechia had come from Slovakia after 1945. Some of these had difficulties in obtaining citizenship in the new republic and were in danger of becoming stateless. The law stated that applicants for citizenship had to have had a clean criminal record for at least five years. This requirement has been criticised as many Romanies had been punished for acts that would not have been considered crimes in a democratic state. Young unmarried women, for example, who stayed at home were sentenced as work-shy and others obtained a criminal record by committing the 'crime' of moving from one town to another without permission. A citizenship law passed in September 1999 remedied the situation for individuals (predominantly Roma) who lacked voting and other rights due to restrictions under the previous citizenship laws. They were enfranchised under the former Czechoslovakia, but were unable to obtain Czech citizenship at the time of the split with Slovakia despite birth or long residency in the Czech Republic.

Prejudice against Gypsies persists and incidents of discrimination and harassment have been reported. In April 2003, the Czech weekly newspaper, *Respekt*, reported that according to a survey of the Prague-based Centre for the Study of Public Opinion, 79 per cent of respondents would not want Roma as neighbours. Attacks on Gypsies by skinheads and right-wing elements which began before the break-up, as early as 1990, have increased and have led to many deaths.

At least twelve Romanies are known to have died in racist violence since 1992 in Czechia. Two Romanies were killed in 1993 in the space of one week in September. Also in 1993 Tibor Danihel was drowned, fleeing from a skinhead gang. In 1994 skinheads threw Molotov cocktails into the homes of Romanies in Jablonec nad Nisou. In 1995 skinheads attacked Gypsies in Breclav and on a train from Chomutov to Klašterec. Tibor Berki was killed in May 1995 in Ždar nad Sazavou. Roman Zigi was killed in the same year. Further attacks took place in Prague, Hlubaha nad Vltava, Jablonec nad Nisou, Olomouc and elsewhere. In 1995 altogether more than eighty attacks by skinheads and right-wing groups on Romanies were reported, twice as many as in 1994. A band of thirteen skinheads attacked two Romani couples in Pilsen, Bohemia early in 1996.

In June 2001, three friends (two of them Roma) were stabbed by a group of skinheads who attacked them in a pedestrian subway in Ostrava. In July that year Ota Absalom was stabbed to death by a skinhead who was sentenced to thirteen years in prison. An estimated 5,000 skinheads were active in the country in 2003 but many observers believe the figure is much higher. In August 2002, in Česky Tešin, thirty Czech men attacked ten Roma outside the Alexandria Discotheque. Norbert G. had his knee broken with a baseball bat. In June 2003, three drunken youths attacked a Romani couple in their home in the northern Moravian town of Jesenik. The youths slashed the husband in the face and chest with a knife and hit his wife in the eye with a cobblestone. A police spokesman stated that the attack appeared to be racially motivated. A court decision in the case was pending at the year's end. In March 2003, the High Court in Prague sentenced Vlastimil Pechanec to seventeen years in prison for the racially motivated murder in 2001 of a twenty-nine-year-old Rom, Oto Absolon, in the town of Svitavy.

There is evidence of police harassment. In June 1994 Martin Červenak died in police custody. In 2002, Vladimir Precha allegedly jumped to his death out of a window in a police station in Brno. In February 2003, six officers in the north-western town of Litvinov physically abused a Romani man, spraying tear gas into his eyes, and repeatedly hitting him on the head with truncheons until he lost consciousness. The case was under investigation at the end of 2003. In May of the same year, five off-duty officers in the north-eastern Bohemian town of Jičin forced their way into the home of the Danis family, in the Popovice quarter, and beat up three people, including a pregnant woman. The officers shouted racial slurs throughout the incident and threatened to burn down the flat. The Inspectorate of the Ministry of the Interior opened an investigation into the case in the same month, and two officers were charged with the crime and dismissed from their posts although the investigation concluded there was no evidence of racism. A trial was scheduled for early 2004. The Government's human rights commissioner criticised a June 2003 ruling by a Karlovy Vary court that the 2001 beating of Karel Billy by five police officers was not racially motivated. Two defendants were acquitted, and three received ten-month suspended sentences. The Ministry of the Interior has since issued special instructions for police searching Romani dwellings.

The Government is actively trying to recruit Roma to serve as police officers and improve police relations with the Roma community. Police trainees attend the National Police Academy's course in Romani language and culture.

There is discrimination in admission to restaurants, bars and discotheques throughout the country. Signs are often posted to prevent Roma from entering public places. Segregation in hospitals and schools has also been reported. While overall unemployment was 10.3 per cent in 2003, unemployment among the Romani population was estimated at over 70 per cent. Although the law prohibits discrimination based on ethnicity, some employers refuse to hire Roma and ask local job centres not to send Romani applicants for advertised positions. In 2003, Marcela Zupkova, a Romani woman from Hradec Kralove in the north-east was denied employment on the basis of her ethnicity. Individual Roma do not have the legal right to file discrimination complaints; such action must come from governmental authorities.

Roma continue to face discrimination in housing. In 2003 it was reported that many municipalities, including the central Bohemian town of Slany and the north-eastern Bohemian town of Jaromer, have attempted to force Romani families to leave. Tactics employed included evicting Roma from municipally owned homes for alleged lapses in rent payments or coercing Roma to sign agreements that they did not understand which were used to curtail their existing housing contracts. While the Human Rights Commissioner criticised such practices publicly, the law allows municipalities substantial autonomy to take such actions.

Romani children continue to be sent to special schools for children with mental or social disorders at a disproportionate rate, thereby perpetuating their marginal position in society. According to unofficial government estimates, 60 per cent or more of pupils placed in these special schools were Romani children, although less than 3 per cent of the population are Roma. Not only are they receiving an inferior education but schooling is provided only until age fourteen in special schools as opposed to age fifteen in standard schools. Children from special schools can also start work at fourteen – one year earlier than normal. While the government reported that approximately 90 per cent of children attended school in 2003, official estimates indicated that less than 20 per cent of the Romani population were still at school at the age of fourteen, and less than 5 per cent completed secondary school. Students leaving special schools are not debarred from attending secondary schools but the curriculum does not prepare students to pass the tests required to transfer to mainstream schools. Some Romani parents chose not to send their children to school regularly due to fear of violence and the expense of books and supplies.

In 1999, twelve Roma families filed suit in the Constitutional Court to protest the '*de facto* segregation' of Roma children into special schools. Although the Constitutional Court rejected the complaint in 1999, an appeal was made to the European Court of Human Rights in Strasbourg. The Ministry of Education later independently began to implement some changes. They began to work on changes to the psychological tests given to Czech children that many claim are psychologically biased against Roma children. Children are assigned to 'special schools' based on poor results in these tests. In January 2002, the Education Minister announced a long-term plan to phase out the special schools and move pupils from them into regular classrooms.

Many districts with large Romani populations hold year-long programmes to prepare children for their first year in school; these programmes are funded by the Government and administered by local NGOs. More than 100 of these schemes were operating throughout the country in 2003. Some districts tracking local Romani students reported that up to 70 per cent of students who attended this preparation successfully entered and remained in mainstream schools. Other positive initiatives include the placing of Romani teaching assistants in primary and special schools and, by 2003, bilingual Romani-Czech language textbooks were being used in sixty elementary schools. The Ministry of Education has also commissioned a textbook for use in schools on the cultural and historical roots of the Romani minority and highlighting successful members of the Romani community. Local NGOs also have supported additional studies and private initiatives to prepare Romani children for mainstream schools.

The continued high numbers of Roma seeking asylum in the UK during 2002 led to the imposition of pre-inspection controls at Prague's international airport. Roma activists in the UK criticised the controls as 'racist' because they appeared to target only Roma. In August 2002 the Czech Prime Minister issued an unprecedented call for Roma to remain in the country and work with the Government and majority population to address their economic and social problems.

The new freedom to form organisations, travel and publish after the fall of Communism in 1989 led to a flourishing of activities. The Museum in **Brno** obtained its own building and Romani was introduced as a degree subject in Prague University in 1991, taught by **Milena Hübschmannová**.

The state funds radio programmes for Roma on public stations and also supports Roma publications. A new magazine entitled *Romano Vodi*, financially supported by the Czech Republic Ministry of Culture and based in Prague first appeared in February 2003. There are many Romani and pro-Romani organisations operating, such as the Foundation for the Renewal and Development of Traditional Romani Values and the Dr **Rajko Djurić** Foundation.

In 2003, in continuation of its Plan for Roma Integration the Government allocated tens of millions of crowns (several million dollars) at various times during the year for projects designed to promote the integration of the Roma. Allocations supported the construction of community centres and educational assistance.

The Inter-Ministerial Commission for Roma Community Affairs includes twelve government and fourteen Romani representatives, as well as the Commissioner for Human Rights and his deputy. There are, however, currently no Roma in the Parliament. David Dudaš became one of the first Romani priests in history when he was selected to serve the Roma community living near the Holy Trinity Church in **Rokycany** in January 2003.

See also CZECHOSLOVAKIA for the period before 1992–3 and SLOVAKIA for the new state after 1992–3.

CZECHOSLOVAKIA. In 1399 the first Gypsy on the territory of Bohemia is mentioned in a chronicle. There are further references, and then in 1541 Gypsies were accused of starting a fire in Prague.

In general, while the provinces were under the **Habsburgs** and the **Holy Roman Empire**, Gypsies were semi-nomadic in the Czech lands, Bohemia and Moravia. They were largely protected over the centuries against central legislation by noblemen who found their services useful on their estates even though Leopold I in the seventeenth century, for example, had declared that all Gypsies were outlaws. He had ordered them to be flogged and then banished if found in the country. In Slovakia they were pressed to settle by **Maria Theresa** and **Joseph II**.

The modern state of Czechoslovakia

was formed in 1918. In 1921 Gypsies were recognised as a minority and able to organise some sports clubs. However, both the nomads and those living in settlements were viewed with mistrust by the majority population. Nineteen Gypsies were tried for cannibalism in **Košice** in 1924 (and eventually found not guilty). In 1928 there was a pogrom against Gypsies in Pobedim after some crops had been pilfered. Slovak villagers killed four adults and two children and wounded eighteen more.

Nomadism by **Vlah** Romanies was strongly discouraged. *Law 117* of 19 July 1927 placed controls on a wide variety of nomadic tradesmen. All Romani nomads had to carry a special pass and be registered if they were over the age of fourteen. Over the next thirteen years, the number of identity cards issued reached nearly 40,000. Local regulations prohibited Gypsies from entering certain areas.

Germany invaded Czechoslovakia in 1938. The country was divided and the Czech lands (Bohemia and Moravia) became a German protectorate in 1939. The first anti-Gypsy decree during the Nazi occupation by the Protectorate Ministry of the Interior on 31 March 1939, prohibited nomadism in the border zones and in groups larger than an extended family. In May 1942 a further decree was passed (on the Fight to Prevent Criminality) by which Gypsies were not allowed to leave their residence without permission and all Gypsies could be taken into 'protective custody.' A count of Gypsies on 2 August 1942, registered 5,830 'pure and half-breed' Gypsies. Two existing work camps at **Lety** and Hodonín were turned into concentration camps for Gypsies. Gypsies were also sent to the main camp at **Auschwitz** in December 1942 and January 1943. The Lety camp received a total of over 1,200 prisoners, and Hodonín a similar number. Conditions in these camps were poor. Food and medical attention were in short supply and the

Czech guards brutally beat the inmates. Over 500 prisoners died in the camps before they were closed in 1943. Then the majority of the surviving inmates were transferred to the Gypsy Family Camp in Auschwitz, together with over 3,000 Gypsies who had previously been left in supervised liberty. Only some 600 persons all told survived the Nazi occupation of the Czech lands.

In contrast to the multinational state that had existed before the Second World War, Czechoslovakia in 1945 was restored as a state for the Czechs and Slovaks, and there was no place in it for the Romanies as a nationality or even as an ethnic group. Little changed with the takeover in 1948 by the Communists who decided on a policy of assimilating the Gypsies.

The first step was to end nomadism and a law to this effect was passed in 1958. The penalty for disobedience was imprisonment. The 10,000 nomads saw their horses were taken away and the wheels removed from their caravans. In 1958 too, the Communists issued a statement saying that Gypsies constituted a socio-economic group (not an ethnic group) that had problems to be solved in a specific manner. In 1965 the government passed the *Resettlement Law*. It was decided that no town or village should contain more than 5 per cent Gypsies. This meant that large numbers would have to be resettled from Slovakia to the Czech lands. Both the Gypsies and the potential host communities resisted this transfer, although some Romanies had already moved west in search of work in the post-war years.

The Government did allow the setting up of the Svaz Cikan Rom (Union of the Romani Gypsies) in 1968, operating throughout Czechoslovakia. Some 20,000 members joined in the first two years. The Union established a recommended orthography for the Romani language and for a time a number of publications were produced. A Czechoslovak delegation attended the first **World Romani Congress** but no one was allowed to travel to the second or third congresses. Lessons in Romani for teachers were organised from 1971 to 1974.

The Soviet invasion of 1968 led, however, to a change in the liberal policy, under Husak's government. In 1973 Gypsy and other organisations were wound up, the magazines ceased to appear and from then until 1989 there were to be very few publications in Romani.

The next attempt to control the Gypsy population was a sterilisation program linked to a decree of 1972. Hints were passed on by word of mouth to social workers and doctors that Gypsies and other mothers of large families should be encouraged to be sterilised. Special inducements were offered to Romani women, classed as 'socially weak' under the decree. After bearing a fourth child a Czechoslovak woman could be sterilised on payment of 2,000 crowns. Romani women, on the other hand, were offered 2,000 crowns to be sterilised after the second child. Some women were treated without them being aware that the operation was irreversible. The civil rights movement Charter 77 organised protests against this programme. It is believed that 9,000 Romani women were sterilised during the program, including some who had had no children.

In the last years of the Czechoslovak Republic, a revival of organisations and publications took place. In the 1990 elections the Roman Civic Initiative (ROI) gained two seats in the federal parliament. In the period 1998–2 there were eleven Roma in the three parliaments – national and federal.See also GERMANY for legislation for Czech territory in the Middle Ages, SLOVAKIA for the period of the Second World War and post 1992/3, as well as CZECH REPUBLIC.

CZIFFRA, György 1915–70. Hungary. Classical pianist.

D

DANIEL, Antonin 1958–96. Czechoslovakia. Teacher and author.

DANIEL, BARTOLOMEJ 1929–. Czechoslovakia. Historian. A scholar working at the **Museum** in Brno, Czech Republic.

DANIHEL, Vincent 1946–. Slovakia. Author and cultural worker.

DANISH TRAVELLERS. References to the **Tatere** (a pejorative term) are found in Danish literature, especially in the writings of Steen Steensen Blicher. After the Second World War the government stopped the children of the Travellers living in caravans and closed such sites as there were. Very few persons (probably less than 100) identify themselves as **Travellers** in Denmark today.

DARÓCZI, Agnes. Hungary. Contemporary civil rights activist and broadcaster. She was active in the cultural association Amalipe, and has been part of the teams preparing the regular radio and TV broadcasts aimed at the Romani population.

DARÓCZI, Jóseph Choli 1939–. Hungary. Poet, translator and civil rights activist. He has translated the four gospels into Romani as well as **Garcia Lorca**'s *Romancero Gitano*, which has appeared in a trilingual edition in Budapest (Romani, Hungarian, Spanish). He was a praesidium member of the **International Romani Union**. In 1979 he became the head of a new political organisation for the Romanies in Hungary – the Orzsagos Ciganytanacs (National Gypsy Council).

DAVID SOTO, José. See MERCE, José.

DAVIDOVÁ, Eva. Czechoslovakia. Twentieth century sociologist. She helped to keep Romani culture alive during the years 1958–89 and was one of the founders of the **Brno Museum**.

DEBARRE, Angelo. France. Contemporary musician. He is a guitarist in the style of Django Reinhardt. The Angelo Debarre Quintet first toured the UK to great acclaim in 2002, producing their first CD *Impromptu* in the same year.

DEBICJI, Edward 1931–. Poland. Poet. His brainchild is the Gypsy music festival in Gorzów Wielkopolski which has run annually since 1989. In addition to music, it has featured films, exhibitions, and book promotions and, more recently, seminars related to Gypsy culture. He is also director of the Gypsy music group Terno and has written a book *Tel Nango Boliben* (Under the Open Sky) published in 1993 (available in Polish and Romani).

DECADE OF ROMA INCLUSION 2005–15. This is a proposal of the **World Bank, Open Society Institute** and the **European Commission**.

DELANEY, Johnny 1988–2003. England, Derby. **Irish Traveller** killed by two teenagers in Liverpool on 28 May after a gang of youths had shouted racist comments at him and his friends. Two teenagers were convicted of manslaughter – not murder – and sentenced to comparatively short prison sentences.

DEMETER family. Russia, Members of the **Kalderash** Demeter extended family now play a leading role in the Romani cultural life of Moscow, including the **Teatr Romen**.

DEMETER Gejza 1942–. Czechoslovakia. Writer. His work includes the novel *O Mule Maškar Amende* (The dead among us).

DEMETROVÁ, Helena 1945–. Czechoslovakia. Author. She has written a book of short stories *Rom Ke Romeste Drom Arakhel* (A Rom finds a way to another Rom).

DENMARK. Estimated Gypsy population: 1,750. The first recorded Gypsies in Denmark came from Scotland in 1505 and then moved on to Sweden. They had a letter of recommendation from King James IV of Scotland to King Hans of Denmark, his uncle. In 1505 other Gypsies came across the border from Germany. Junker Jørgen of Egypt came to Jutland and got a letter of safe conduct from Duke Frederik. In 1536, however, tatere (Gypsies) were ordered to leave Denmark in three months. This order was not obeyed. In 1554 King Christian III circulated a letter accusing many noblemen and others of supporting the Gypsies, although they were believed to be "wandering around and deceiving the people". Anyone who gave them refuge would be punished, anyone who killed a Gypsy could keep his property, any local authority official who did not arrest the Gypsies in his area would have to pay for any damage they did. The main effect of this letter was that the Gypsies started travelling in smaller groups. A further letter was issued in 1561 by Frederick II, in a milder form than Christian's. A certain Peder Oxe was sent to arrest all Gypsies in Jutland and bring them to Copenhagen to work as smiths or in the galleys.

In 1578 the Bishop of Fyn told his priests not to conduct marriage ceremonies for Gypsies and to have them buried outside the churchyard as if they were Turks. In 1589 the original edict, ordering Gypsies to leave the realm inside three months, was reissued with the addition of capital punishment for those who remained. Immigration ended and with the strong laws, the Gypsies resident in Denmark merged with the indigenous nomadic population forming a group of Travellers, popularly still called tatere. There was a small immigration of **Sinti** and **Jenisch** families at the beginning of the nineteenth century. The laws against Gypsies were eased in 1849 and re-imposed in 1875 with the threat of a large-scale immigration of **Vlah** Romanies. From 1911 this law was carried out more effectively

with the creation of a national police force. A travelling musical group known as Marietta's gang were probably the last to be expelled, in 1913, and by 1939 very few families of Gypsies, if any, lived in Denmark and the Travellers had all but disappeared.

After 1945, the government banned anyone who had not been born in a caravan from nomadising. Around 1970 there was a camping site at Islands Brygge near Copenhagen that was used by Scandinavian Travellers and Gypsies and from time to time by Dutch Travellers. After the repeal of anti-Gypsy legislation in 1953 small numbers emigrated from eastern and central Europe. They are settled in houses and flats in Copenhagen and Helsingör. The ERRC has criticised the practice of racial segregation in schools in Helsingor County (Municipality), Denmark. There are classes designed for children with special requirements but the classes for Roma children are focused on a particular ethnic group. Helsingor municipality has stated that the classes are for "Roma pupils, who cannot be contained in normal classes or special classes".

Stevica Nikolic was the representative of the **Comité International Rom** until he moved to Holland. The organisation Romano led by Eric Thulstrup is currently active.

DEPP, Johnny 1963–. US. Actor. He played the part of a Romani in the film *Sophie's Tears* and a Traveller in *Chocolat*. Johnny Depp has taken a special interest in promoting the music group **Taraf de Haiduks**.

DERBY. England. Horse race. It has for a long time been one of the important events in the Gypsy calendar. Gypsies maintain that they were the first to race on the **Epsom Downs** where the Derby takes place and have gathered there for many years from the Sunday before the race (known as Show Sunday). Apart from being a source of income for fortune-tellers and racing tipsters, it is also a social gathering. Since 1937 several attempts have been made to stop Gypsies attending. In that year Gypsies camped instead on the land of a sympathiser, Lady Sybil Grant. Currently a fenced-in field has been allocated for Gypsy families and their caravans, while the fortune-tellers park separately. The moving of the Derby from Wednesday to Saturday (when it clashes with the **Appleby Fair**) has led to a reduction in the number of Gypsies attending.

DEVEL (DEL). The Romani word for 'God.' It is cognate with Latin *Deus* and Greek *theos*. Early writers on Gypsies were confused by the similarity of Devel and 'Devil' and thought the Gypsies worshipped the Devil. The Romani word for 'Devil' is **Beng**.

DEVLIN, Bernadette. See McALISKEY, Bernadette.

DEWUS, Reinhard. The Netherlands. Contemporary singer. Reinard Dewus is a **Sinto** whose songs have lyrics in the Romani language set to well-known Dutch melodies. The film, *Soeni* (The Dream) by Carin Goeijers, combines elements of music video with intimate glimpses of his family.

DIMIĆ, Trifun 1945–2000. Serbia. Writer. He has translated the New Testament and the *Epic of Gilgemish* into Romani. He also translated and produced a first reader for children.

DIMITRIEVITCH, Valja. Russia. Contemporary singer. Formerly living in Russia. She is married to the Brazilian consul in France.

DJURIĆ, Rajko 1947–. Serbia. Journalist and poet. He studied in the Faculty of Philosophy at Belgrade University from 1967 to 1972, and went on to obtain a Doctorate of Sociology in 1986. Until 1991 he was editor of the cultural section of the daily newspaper *Politika*. As an opponent of the government and the war in Bosnia, he had to flee in October 1991 to Germany where he still lives. He has written poetry and prose in both Romani and Serbo-Croat. At the third **World Romani Congress** he was elected secretary and he served as president between the fourth and fifth Congresses. His literary works have been translated into more than five languages. They include a collection of lyrics, *Than telal o kham* (A place under the sun) and a survey of Roma writers.

DODDS, Norman 1903–65. England. Politician. He was a Labour member of Parliament in the United Kingdom who fought for Gypsy rights. At one time he opened a caravan camp on his own land. He was to die before seeing the fruits of his efforts in the **Caravan Sites Act of 1968**.

DOHERTY, John 1895–80. Ireland, Donegal. He took up the fiddle in his teens and soon was in much demand to play at the local village houses of entertainment (known as 'Ceilidh houses'). The Dohertys would travel around the Bluestack Mountain region calling in cottages in this sparsely populated area.

In the 1960s, John Doherty was 'discovered' and made a recording for the BBC. He went on to make several other recordings such as *The Peddlers Pack*, *Bundle and Go* and *The Floating Bow*. He was also the subject of a documentary, *Fiddler on the Road*, made by an Ulster TV producer.

DOHERTY, Tommy d. 2003. Ireland. Political activist. Brought up in Northern Ireland, he founded the Society of Travelling People in 1959 in Dublin. After moving to England, he joined the **Gypsy Council** in 1966 and was for many years the Chairperson. He continued working locally in Leeds and Sheffield where he advised on a study conducted at the University on the health of Gypsies and Travellers. His last public appearance was at the **Irish Travellers**' Heritage Day in London in February of the year of his death.

DOM. (i) Dom is an earlier form of the words **Rom** and **Lom**. Originally in Sanskrit it meant 'man' and was the self-ascription of many clans, some of whom emigrated west and helped to form the Romani people. However, in some parts of India it now has a pejorative meaning referring to a lower caste person.

(ii) See NAWWAR

DOMARI (The Society of Gypsies in Israel). Est. 1999. Spokesperson Amoun Sleem. Estimated population of **Nawwar** (Dom): 1,200 in the old city of Jerusalem in the neighbourhood Migdal ha-Chasidah. They are recognised as a separate community but classed as Israeli Arabs. They are no longer nomadic.

DORAN, Felix 1915–72. Ireland. Musician. An **Irish Traveller**, piper and brother of Johnny Doran. He won the first prize for the pipes at Fleadh Ceoil na h-Eireann, the national competition. He moved to Manchester where he became a haulage contractor and continued to play and record.

DORAN, Johnny 1907–50. Ireland. Musician. He was an **Irish Traveller**, piper and brother of Felix Doran. Johnny and Felix Doran were descendants of John Cash, a famous piper in Wicklow in the nineteenth century. Johnny Doran travelled in a horse-drawn caravan throughout Ireland but principally in County Clare, before he was killed in an accident.

DORTIKA. A variety of Greek with Romani words.

DOUGHTY, Louise 1963–. England. Author, journalist and broadcaster. She has written three novels. The most recent of her books, *Fires in the Dark*, is the first of a trilogy based on the history of the Romanies. The next volume in the series is set in Britain and deals with the lives of Romanies in the late nineteen and early twentieth centuries.

DOUGLAS, Charles MBE. Scotland. Contemporary campaigner for civil rights. A **Scottish Traveller,** he was active in the 1970s and was involved in setting up the Scottish Gypsy Council which worked in co-operation with the **Gypsy Council**. He has been one of the representatives of Travellers on the A**dvisory Committee for the Secretary of State for Scotland**.

DRAKHIN (Grapevine). A website for Romanies conducted in the Romani language.

DRAMA. The establishment of the **Teatr Romen** in Moscow led to the writing of plays in the USSR celebrating the transmutation of nomadic Gypsies into collective farmers and factory workers. After 1945, a few writers have created original plays in Romani. The works of **Mustafa Aliev** (Romanov Manush) in Bulgaria were apparently confiscated by the police some years after the Sofia Gypsy theatre was closed. See GINA, Andrej; KRASNICI, Ali; LACKOVA, Elena.

DRINDARI. Quiltmakers' clan in Kotel, Bulgaria. Their name comes from the sound made by a mallet carding wool for quilts. They are also known as Musikantsi (Musicians) and Katkaji as they use the word katka (here) in their dialect as opposed to the majority of Bulgarian Gypsies who say kate. Bernard Gilliatt-Smith described in the *Journal of the Gypsy Lore Society* their dialect which resembles that of Sliven and others in eastern Bulgaria.

DUBLIN TRAVELLERS' EDUCATION AND DEVELOPMENT GROUP. Ireland. Est. 1983. Part of its programme includes legal advice and training courses for young adults. It is now known as **Pavee Point** after the name of its headquarters and to reflect its nationwide role.

DUDAROVA, Nina. USSR. Contemporary teacher and poet. In the 1930s, she was employed to teach Romani at the famous **Teatr Romen** in Moscow.

DUENDE. A Spanish term describing a mysterious power held by some flamenco singers and dancers.

DUKA, Jeta 1948–. Albania. Civil rights activist. She is a Romani civil rights worker and collector of folk tales. During the transition period after the end of the Communist regime, she was employed as an adviser on women's issues. She currently works as a university language assistant and is co-author of a Romani-Albanian dictionary covering several dialects.

DUNN, Sylvia. England. Contemporary civil rights activist. She is a leading figure in the UK **National Association of Gypsy Women.**

DUO Z. The professional name used by the singers **Rudko Kawczynski** and Torando Rosenberg from 1979. The Z stood for the concentration camp designation of Gypsies (*Zigeuner*). Their aim was to sing for the non-Gypsies to confront them with the problems of their people. One of their successes was a reworking of the German folk song *Lustig ist das Zigeunerleben* (Gypsy life is carefree) with words referring to the persecution during and after the Holocaust.

DURBAN CONFERENCE. 2001. Several Romani organisations including **Aven Amentza** from Romania, took part in the NGOs meetings alongside this World Conference against Racism.

DZENO FOUNDATION. Czech Republic. A foundation that aims at the renewal and development of traditional Romani values. Among its activities are the magazine *Amaro gendalos* and the Internet radio ROTA.

E

EAST ANGLIAN GYPSY COUNCIL. UK. Est. 1976. Secretary: **Peter Mercer**. A regional body based in Peterborough. The Liberal MP Clement Freud is a patron.

ECONOMIC AND SOCIAL COUNCIL OF THE UNITED NATIONS (ECOSOC). In 1979 the **[International] Romani Union** was recognised as a non-governmental organisation representing Gypsies and **Travellers**. In 1993 it was upgraded to category II status which gave it the right to speak at meetings. *Etudes Tsiganes* is also recognised by ECOSOC. See also UNITED NATIONS.

EGYPTIANS. (i) The name first given to Gypsies when they reached Western Europe, as it was thought they came from Egypt. (ii) A number of groups in the Balkans previously thought to be Romani Gypsies but who no longer spoke the Romani language began in the last few years to claim that they were not Gypsies but descendants of Egyptian immigrants to Europe. They number several thousand and are found in Albania, Kosovo and Macedonia. In Albania they are known as *Evgjit* or *Jevg*, where their non-Romani origin has been accepted for longer. They asked to be recognised as an ethnic group for the Yugoslav, Serbian and Macedonian censuses of 1991 but no separate figures have been published listing them. The Serbian-led government in Belgrade was pleased to welcome the emergence of the Egyptians as they helped to diminish the percentage of Albanians in Kosovo and the ethnologist, Hadži Ristić, stated that he had found traces of Egyptian presence in Macedonia. It seems likely that the Egyptians emerged from the population of Albanian-speaking Roma who found, after 1990, that there was no advantage in being Albanian in either Kosovo or Macedonia. However, they had little inclination to call themselves Roma because of the low social status of this group.

There is a tale of an Egyptian shipwrecked on the coast near Durres around the year 825, being able to converse – in Coptic, presumably – with local Egyptians.

EINSATZGRUPPEN. Nazi Task Forces that murdered some 20,000 Gypsies in the occupied regions of the Soviet Union between 1941 and 1943. Their primary targets were 'Jewish Bolshevists.' During a visit to Minsk in August 1941, Heinrich Himmler extended the original orders of the Task Forces to kill all Gypsies – men, women and children.

EL BARULLO. See MONEO, Manuel.

EL CHOCOLATE. See MONTOYA, Antonio Nunez.

EL FARRUCO. See FLORES, Antonio Montoya.

EL FARRUQUITO. See FLORES, Antonio Montoya.

EL PELE. See CERIFINO, Jiménez.

ENCYCLOPAEDIA. The fourth **World Romani Congress** set up an Encyclopaedia Commission with the remit of preparing an encyclopaedia in Romani. The work was taken over by a working party under the auspices of the now defunct **Centre de Recherches Tsiganes**. Some draft entries and a call for contributors were circulated with Interface early in 1997. The future of the project is in doubt.

ENGLAND. Estimated Gypsy population 300,000, including **Irish Travellers**. Some 40,000 live in caravans. The census figures for January 2003 show some 6,000 caravans on official council sites, over 4,500 on authorised private sites and 3,000 unauthorised encampments.

It is likely that the first Gypsies came to England from France at the turn of the fifteenth century. The first written record dates from 1514 and refers to a fortune-teller from Lambeth who had left England some time previously. Further references occur between 1513 and 1530. A distinctive costume was common in England early in the sixteenth century, as there are records of court ladies dressing up as Gypsies as early as 1517.

There were soon a large enough number of Gypsies to worry the authorities and the first anti-Gypsy law was passed in 1530 under Henry VIII. This banned '**Egyptians**' from entering the country and ordered those already there to leave within fifteen days. In 1540 a group of Gypsies was released from Marshalsea Prison and put on a ship bound for Norway. Others were expelled to Calais, still an English colony. In 1554 and 1562 the law was strengthened, with the death penalty extended to anyone consorting with the Gypsies. In 1577 in Aylesbury, six persons were hanged under this law, a further five in Durham in 1592 and nine in York in 1596. At least thirteen more were executed under this law before it and most legislation concerning Gypsies were repealed in 1783. Between 1598 and 1868, many Gypsies were deported to the colonies in Australia and America under the 1598 *Act for the Punishment of Rogues, Vagabonds and Sturdy Beggars*. In some parts of the country, however, no action was taken against Gypsies, and they were also protected by landowners who found it useful to have Gypsies available for entertainment and casual work.

Fortune-telling was evidently an important occupation. In 1602 **William Shakespeare's** Desdemona refers to a handkerchief that an Egyptian woman who could read minds had given to her mother. The wife of the diarist Samuel Pepys went to see Gypsies at Lambeth with a friend to have their fortunes told. However, a male was apparently burned at the stake in Warwickshire for telling fortunes, if the story is to be believed.

The policy of expulsion from the country failed and in the nineteenth century settlement and assimilation became the aim. Various Christian missions took an interest in the Gypsy nomads and special schools were opened. In 1815 John Hoyland was commissioned by the Society of Friends to collect information about Gypsies with a view to improving their condition. This was the first survey made and gave James Crabb, among others, the impulse to start his mission. Assimilation was the aim, but this was thwarted by police and local authorities who continued to move Gypsies on. In 1822 and 1835 (the Highway Act) penalties were introduced for Gypsies camping on the highway. Attempts by **George Smith** to control the nomadic Gypsies with the Moveable Dwellings Bills in Parliament failed, however, owing to the opposition of circus and fair owners. The Gypsy population around this time has been estimated at about 10,000.

Popular novels in England – as elsewhere – featured Gypsies who stole children or pronounced curses that could not be avoided. In the late nineteenth century **Gypsylorists** emerged.

A new immigration started in the second half of the nineteenth century and there are reports of "foreign Gypsies" – certainly belonging to **Vlah** clans. At the beginning of this century England was visited by bear trainers, "German Gypsies" (probably **Lovari**) and the first of the **Kalderash** families who were to become regular visitors. Legislation against 'aliens' aimed at Jewish immigrants from Eastern Europe, was used to prevent Romanies landing and to expel them rapidly. Nevertheless, in the 1930s, the Kalderash Stirio and Yevanovic families established themselves in England, and their descendants form a compact Romani-speaking community today. **Irish Travellers** have been coming to England and the rest of Britain, since the middle of the nineteenth century. They number some 10,000 in England.

Between the two world wars (1918–39) much legislation was enacted affecting the nomadic Gypsies. The 1936 *Public Health Act* (Sec. 268) defined tents, vans and sheds as 'statutory nuisances.' In 1937 the first of many attempts to stop the Gypsies' annual gathering for the **Derby** horse race failed. During both wars Romanies served in the armed forces, and many were awarded medals for valour.

In the highly industrialised England that arose after 1945, nomadic Gypsies found life much harder. Their traditional camping places were built on and, with increased and faster traffic, stopping on the roadside became dangerous and – in many cases – banned. The 1947 and 1950 *Town and Country Planning Acts* restricted the use of land by caravans and then the **Caravan Sites Act 1960** led to the closure of many sites.

A civil rights movement began to emerge in the 1960s with the Society of Travelling People in Leeds (1965) and Tom Jonell in the south. In 1966 the **Gypsy Council** was founded at a meeting in Kent. Under its secretary **Grattan Puxon**, it began a campaign of passive resistance to the forced moving-on of caravans from public land, which obtained considerable press and television publicity. It organised the first caravan school at Hornchurch aerodrome with volunteer teachers including **Thomas Acton**. Others followed.

Under pressure from **Norman Dodds**, a Member of Parliament, the central government began to take an interest in Gypsies. The Ministry of Housing and Local Government produced a report *Gypsies and other Travellers* (1967) which was the first official study of Gypsies in England and Wales. With pressure from inside and outside Parliament, the **Caravan Sites Act 1968** was passed, applying to England and Wales only. This act placed a duty on county councils in particular to provide caravan sites. However, areas of the country could then be 'designated' as areas where Gypsies could not park their caravans unless they found a pitch on the official sites. The first of these designations were made in 1973.

In 1980 the *Local Government* Planning Land Act removed the word 'Gypsy' from the 1835 Highway Act. This was no longer necessary because of the provisions of the 1968 *Caravan Sites Act*. Gypsies were no longer singled out for punishment for camping on the roadside, unless it was a 'designated' area. In 1994 the **Criminal Justice and Public Order Act** imposed stronger penalties for camping anywhere in England and Wales outside official sites. At the same time the duty on councils (laid down by the 1968 *Caravan Sites Act*) to provide such sites was removed, and Gypsies were told that they had to buy land, get planning permission and make their own caravan sites. Many have bought land and then found that they could not get planning permission. The local authorities then take them to court in order to remove them. The evictions of the 1960s from public land have been replaced by evictions from the Gypsies' own land. During 2003 bailiffs evicted by force two such encampments, Woodside Park in Bedfordshire and Cow Roast in Hertfordshire.

In 1996 it was estimated by the authorities that 50,000 nomadic children aged 0–16 lived in England. This figure includes some **New Travellers**. The majority of primary age children (5–11) attend school but the situation is not so satisfactory for secondary school children (age 11–16). The Department for Education and Science funds Traveller Education Support services as part of the Vulnerable Children's Grant. Continuing education after the age of sixteen is not common. Many Gypsies and Travellers attending further and higher education colleges conceal their origins and no figures are available.

There have been some incidents of stone-throwing at caravans but most anti-Gypsy violence has been directed at asylum seekers. In May 2000 Roma experienced three separate physical attacks across the country in a week. A refugee in Salford had a brick thrown through his window while attempts were made to kick down his door. He was also subject to racist abuse screamed from the street. The City Housing Service refused to help or re-house the man. The North West Refugee Consortium said it had yet to determine whether the attack was racially motivated – it could have been attempted burglary. A group of Roma living in Middlesborough were so shaken by the attacks they experienced that some of them decided to return to Slovakia, saying that if they were going to die, they would prefer it to be in their own country. Several thousand Roma from Eastern Europe had come to Britain in the years after 1990 as asylum seekers but very few were accepted as refugees. With the accession of several countries to the European Union in May 2004 many will have the right to remain in the country as workers.

Gypsies in England today are mainly self-employed with such trades as tarmac-ing and block-paving, landscape gardening and house repairs. As musicians they are known in folk club circles but not to the general public. See also SCOTLAND and WALES.

EPSOM DOWNS. A gathering place for English Gypsies at the time of the **Derby** horse race. Howard Brenton wrote a play *Epsom Downs* first performed by the Joint Stock Company at the Roundhouse, London, in 1977 and featuring the Gypsy presence. Sporadic attempts by the authorities to stop Gypsies bringing their caravans to the Downs have failed.

ERKÖSE BROTHERS, ERKÖSE ENSEMBLE. Turkey. The three brothers Ali (zither), Barbaros (clarinet) and Salahaddin (lute) are contemporary folk musicians, originally from Bursa. They have played concerts abroad and made recordings. CD. *Tzigane*.

ERLIA, ARLIA. A term used by Romanies in the Balkans to describe sedentary Gypsies and their dialects, as opposed to nomads. The derivation is from the Turkish word *yerli* (local).

ESMA. See REDJEPOVA, ESMA.

ESSEX, David. See COOK, Albert David

ESTONIA. Estimated Gypsy population: 1,000. The first record of a Gypsy in the territory of present-day Estonia dates from 1533 when the presence of at least two Gypsies in Tallinn was noted. Estonia was under the rule of various countries until 1918 and their laws would have applied. Numbers have never been high and, during the Nazi period, the German occupiers murdered almost all the Gypsies in the years 1941–3. The dead included the whole of the Lajenge Roma, a distinct clan with their own dialect of Romani. The Estonian writer Tuglas Friedbert is of Romani origin.

ETAPE 29. France. An organisation which campaigns for better camping facilities, schooling for children and the abolishment of strict laws which make it illegal to camp on public land.

EUROPEAN COMMISSION. A body of the **European Union**. It initiated a newsletter with project partners in Bulgaria, Poland, Slovakia and the **Minority Rights Group** (MRG) in London. The newsletter's purpose was to inform anyone involved in Romani rights and education.

EUROPEAN COMMISSION ON HUMAN RIGHTS. Established by the Council of Europe in 1950 it merged into the **European Court of Human Rights** in 1993.

EUROPEAN COMMITTEE ON MIGRATION (CDMG). On the instructions of the Committee of Ministers of the Council of Europe, the CDMG carried out an in-depth study in 1994 on the situation of Gypsies in Europe.

EUROPEAN COMMITTEE ON ROMANI EMANCIPATION (ECRE). UK. Spokesperson: Len Smith. ECRE was established to promote common rights of equity of treatment, protection and improvement in the conditions of the Roma in Europe.

EUROPEAN COMMUNITIES. See EUROPEAN UNION.

EUROPEAN CONGRESS. 1994. Seville, Spain. The Congress was organised originally with the primary purpose of looking at education but its remit expanded and it took on the air of an international congress. The King and Queen of Spain patronised the proceedings.

EUROPEAN COURT OF HUMAN RIGHTS. A number of cases involving Gypsies have been taken to this Court. Several concerned with police harassment in Eastern Europe have been successful but attempts by English Gypsies (such as Mrs Chapman) to overturn negative planning decisions for caravan sites have met with failure.

EUROPEAN DIALOGUE UK. Est. 1990. An independent membership organisation launched in 1990 as part of the pan-European civic network the **Helsinki Citizens Assembly**. It sponsors a number of initiatives in the Romani field.

EUROPEAN PARLIAMENT. See EUROPEAN UNION.

EUROPEAN ROMA (AND TRAVELLER) FORUM. A proposal of the Committee of Ministers of the **Council of Europe** put forward by Finland, originally in 2001. Anne-Marie Nyroos chairs a working party (GT-ROMS) on the project which could come into effect in 2004. The aim would be to set up a body to represent all the Gypsy organisations which would meet twice yearly and have an office in Strasbourg.

EUROPEAN ROMA RIGHTS CENTER. Hungary. Est. 1996. Director: Dimitrina Petrova. An autonomous non-governmental human rights organisation in Budapest, Hungary, governed by a nine-member board to monitor and defend the human rights of Romanies in Europe. Initial funding came from the **Open Society** Institute. It publishes a quarterly magazine *Roma Rights* and several reports on conditions for the Roma in various countries.

EUROPEAN UNION. The European Union (previously known as the European Communities), based in Brussels, has taken a number of initiatives in Gypsy matters.

In May 1984, the European Parliament passed a resolution on the situation of Gypsies in the Community. It called on member states to eliminate existing discriminatory provisions that may exist in their legislation and to make it easier for nomads to attach themselves to a state (in accordance with recommendation R(83)1 of the **Council of Europe**).

Five years later, in May 1989, the council passed a resolution on School Provision for Gypsy and Traveller Children. The programme of action to be taken included the following: experiments with distance learning and training and employing Gypsies and Travellers as teachers wherever possible.

The Union has financed a number of projects in the spirit of these recommendations. Governments were to let the European Union know the results of their measures so that a combined report could be presented to the Council by 31 December 1993. The report was eventually published in 1996. This showed, as might have been expected, that some states had done more than others in implementing the recommendations.

Recent action has been less directed at nomads in the west but rather with improving conditions for the Roma in the Eastern European countries that will be joining the Union.

EUROROMA. A civil rights programme run by the **Autonomia Foundation** in Hungary. It covers Bulgaria, Slovakia, Hungary and Romania and is financed by the **European Union**. Its aim is to foster self-help initiatives among the Romani communities in the partner countries. The first meeting of the partner organisations from the four countries took place in Budapest in January 1996.

EVANGELICAL CHURCH. See CENTRE MISSIONAIRE EVANGELIQUE ROM INTERNATIONALE; PENTECOSTALISM.

EVENS, Reverend George Bramwell 1874-1943. England. Religious leader. Known as 'Romany,' he was the son of Tilly Smith, the sister of Rodney Smith, and Salvation Army lieutenant George Evens. He was a broadcaster of BBC *Children's Hour* programmes in Manchester from 1933 to 1943, when he unexpectedly died. His wife, Eunice Evens, published a biography of her husband entitled *Through the years with Romany.*

ETUDES TSIGANES. France. Est. 1949. President: Jacqueline Charlemagne. An organisation with mainly non-Gypsy members, founded in Paris after the Second World War. Since 1955 it has published the journal of the same name (current editor is Alan Reyniers) and has held two scientific conferences: the first in Sevres in 1986 and the second in the Centre Pompidou in Paris.

EVGJIT. See EGYPTIAN.

EXPERT GROUP (of the Council of Europe). See SPECIALIST GROUP ON ROMA/GYPSIES.

EYNARD, Giles. France. Contemporary civil rights activist. He was a member of the committee of the Comité Rom de Provence and the West European **Gypsy Council**. He is currently treasurer of **Tchatchipen**.

F

FAA, FAW. The surname of several Scottish Traveller families. The name was also adopted by some Romanies who came to Scotland.

FAA, Johnny C15th. Scotland. Scottish **Traveller**. According to legend, he rescued two sisters from the clutches of their uncle in 1470. The uncle had thrown them into a cellar to make off with their inheritance.

FABIANOVÁ, Tera 1930–. Czechoslovakia. Writer. She was one of the first Czech Gypsies to write in Romani. In 2003, she received the Roma Literary Award for Fiction.

FAMULSON, Victor. Finland. Contemporary political activist. A **Vlah** Romani living in Finland, he is a vice-president of the **International Romani Union** (elected 1990).

FARRUCO, El. See FLORES, Antonio.

FARRUQUITO, El. See FLORES, Antonio.

FAYS, Raphael 1959–. Italy. Musician. An Italian **Manouche** guitarist and the son of the guitarist Louis Fays, he plays classical as well as jazz and Latin American music. He is currently playing in the **Django Reinhardt** style with a trio.

FEKETE VONAT (Black Train) (i) A name given to the train carrying Gypsy workers to and from Budapest for a weekend break in their homes in eastern Hungary.
(ii) A rap group. They appear on the CD

Rough Guide to Hungarian Music.

FELDITKA ROMA. A term used for the Lowland Gypsies in Poland.

FERKOVÁ, Ilona 1956–. Czechoslovakia, **Rokycany**. Writer. Ilona Ferková began to write in Romani after getting acquainted with the works of **Tera Fabianová** and **Margita Reiznerová**. Her works include a short story, *Mosarxa Peske o Dživipen* (She spoilt her life).

FERRÉ, Boulou. France. Contemporary musician. Gypsy jazz guitarist and the son of **Matelo Ferré**, both he and his brother Elios tour widely as a duo in the style of **Django Reinhardt**. They have made several recordings.

FERRÉ, Matelo 1918–. France. Musician. A jazz guitarist, he is the last survivor of the senior Ferré brothers. As a **Gitano** living in Paris, he and his brothers composed many waltzes. His three sons – **Boulou**, Elios and Michel – all follow in his footsteps as musicians.

FICOWSKI, Jerzy. Poland. Contemporary historian. He is an authority on Romani history and culture, his first major publication being *Cyganie Polscy* (The Gypsies of Poland) in 1953. He has since published several works in Polish as well as one book in English on the Gypsies in Poland. Jerzy Ficowski was instrumental in introducing the Romani poet **Bronislawa Wajs** (Papusza) to the Polish public.

FILM. Many films have been made by non-Gypsies on the theme of Romanies, for example:

Gypsy (Great Britain, 1936)

Gypsy Wildcat (US, 1944)

The Gypsy and the Gentleman (Great Britain, 1957)

I even met Happy Gypsies (Skupljace perja) (Yugoslavia, 1967)

Angelo My Love (US, 1982)

The Time of the Gypsies (Yugoslavia, 1989) – **Rajko Djurić** was the advisor.

American Gypsy (US, 2000)

Some other films have been made by Gypsies or with their involvement at production level:

The Raggedy Rawney (Great Britain, 1987), **Bob Hoskins** directed and starred in the title role (an army deserter dressed as a Gypsy girl).

A large number of documentaries have also been produced including the first two parts of a trilogy by **Tony Gatlif:** *Les Princes, Latcho Drom* completed by the fictional *Dinilo Gadjo*. A Spanish film *The Three Thousand* (aka *Seville South Side*), made in 2003, deals with a Gypsy community resettled in Seville and *Into the West* (Irish Republic, 1992), a film featuring Irish Travellers.

'FINKS' Finks was a Latvian Rom who was a renowned fortune-teller. It is said he predicted in the 1930s that Latvia would prosper under a woman's leadership and that the country would re-emerge from Soviet occupation in 1991.

FINLAND. Estimated Gypsy population: 8,000. From approximately 1200 to 1809, Finland was under Swedish control. Eight workhorses were confiscated from Gypsies on the island of Åland in 1559 – the year of their arrival. They were reputedly the first Gypsies in Finland. Many of this group were sent back to Sweden. The first record on the mainland dates from 1580. In the 1600s Finland's Romani population grew with immigration occurring from the east as well as from Sweden. In 1660 the ruler Per Brahe settled 140 Gypsies on farms in the Kajaani Castle area. These were farms abandoned by Finnish peasants after the crops had failed. He wanted the Gypsies to serve as spies and guards on the eastern border. It seems then that they did not settle down and in 1663 Per Brahe issued a warning that if they did not settle by the next year on the plot of land given to them they would be banished from the whole of the Swedish empire. The Swedish law of 1637, which applied to Finland too, stated that all Gypsies should be banished or hanged but this was ineffective. The Gypsy population carried out traditional nomadic trades in Finland – horse selling, veterinary care, castration of pigs, ironwork, smithing, making and selling lace, fortune-telling and seasonal agricultural work.

In 1809 Russia occupied Finland. In 1812 a decree was issued that all the disabled, wandering **Tartars**, Gypsies and other vagabonds of poor reputation who were not capable of ordinary work were to be dispatched to workhouses. In 1863, any Gypsies in ordinary workhouses were removed and placed in special stricter workhouses in Hameenlinna. The year 1862 saw Gypsies arriving from abroad being sent back even if holding genuine passports. A census in 1895 recorded 1,551 Gypsies, a figure seen as too low.

Finland became independent in 1917. In 1906 a Gypsy mission had been founded by Oskari Jalkio, whose aim was to remove Gypsy children from their families and give them a normal education. The first attempts to set up children's homes in the 1920s were not successful. By 1953 a new commission was set up with various recommendations including once again the use of children's homes and enforcing school attendance. By 1963 five homes were established, and 100-150 children lived in them.

After the Second World War, the industrialisation of Finland decreased the demand for the Gypsies' trades and seasonal work was no longer available. In addition, the Gypsy community of Karelia, taken over by the Soviet Union, decided to migrate from their former living areas into Finland proper. Gypsies had to move into towns where they soon found themselves living on welfare benefits. In 1960 a report of the Helsinki City Special Committee published a survey of the situation.

In 1967 the Suomen Mustalaisyhdistys Ry (Finnish Gypsy Association) was formed, with the aim of bringing pressure on the government to improve the standard of living of the Gypsies and to stop discrimination in Finnish society. For several years the magazine *Zirickli* (The Bird), edited by Kari Huttunen, was a mouthpiece for Gypsy civil rights.

In 1968 the State Committee for Gypsy Affairs was re-established. The committee included three members representing the association and two from the Lutheran Gypsy Mission. They set about making two studies, one on the social needs of Gypsies and one on housing, which were published by the committee. In 1970 an act of Parliament prohibited racial discrimination. In 1971 the *Social Welfare Act* was reformed, and the government then refunded half of any welfare assistance that the local authorities gave to their Gypsy population. At this time, three-quarters of the Gypsies were receiving welfare payments and faced diminished health, family breakdown and unemployment. The aim of the reform was to make it easier to obtain welfare payments and provide more systematic and better-planned support to promote assimilation. The Ministry of Education encouraged adults to join classes in literacy and technical subjects, as well as studying Gypsy history. The National Board of Education then printed a history book for the Gypsies. The Work Group for Vocational Training set up by the Ministry of Labour proposed in 1972 linking vocational and basic education into one course.

In the 1980s 2,000 Finnish Gypsies emigrated to Sweden. Most left for better housing and employment conditions, and the Finnish Romani Association in Stockholm was created to assist the Gypsies there. Meanwhile, living conditions in Finland itself improved.

At the end of the 1960s Gypsy musicians were very popular in Finland, with Hungarian and Russian Gypsy music proving particularly popular with Finnish people of all classes. The Folklore Archive of the Finnish Literary Society started to collect Gypsy songs in 1968 and now has over 1,000 titles. In 1972 the Folklore Archive and Love Records jointly produced an anthology called *Kaale dzambena* (Finnish Gypsies Sing). Singers and musicians include **Olli Palm**, the band **Hortto Kaalo**,

Anneli Sari and the classical violinist Basil Borteanou.

The language of the Finnish Gypsies is a distinct dialect that was falling into disuse among the younger generation. However, there has recently been a revival of the Romani language, and textbooks have been prepared for children.

FIRLE BONFIRE, Lewes, Sussex. In November 2003 the Firle Bonfire Society burnt a caravan with models of Gypsies looking out of the window. Anti-Gypsy graffiti were painted on the caravan. This was in line with an annual tradition of burning effigies of political figures but this time the authorities felt the ceremony had gone too far and several members of the organising committee were arrested and charged with incitement to racial hatred. Following this, there were a number of initiatives to move forward in a constructive way and Lewes Council was to form a working party to develop new strategies relating to caravan sites.

FIZIK, Ladislav. Slovakia. Contemporary political activist. He is the chairperson of the **National Roma Parliament**.

FLAG. In the years after 1945, a Romani flag appeared with green, red and blue horizontal stripes. By 1962 its had spread widely. It was said that green represented the grass, red the fire and blue the sky. Because of the alleged Communist connection of the red stripe, some groups changed it to a fire-shaped emblem. The most commonly used flag nowadays is one with blue and green horizontal divisions and a superimposed wheel. This flag was decided at the first **World Romani Congress**. According to the congress decision the wheel is to be identical with the *ashoka* symbol on the Indian flag.

FLAMENCO. A form of song and dance that emerged in the south of Spain in the nineteenth century. It is considered to be the result of a combination of Gypsy, Moorish and Andalusian dance and music. Gypsies are the prime performers of flamenco which has spread from Andalusia to the rest of Spain. The Spanish word *flamenco* means Flemish – that is 'exotic.' The **Presencia Gitana** research team has listed 240 Gypsy singers in Spain from 1749 to the age of the flamenco while Bernard Leblon in his book *Gypsies and Flamenco* gives details of 200 and lists one hundred further names. This dictionary has entries for some forty of the best known from the beginning of the twentieth century onwards.

FLORES, Antonio Montoya (El Farruco) 1936–97. Spain. Dancer. He performed with Pilar Lopez and Jose Greco. His son, El Farruquito, died tragically and his grandson son, El Mani, now performs under that name.

FLORES, *Lola (La Faraona)* 1923–95. Spain. Singer. She is a **flamenco** artist who considered herself to be a Gypsy *adentro* (through and through).

FOLK LITERATURE. The Romanies' oral literature consisted of ballads, songs and tales as well as riddles and proverbs. These began to be collected and published in the nineteenth century by non-Gypsies. After 1945 several Gypsies have begun to collect their oral literature in anthologies that are listed in the bibliography.

FONSECA, *Isabel*. US. Contemporary writer. Currently, Isabel Fonseca resides in England and is married to the writer Martin Amis. After several visits to meet Gypsies in Eastern Europe, she wrote the controversial travel book *Bury Me Standing*.

FORTUNE-TELLING. Although comparatively few Gypsy women practise fortune-telling, it provides a useful first or second income for those families who pursue this profession. Many **Kalderash** families specialise in fortune-telling with the daughters learning from their mothers. But **Sinti** also have traditionally told fortunes. In Western Europe fortune-telling is usually done by palm-reading while in Eastern Europe coffee beans are often used. In England and Wales fortune-telling was controlled until recently by the Vagrancy Act of

1824. Any person professing to tell fortunes could be arrested without a warrant. In fact, prosecutions normally take place under section 15 of the Theft Act, where, for example, a fortune-teller takes money away to be blessed and does not return it. The Fraudulent Mediums Act of 1951 is rarely used against fortune-tellers.

FOUNDATION FOR THE RENEWAL AND DEVELOPMENT OF TRADITIONAL ROMANY VALUES. Czech Republic. Director: Ivan Vesely. An organisation in Prague which is the Czech partner of the **Minority Rights Group.**

FRAMEWORK CONVENTION FOR THE PROTECTION OF NATIONAL MINORITIES. Est. 1998. Countries who are signatory to the declaration have to report their progress on protecting national minorities each year.

FRANCE. Estimated Gypsy population: 310,000. The first Gypsies came to France, to the town of Colmar in 1418. In 1419 more Gypsies arrived in Provence and Savoy. Nine years later the first Gypsies were recorded in Paris. In 1504 Louis XII issued the first of many decrees ordering the expulsion of the Gypsies. Further decrees followed in 1539, 1561 and 1682. In the latter year Louis XIV recognised that it had been impossible to expel the Gypsies because of the protection they had received from nobles and other landowners. During the eighteenth century, there are reports of armed Gypsies resisting arrest and expulsion. Others served in the French army as soldiers and musicians. Often this was the only alternative to imprisonment. Jean de la Fleur, born in Lorraine, served as a mercenary in several armies. In 1802 there was a determined campaign to clear Gypsies from the French Basque provinces. More than 500 were captured and imprisoned pending their planned deportation to the French colony of Louisiana. The colony was, however, sold in 1803 to the United States. It was 1806 before the last of the captives were released, four years during which many had died from disease and malnutrition.

Gypsies, such as Liance, were well known in France as dancers and are mentioned several times by the playwright Molière. In 1607 they danced before King Henri IV at Fontainebleau Castle, although legally they had no right to be in France. It was not until the twentieth century that instrumentalists such as **Django Reinhardt** attained the fame of the Gypsy dancers.

The first Romanies to come to France appear to have merged over the years with indigenous nomads to form the community known today as *Voyageurs* (**Travellers**). They no longer speak Romani but a variety of French with Romani words. In the south of France many families speak **Caló**. There have been two migrations from Germany of families of the **Sinti** and **Manouche** clans. **Vlah** Gypsies arrived from the end of the nineteenth century onward, both from Romania directly and via Russia.

It was probably the newcomers that led the French government to introduce new measures to control the nomadic population. In 1898 a report gave the exaggerated figure of 25,000 nomads travelling in bands with caravans. As a result, in 1912 the authorities introduced a special identity card – the *carnet anthropométrique* – for nomads. This carried the photograph and fingerprints of the owner and other details such as the length of the right ear. It was not to be abolished until after 1945.

When Germany occupied most of France during the Second World War, nomadic Gypsies were interned in some twenty-seven camps run by the French police. The camps at Jargeau, Les Alliers, Montreuil-Bellay, Rennes and St Maurice held internees for most of the war. Other camps were closed as the conditions in them worsened, and the prisoners were transferred from camp to camp. In some places Gypsies were allowed out to work under supervision. Conditions in these camps were poor and many prisoners died from disease and malnutrition. A small number were deported to concentration camps in Poland. Others, who had Belgian nationality, were released, only to be rearrested by the Germans in Belgium and northern France and sent to **Auschwitz**. House-dwelling Romanies were not affected by any special regulations.

The years following 1945 witnessed the arrival of large numbers of Gypsies from Eastern Europe, in particular Yugoslavia. They came as factory workers and settled in houses and flats in Paris and elsewhere. Meanwhile, nomadic Gypsies found that there were few official campsites and many districts prohibited the stationing of caravans. It was on French territory that **Vaida Voivod III** and **Vanko Rouda** founded the first international Gypsy organisations while the **Études Tsiganes** association pioneered serious research into Romani history and culture. There are writers who have written in French, such as **Matéo Maximoff** and **Sandra Jayat**. In France, too, **Pentecostalism** first took hold among the Gypsies.

In 2003 a new internal security bill proposed fines of 3,750 euros for Travellers who occupy land belonging to someone else while the 1999 **Loi Besson** encouraged the provision of council-run sites. In practice few sites have been built and in October 2002 a delegation representing a dozen Gypsy organisations met the Minister of Home Affairs, Nicola Sarkozy, to press for more sites and better conditions on those which have been built.

FRANKHAM, Eli d. 2002. England. Poet and political activist. He was the founder of the **National Romany Rights Association**.

FRANKHAM, Johnny. England. Twentieth-century boxer. He held the British light-heavyweight title from June to October 1975.

FRANZ, Philomena 1922–. Germany. Author. Now living near Cologne, she survived internment in **Auschwitz**, Ravensbrück and Oranienburg concentration camps. She has written her autobiography and tales in the folk idiom.

FREDRIKSSON, Malik Faltin 1977–. Sweden. Entertainer. A **Traveller**, he is a break dancer and rap singer who performs under the name Tattarprinsen (Gypsy prince).

FRIENDS, FAMILIES AND TRAVELLERS' ADVICE AND INFORMATION UNIT. UK. Est. 1993. Founder: Steve Staines. Originally based in Glastonbury and working mainly with **New Travellers** it has its headquarters in Brighton and serves all Gypsies and **Travellers**.

FUHLER, Lee. Australia. Contemporary poet and political activist. President of the **Romani Association** of Australia, a collection of his poems was published under the title *Dog Days*.

FUREY, Eddie and Finbar. Pipers of **Irish Traveller** origin. In 1967 they moved to Scotland as labourers but then developed a successful musical career. They have played at the Edinburgh Festival and toured widely in Britain. Apart from their recordings, the Furey brothers have appeared on both Scottish and English TV.

FUREY, Martin. Ireland. Contemporary Musician. An **Irish Traveller**, he currently resides in England and is a musician in the folk rock group, Bohinta.

G

GADES, Antonio 1936–. Spain. Dancer and choreographer. He has produced a stage version of *Carmen* as well a film version in conjunction with Carlos Saura. He dances in the **Flamenco** style.

GADJO. See GAJO.

GAISFORD, Paul 1960–. English. Painter and teacher. He is of Romani descent.

GAJO. The Romani word for a non-Gypsy. The etymology is disputed but it probably comes from a Greek word for 'farmer.' Another suggestion is from the Sanscrit word *gramaja* (villager) which survives in some modern Indian languages as *gajja*. In Romani the feminine is Gaji and the plural Gaje. It is also spelled Gadjo and, traditionally, in English, as Gorgio.

GAMMON. (i) An alternative name for **Irish Travellers' cant**. (ii) One of the suggested sources of vocabulary for this cant. It is a secret vocabulary from the Middle Ages formed by reversing or changing the order of the letters in a word. An example is the word gred (money) from Irish *airgead*. The name Gammon itself is probably formed from the word Ogam, an ancient alphabet used in Britain and Ireland.

GANDHI SCHOOL. Hungary, Pecs. Est. 1994. The school was set up to teach mainly children of the **Bayash clan**. There is a strong Romani cultural element in the timetable. Its first graduating class had eighteen pupils, sixteen of them seeking higher education. Classes in at least two Gypsy dialects are compulsory at the school. It is hoped that the experience gathered by the school will prove invaluable for similar institutions elsewhere. The Principal, Erika Csovcsics, received the US Human Rights Prize.

GARCIA LORCA, Federico 1898–1936. Spain. Poet and playwright. In 1922 he organised a festival in Granada that paid tribute to Gypsy traditions. His *Romancero Gitano* (Gypsy Ballad Book) was published in 1928 and demonstrates his empathy with the Romani community. He had already shown this sentiment two years earlier by opposing the brutal expulsion of Gypsies from Alpujarra. Speaking of this book, he said, "I gave it the name Gypsy Ballads because the Gypsies are the highest, the deepest and the most aristocratic people of my land." The **Pralipe** Theatre perform Federico Garcia Lorca's play *Blood Wedding* in their repertoire, and the Hungarian Romani poet **Jószef Choli Daroczi** has independently translated it into Romani.

GATLIF, Tony. 1948– Algeria. Contemporary film producer. He is now resident in France and has made several documentary films about Gypsies: *Corre Gitano*, *Les Princes* and *Latcho drom* (1993), in addition, two fictional films *Canto Gitano* (Gypsy Song) (1981) and *Gadjo Dilo* (Foolish non-Gypsy) (1997). A later film is *Swing* (2001), a feature, richly larded with Gypsy jazz, about a lonely young boy who befriends a Gypsy girl.

GELEM, GELEM. The Romani national anthem, chosen at the first **World Romani Congress**. The first lines are as follows:
Gelem gelem lungone dromensa,
Maladilem bahtale Romensa.
[We went, we went down long roads,
We met happy Gypsies.]
    The tune is traditional and was featured in the film *Happy Gypsies*. The new lyrics were composed by **Žarko Jovanović** during the Congress.

GENOCIDE. See HOLOCAUST

GEORGIA (previously USSR). The official figure for Gypsies is 1,744 (1989 census) but, in fact, there are several thousand living in the Republic. Their economic and social situation is not good. Few are educated and those were taught Russian rather than Georgian which puts them at a disadvantage in the job market. Many have Moldavian rather than Georgian citizenship which debars them from welfare payments. Police harassment of market traders is common. In August 2003, a market incident in Tbilisi escalated into a pogrom: after a non-Roma woman was beaten up by a merchant, the local people then dispersed and began beating and menacing the Roma community, destroying their places of trade by burning them to the ground. It has been alleged that market officials provoked the incident in order to gain control of Romani trading stalls. A Roma Rights Defence Centre has been established.

GEORGIEV, Mihail. Bulgaria. Contemporary political activist. Executive Director of the **Romani Baxt Foundation** in Sofia.

GEORGIEVDEN. See ST GEORGE'S DAY.

GERMAN, Aleksandr 1893–1955. Russia. Writer and translator. A cultural worker and active in the All-Russian Union of Gypsies in the 1920s. He translated Russian literature into Romani as well as writing original works.

GERMANY. Estimated Gypsy population: 100,000. Records state that in September 1407 wine was given to Gypsies ('**Tartars**') while their papers were being checked at the town hall in Hildesheim. Another early description is of a group of acrobats in Magdeburg who danced on each other's shoulders and did "wonderful tricks". They were rewarded with food and drink. In 1416 we find the first anti-Gypsy action in Germany when the Margrave of Meissen ordered the expulsion of Gypsies from the territory under his authority. In September 1498 the Parliament of the **Holy Roman Empire**, as the German Empire was then called, meeting in Freiburg under Maximilian I, ordered them to leave the country by the following Easter. Any

who did not leave would be regarded as outlaws. It would then not be a crime to beat, rob or even kill them. In 1516 they were forbidden to enter Bavaria. By the eighteenth century the laws were becoming more severe. Saxony ordered Gypsies to be executed if they reappeared in the state after once being expelled. In 1714 Mainz decreed the execution of any Gypsy men captured, while their wives and children would be flogged and branded. In Frankfurt-am-Main in 1722 it was stated that children would be taken away from their parents and placed in institutions while their parents would be branded and expelled from the district.

The harsh laws led to some emigration when some of the **Sinti** and all of the **Manouche** clans left for France and other Sinti went east to Poland and Russia and south into Italy. The existing laws gradually fell into disuse, and in the nineteenth century we find assimilation programmes replacing expulsion. Schools for Gypsies were set up in a few places. When Otto Bismarck became chancellor of Germany in 1886 he recommended the expulsion of all foreign Gypsies. Anti-Gypsy actions by the authorities then increased. In March 1899 an Information Service on Gypsies was set up at the Imperial Police Headquarters in Munich. There, the registration and surveillance of the entire Gypsy population group was organised. This included the **Vlah** Romanies who were immigrating from the east. Alfred Dillmann, an officer of the Munich police, published in 1905 his Zigeunerbuch (Gypsy Book), giving details of over 3,500 Gypsies and persons travelling as Gypsies. By 1925 the Service already had 14,000 individual and family files for Gypsies from all over Germany.

Two years after the Nazi Party came to power, the **Nuremberg Laws** made Gypsies, alongside Jews, second-class citizens. The first internment camps for nomadic Gypsies were established in the towns of Cologne and Gelsenkirchen in

1935. More camps followed and settled Gypsies were removed from their houses and also interned. In 1936 the Race Hygiene and Population Biology Research Centre was established under the direction of **Robert Ritter**. Its role was to search out, register and classify Gypsies as pure or mixed race. The first mass arrests came in the week of 13–18 June 1938, when many Gypsies were deported to concentration camps. In October of the same year the National Centre for the Fight against the Gypsy Menace was set up. In 1940 a policy of making Germany Gypsy-free began when 2,800 Gypsies were deported to German-occupied Poland. Then, starting in March 1943, the mass deportation of some 10,000 Gypsies – both Romanies and Sinti – to the concentration camp of **Auschwitz** was organised. It is estimated that 15,000 died there and in other camps – three-quarters of the Gypsy population of Germany (some 15,000 persons).

After the end of the Second World War those who had survived found it difficult to get reparations as compensation for their suffering. In 1956 Oskar Rose founded an organisation, the Union and Society for Racially Persecuted German Citizens of non-Jewish Belief, the first organisation for Sinti and Romanies. In 1979 the **Verband der Deutscher Sinti** was recognised throughout the republic as the representative body for Sinti. It has some non-Sinti members.

Many Romanies have come to Germany since 1945 as guest workers, particularly from Yugoslavia. Others arrived from Poland and more recently, from Romania as asylum seekers. This explains the high estimated Gypsy population. **Rudko Kawcinski** in Hamburg set up the **Romani National Congress** which represents the interests of these recent arrivals.

Germany and Romania have now signed a formal agreement, whereby Germany will deport asylum seekers back to Romania which accepts them in exchange for monetary assistance to the Romanian government. Repatriation of Romanies to Macedonia and Bosnia is also taking place.

The Romani language has been recognised as an official minority language in the state of Hesse. In general the press and the public have little sympathy for the Gypsies. Some towns have set aside stopping places for the few nomadic families.

GESELLSCHAFT FÜR BEDROHTE VÖLKER (SOCIETY FOR ENDANGERED PEOPLES). Germany, Göttingen. An organisation led by Tilman Zülch that helped the German **Sinti** develop their own representative bodies. It supported the third **World Romani Congress** and its journal *Pogrom* often has articles on Gypsies.

GHAZA AND THE WEST BANK. A number of Dom (**Nawwar**) families live in this territory.

GHEORGHE, Nicolae 1940–. Romania. Sociologist and civil rights worker. He is active on the international scene and has represented Romani interests at many international conferences. Nicolae Gheorghe organised the rebuilding of Romani communities that had suffered from pogroms in Romania. He has travelled extensively in Europe investigating the situation of the Romanies and has made reports to major international organisations.

GIESSEN. A town in Germany where a project to encourage the culture and educational prospects of Romanies and **Sinti** has been running. The programme includes a publication called Giessener Zigeunerhefte.

GILDEROY, Jack Scamp 1812–57. England. Bare-knuckle boxer. 'King' of the Kentish Gypsies. His several brothers worked in the scissors-grinding trade. His striking appearance in a top hat, given to him by Baron Rothschild in return for his vote in the Hythe Parliamentary elections, was well known to contemporaries. Jack Gilderoy also took part in pony-trap races.

GILLIAT-SMITH, Bernard 1883–1973. England. Diplomat and amateur scholar of the Romani language. He was a regular contributor to the journal of the **Gypsy Lore Society** and also translated *St. Luke's Gospel* into Romani.

GINA, Andrej 1936–. Czechoslovakia. Writer. He has written a novel in Romani entitled *Biav* (Wedding). He received the 2003 Roma Literary Award for Fiction.

GINA, Ondrej. 1936–. Czechoslovakia. Contemporary musician and political activist. He is a leading member of the Romani community in **Rokycany**. He was a member of Parliament in the first post-communist parliament in Czechoslovakia.

GIRCA ASSOCIATION. Switzerland. Est. 2000. The Association organises actions aiming at obtaining recognition for Gypsy communities' rights and more specifically to get indemnification for the death of many thousand Gypsies in the Nazi period (1933–45). GIRCA is headed by **May Bittel**.

GITANO-S, GITAN-S. The Spanish and French (alongside Tsigane) names for Romani Gypsies, deriving from the words 'Egitano' and 'Egyptien'. The terms are particularly used of Romanies in Spain and the South of France. See EGYPTIAN (i).

GJUNLER, Abdula. Macedonia. Contemporary poet. Abdula Gjunler currently resides in Holland. A book of his poems in Dutch and Romani was published in 1995 under the title *Bizoagor/Eindeloos* (Without End).

GOLEMANOV, Dimiter 1938–94. Bulgaria. Poet and teacher. His father was active in trade union politics as early as the 1930s and honoured as a fighter against fascism. Dimiter Golemanov became known to the world of Gypsy studies through a version of the Balkan tale, *Song of the Bridge,* that **Lev Cherenkov** had published in the *Journal of the Gypsy Lore Society*. Dimiter Golemanov had a great love for the Russian language, which he had studied at Sofia University and he wrote poetry and songs in Russian as well as Bulgarian and Romani. He attended the second **World Romani Congress** in Geneva. He died of a heart attack shortly after the political changes in Bulgaria.

GÓMEZ, Heliós. Spain. Twentieth-century political activist. Born in Seville, he was one of the founders of the Anarchist Trade Union but then joined the Communist Party. Gómez was detained seventy-two times, faced forty-two criminal charges and was expelled from Spain, France, Belgium and Germany. He then worked in the Kuznetsoy factory in Siberia. He returned to Spain in 1936 after the election victory of the left-wing government. He was in Barcelona when the civil war broke out and he fought there and later in Aragon. He was the political commissar of the Balearic command. During the war many Gypsies were members of the Catalan Nationalist Party and fought for the government. Following Franco's victory, he sought refuge in the USSR again.

GORGIO. See GAJO.

GRANICA. Town in Kosovo, Yugoslavia. Since 1945 it has become a place of Gypsy pilgrimage on the Orthodox Feast of the Assumption (27–28 August).

GRASS, Günther 1927–. German. Author. He told a conference against racism that Gypsy representation in international bodies was the only way to overcome the discrimination they encountered in many European states. "At the end of a century during which we were brought to the edge of the abyss by totalitarianism and racism, world wars and genocide, destructions and mass expulsions, it should be possible to make room and give a voice to the Roma nation (the Gypsies), Europe's largest minority, in the European Parliament," he said. He was awarded the Spanish **Premio Hidalgo**.

GREAT BRITAIN. See separate entries for ENGLAND, SCOTLAND, WALES and NORTHERN IRELAND. Legislation passed in the London Parliament will generally apply in Wales.

GREECE. Estimated Gypsy population: 350,000. At an early date Gypsies were recorded on the islands of the eastern Mediterranean. By 1384 Gypsy shoemakers were established on the mainland of Greece in **Modon** (then a part of the Venetian Empire), and by the end of the fourteenth century a large number of Gypsies were living on the Peloponnese peninsula. As the Turks advanced into Europe, many Romanies fled to Italy and other countries of Western Europe. Under the **Ottoman Empire** those Gypsies who remained were given comparative freedom provided they paid their taxes to the Turkish rulers. In 1829 Greece gained its independence. There have been a number of population exchanges between Greece and Turkey and some Muslim Gypsies have taken the opportunity to migrate eastwards, to Turkey.

Towards the end of the Second World War, the Germans began to arrest Gypsies to use them as hostages but the majority survived unscathed.

In Greece today many Gypsies are settled and ignored except by some educational authorities. Perhaps half are living in barely tolerated tent and shanty towns. As many of these are not registered as citizens their children are refused entry by schools. In 1997 some 3,500 Gypsies living in tents were ordered to leave the land in Evosmos (Salonica) where they had been living for thirty years. It was intended to rehouse them in a converted army barracks. A number of other Gypsy settlements have been destroyed, some in preparation for the Olympic Games.

A positive note is the establishment of a museum of basket making in Thrace. Gypsy musicians are popular. They include the singers Eleni Vitali, Kostas Pavlides and Vasilis Paiteris, together with the clarinettist Vasilis Saleas. An extremely popular TV soap opera entitled *Whispers of the Heart* transformed public attitudes towards the Roma for a short time in 1998. Chroni-cling the love story of an upper-class Greek architect and a young Romani woman, it was one of the most successful shows ever on Greek television.

See also BYZANTIUM.

GRELLMAN, Heinrich 1756–1803. Germany. Author. Wrote a treatise in 1783 entitled *Die Zigeuner. Ein historischer Versuch*. In 1787 this was translated into English as *A Dissertation on the History of the Gypsies*. The English edition was influential in affecting thinking on the treatment of Gypsies and inspiring the evangelical movement of persons such as John Hoyland and Samuel Roberts to start missions to the Gypsies in Britain in the nineteenth century. Some Dutch scholars see Grellman as the founder of a Gypsy identity which did not exist before his book.

GROOME, Francis Hindes 1851–1902. England. Writer and scholar. Possibly related to George Borrow. He left university without taking a degree and lived with Gypsies in England and Europe including an English Romani Esmeralda Locke whom he later wed, although the marriage was not to last. He was joint editor of the first series of the Journal of the **Gypsy Lore Society**. Francis Groome also wrote a novel *Kriegspiel* with a Romani theme and edited a collection of Gypsy folk tales.

GROTA BRIDGE. A bridge in Warsaw. In 1994 hundreds of Romani refugees from pogroms in Romania found shelter under this bridge. In 1995 the settlement was broken up by police.

GURBET(i) A **clan** in Yugoslavia. Archaic features in their dialect suggest that they were amongst the first Roma to reach Europe. (ii) A name given to the Muslim Gypsies of Cyprus.

GYPSIES FOR CHRIST. A **Pentecostal** movement in England and Wales. They are now independent of the international organisation.

GYPSY. In this dictionary 'Gypsy' is used as a synonym for 'Romani' except in articles on the Middle East and Asia. There the term applies to industrial nomads (peripatetics), mainly of Indian origin.

The word is derived from '**Egyptian**' because, when the Romanies first came to Western Europe, it was wrongly thought they had come from Egypt. Some authors suggest that the name may come from a place called Gyppe in Greece. Early English laws and authors such as **William Shakespeare** write 'Egyptian' (e.g. in the play *Othello*). The Spanish word *gitano* and the French word *gitan* are of the same derivation.

'Gypsy' is not a Gypsy word and there is no single word for Gypsy in all Romani dialects. **Rom** (plural Rom or Roma) is a noun meaning 'a man belonging to our ethnic group' but not all Gypsies call themselves Roma. The **Sinti**, **Manouche** and **Kaale** in Finland use the word Rom only in the meaning of 'husband'. There is, on the other hand, a universal word for non-Gypsy, which is **Gajo**.

In the Western European image of a Gypsy the idea of nomadism and self-employment is predominant. So we find, for example, an Intenet site on the World Wide Web proclaiming: "We are Cyber Gypsies – we roam the Net". An international tennis player or football manager is described in the media as leading a Gypsy way of life. In Eastern Europe, on the other hand, we find a paradox, with the Gypsies considered at the same time as lazy but taking on the dirtiest work, and foolish and at the same time cunning. Nomadism is not seen as a fundamental meaning of the equivalent of the word Gypsy (usually '*Tsigan*') in Eastern Europe.

In British law (as defined by the *Caravan Sites Act* **1960** and subsequently refined by judges) the term 'Gypsy', when used in planning law, does not apply to an ethnic group but anyone travelling in a caravan for an economic purpose. With regard to race-relations legislation, however, 'Gypsy' is considered to be a synonym for the ethnic term 'Romani'.

GYPSY AND TRAVELLER LAW REFORM COALITION. See TRAVELLER LAW REFORM COALITION.

GYPSY BROTHERS. Sweden, Malmö. Group playing traditional music, comprising keyboard player Ivan Nikolizsson, **Monica Caldaras** and their three sons. CD: *Gypsy Brothers*

GYPSY COUNCIL. UK. Est. 1966. The first secretary was **Grattan Puxon**. It carried out a campaign of passive resistance to the moving on of caravans by the police and local authorities. The campaign was a major factor in persuading the government to take some action over the problem of sites for Gypsies, culminating in the **Caravan Sites Act 1968**. Realignments within the Gypsy civil rights movement led to the formation of the **Romany Guild** in 1972, the **National Gypsy Council** in 1974 and **the Association of Gypsy Organisations** in 1975.

The National Gypsy Council has recently readopted the name Gypsy Council.

GYPSY COUNCIL FOR EDUCATION, CULTURE, WELFARE AND CIVIL RIGHTS. UK. At the time of writing this is the new name of the **National Gypsy Education Council**. It took over the latter's constitution but has had a wider brief than education (as the name indicates). There is a proposal to shorten the name to The Gypsy Council.

GYPSY CZARDAS. (i) A poem written by the nineteenth-century Russian poet Appolon Grigoriev after his beloved Leonida married another man. Ivan Vasiliev, conductor of a Gypsy choir, composed the music and it became popular with Gypsies in both St Petersburg and Moscow. The tune is often sung with different words but in recent years the original lyrics have returned to popularity.

(ii) A variety of the Hungarian Czardas danced by Gypsies without hand contact.

GYPSY EVANGELICAL MOVEMENT. See PENTECOSTALISM.

GYPSY GROOVZ. Gypsy brass band from Vranjska Banja in Serbia. The leader is trumpeter Ekrem Sajdic. Their album

Rivers of Happiness relates to the struggle of the villagers to get their water supply restored.

GYPSY KINGS. A band playing folk rock. It was first formed under the name Los Reyes in 1972 by younger members of the Reyes and Baliardo families in the south of France and in 1982 adopted the name Gypsy Kings. Their first record appeared in 1987 and they have toured widely since. An early hit was the song *Bamboleo* which reached the Top Ten in the United Kingdom. Another well-known song is *Djobi, Djoba*. They sing in a number of languages, including **Caló**.

GYPSY LORE SOCIETY. US. Est. 1888. Founder David McRitchie. The oldest society for the study of Gypsies. It ceased activities in 1892 and was revived in 1907. In the early days few meetings were held but it published the *Journal of the Gypsy Lore Society* (JGLS). Members of the newly created American chapter of the society took over its running in the 1980s and it has since had its headquarters in the United States. In addition to the journal (now called *Romani Studies*) there is now a newsletter. Annual meetings are usually held in America but four have taken place in Europe: in Leicester, Leiden, Turin and Budapest (2002).

GYPSY RONDO. The final movement of a piano trio by Haydn.

GYPSY SCALE. Also known as the Hungarian scale. This is a scale with the notes c – d – e flat – f sharp – g – a flat – b – c, popular in Hungary in the nineteenth century.

GYPSY SITES MANAGEMENT AND WELFARE COMMITTEES. UK. These are two committees set up by the **Association of Gypsy Organisations** (AGO) which still operate a small number of projects originally established by AGO.

GYPSY STUDIES. Gypsy studies were largely amateur until the 1950s. Since then, departments for courses in Gypsy Studies have been set up at a number of academic institutions in Europe, for example, St Charles University in Prague (Romani language), Greenwich University in England and the pedagogical college in **Košice** in Slovakia.

GYPSY WELFARE COMMITTEE. UK. See **GYPSY SITES MANAGEMENT AND WELFARE COMMITTEES**

GYPSYLORISTS. A term used for non-Gypsy amateur scholars in the nineteenth and early twentieth centuries who saw the Gypsy life as romantic, at least for short periods in the summer. They used to travel in horse-drawn wagons and make campfires around which they sang their own translations into Romani of popular songs. So, the student song *Gaudeamus igitur* was translated as Kesa paias kana 'men tarniben atchela (Let us make merry while we still have youth). They have been criticised for ignoring the harassment suffered by the Romanies they studied.

H

HABSBURG EMPIRE. The Habsburg family ruled much of Central Europe from 1438 to 1745. **Maria Theresa** and her son **Joseph II** inherited part of the Habsburg Empire.

HADLOW. On 20 October 1853 thirty Gypsy hop-pickers were drowned when the flooding river swept away their wagons as they were crossing Hartlake Bridge near Hadlow. The people, of Hadlow decided to erect a memorial to the dead Gypsies in the form of a pyramid-shaped tablet in the corner of the graveyard beneath a yew tree. The names of those who perished are now displayed inside the church doorway. The event was also commemorated in a song.

HAGA, Antonia 1960–. Hungary. Teacher,

political activist and politician. She was previously a member of the Hungarian Parliament, and is currently president of the Ariadne Foundation, a cultural organisation.

HALADITKA (Haladitko). The name given to a large clan of Gypsies living in Russia and adjoining countries. Their dialect is called haladitko. Many members of the clan consider the term (which means 'soldier') as being pejorative and prefer being called Russian Gypsies.

HALITI, Bajram 1953–. Kosovo. Poet and editor. From Gniljane, Bajram Haliti was the editor of the journal *Ahimsa*. He set up a Memorial Centre for Holocaust Studies, holding some 4,000 books and other items, all of which were lost when his house was burnt down. Bajram Haliti was seen as pro-Serb during the hostilities of 1999-2001 and was barred from entering the European Union countries for a time.

HALL, George C19th. England. Cleric. He was a supporter of the Romani way of life in the Midlands.

HANCOCK, Ian 1942–. England. Lecturer, writer and political activist. He is now teaching in Texas. He was at one time vice-president of the **International Romani Union** and on the board of the US **Holocaust** Museum.

HAVEL, Vaclav 1936–. Czechoslovakia. Political leader. The president of Czechoslovakia and later of the Czech Republic. Addressing the international Romani festival, Romfest, in **Brno** in July 1990, he stressed the right of Romanies to their own ethnic consciousness, and said that they should enjoy the same rights and duties as all citizens of the nation.

HAYWORTH, Rita 1918–87. US. Film actress. Born in Brooklyn, New York, she was the daughter of an American mother and a Spanish Gypsy father. Starting her career as a dancer at the age of twelve, she became the star in many popular Hollywood films.

HEARN, Patricio Lafcadio 1850–1904. Greece. Author. Son of a Cypriot Romani mother and a British Romani father, he was one of the first writers to create the modern-day journalistic style. He studied in the US where he met his wife who was African-American, and spent the end of his life living in Japan.

HEDMAN, Henrik 1954–. Finland. Pastor. He is leader of the Lutheran Mission to Gypsies in Finland and a translator of the *New Testament*.

HEINSCHINK, Mozes 1939–. Austria. Civil rights activist and scholar. Without having pursued an academic career, he received an honorary title of Professor from the University of Vienna for his studies of Romani speech and music. Devoting most of his free time to the Roma, he is closely involved with the **Romano Centro** in Vienna. His documentation of widespread and rare Romani dialects and music is legendary. His collection of over 700 hours of Romani speech and music is housed in the Phonogram archives in Vienna.

HELSINKI CITIZENS' ASSEMBLY (hCa). Est. 1990. The Helsinki Citizens' Assembly is an international coalition of civic initiatives, east and west, working for the democratic integration of Europe. At its Ankara Assembly, several workshops were devoted to the problems of the Romanies, and an hCa Roma Committee with Romani and non-Romani members was established in March 1994. It has its headquarters in **Brno** where **Karel Holomek** is the contact.

HELSINKI FOUNDATION FOR HUMAN RIGHTS. Poland, Warsaw. The foundation's aims include producing a handbook to enable activists and non-governmental organisations to gain access to information about Romanies' rights and educational possibilities.

HEREDIA, Jose. Spain. Contemporary scholar. He is professor of modern Spanish literature at Granada University.

HEREDIA, Juan De Dios. See RAMIREZ, Juan De Dios.

HIDRELLEZ/HEDERLEZI. Turkish feast celebrated by Gypsies, corresponding to St George's Day (6 May).

HIGGINS, Lizzie. Scotland. Contemporary singer. A **Scottish Traveller** singer, she is **Jeannie Robertson's** daughter and related to the Stewart family of musicians and singers.

HIROSHIMA FOUNDATION, Sweden. The Foundation works to support peace activities in the cultural field. It was founded in memory of the Swedish-born author Edith Morris whose best-known novel is *Flowers of Hiroshima*. In 2002 the Foundation elected to bestow its awards on individuals who have played key roles in preserving and promoting Romani culture including **Valdemar Kalinin**, **Rahim Burhan** and **Roberto Ciulli**.

HOLLAND, See the Netherlands.

HOLOCAUST. The Nazi genocide of Jews, Gypsies and others, particularly in the period following 1941.

When the Nazi party came to power in 1933, it inherited laws against nomadism already in operation. From the beginning, the National Socialists considered the Romanies and **Sinti** – whether nomads or sedentary – as non-Aryans. Together with the Jews, they were classed as alien and considered a danger to the German race. Already by 1935 they had been deprived of citizenship and given the second-class status of 'nationals'. In the same year the Law for the Protection of German Blood made marriages between Gypsies and Germans illegal. There was no place in the image of Germany under the New Order for a group of people who travelled around the country freely, worked as craftsmen and sold their wares from door to door. A quasi-scientific research programme was set up, under the leadership of **Robert Ritter**, in Berlin. Later this programme was carried out at the Race Hygiene and Population Biology Research Centre. The researchers had to accept the historical and linguistic fact that the Romani and Sinti peoples came originally from India and therefore should count as Aryan but they claimed that on the route to Europe they had intermarried with other races and as a 'mixed race' had no place in Nazi Germany. Allegations were made against the whole race in pamphlets and articles.

Internment camps were set up on the outskirts of towns in Germany, and both caravan and house-dwelling Gypsies were sent there. Discipline was strict and the internees were only allowed out to work. In 1938 several hundred Gypsy men were deported to Buchenwald and Sachsenhausen concentration camps as "people who have shown that they do not wish to fit into society" under the Decree against Crime of the previous year.

Heinrich Himmler, who became police chief in 1936, was particularly interested in the Gypsies and led the campaign against them. In 1938 he signed the Decree for Fighting the Gypsy Menace under which Ritter's Research Centre was linked with an established Gypsy Police Office and the new combined institution was put under the direct control of police headquarters in Berlin. The first task of this institution was to classify all nomads by their ethnic origin. To be classed as a 'Gypsy of mixed race' it was sufficient to have two great-grandparents who were considered to have been Gypsies which meant that part-Gypsies were considered to be a greater danger than part-Jews. In general, a person with one Jewish grandparent was not affected in the Nazi anti-Jewish legislation whereas one-eighth 'Gypsy blood' was considered strong enough to outweigh seven-eighths of German blood – so dangerous were the Gypsies considered.

Alongside the programme of registration and classification, new laws were imposed on the Romanies and Sinti. Any children who were foreign 'nationals' were excluded from school; the German Gypsies could be excluded if they represented a 'moral danger' to their classmates. The race scientists discussed what should happen next. Eva Justin proposed sterilisation except for those 'with pure Gypsy blood' while Ritter himself wanted to put an end to the whole race by sterilisation of those with one-eighth or more Gypsy blood. In fact, a law of 1933 had already been used to carry out this operation on individual Sinti and Romanies.

In the end, the Nazi leaders decided in 1940 that deportation was the means to clear Germany of Gypsies. Adolf Eichmann was responsible for the transporting of Gypsies alongside the Jews. In a first operation 2,800 were sent to Poland and housed in Jewish ghettoes or hutted camps.

In 1941, however, the Nazi leaders had carried out an experiment with Zyklon B gas in **Auschwitz** where they had murdered 250 sick prisoners and 600 Russian prisoners of war in underground cells. The discovery of this cheap and rapid method of mass murder led to a change in the treatment of the Jews. Deportation was replaced by death, and in 1942 Himmler decided that the same 'final solution' should be applied to the Gypsies.

On 16 December 1942 he signed an order condemning all the German and Austrian Gypsies to imprisonment in Auschwitz, and in February of the following year the police began rounding up the Romanies and Sinti. Within the first few months 10,000 persons had been transported to the camp. Children were taken out of orphanages and Germans were asked to inform the police of any Gypsies living in houses that might have been missed. We are not yet in a position to say how many German Gypsies remained outside the camps. They can be numbered in hundreds and lived under strict police control.

When Austria was annexed to Germany in 1938 it was announced that the Gypsies there would be treated as those in Germany. Two years later a camp was opened in Lackenbach just for the Austrian Romanies and Sinti. The western part of Czechoslovakia was also annexed but many Romanies succeeded in escaping across the border to the puppet state of Slovakia. Two internment camps were opened in 1942 in the German-controlled provinces of Bohemia and Moravia. The majority of the nomads were immediately locked up in the new camps and later several hundred of them were sent to Auschwitz from the camps when they were closed – together with the sedentary Gypsies. Only a handful of the Czech Gypsies survived the occupation.

The Romani population in Eastern Europe was mainly sedentary and integrated into the life of town and village. Many had been to school and had regular work. They had cultural and sports clubs and had begun to develop Romani as a literary language. Nevertheless, the German troops carried out the same policies of murder against these populations as against the nomads.

The Romanies who lived in Poland were crammed into the Jewish quarters of towns and villages. The Germans forced the Jews to give up their houses and move in with other families and then the Romanies were allocated the empty houses. In addition, a transport of 5,000 Sinti and Romanies were brought from Germany and Austria and housed in the Jewish **Lodz Ghetto**. An epidemic of typhus broke out but no medical help was provided. In the first two months 600 died. When spring arrived the survivors were taken to Chelmno and gassed.

The task of murdering the Romanies in the occupied areas of the Soviet Union was allocated to the Task Forces (**Einsatzgruppen**) who were given their orders soon after the invasion. Their orders were to eliminate 'racially undesirable elements' and most reports of the Forces mention the killing of Gypsies. In all, they murdered over 30,000 Romanies.

After the rapid capture of Yugoslavia in 1941, Serbia came under German military rule and the Romanies were compelled to wear a yellow armband with the word Gypsy on it. Trams and buses bore the notice 'No Jews or Gypsies.' A new tactic was used to kill the Romanies. They were shot as hostages for German soldiers who had been killed by the partisans. In Kragujevac soldiers with machine guns executed 200 Romanies, alongside 7,000 Serbians, in revenge for the death of ten German soldiers. These executions were carried out by regular soldiers of the German army. After so many of the men had been shot, the occupying forces were faced with the problem of a large number of women and children with no breadwinners. A solution was easily found. Mobile gas vans were brought from Germany, women and children were loaded into these vans, taken to the forests, gassed and buried. Their possessions were sent to Germany to be distributed by charitable organisations to the civilian populations.

In most of the countries that came under German rule the alternative was often between death on the spot and a journey without food or water to a concentration camp. Nearly all the larger camps had their section for Romanies: Bergen-Belsen, Buchenwald, Mauthausen, Natzweiler, Neuengamme, Ravensbrück, Sachsenhausen, Theresienstadt and others. From 1943 on the camps were merely waiting rooms for the journey to death by gas or shooting. Chelmno, Sobibor and Treblinka were names that meant immediate death on arrival. From all the camps where Romanies and Sinti were held, the best records available are for Auschwitz where Jewish prisoners kept secret notes.

It is also known that Romanies and Sinti were used in the camps for experiments with typhus, salt water and smallpox, but perhaps the most horrifying were the attempts to find new quick methods of sterilisation. These were to be used on all the races considered inferior so that they could be used as a workforce while preventing the birth of a new generation.

As Soviet and Allied troops advanced in 1944, the last tragic phase began in the life of the concentration camps. The remaining prisoners were evacuated on foot in the direction of Austria and Germany. Anyone who could not keep up during these marches was shot.

During the Hitler period, the Romanies and Sinti of Europe suffered a terrible blow from which they have not yet fully recovered. Some estimates of deaths are as high as 500,000. It should not be forgotten that this figure does not give the whole extent of the persecution of the many thousands more who suffered internment or other repressive measures. See also REPARATIONS.

HOLOMEK, Karel. Czechoslovakia. Contemporary political activist. He is currently the Romani contact, based in **Brno**, for the **Helsinki Citizens' Assembly**. He was a member of the national Parliament before the break-up of Czechoslovakia.

HOLOMEK, Miroslav 1925–89. Czechoslovakia. Political activist and sociologist. He was one of the founders of the Romani civil rights and cultural movement in the Republic in the 1970s.

HOLOMEK, Tomas 1911–88. Czechoslovakia. Lawyer and writer. He was one of the founders of the Romani civil rights and cultural movement in the Republic in the 1970s.

HOLY ROMAN EMPIRE. 1962-1806. This term was applied to the German Empire, and from 1438 it can be considered for practical purposes the same as the **Habsburg Empire**. Its boundaries varied. For the policy of the Empire toward Gypsies, see GERMANY; JOSEPH II; MARIA THERESA.

HOME MISSIONARY SOCIETY. England. The Society carried out some reform work with Gypsies in the 1820s with the aim of encouraging them to settle and take up regular employment.

HORSMONDEN. The Horse Fair at Horsmonden in Kent in October, together with the Barnet Fair, was one of the last events in the English Gypsies' calendar before the winter set in. Unlike some of the other fairs, Horsmonden has been an all-Gypsy event. It is not a 'charter fair' and is popularly believed to have grown out of a nineteenth century hop-pickers' Sunday holiday. Attempts have been made over the years to stop the fair or move it to another location. In 2001 the local authorities made their most determined effort yet to stop the fair and the Home Secretary declared the village an 'exclusion zone'. The **Gypsy Council for Education** has maintained a token presence each year since then in the hope of keeping the tradition alive and eventually restored.

HORTTO KAALO. Finnish Gypsy music group, playing traditional music, founded in 1970 by the two brothers Feija Akerlund and Taisto Lundberg together with Marko Putkonen. Their first record was a protest song against discrimination *Miksi ovet ei aukene meille*? (Why are the doors not open for us?) which reached the Top Ten in Finland. Their repertoire is varied: Russian-style Gypsy songs, folk songs from various countries and their own compositions. They have toured in Scandinavia and appeared regularly on television.

HORVATH, Aladar 1964–. Hungary. Civil rights activist. Once a teacher, now a politician, Horvath was president of the Roma Parlament in Hungary and, standing for the Free Democrat Party, he was one of the first two Romani MPs in the Hungarian Parliament (1990–4). Since 1995 he has run the Foundation for Romani Civil Rights in Budapest and set up the Roma Press Centre.

HOSKINS, Bob 1942–. British. Film actor and producer. His films include *The Raggedy Rawnie* in which an army deserter disguises himself as a Gypsy girl.

HOST (Hnuti Obcanske Solidarity a Tolerance: Citizens' Solidarity and Tolerance Movement). Czech Republic. Est. 1993 The movement was founded in Prague late in 1993 after four people, including two Romanies, were killed in violent attacks in one month. Its aims include monitoring ethnic violence and opposing discrimination. Gypsies are only part of HOST's work.

HRISTO, Kyuchukov 1962–. Bulgaria. Educationalist. The first Romani psycholinguist, he earned a PhD from Amsterdam University. He is currently training potential teachers in Bulgaria.

HÜBSCHMANNOVÁ, Milena 1953–. Czechoslovakia. Scholar and civil rights activist. She helped to keep Romani culture alive during the period 1973–89 when it was discouraged by the government in Czechoslovakia. She was instrumental in small-scale publishing during this period, including *Romane Gil'a*, a book of songs in Romani, as well as teaching the language. Milena Hübschmannová has written many articles and books in and on the language. She is the editor of the learned journal *Romano Džaniben* (Romani Knowledge) and teaches Romani at Prague University.

HUMAN RIGHTS PROJECT. Bulgaria. Est. 1992. Director: Emil Cohen. This organisation documents human rights abuses against Romanies and others, as well as providing free legal services to combat discrimination. It publishes a newsletter, *Focus*, as well as a number of reports and arranges training meetings for activists. It is based in Sofia with branches in Montana, Pleven, Shumen and Stara Zagora. In 1999 the Project initiated work on the Framework Plan for integrating the Romanies into Bulgarian society.

HUNGARIAN GYPSY MUSIC. Apart from the groups playing what is popularly regarded as Gypsy music in Hungary, such as waltzes and polkas by Strauss, there is also a strong singing tradition amongst the **Vlah clans** in the country. This includes slow songs for listening and fast songs for dancing. The slow song (loki gili) is often sung in harmony when others join in with the soloist, often improvising the words. The dance song (khelimaski gili) is used for the

Gypsy **csardas** and much of the text consists of nonsense syllables (mouth music). They are accompanied by other singers imitating various instruments such as the double-bass and percussion (snapping fingers, spoons, etc.). Finally, there are the 'stick songs' which usually have short verses and accompany stick and other solo dances (*csapás*). Groups such as **Kalyi Jag**, playing a type of folk rock, have become popular among both Gypsies and Hungarians.

HUNGARY. Estimated Gypsy population: 750,000. Gypsies may have reached Hungary by 1316 but the first certain reference to Gypsies refers to musicians who played on the island of Czepel for Queen Beatrice in 1489. However, others certainly passed through the country earlier in the fifteenth century. Sigismund, the king of Hungary and of the Holy Roman Empire, attended the Empire's Great Council in 1417 at Constance on the lake of the same name. While he was spending some free days in the neighbouring town of Lindau, some Gypsies arrived from Hungary and asked him for a letter of safe conduct. In 1423 Sigismund gave a safe conduct letter to another Gypsy leader, Ladislaus, and his company, in Slovakia (then part of the Hungarian Empire). These Gypsies then travelled to Germany where they used Sigismund's letters to get food and lodging from the authorities. Later in 1476 Gypsies were sent to work by King Matthias Corvinus as smiths in Sibiu in Transylvania (part of Hungary at that time). In these early years, Gypsies in Hungary were under the jurisdiction of their own leaders. Things were to change with the rule of **Maria Theresa.**

From 1758 Empress Maria Theresa legislated to assimilate the Gypsies, or New Hungarians (*Ujmagyar*) as they were thenceforth to be called. They were to settle and farm the land. Her son **Joseph II** continued his mother's policies. The 1893 census recorded 275,000 Gypsies, of whom over 80,000 spoke Romani. The vast majority were sedentary as a result of Maria Theresa's intervention.

Apart from the musicians, Gypsies have been viewed with mistrust. From the mid-1930s calls were made in the Hungarian Parliament for the internment of Gypsies in labour camps. However, although Hungary was allied to Germany in the Second World War, it was not until German troops occupied Hungary in March 1944 that mass deportations of Romanies to concentration camps began. The accession to power of the fascist Arrow Cross party in October 1944 gave a new impetus to the persecution and, with the Soviet army approaching Budapest, killing increased. Over 100 were shot in a wood near the town of Varpalota in February 1945. One post-war report suggests that 28,000 died in the camps but this figure may be too high.

After the liberation of Hungary in 1945, the policy was that the Romanies had the same rights and responsibilities as other Hungarians. This policy was meaningless because it did nothing to remedy the neglect of years and the general prejudice against the Roma. They continued to live in isolated settlements and many children were not accepted into schools.

On coming to power the following year the Hungarian Workers Party adopted a policy of assimilation. Prime Minister Matyas Rákosi referred to them as New Hungarian Citizens, a similar term to that of Maria Theresa. Nomadism was prohibited. The Kadar regime (after the 1956 counter-revolution) took more interest in the Romani population and in 1958 the Politburo of the Hungarian Socialist Workers Party (MSZMP) adopted a policy of active support for minority culture and education. Part of this policy included the creation of the Cigányszövetség (Gypsy Union), the first Romani organisation officially operating in Hungary (1958–61). A report revealed that two-thirds of the Gypsies then lived in substandard housing, mainly in rural Gypsy settlements or separate quarters in towns. A re-housing programme began in 1964 with low interest long-term loans.

A debate in 1961 concerning whether the Romanies were an ethnic minority resulted in the conclusion that they were not and that Romani should not be taught in schools. The Gypsy Union was closed in the same year. *Rom som* (I am a Romani), a bilingual journal, published its first issue in January 1975. It was produced with stencils by the Romani cultural club in District 15 of Budapest but circulated outside the capital. By 1982 it had disappeared, although the title has now been revived in a printed format.

In 1976 the government ordered measures to ensure full employment for men and pre-school nursery education for children in an attempt to integrate the Gypsy population. By 1986 the need to support a political organisation for the Romanies was acknowledged and the Orzsagos Cigánytanacs (National Gypsy Council) came into being. The head of the new body was **József Choli Daróczi**. The establishment of the national body was soon followed by the creation of councils in each county which dealt with individual cases of discrimination. A further body, the Ungrothemeske Romane Kulturake Ekipe (Hungarian Romani Cultural Association), was created in 1986 to encourage and sponsor Gypsy artists and support Romani culture. It received a large grant to assist over 200 cultural groups and forty dance troupes. The president was **Menyhért Lakatos**. In 1979 the Gypsies in Hungary were finally recognised as an ethnic group.

In 1989 multi-party democracy came to Hungary and Dr Gyula Naday formed the Magyar Cigányok Demokrata Szövetség (Democratic Union of Hungarian Gypsies), and Pal Farkas became chairman of the Social Democratic Party of Gypsies of Hungary. The Hungarian Roma Parliament was set up in the same year, as was the organisation **Phralipe** under **Bela Osztojkan**. The Minorities Law, passed in July 1993, defined the rights of minorities in Hungary and led to the creation of the short-lived Minorities Round Table, a body that negotiated with the government Office of National and Ethnic Minorities. In 1994 the Romanies were able for the first time to elect local Romani councils and, in April 1995, a Hungarian National Council of Romani Representatives was formed with Florian Farkas as its president.

Independent Romani political parties have been able to put up candidates at the recent general elections: Magyarorszagi Ciganyok Bekepartja (Hungarian Gypsies' Peace Party), led by Albert Horvath, Magyar Cigányok Antifasiszta Orszagos Szervezet (National Organisation of Gypsy Antifascists) and Roma Parliament Választási Szövetség (Romanies' Parliamentary Electoral Alliance). The Magyar Cigányok Szolidaritás Partja (Hungarian Gypsies Solidarity Party) presented three candidates, including Bela Osztojkan.

Ethnicity is not registered officially, so voting on the recently established local minority self-governments is not limited to the minorities themselves. The Democratic Romani Coalition, under the chairmanship of Aladar Horvath, swept to victory in the National Gypsy Minority Self-Government elections, defeating Lungo Drom.

In 2003 there were four Romany MPs. Romany mayors headed four municipal governments and 544 Roma sat on local and county government assemblies. A Rom, Laszlo Teleki, was appointed as First Secretary for Roma Affairs in June 2002. The Government is appointing special commissioners for Gypsy affairs at six ministries.

Democracy has also meant freedom for right-wing nationalists and skinheads to organise and racist attacks against Romanies have occurred in Eger and other towns. Three Romanies were killed in 1992 but the government denied any racist motivation. In September 1992 there was an arson attack on Romani homes in Ketegyhaza. Heavy-handed police raids have taken place in Arantyosapoti, Orkeny and elsewhere. In 1995 two assaults took place in Kalocsa. Joszef Sarkozi was shot after an argument in a bar in Pilisvorosvar in July 1996 and a Romani man was beaten up in a police car near Nyíregháza in February 1997. In 1999, Laszlo Vidak from the Roma settlement in the town of Bag filed a complaint alleging that he had been beaten by police officers during interrogation in October of that year, and three police officers were later given suspended sentences. Following on from this, it has been suggested that a February 2001 incident where police raided a Romani settlement in the town of Bag may have been intended to intimidate Laszlo Vidak. More recently, in November 2003, a Romani man burnt to death in a 'rubber cell' at a prison in Zalaegerszeg, Zala County.

Physical attacks are at a lower level than in other Eastern European countries. Nevertheless prejudice remains. A petition signed by 827 residents in Szentetornya in 1994 called for the expulsion of all Gypsies in the area. A poll taken earlier by Helsinki Watch found that one third of the Hungarian population supported the idea of compulsory repatriation of the Romanies to India. In another poll by the Median agency, three quarters of those asked expressed anti-Gypsy sentiments.

Despite the existence of an anti-discrimination law, Roma continue to be widely discriminated against, even by the judiciary. In one recent case, two Roma men who had served fifteen-month prison sentences were released from custody in November 2003 having been found innocent. They decided to sue for compensation but were not awarded the requested amount as the court stated that the individuals were more 'primitive' than average and did not merit the greater compensation. An appeals court went on to uphold the judgement; however, the Prime Minister reprimanded the presiding judge.

In January 2003, a police investigation into the Minority Affairs Ombudsman's allegation of housing discrimination against Roma removed to villages surrounding the town of Paks in September 2002, concluded that there was no violation of the law and the case was closed.

The unemployment rate for Roma is estimated at 70 per cent, more than ten times the national average. That the Government reduced the limit on unemployment benefits from one year to nine months in 2000 has only served to exacerbate the poverty of the Roma. The Hungarian government has, however, recently committed two billion forints (£16 million) towards improving the plight of the Gypsy minority. Some Gypsy leaders have called for a larger twenty-year programme.

Romany children are often segregated by being placed in 'special schools' designed for children with mental disabilities or poor academic performance. The Government states that these schools are intended to provide intensive help for disadvantaged children. The opening of a selective English style 'public (i.e. private) school' in the town of Jaszladany caused great resentment for the town's 30 per cent Romany population who feel discriminated against and socially excluded, as the high tuition fees at the school mean that their children are essentially barred from attending. Nevertheless, there are signs that the government is committed to increased efforts at various levels of Gypsy education. Pecs University launched the country's first post-graduate programme in Gypsy studies with a department of Romology. The teachers' training colleges in Pecs and Zsambek also have departments of Romany studies and the Romaversitas programme supports Roma students completing degrees in colleges of higher education.

A high school with special responsibility for Gypsy education has been opened at Szabolcs, a deprived region of eastern Hungary. A kindergarten catering almost exclusively for Gypsy pupils has also been opened in Csepel, a poor Budapest suburb. The cities of Ozd and Szolnok have just signed an agreement with the Ministry of Education for the creation of student hostels providing 400 spaces to Gypsy pupils engaged in further education. Additionally, there are scholarships available to Roma at all levels of education through the public Foundation for the Hungarian Roma.

Music has always been a popular profession for the Gypsies of Hungary. In 1683 it was said that every nobleman in Transylvania had either his own Gypsy violinist or locksmith. In 1839 the first Hungarian Gypsy orchestra visited Western Europe and in 1847 **Barba Lautari** met the composer **Franz Liszt**. In 1938 the Federation of **Hungarian Gypsy Musicians** arranged a Gypsy music festival to commemorate the 500th anniversary of the Gypsies' first appearance in Hungarian territory. Apart from the polkas and waltzes that they play in restaurants, there is **Hungarian Gypsy music**. The **Vlah** Romanies have a lively culture of their own with ballads and songs to accompany dancing.

Three main groups of Gypsies live in Hungary: the Hungarian Romanies, who form some 70 per cent of the population, very few of whom speak (the Carpathian dialect of) Romani; the Vlah, some 20 per cent, and the **Beyash**, who speak a dialect of Romanian.

Weekly radio and television programmes are aimed at Gypsies but also have a Hungarian audience. **Agnes Daróczi** was originally on the teams that produce these programmes. In 2001 Budapest's Roma gained their own radio station with the launch of Radio C, a station run by and for Gypsies. The current director is David Daroczi. The station is noted for its breadth of musical coverage including Romani rap, such as the band **Fekete Vonat**. See also MINORITY SELF-GOVERNMENT (HUNGARY).

I

ICELAND. Apart from short visits early in the last century by horse-dealers from Scandinavia (and one woman and her child on their way to America in 1933), there has been no migration of Gypsies to Iceland.

ILIEV, Jony. Bulgaria. Contemporary musician. In his own country he plays turbo-folk but his CD *Ma maren ma* (Don't beat me) is more traditional.

ILIJAZ, SABAN. Macedonia. Contemporary poet from **Shuto Orizari** in Macedonia.

INDIA. It would take a volume on its own to look at tribes and castes in India and Pakistan who might be related to the Romanies of Europe and the Doma (**Nawwar**) of the Middle East. We would need to consider all the groups of industrial nomads who speak a north Indian language. However, there are three names that spring to mind because of links that have already been made. The first is Banjara, who took an active part in the Second World Romani Congress in Geneva. Dr Shyamala Devi, who later was to be one of the first of the **clan** to go through university, has visited Europe many times and written about the Banjara-Romani connection

The Sapera (snake-charmers) – also known as **Kalbelia** – live mainly in Rajasthan. Sapera dancers have visited Europe several times and are featured in **Toni Gatlif's** film *Latcho Drom*. English Gypsies were invited by the Indian High Commission to a showing of a documentary on this tribe in 1984. The Romani viewers immediately claimed to recognise the whistles used to call dogs – which had survived in their folk memory for nearly a millennium since the departure from north India.

A study association has been set up in Rajasthan with the aid of Dr **Milena Hübschmannová** from Prague, herself a specialist in Indian languages. More research on the Kalbelia would be useful but so far the Association has not been as active as **W.R. Rishi's** circle in Chandigarh and the Kalbelia themselves are not as politically organised as the Banjara.

It has been suggested that, at the same time as the ancestors of the European Gypsies moved west, a small group of nomads migrated south, the **Vaghri** or Nari-kuravar. They speak a north Indian language and their main occupation today is catching birds – *nari-kuravar* in Tamil. In 1961 a Tamil named K. Raghupathi gave up his work with a bus company and started a day school in Trichi. Six years later he set up a meeting with sixty-seven leaders of the community to form the Nadodi Nalvazue Sangam. Raghupathi married a woman from the tribe, Jnasundari, which made him more accepted by the people with whom he was working. In 1972 he set up the first boarding school in Madras against much initial opposition from the parents of the children, since when further school projects have been initiated.

The Vaghri – like the Sapera – have not reached the political maturity of the Banjara and links between them and European Romanies have been solely through the missionaries of the **Pentecostalism** movement.

INDIAN INSTITUE OF ROMANI STUDIES. India, Chandigarh. Founder: The late **W.R. Rishi**. The Institute is now under the directorship of his son, Veerendra Rishi.

INDIAN ORIGIN. Some references to Indian origin are made in the early accounts of Gypsies in Europe. This was then forgotten both by Gypsies and non-Gypsies and replaced by the theory that they came from Egypt. However, investigations into the Romani language showed that it originated in North India and had been brought to Europe by the Gypsies. A small number of writers have recently denied the Indian origin and claim that the Gypsies are Europeans who acquired the language through contact with Indian merchants.

Many Gypsies are actively aware of the Indian connection. They like to watch Indian films and play the music of these films, and some even have statuettes of Indian gods in their houses. The **Teatr Romen** in Moscow includes translations of Indian plays in its repertoire. Some contemporary writers, in particular poets, have introduced Hindi words into their works. In India itself the connection was recognised by the Prime Minister Indira Gandhi, the two **Chandigarh Festivals** and the activities of the **Indian Institute of Romani Studies**

INDORAMA. Bulgaria. Est. 1991. President: Vasil Danev.

An association founded in Bulgaria in 1991 whose vice-president was the businessman and sometime poet Georgi Parushev.

INFORMAL CONTACT GROUP ON ROMA OF THE INTERGOVERNMENTAL ORGANISATIONS The Group is composed of representatives from **OSCE/ODIHR**, the **Council of Europe**, the European Commission and the **European Union**.

INFOROMA. Bratislava, Slovakia. It collects documentation and runs training courses. It is supported partly by **Open Society**.

INSTITUTO ROMANO. (i) A cultural and welfare organisation in Barcelona affiliated to the **Unión Romani**. The secretary is Juan Reyes Reyes.
(ii) The Romani title of the **Romani Institute** of Britain.

INTERFACE. (i) The newsletter of the **Centre de Recherches Tsiganes**. It was published in several Western European languages.
(ii) The Interface Collection, a publica-

tion programme of educational books by the Centre.

INTERNATIONAL COVENANT ON ECONOMIC, SOCIAL AND CULTURAL RIGHTS. The Covenant was set up by and is monitored by the **United Nations**. The ERRC and other bodies have submitted regularly evidence to the UN showing that many countries, most recently Russia and Slovakia are not following the Convention.

INTERNATIONAL MEETINGS. The first meeting mentioned in some books is the **Cannstadt Conference** of 1871. Recent research has discovered that this was a story made up by a newspaper. Some books also mention an international **Sofia Congress** in 1905. However, it seems that this gathering was just for Gypsies living in Bulgaria. In 1934 the Romanian Gypsy Union organised what can be considered the first international meeting, the **Bucharest Conference**, although few, if any, foreigners participated. After the Second World War, six international congresses have been held as well as a **European Congress** in Seville. Both Catholic and Protestant organisations arrange international conferences and meetings.
See WORLD ROMANI CONGRESS. PARIS CONGRESS and LODZ CONGRESS.

INTERNATIONAL ROMA CONTACT GROUP. Est. 2000. Group established at the initiative of **ODIHR**. It includes representatives of the **International Romani Union**, the **Roma National Congress**, elected Romani representatives, experts on the Romanies and the ODIHR/**CPRSI**.

INTERNATIONAL ROMA WOMEN'S NETWORK (IRWN). Sweden. Est. 2003. President: Soraya Post. The IRWN was launched on 8 March (International Women's Day) by Roma women from eighteen European countries to lobby governments for better living conditions and to fight for Roma women's rights. Activists are drawn from Roma, **Sinti** and **Traveller** communities and cover

west, central and Eastern Europe.

INTERNATIONAL ROMANI UNION. Est. 1978. President: Emil Sčuka. Since the second **World Romani Congress (1978)** the Union has operated between congresses as the official body representing Gypsies, replacing the role of the **Comité International Tzigane**. It is recognised as a representative body by the major international organisations and was awarded roster status by the **Economic and Social Council of the United Nations** as long ago as 1979 and later by UNICEF.
See WORLD ROMANI CONGRESS

INTERNATIONAL ROMANI WRITERS ASSOCIATION. Finland. Est. July 2002. President: **Veijo Baltzar**. Arising initially from a meeting in Cologne in November 2001, the Association was formed in July 2002 when some thirty Romani writers from nine countries came together in Karis in Finland to found this association. The main aim of the organisation is to promote multi-lingual Romani literature and to strengthen the language and culture of the Romani people.

INTERNATIONAL ROMANI GUILD. UK. Spokesman is Michael Veshengro Smith.

INTERNATIONAL ROMA NEWS AGENCY. Berlin. The Agency is under the direction of **Rajko Djurić.**

INTERNATIONAL UNION OF THE ROMA OF THE BALTIC STATES AND THE CIS. Est. 2003. Chairperson: **Oleg Kozlovski.** At a conference in Smolensk (Russia) in early 2003 this Union was established linking thirty-two Romani organisations throughout the region. Oleg Kozlovski was elected as Chairperson but this appointment has not been recognised in all the states

IRAN. The Roma passed through Iran on their journey from India to Europe, enriching their language with loans from Farsi. Some remained in the country. Their descendants include the **Koli**.

IRAQ. The 1976 census recorded 5,519 Gypsies (presumably **Nawwar**) and 2,569 Karach (indigenous commercial nomads) but the real figure is perhaps twice this. In 1979 the Government granted citizenship to all the Gypsies provided they knew Arabic and had a trade. Saddam Hussein settled several thousand in Abu Ghreib near Baghdad where they came into conflict with the locals for selling alcohol. After the US-led invasion the Muslim Iraqis forced the Gypsies to leave their homes.

IRELAND. See IRISH REPUBLIC and NORTHERN IRELAND.

IRISH REPUBLIC. Estimated population of **Irish Travellers**: 45,000 in caravans and houses. They form a separate social group and are distinguished by main-stream Irish society even when they are settled in houses. About a third live in caravan camps run by local councils, while the others nomadise or settle on unofficial sites. Their main occupation is recycling waste material. There is con-siderable discrimination, for example, in entry to hotels and bars. Two farmers attacked a roadside camp in County Kilkenny in August 1965 and killed a 41-year-old Traveller, father of ten children. The assailants were found guilty only of manslaughter and sentenced to two years in prison.

In 1960 the Irish government estab-lished a Commission on Itinerancy whose report was published three years later. This report was the basis for a later assimilation programme. Around this time a civil rights movement emerged amongst the Travellers.

In 1963 a school for Travellers, St Christopher's School, was built by Johnny MacDonald and others on an unofficial site at the Ring Road, Ballyfer-mot, Dublin. On 6 January 1964, it was burned down by Dublin Corporation employees together with several huts used as accommodation. The school was later rebuilt on Cherry Orchard.

At the end of 1963 the Itinerant Action Group was set up to fight for better living conditions and access to education. The first demand was for a water supply at the Ring Road site. In 1981 Travellers took a test case to the **International Court of Human Rights** in Strasbourg. They claimed that their constitutional right to educate their chil-dren was denied by their being moved constantly without caravan sites being available. Families sought the ruling that they could not be evicted unless an alternative site was provided. The court ruled favourably. So, in that same year, a new report was requested, and the Trav-elling People Review Body was set up by the Minister of Health. It consisted of twenty-four members, including repre-sentatives of the National Council for Travelling People (a network of settle-ment committees) and three Travellers. Its remit was to review current policies and services for the Travelling people to improve the then current situation. The group reported in 1983. The thrust of this report, as that of 1963, was the need to provide official stopping places for the Travellers' caravans and to help with education and employment.

Task Force on the Travelling People was set up in 1993 and published yet another report two years later. In March 1996 a National Strategy for Traveller Accommodation was announced to pro-vide 3,100 units of accommodation. This would consist of 1,200 permanent cara-van pitches, 1,000 transit pitches and 900 houses. A Traveller Accommodation Unit was established at the Department of the Environment to oversee the strat-egy. It was intended to initiate legisla-tion that would require local authorities to draw up five-year plans for Traveller accommodation. This emerged in *the Housing (Traveller Accommodation) Act* of 1998. Provision of caravan sites has been slow and only some 850 units of accommodation have been provided. Nevertheless, in 2002 the Government introduced the *Housing (Miscellaneous Provisions) Act* which made trespass a criminal act. The **Irish Traveller Move-ment** picketed the Dáil (Parliament) on 2 July to protest against the law. Many Travellers have been evicted from unau-thorised camps and in some cases their caravans were confiscated, forcing them to sleep in their cars.

The main organisations are the Irish Travellers Movement and **Pavee Point** (previously known as the Dublin Traveller Education and Development Group). There is also a national co-ordinator appointed by the Department of Education.

See also IRISH TRAVELLERS.

IRISH TRAVELLERS. Estimated population: 45,000 in the Irish Republic, 22,000 in the United Kingdom and Northern Ireland, 12,000 in the US. The origins of the Travellers are unknown. Some writers would trace the Irish Travellers back in history to as early as 2000 BC when newly arrived metalworkers travelled the country with their families. These families would then have been joined by itinerant musicians and later by some Druid priests as Christianity gained in popularity, forming the core of the Traveller population. Others may have joined them when tenants were later dispossessed of their lands. By 1834 the travelling community was clearly distinguished from other poor who wandered the land in the report of the Royal Commission on the Poor Laws in that year.

Migration of Irish Travellers to England probably started soon after invaders from Britain landed in the country in 1169. It may be more than a coincidence that the first appearance of '**tinker**' as a trade or surname in Britain was six years later. In 1214 a law was passed for the expulsion of Irish 'beggars' from England and in 1413 all Irish (with a few exceptions) were to be expelled.

Several hundred Irish Travellers emigrated to mainland Britain from 1880 onward. There are now well over 1,000 Irish Traveller families living in caravans in Great Britain, including children who were born in the country. In spite of some intermarriage with the English Romanies, they form a separate ethnic group, partly because of their strong Catholicism. It is estimated that there are also 10,000 people of Irish Traveller descent in the United States whose ancestors left Ireland even before the nineteenth-century famine.

The Travellers used to speak Irish with two special vocabularies called respectively **Cant** and **Gammon** by their speakers and **Shelta** by scholars. By the twentieth century the vast majority spoke English, again with a special vocabulary. A strong musical tradition thrives among the Travellers.

Irish Travellers were recognised as an ethnic group in England and Wales in 2000 as a result of a court case concerned with discrimination (CRE v. Allied Domecq)

They had already been acknowledged in Northern Ireland in 1997 in the Race Relations (Northern Ireland) Order. The Irish Republic protects Travellers against discrimination in Section 2 of the Equal Status Act of 2000 without accepting them as an ethnic group.

IRISH TRAVELLERS MOVEMENT (ITM). Ireland. Est. 1990. Chairperson: Catherine Joyce. A national association in the Irish Republic, linking a number of local groups from all parts of Ireland in its membership. The Irish Traveller Movement consists of a partnership between **Travellers** and settled people committed to seeking full equality for Travellers in Irish society. This partnership is reflected in all of the structures of ITM.

ITM BRITAIN. UK. Est. 1999. Chairperson: Joe Browne. The aim of ITM Britain is to establish and facilitate a national network of groups, organisations and individuals working with and within the Traveller community, to promote the interests and welfare of the **Irish Traveller** community in Britain. The ITM was formed due to a recognised need, which arose from conferences organised by Brent Irish Advisory Service in consultation with local Traveller projects throughout the country. These three conferences highlighted a lack of representation at a local and national level for Irish Travellers. The main activities of the organisation are to promote the recognition of Irish Travellers as a nomadic ethnic group, to bring together in partnership Travellers and settled people who are committied to achieving full equality for Travellers and to challenge the racism and discrimination – individual, cultural and institutional – that Irish travellers experience.

ISLE OF MAN. Gypsies are rare on the island. Around 1950 a Gypsy caravan stopped on Douglas Head then disappeared because of the banning of camping on the island. In 1975 a fortune-teller operated in Douglas. There were also at that time a few families – some dealing with scrap metal – living in houses, also in Douglas.

ISRAEL. A small community of **Nawwar** (Dom) live in Jerusalem and are well organised politically. See DOMARI.

ISTANBUL ORIENTAL ENSEMBLE. The ensemble who play alongside **Burhan Ocal**, brings together some of the best Romani musicians of Turkey playing Turkish and Thracian Gypsy music of the eighteenth and nineteenth century.

ITALY. Estimated Gypsy population: 100,000. In 1422 the first company of Gypsies came from the north into Italy, to the town of Bologna, in the shape of Duke Andrew of Little Egypt with a party some 100 strong. They had a letter of safe conduct from King Sigismund of Hungary and said they were on their way to Rome to see the **Pope**. The local priests in Bologna threatened to excommunicate anyone who had their fortune told by the Gypsies. There is no record of them being received by the pope at that time. We later find a series of edicts from different parts of Italy that, on the one hand, enable us to follow the travels of the Gypsies but, on the other, reveal the antipathy toward these nomadic groups. The first edict was in 1493 in Milan where the duke ordered all the Gypsies in the area to leave under the threat of execution. Similar decrees followed in Modena (1524), the Papal states (1535), Venice (1540), Tuscany (1547) and

Naples (1555). These decrees did not succeed in banishing the Gypsies from Italy, however. We find them depicted by Leonardo da Vinci and Caravaggio and other artists. In Lombardy and Piedmont Gypsies nomadised with their crafts without attracting the same attention of lawmakers as had the companies led by the dukes.

Following a different route, across the sea from the Balkans, Gypsies came to central and southern Italy – Abruzzi and Calabria – in the period 1448–1532, along with Greeks and Albanian immigrants, fleeing from the advancing Turks. They settled here and only travelled in limited areas, up to and including Rome. Later, **Sinti** Gypsies came from Germany into northern Italy and toward the end of the nineteenth century, **Vlah** Gypsies from Romania. Some Yugoslav Gypsies nomadised in Italy between the two World Wars (1918–39).

Under the fascist regime of Mussolini, Gypsies were harassed and imprisoned. Even before the Second World War many were arrested and expelled from the mainland to Sicily and smaller islands. Then from September 1940 internment camps were set up and the first official instructions for the incarceration of Italian Gypsies were issued. From 1942 Agnone in the south was a camp solely for Gypsies. When Italy signed an Armistice with Britain and the Allies in September 1943, the Germans took over the north of the country and began to send Gypsies to the concentration camps in Poland.

The years after 1945 witnessed a great influx of Romanies from Yugoslavia. Most of these live in shanty towns on the outskirts of the cities. There have been a number of anti-Gypsy actions by right-wingers. In March 1995 a bomb was thrown at two children who were begging by the roadside near Pisa. Local authorities have evicted nomadic families from sites in Florence, Milan, Turin and Verona. The right-wing National Alliance (AN) has organised demonstrations against Gypsy camps in Rome and elsewhere. The Northern League in Verona has distributed a pamphlet alleging that "Gypsies are parasites." In Genoa in June 1996 two demonstrations against Romani immigrants were held. Heavy-handed police action against new immigrants has been alleged, and at least one death in police custody has occurred, that of Zoran Ahmetovic in 1996.

On the other hand, the voluntary Opera Nomadi organisation has worked to get education to the children of nomadic families and those in the shanty towns while the **Centro Studi Zingari** published for many years the informative journal *Lacio Drom*. Vittorio Pasquale Mayer and Zlato Levak are amongst the Romanies who have contributed to the journal. One of the foremost cultural activists is **Santino Spinelli**.

ITINERANTS. A pejorative term sometimes used in Ireland for **Travellers**.

J

JAKOWICZ, Wladyslaw 1915–. Poland. Writer and dancer. Born in Krakow, but lived in Russia 1939–45. On his return to Poland, he earned his living as a dancer and then emigrated to Sweden where he worked as a teacher. Wladyslaw Jakowicz wrote the poem *O Tari thaj e Zerfi* (a ballad of two lovers) in the Romani language in 1981.

JASENOVAC. Concentration camp set up by the puppet Croatian government in 1941. Some 28,000 Gypsies were killed there, alongside Jews, Serbs and leftwingers, by the Ustashe guards. The majority were killed on arrival. Men and women were separated and then taken across the River Sava to extermination units at Gradina and Uštice. A small number of men were set to forced labour in a brick factory where they soon perished through the poor conditions. A few Gypsy survivors escaped while being led to execution. The Croatian authorities have not been helpful to Roma wishing to attend commemoration events at the site of the camp.

JAYAT, Sandra. Italy. Contemporary poet and artist. A **Manouche** Gypsy and self-taught, she describes herself as "a daughter of the wind". Born in Italy, she is related to the renowned guitarist, **Django Reinhardt**. She left Italy, where her parents lived, as a teenager and worked as a commercial artist in Paris. Small exhibitions culminated in having her work shown in the Grand Palais Salon. In 1985 she organised an international exhibition of Gypsy art in Paris and in 1992 exhibited at the Musée Bourdelle. The French government then commissioned her to create a postage stamp depicting 'travelling people' in the same year.

Among her collections of poems are *Herbes Manouches* (1961), illustrated by the writer Jean Cocteau, and the 1963 publication, *Lunes Nomades* (Nomad Moons), translated into English by Ruth Partington in 1995. She has also written a novel, *El Romanes*. Her many honours include the 1972 Children's Literature Prize (Paris), the Poetry Book Prize (Stockholm) in 1978 and an international prize for painting also in 1978.

JENISCH; Yéniche. A **clan** of **Travellers** originally established in Germany, some of whom later migrated to Austria, Belgium, France and Switzerland. They may well number 10,000. They speak a variety of German with loan words from Romani as well as Yiddish. Traditionally, they were basket-makers and peddlers. Some scholars say they originated with a group of basket-makers and broom-makers in the Eifel region of Germany from where they spread out. During the Nazi period in Germany, many of the Jenisch were sent to concentration camps as 'antisocial' and perished. In occupied France they were kept alongside Romanies in internment camps for nomads during the period of the Second World War. For many years a Swiss mission took Jenisch children away from their parents and sent them to be brought up in children's homes. In both France and Germany small numbers continue to survive as semi-nomads. The Jenisch in Austria have formed their own cultural organisation.

JETHRO. It has been said, with little justification, that Jethro (Moses' father-in-law) was a Romani.

JEWS. The destiny of the Gypsies and the Jews has been intertwined ever since the former arrived in Europe some years after the latter. For example, in Spain the deportation of the Moors and the Jews and the attempted deportation of the Gypsies happened at about the same time. In the Russian Empire some Gypsies were converted to Judaism. They survived the Nazi occupation because they were thought not to be ethnically Jewish or Gypsy.

Many Jews have written about the genocide of the Roma and **Sinti** during the **Holocaust** (e.g. **Miriam Novitch** and Ben Sijes) while **Dora Yates** served many years as the voluntary Secretary of the **Gypsy Lore Society**.

JOHN, Augustus 1878–1961. England. Artist. He painted Romanies and Gypsy themes. Augustus John learned many Romani words that he used in correspondence with his closest friends.

JONES, Nella (née Saunders) 1932–. England. Psychic and healer. A Romani Gypsy who was brought up at Belvedere Marshes in Kent. She reputedly assisted in solving many cases for the police headquarters at Scotland Yard. They included the famous 'Yorkshire Ripper' case – that of Peter Sutcliffe who was sentenced at the Old Bailey in 1981 for the murder of thirteen women. She also helped to locate Stephanie Slater, a kidnap victim.

JORDACHE, Toni. Romania. Contemporary musician. He played the **cimbalom** in the years after the Second World War.

JOSEPH, Charles Louis 1833–96. Austria. Writer and politician. The Archduke of Austria, he published a number of works at the end of the nineteenth century on the Romani language in Hungary.

JOSEPH II 1741–90. Austria. **Habsburg** Emperor of Austria-Hungary (part of the **Holy Roman Empire**) from 1765, he was the son of **Maria Theresa** and continued her assimilationist policies towards Gypsies. The Romani language and dress were banned and music was only allowed on feast days. Schooling and church attendance were made compulsory. Resistance by the Gypsies led to Joseph modifying some of his decrees.

JOVANOVIĆ, Žarko d. 1997. Serbia. Balalaika player and singer. During the Second World War he escaped from the concentration camp of Zemun and joined the partisans. Žarko Jovanović made many recordings in the years after 1945. He wrote the lyrics of the Romani **National Anthem, Gelem, Gelem.**

JOYCE, Nan. Ireland. Contemporary civil rights activist. An **Irish Traveller** herself, she stood unsuccessfully in Dublin for election to the Irish Dáil (Parliament) to draw attention to the Travellers' needs.

JUSTIN, Eva. Germany. Twentieth-century scientist. Working with **Robert Ritter** in the Race Hygiene Research Centre in Nazi Germany. She saw sterilisation as the way to solve the 'Gypsy problem.' See HOLOCAUST.

JUSUF, Shaip (Šaip) 1932–. Macedonia, **Skopje**. Teacher and writer. He helped in the establishment of the **International Romani Union** and was a scholar of Romani grammar. Shaip Jusuf visited the first Chandigarh Festival and used many loans from Indian languages in his writing. He published a biography of Tito in Romani in 1978 and a Romani grammar in 1980.

K

KAALO. The term used for self-ascription by Finnish Gypsies. It is from the Romani word (**kalo**) meaning 'black'.

KAL. Serbia, Valjevo. Band led by brothers Dragan and Dušan Ristić (vocals and guitar) who play in the style of the many traditional musicians from the Serbian village of Grabovica. The name comes from Romani **kalo** (black) and also the Greek God Kal.

KALBELIA. The Kalbelia are nomads in Rajasthan, also known as Sapera, one of whose occupations is snake charming. They are considered by many scholars to be close cousins of the European Romanies. Kalbelia dancers from Rajasthan have appeared several times in Western Europe with folk dance groups from India. Gulab and Mera, who danced with the Surnai Company in Rajasthan, came to London and performed at the Albert Hall in March 1986. They also appear in the documentary film *Latcho drom* (Good Road).

KALDA, Jozef. Czechoslovakia. Contemporary poet. A Moravian poet who had a success with a series of poems supposedly written by a farmer's son who falls in love and runs off with a Gypsy. The poems inspired the composer Janaček to write the song cycle *The diary of one who disappeared.*

KALDERASH (i) Name of a **clan** derived from the Romanian word *calderar* (coppersmith). Many emigrated from Romania after the end of slavery in the nineteenth century. They are probably the largest Romani clan, numbering nearly one million, spread throughout the world. Many men still work in the traditional trade of repairing copper utensils while their womenfolk practise palmistry.

(ii) A dialect of Romani.

KALI. An incarnation of God in the Hindu religion. When the Gypsies came to Europe they transferred their adoration of Kali to the many black statues of the Virgin Mary in Poland and elsewhere, as well as St Sarah at **Saintes Maries de la Mer**. There is a report from 1471 of a "Duke Paul of Egypt" making a pilgrimage to Compostela to see the **Black Virgin** of Guadalupe.

KALININ, Valdemar 1946–. Belarus. Teacher, poet and translator. He currently resides in London. Valdemar Kalinin has translated the New Testament into Romani, and is currently preparing the Old Testament for publication. He is the winner of the 2002 **Hiroshima Foundation Award** and the Roma Literary Award for translation. His son Nikolai (b. 1977) is a counsellor for Roma at the Belarus branch of the International Society for Human Rights.

KALO. The Romani word for 'black'. The north Welsh and Finnish Gypsies use Kalo/Kaalo as a self-ascription rather than 'Rom'. It is likely that many of the Finnish Gypsies came from Spain via Britain, and there are some similarities in the dialects. The connection with the **Koli clan** in Iran is unclear.

KALYI JAG (Black fire). Hungary. The first group to play **Vlah** music in a popular style for a wider audience. Their music has developed from traditional dance tunes with the accompaniment of mouth music and improvised percussion instruments.

KALYI JAG ROMA SCHOOL. Hungary. A vocational comprehensive school in Budapest.

KANNAUJ. A city in India on the Ganges captured by the Muslims in 1018. All of its inhabitants were apparently taken as captives to Khorasan. The linguist **Marcel Cortiade** has put forward the hypothesis that these captives were the ancestors of the Romanies.

KANTEA, GEORGI. Moldava. Contemporary poet. A collector of folklore, he is a member of the **Ursari clan**.

KARDERASH. A **Vlah clan** in Bulgaria.

KARISLAMA. Turkey. Romani band, whose music appears in **Tony Gatlif's** film *Latcho Drom*.

KAROLY, Bari. Hungary. Contemporary writer. He edited an anthology of poetry and tales and has many books of his own poetry. He has also compiled a collection of Hungarian and Romanian Gypsy folklore music, *Cigány Folklór*.

KARRNER. A **clan** of **Travellers** in Austria.

KARSAI, Ervin. Hungary. Contemporary teacher and poet.

KARWAY, Rudolf. Poland. Twentieth-century civil rights leader. A **Lovari** who emigrated to Germany, he was president of the Zigeunermission, a civil rights movement based in Hamburg that was active in the 1960s. In 1968 the mission organised a delegation to the European Commission on Human Rights in Strasbourg protesting against discrimination. Rudolf Karway visited England in 1970.

KATITZI. Character, largely autobiographical, in a series of thirteen books for children written by **Katarina Taikon** 1975–6. In 1979 the books came out in cartoon form and there was also a film. **Hans Caldaras** recorded the song *Katitzi* in Katerina Taikon's honour. In 2003 the books were turned into a play. The books are still popular and have been translated into several languages.

KAVALEVSKY, Sonya. Sweden. Academic. In 1884, Sonya Kavalevsky, whose mother was a Gypsy, became the first woman professor in Sweden. She taught mathematics at Stockholm University.

KAWZCYNSKI, Rudko. Poland. Contemporary civil rights activist. He came to Germany as a refugee in the 1970s. He was a singer in the Duo Z. Later, he entered the Gypsy civil rights movement and set up the **Romani National Congress** in Hamburg. He was also active in establishing Eurom. Rudko Kawcinski has organised many demonstrations such as the *Bettlermarsch*, a march across Germany to the Swiss frontier, and the occupation of the Neuengamme concentration campsite. He recently arranged the international **Lodz Congress** and takes part in conferences organised by intergovernmental organisations.

KAYAH 1960–. Poland. Popular singer. Exceptionally, she made the largely folk music CD *Kayah-Bregovic* (1999). There is no connection with the Finnish pop group of the same name.

KEENAN, Paddy 1950–. Ireland. Musician. **Irish Traveller** piper in the style of **Johnny Doran**. He was part of the band called the **Pavees** and has recorded as a soloist.

KENITES. A tribe of nomadic smiths in biblical times living in Judah. They are unrelated to the Romani Gypsies but appear on some maps.

KERIM, Usin 1928–. Bulgaria. Poet. He has written in Bulgarian and, later, Romani. His first book of poems was entitled *Songs from the Tent* (1955).

KETAMA. Contemporary folk rock group in Spain founded by Ray Heredia, Jose Soto and Juan Carmona. The Carmona family of Madrid have been musicians for three generations, starting with Tio Habichuela, the grandfather of Juan. Later they were joined by Antonio Carmona. Their first recording was issued in 1985. Ray Heredia left the group to be a solo act but died shortly afterward. Josemi Carmona, a cousin of Jose and Juan, then joined the group before their third recording *Songhai 1*, which incorporated a fusion of **flamenco** and Mali music. In 1992 the sixth recording was *Pa gente con Alma* in collaboration with the Dominican jazz pianist Michel Camilo. Soto has now left the group, and Ketama consists of the three Carmonas. In their first album as a family trio *El arte de lo invisible*, salsa predominated over flamenco. They have also played in films such as Saura's *Flamenco*. Their latest recording, *Aki a Ketama*, is a mixture of flamenco, jazz and funk.

KHAMORO. (Little sun). Cultural festival first held in Prague in 2000.

KIEFFER, Jane. France. Contemporary poet. The collection *Cette Sauvage Lumière* (This savage light) appeared in 1961, followed by the collection *Pour Ceux de la Nuit* (For Those of the Night) in 1964.

KINGS. When the Romanies first came to Europe their leaders adopted European titles and we find in the records references to dukes in particular. The use of the titles king and queen started perhaps in the nineteenth century. In some cases the person designated 'king' is not the real leader – a device to deceive the authorities. Most kings and queens only have authority over their own extended family.

KIRK YETHOLM. Village in Scotland near Kelso. In 1695 a Gypsy named Young saved the life of Captain David Bennet at the Siege of Namur. In a gesture of generosity, the grateful officer gave some cottages to the Gypsies in Yetholm. The twin villages of Yetholm and Kirk Yetholm then became home to as many as 250 Gypsies for more than two centuries. They wintered in the Borders villages and took to the roads in the spring to sell their wares and their horses. Smuggling tea, salt and alcohol from across the Border in England is said to have provided a valuable additional source of income. The romantic but harsh lifestyle changed radically in 1839 when the Reverend **John Baird** became minister at Yetholm. He persuaded the elders of the tribe to board out their children with local families so that they could become pupils at Scotland's first ragged school.

A so-called Gypsy Palace—in reality a modest-sized cottage—still stands but otherwise there are no tangible signs that generations of the Romani race settled there. The Romanies are now to be honoured with a memorial in the village which claims to be the country's Gypsy capital.

Descendants of the original Yetholm Gypsies continue to live in the area although the current heir to the **Faa** 'throne' is an Edinburgh housewife who has shown no interest in claiming the title.

KISFALU CONFERENCE. A meeting of Gypsies held in Hungary in 1879. The participants were from Hungary only.

KLIMT, Ernst d. 1892. Germany. Political activist. A post-1945 political leader of the **Sinti** in Hildesheim and Lower Saxony. His family lived in the Sudetenland where his father was a miner. The family was arrested and taken to **Auschwitz** where Klimt arrived still wearing his Hitler Youth uniform. He was transferred, as being fit for work, to Buchenwald, where he took part in the internal camp resistance movement and helped to free the camp just as the US Army arrived. In 1965 he gave up his business activities and devoted himself to civil rights. His life story was turned into a musical play by the Theater Fahrenheit in Germany.

KOCHANI (KOČANI). A brass band from Macedonia. They have toured widely abroad.

KOCHANOWSKI, Vanya de Gila 1927–. Poland. Linguist. Born in Poland but brought up in Latvia, he is now living in France. Vanya Kochanowski wrote *Gypsy Studies* (1963), for which he earned a doctorate, a novel *Romano Atmo* (L'Ame Tsigane) and *Parlons Tsigane*.

KOCI, Ferdinant (Ferdinand). Albania. Contemporary artist. Now living in England, he has illustrated several publications including *Bibaxtale Berša*, a Romani edition of Donald Kenrick and Grattan Puxon's *Destiny of Europe's Gypsies*.

KOGALNICEANU, Mihael 1817–91. Romania. Politician. He strove for the emancipation of the Gypsy slaves in the nineteenth century.

KOIVISTO, Viljo. Finland. Contemporary writer and translator. He attended the first **World Romani Congress**. He writes for the religious bilingual periodical *Romano Boodos* (Romani Information) and has translated parts of the *New Testament* as well as producing an ABC primer.

KOLI. A **clan** of Indian origin in Iran. In recent years some members have visited Italy, mainly trading in gold.

KOPTOVÁ, Anna. Slovakia. Contemporary writer and cultural worker. She founded the **Romathan** theatre in **Košice**.

KOŠICE. Town in Slovakia that is home to the **Romathan** Theatre and a college that has a faculty for training Romani teachers.

KOSOVO. Province in the Balkans, currently part of Serbia-Montenegro. Estimated Gypsy population today: 40,000. The 1971 census showed 14,493 Roma in Kosovo, while in 1991 a more realistic figure of 45,745 was recorded. The estimated Romani population before the recent conflict was, however, at least 100,000. During the weeks preceding the 1971 and 1981 censuses both ethnic Albanians and Turks tried to persuade Roma to declare themselves as Albanians or Turks respectively while the Serbs encouraged them to register as Roma, in order to reduce the nominal percentage of Albanians in the country.

During the Second World War, it was garrisoned by Albanian fascists. Gypsies were made to wear distinctive armbands and recruited for forced labour. **Ljatif Sucuri** is regarded as having personally saved the Gypsies of Kosovo from massacre. Many Romanies joined the partisans.

Kosovo was a strong centre for Romani culture from 1945 until the recent hostilities. In 1983 radio broadcasts in Romani began in Pristina, amongst the earliest in Europe, and these continued for many years, while weekly television broadcasts started in the same town three years later. There was a regular TV programme from Tetovo as well as a locally produced magazine called *Amaro Lav* (Our Word). A group of young poets received acclaim well beyond the province largely because of the efforts of **Marcel Cortiade** in getting their work published. Two magazines – *Rota* and *Ahimsa* – were being published in Pristina. Formal education was rather less successful since, although some schools introduced Romani in 1985, this was without a curriculum or any textbooks. In this region the **Erlia** and **Gurbet** dialects were widely spoken.

In 1990, following the example of some Romanies in Macedonia, an **Egyptians'** Association was set up in Kosovo. It claimed that several thousand 'descendants of the Pharaohs' lived in the province. In spite of pressure both from Serbs and ethnic Albanians on the Roma to align themselves with one of the larger groups, the Association of Roma People of Pristina had a membership of more than 10,000. Its president, Baskim Redjepi, was a deputy in the Pristina city council while the poet, **Bairam Haliti**, worked in the Centre for Minority Languages and Culture in Pristina. Later, he was to flee to Zemun in Serbia after being denounced as a collaborator and war criminal by Albanians.

The province of Kosovo is currently still *de jure* part of Serbia-Montenegro, following the twelve-week war in 1999, waged by NATO against rump Yugoslavia to prevent the ethnic cleansing of the indigenous Albanian inhabitants. *De facto*, however, it is now controlled by Kosovar Albanians and the successors to their guerilla force, the Kosovo Liberation Army (KLA).

From 1981 the desire of many Kosovar Albanians for a fully independent Kosovo strengthened. Sometimes this turned to violence against Serbs but also against the Roma, whose leaders supported the Serbs. Such attacks only served to reinforce the alignment of the Roma with the dominant Serbs. When Yugoslav government tanks arrived in Pristina prior to the autonomous status of Kosovo being revoked in 1990, the Romani population unwisely had turned out to welcome them.

As economic and social segregation intensified, Albanians voluntarily or unwillingly left their jobs under the Serbian-led administration and many Roma took over the vacant posts, a move that was not to endear them to the Albanians. In social life Serbs replaced Albanian musicians by Roma while the Albanians themselves employed Albanian musicians in preference to Roma.

Albanian resistance against the Serbs continued and in 1998 the central government of Yugoslavia launched an offensive against the KLA, leading some 2,000 Roma to leave Kosovo for Voivodina in northern Serbia to flee the hostilities. After Serbian troops recaptured Orahovac from the KLA and massacred some 200 civilians, Roma were used to load corpses onto lorries. The use of Roma as gravediggers was to escalate during the period of the NATO raids the following year.

A decade later, in a rapidly deteriorating situation, the Yugoslav delegation to the Paris peace talks on Kosovo in 1999 included Albanians and Turks, Kosovan Roma and the newly discovered minority of Egyptians, alongside a Serbian majority. Amid this claim of multiculturalism, the delegation refused for several days to have direct talks with the KLA, whom they persisted in calling 'terrorists'. For the Romani and Egyptian delegates, Ljuan Koka and Cherim Abazi, their participation in the talks was to lead to their enforced flight to Serbia to escape Albanian hostility.

Then came the period in 1999 during which NATO carried out intensive bombing raids. We will not pre-empt history's judgement on whether Serbian atrocities against Albanians escalated during that time, although at the very least they continued. During this dramatic period when they were the victims of both warring groups, Roma were swiftly enrolled by the Serbs to help them terrorise the ethnic Albanians. Men of military age were forcibly recruited into the army and others were posted at the doors of food shops to keep the Albanians out. In self-defence, interpreted as complicity by the Albani-

ans, the Roma in several villages marked an R on their doors to distinguish them from the Albanian houses when the Serbian auxiliaries arrived to burn and kill. Some Roma had worked as gravediggers before the bombing started. Now their services were called upon by the Serbs to bury their Albanian victims. But the number of victims was such that extra hands were needed and unskilled Roma were recruited for the task.

Other Roma fled the country, either to escape NATO bombing raids or because – as Muslims – they, too, were being targeted by the Serbian auxiliaries. Some 2,000 fled to Macedonia where they were helped by Romani organisations and individual families in the face of discrimination by Macedonian agencies. Some 20,000 more took refuge in Serbia, over 800 in Albania, 8,000 in Montenegro and a smaller number in Bosnia. In June 1990, after Serbian President Milosevic agreed to peace terms with the NATO forces, they entered the province as so-called K-FOR peacekeepers. As the Serbian troops withdrew from Kosovo they looted the houses of Albanians who had fled during the period of the air strikes. The Serbs forced the Roma to load the most valuable items onto their lorries and then told the Roma to take what was left. Undoubtedly, some did so.

The departure of the Serbian army and police was soon followed by a series of retaliatory attacks by Albanians from Kosovo and from Albania proper on both civilian Serbs and Roma. By 12 August 1999 UNHCR estimated that 170,000 Serbs had already fled in the days since K-FOR arrived, leaving only 30,000. The Roma were to follow.

Many of the Albanians who returned from refugee camps in Macedonia and Albania were to take revenge on the Romani community as a whole because of those members who had actively helped the Serbs. It is not yet clear how much of the ethnic cleansing of Roma that was to follow can be attributed to

Kosovar Albanians and how much to intruders from Albania proper. Whoever the perpetrators were, the Roma were now to suffer what the Albanians had suffered from the Serbs.

Pogroms since the end of the conflict include the following. In June 1999 the Romani quarter in Mitrovica was burnt down and the inhabitants fled to Pristina. Roma in Kosovo Polje (near Pristina) also came under threat and 3,500 took refuge in a school. Roma and 'Egyptians' in Djakovica and elsewhere were told they would be killed if they stayed. On 29 June twelve houses were burnt down in Sitinica, a mixed village inhabited by Roma and ethnic Albanians. The Romani quarter of Dusanova in Prizren has also been burned down, as have many houses in Obilic and the quarter of Brekoc in Djakovica.

German K-FOR troops discovered fifteen injured Roma in a police office that had been taken over and used by the KLA as a prison in Prizren. A sixteenth man had been beaten to death. It was alleged the victims had taken part in looting. Romani victims of Albanian violence, however, have included many who could have taken no part in helping the Serbs. For example, a nine-year-old girl, JQ, was beaten in the Fabricka Street quarter in Kosovska Mitrovica and in the same quarter three elderly Roma died in their houses when these were set on fire by Albanians.

Shukrije Bajrami fled from the fighting to Vucitrn to the house of a relative with her four-year-old daughter. There the local Albanians told the Roma: "Leave because we are going to kill you." As she spoke to a reporter another Romani house went up in flames. A young man wearing a KLA beret watched the house burn (*Financial Review*, 25 June 1999). Many reports have also been filed of rapes of Romani women by men in KLA uniforms.

In addition to the improvised refuge in Kosovo Polje, K-FOR built a camp housing 5,000 'internally displaced' Roma at Obilic (near Pristina) in a pine forest and surrounded it with barbed wire covered with plastic sheeting. Albanians removed the protective sheeting so they could hurl insults and missiles against the Roma in the camp. In December 1999 the residents were moved to an army barracks in Plemetina. Roma elsewhere have complained that K-FOR does nothing. There are countless reports of Roma seeing their homes looted and burnt while British and other K-FOR troops stood by unable or unwilling to help.

Although ethnic Serbian refugees from Kosovo were reluctantly accepted into Serbia proper, many Roma were stopped on the border and told to go back to their homes by the police. Meanwhile, thousands of Roma from Kosovo have taken refuge in several countries. As attacks increased, over 2,000 Roma fled to Italy in June and July 1999 but in August the Italian authorities said they would no longer accept refugees from Kosovo as the fighting was over. Nevertheless, Roma still attempt the sea crossing, sometimes with tragic results.

An OSCE Report in January 2000 suggested there were some 25,000 Roma of various **clans** still in the province, living in a 'precarious' state and the new millennium has seen further attacks. Amongst the reports we read that seven Roma were murdered between February and May 2000, an eleven-year-old boy was beaten and thrown into the river at Klina in March, while sixteen Roma families were forced out of Ogoste by ethnic Albanians displaced from an Albanian settlement on the other side of the Kosovan border in southern Serbia.

In 2003 the UN High Commissioner for Refugees reported that: "Roma, **Ashkali** and Egyptian communities continue to face serious protection problems. The problems include grenade attacks and physical harassment, in addition to acute discrimination and marginalisation." Most of the Romani intelligentsia have fled and it seems that the conflicts in this region have extinguished what had once been an inspirational example to Roma elsewhere.

KOUDELKA, Joseph 1938–. Czechia. Photographer. In 1961 he started to photograph the Gypsies of Slovakia. His pictures were exhibited in Prague in 1967. In 1968 he also worked with Gypsies in Romania and took photographs of the Soviet invasion of Czechoslovakia which were published anonymously abroad. In 1970 he was granted asylum in Britain and later became a French national. *Gypsies* (1978) contains his photographs from Slovakia.

KOZLOVSKY, Oleg. Belarus. Contemporary political activist. Chairman of the Union of CIS and Baltic Roma.

KRASNICI, Ali 1952–. Yugoslavia. Writer. As well as short stories, he has written two plays in Romani: *Čergarendje jaga* (Nomad fires) and *Iripen an-o živdipen* (Return to life).

KRIS. The legal system of some **clans** of the Romani people. Some writers think this practice goes back to the village courts of India. The Kris is an assembly of the elders of a group of extended families or, in the case of a serious problem, the whole clan.

KOSTURI, Demir 1928–98. Albania. Political leader. Romani community's chief judge for internal justice in Korca and neighbouring districts. He was the first Albanian Rom to lead a delegation abroad when he attended the Fourth Romani Congress in 1990. He has also organised musical and theatrical events within Albania.

KUPATE. Bulgaria. **Zlato Mladenov** is the main figure in the organisation. It has a central office in Sofia and works with several local councils. A cultural centre is planned for the capital.

KWIEK DYNASTY. One of several families named Kwiek emigrated to Poland from Romania, via Hungary, at the beginning of the twentieth century. They established a royal dynasty, which continued until shortly after the end of the Second World War. These kings were not recognised by the long-settled Polish Romanies, who had their own chief called Shero Rom. In the period between the two world wars there was sometimes more than one claimant for the title of king.

King Michal II (elected in 1930) was invited to the **Bucharest Conference** in 1934 and addressed a meeting in London's Hyde Park later that year, putting the case for a Gypsy state in Africa. Janusz Kwiek was crowned king in 1937 by the Archbishop of Warsaw. He, too, was influenced by Zionism and asked Mussolini to grant the Gypsies an area of land in recently conquered Abyssinia (present-day Ethiopia). He disappeared during the Nazi occupation of Poland. In 1946 Rudolf Kwiek was declared king but, living in a Communist state, he changed the title to that of president of the Gypsies. He died in 1964.

KYUCHUKOV, Christo 1962–. Bulgaria. Educationalist. He compiled the educational material on Romani culture for schools. He is currently training Romani teachers at the University of Veliko Tarnovo.

L

LA CANILLAS. See ABAD, Marina

LA CHUNGA. See AMAYA, Micaela

LA CHUNGUITA. See AMAYA, Lorenza Flores

(LA) MINA. See under MINA (LA)

LABOUR CAMPAIGN FOR TRAVELLERS' RIGHTS. UK. Est. 1986 Secretary: Andrew Ryder. A recognised Labour Party group open to all members of the British Labour Party. Its aims include sensitising members of the Party to the needs of Gypsies and **New Travellers**.

LACIO DROM (Good road). (i) An academic journal founded in Italy in 1964 and published by the **Centro Studi Zingari**. It has now ceased publication. The editor was Mirella Karpati.

(ii) The Lacio Drom schools were established to further the education of Gypsy children in Italy.

(iii) As *Latcho Drom*, the title of a film by **Toni Gatlif.**

LACKOVÁ, Elena. 1921–2003. Slovakia. Writer. She was born in a Romani settlement to a Polish mother and a Gypsy father. One of nine children, she was the only girl in her community of 600 to complete primary school. In 1944 the settlement where she lived with her husband was set on fire by fascists and she was forced to flee into the forest, where one of her twin daughters died of hunger in her arms. Her first work, a play in the Slovak language, drew on her wartime experiences and was entitled *Horiaci cigansky tabor* (The Gypsy Camp is Burning) (1947).

Later on, she wrote in Romani. Having obtained a university degree in the 1970s, she set up and then became President of the Cultural Association of Romani Citizens (Kulturny Zvaz Obcanov Romskej Narodnosti na Slovensku), founded a Romani periodical, *Romano Llil* (Gypsy Newspaper)

while continuing to write. Her autobiography was published in English as *A False Dawn* and was well reviewed throughout Europe.

LAFERTIN, Fapy 1950–. France. Musician. A **Manouche** jazz guitarist and violinist renowned for his performances in the Belgian-based Gypsy group Waso and for his forays into British jazz. **Fapy Lafertin** has been fascinated from childhood with the 12-stringed Portuguese guitar and mastered the 'fado', a Portuguese love-song style. He plays regularly with the British band Le Jazz and his own group, the Hot Club Quintet.

LAGRÈNE, Bireli 1966–. France, Alsace. Musician. He is a **Sinto** jazz guitarist. Taught by his father, Fiso, from the age of four, he began touring at an early age. He started recording at the age of eleven. Switching to the electric guitar, he developed a style of fiery speed and versatility, moving away from mere imitation of **Django Reinhardt**. CDs: *Routes de Django* (1981), *Acoustic Moments* and *Bireli Swing*.

LAGRÈNE, Jean (Pere). France. Artist's model. Edouard Manet painted him in 1862. The painting, *The Old Musician*, is in the National Gallery of Art in Washington.

LAGUILLER, Arlette 1940–. France. Political activist. A **New Traveller** who was an unsuccessful candidate for the European Parliament in southern France in 1995.

LAKATOS, Anka. Hungary. Contemporary poetess. The daughter of Menyhért Lakatos, she writes in Hungarian.

LAKATOS, Menyhért 1926–. Hungary. Writer. A novelist who writes in Hungarian. His first novel *Füstös képek* (Bitter Smoke) has been translated into German as *Bitterer Rauch*.

LAKATOS, Roby 1965–. Hungary. Violinist

and composer. Descended from **János Bihari**, he studied at the Budapest Conservatory, then moved to Belgium where he formed his own orchestra which played at the Les Ateliers club. Now he tours internationally, playing mainly traditional music in his own idiom.

LALORE SINTI. Literally 'dumb Gypsies'. The name given by the **Sinti** Gypsies of Germany to all those in the country who did not speak their dialect. During the Nazi period, the Lalore Sinti were classed as German Gypsies because it was said they had lived among Germans in Bohemia and Moravia. This did not save them from the concentration camps.

LAMBRINO, Zizi. The first wife of King Carol II of Romania (married 1919). She was Jewish rather than, as some books suggest, Romani.

LAS TRES MIL. Neighbourhood in Seville called Las Tres Mil Viviendas (the 3,000 apartments) built around 1970. Many Gypsies were moved there from the shanty town, Triana. It is featured in Dominique Abel's documentary film *Seville Southside.*

LATVIA. Estimated Gypsy population: 8,000. The official population according to the 1989 census was 7,044, with 84 per cent speaking Romani as their mother tongue. Latvia was an independent country in the period 1919–40 and from 1991. By the twentieth century the majority of Romanies living in the country had been sedentarised during the years of Russian rule. In 1933 **Janis Leimanis** translated St John's gospel into Romani.

Soon after the German occupation in 1941, the **Einsatzgruppen** began killing Gypsies. At Ludza Gypsies were locked up in a synagogue then taken to the nearby forest and shot. Only in Talsen and Daugawpils were local Latvian officials able to protect the Gypsies. It is thought that about 2,000 were killed in all, a third of the population.

Since 1944 when Soviet troops reoccupied the country, there has been immigration by Gypsies.

Some anti-Gypsy activity perists today. Joachim Siegerist, leader of the People's Movement for Latvia, was convicted in Germany for incitement to racial hatred as a result of distributing more than 17,000 circulars in which he wrote: "Gypsies produce children like rabbits" and they are "a seedy criminal pack who should be driven out of the country." His party gained 15 per cent of the vote in the general election of October 1995 in Latvia.

Notable Roma include Karlis Rudjevics, artist, poet and cultural worker, and **Janis Neilands**, leader of a small educational movement that has opened two Romani schools and initiated the production of an ABC primer in the local **Chuhni** dialect. The former MP Normundas Rudjevics is active in promoting Romani cultural and social issues.

LAU MAZIREL ASSOCIATION. Netherlands. Est. 1981. An organisation that has been working in the interests of the Romanies. It published the journal *Drom* and also has given help to individual Gypsies and organisations in the Netherlands. The association is named after Lau Mazirel (d. 1974), a lawyer who supported the rights of minorities.

LAUTAR (Romanian – fiddler). The term is used for Gypsy and non-Gypsy violin players in Romania.

LAUTARI, Barba. A Gypsy violinist in Moldavia in the nineteenth century. He was an acquaintance of the composer **Franz Liszt**.

LAZURICA, Lazarescu. A civil rights activist in Romania between the world wars. At first he worked with **Popp Serboianu** then in 1933 he set up his own organisation, Uniunea Generala a Romilor din Romania (the General Union of the Gypsies of Romania). A year later he handed over the presidency to **Gheorghe Niculescu.**

LE COSSEC, Clement. A Breton lay pastor in the years after the Second World War. He was the initiator of **Pentecostalism** among Gypsies in 1952. Clement Le

Cossec was preaching in Lisieux when a **Manouche** couple, Mandz Duvil and his wife (by Romani custom), came to his prayer meetings and were converted. They spread the message among their relatives and friends. The number of converts grew and in 1958 the pastor decided to devote himself to work among the Gypsies.

LEE, Tom 1923–2002. England. Political leader and civil rights activist. He was born in a horse-drawn wagon and fought in the Second World War. A talented campaigner, he made headlines in 1970 when he parked his caravan close to Downing Street to persuade the Government to pressure local authorities to provide fit sites for travellers to rent. Later, he began to regard officially provided sites as unsuitable for Gypsies and argued that they should be allowed to buy their own sites and let pitches for other Gypsy caravans. He set up a private caravan site in Stratford, East London, and following the trend for urban farms, encouraged schools to visit the horses, chickens and doves he kept on it. After falling out with members of the **Gypsy Council**, he founded the **Romany Guild** in 1972, although the two organisations later reunited for a short time as the **National Gypsy Council.**

LEIMANIS, Janis 1886–1954. Latvia. Social rights worker. From 1915 he worked alongside Romani refugees helping with welfare and taking care of their cultural needs. Involved in collecting the literary heritage of Gypsies in Latvia, in 1931 he established the society Ciganu draugs (Friends of the Gypsies), an Orthodox Christian organisation. He translated St John's Gospel into Latvian Romani (**Chuhni** dialect) in 1933 and in 1939 published the book *Cigani Latvjas mezzos un lakos* (Gypsies of the forests and lakes of Latvia).

He tried, with little success, to persuade the German occupiers during the Second World War to stop the killing of Gypsies in Latvia. After the war, until his death, he continued to take part in the ministry amongst the Rom.

LESHAKI. A sub-dialect of Polish Romani.

LETY. Two work camps were established by the Czech government in Lety and Hodonín. In 1942 they became camps for Romanies. The site of Lety is now occupied by a pig farm and this has angered the survivors but the Czech government has pleaded the cost of removing the pig farm for its inaction.

LIANCE. A famous dancer in France in the seventeenth century. She was fêted by poets and nobles and had her portrait painted by Beaubrun. Her husband was arrested for highway robbery and executed. After this incident Liance wore mourning clothes for the rest of her life and never danced again.

LIOZNA. A collective farm in the Soviet Union, near Vitebsk, in the years between the world wars. Originally a Jewish collective farm, the authorities moved the Jewish farmers out and replaced them by Romanies. Later, the Gypsies in their turn were displaced, as Stalin decided that Gypsy nationalism was dangerous.

LISZT, Franz 1811–86. Hungary. Musician. He was fond of Gypsy music as a child and between 1840 and 1847 he published twenty pieces based on Hungarian Gypsy music. These became the basis for his *Hungarian Rhapsodies* (1851–53).

LITERATURE, GYPSIES IN. Many famous authors have put Gypsy characters into their novels and plays or written poems on Gypsy themes. Amongst them are Guillaume Apollinaire, Louis Aragon, Matthew Arnold, Charles Baudelaire, Vicente Blasco Ibañez, Charlotte Brontë, Robert Browning, Miguel de Cervantes, Arthur Conan Doyle, the Greek writer Drossinis, George Eliot, Ralph Waldo Emerson, Henry Fielding, Wolfgang von Goethe, Oliver Goldsmith, Ernest Hemingway, Ben Jonson, John Keats, Jack Kerouac, Blaze Koneski, D. H. Lawrence, **Federico García Lorca**, Antonio Machado, Osip Mandelstam, Boris Pasternak, Ezra Pound, **Aleksandr Pushkin**, Walter

Scott, Jules Verne, Tennessee Williams and Virginia Woolf. It might almost be easier to list famous authors who have never created a Gypsy character.

LITERATURE, GYPSY. Until the twentieth century, Romani literature was almost entirely oral – songs and folktales. The temporary encouragement of the **Romani language** in the newly founded Soviet Union led to a flourishing of literature in the period between the world wars. Since 1945 much poetry, short stories and drama has been written. Many Gypsy writers, such as **Matéo Maximoff** and **Veijo Baltzar**, have written novels in the majority languages of the country where they live. See DRAMA; FOLK LITERATURE; POETRY and section VI.5 in the Bibliography.

LITHUANIA. Estimated Gypsy population: 5,500. The official population, according to the last Soviet census (in 1989), was recorded as 2,700 with 81 per cent speaking Romani as their mother tongue. The earliest reference to Gypsies on the territory of present-day Lithuania dates from 1501 but it is likely that they had been there for some years before. In that year Earl Alexander granted the right to Vasil to govern the Gypsy **clans** in Lithuania, Poland and Belarus, the Gypsies being permitted to nomadise under the authority of their own leader. In 1564, however, Gypsies were invited to settle or leave the country. In 1569 Poland and Lithuania became one country. A new decree was issued, confirming the existing policy of expelling nomads, in 1586. Some Gypsies left, some settled down, and a third group continued to nomadise in spite of the prohibition.

In 1795 the Russian czar became ruler of the country. From 1919 to 1940 Lithuania was independent then it was taken over by the USSR for one year until Nazi Germany invaded.

During the German occupation (1941–4) about half of the Gypsies were killed with the collaboration of Lithuanian nationalists. One transport of twenty persons was sent to **Auschwitz**; the others were killed in Lithuania itself.

In 1944 the Soviet Union once more occupied Lithuania. The country finally became independent again in 1991.

Nationalist feelings against the Russians spread to incorporate the Gypsy minority. In 1992 there was a pogrom in Kaunas. Some Gypsies were killed, cars were set on fire and homes were ransacked.

The majority of the present population are Catholics, the rest Orthodox. Three dialects of Romani are spoken: Litovski, Lotfitka and **Chuhni**. A Gypsy organisation has been set up, and a project to develop Romani as a written language is under way

LITTLE EGYPT. When the Gypsies moved west again in the fifteenth century, many came in groups of sometimes over a 100 persons, led by a Duke of Little Egypt. It is thought that Little Egypt referred to a part of Greece.

LIULI see LYULI.

LODZ CONGRESS. May 2002. This Congress is also known as the Second World Congress with the Coronation of the Polish Romani King in 1935 counted as the First. The event was initiated by the **Romani National Congress** with the strong support of the **European Union**. It was preceded by a period of discussion via the Internet and the Congress was partially online with the opportunity to vote via the Net. There were some fifty participants including Roma from thirty organisations.

The first day of the Congress was taken up with keynote speakers, including **Nicolae Gheorghe**. On the second day of the Congress a ceremony was held at the site of the **Lodz Ghetto**, set up by the Nazis during the Second World War. In the afternoon and on the following day three working groups met.

The three groups looked at Romani representation at the international level, compensation for the **Holocaust** and the question of refugees and other migrants.

It appointed an Executive Committee

to serve for one year. Six members were elected including **Agnes Daroczi, Ondrej Gina** and **Rudko Kawzynski**. The seventh place was to be left open for a representative of the **International Romani Union**. The Committee was given the task of setting up a body to be called the Romani Council of Europe. The Congress supported the idea of a **European Roma Forum** with a membership open to all Roma organisations and leaders.

The organisation Drom from Kumanovo (Macedonia) had featured the peace song 'Is love enough?' for its celebrations of 8 April – **Roma Nation Day** – and the song was adopted as the song of the Congress.

LODZ GHETTO. In October 1941 the Germans ordered the Jews imprisoned in the ghetto at Lodz to evacuate several streets that were then wired off and used to house 5,000 Gypsies, mainly from Austria. An epidemic of typhus broke out and several Jewish doctors volunteered to treat the sick. Apart from those who died of typhus, many Gypsies were beaten to death in the first weeks. The fate of 120 adults who were apparently sent to work in a factory in Germany is not known. Early in 1942 the remaining Gypsy prisoners were taken to the Chelmno extermination camp and gassed.

LOI BESSON. France. The adoption by Parliament in 1999 of Article 28 of the Loi Besson was intended to lead to the establishment of caravan sites for nomads. It requires every town with a population greater than 5,000 to provide camping facilities to *Gens du Voyage* (travelling people). It was hoped to attain a figure of 30,000 plots. By the year 2000 only a third of these had been provided and further progress has been slow.

LOLI PHABAI (Red Apple). The first international journal all in Romani was published in Greece in the 1970s under the editorship of **Grattan Puxon**. Three issues appeared. The contents included articles by **Shaip Jusuf, Lázló Szegö** and others, as well as folktales and reprints from Soviet literature of the interwar period.

LOM. A **clan** of Gypsies calling themselves Lom who are believed to have originated in north-west India, together with the Roma, and who are now resident in Armenia, other parts of the CIS (Georgia, Nagorno-Karabakh) and Turkey. In Armenia they live in the capital, Yerevan, and in a number of villages. The Lom of Armenia migrated there from the Erzerum region of so-called western Armenia (in eastern Turkey) following the Russo-Turkish war at the beginning of the nineteenth century. The name Lom is considered to be derived from **Dom**.

The Lom make their living from trade selling hand-made sieves, candles, straw baskets and boxes and also deal in honey. The women, unusually for Gypsy tribes, do not tell fortunes. They are practising Christians, and attend the Armenian Church, although, like Muslims, they often marry blood relatives, which is not permitted under Armenian Christian tradition. They now speak a variety of Armenian with words of Indian origin, known as Lomin or Lomavren.

LONGTHORNE, Joe 1956–. England. Singer. He performs in concerts and on television in the country and western idiom.

LORCA, Federico García. See *GARCÍA LORCA, Federico*.

LOVARI. A **clan** living mainly in Hungary and in Poland. In the past many were horse-dealers and some still carry on this trade. From 1870 onward small numbers nomadised in Western Europe, though they were never as numerous as the **Kalderash**. The Romani spoken by the Lovari belongs to the **Vlah** dialect cluster. The Lovari rarely play music for the public though they have a strong tradition of singing and dancing.

LOVERIDGE, Samuel. The fictitious author of *Being the Autobiography of a Gipsy* published in 1890. Although allegedly written by a Samuel Loveridge, it was in fact compiled by A. Way.

LOYKO. A partly Gypsy trio of musicians from Russia, including Sergei Edenko and Oleg Ponomarev, now resident in Ireland. Vladim Koulitskii replaced the original guitarist Igor Staroseltsev. They have toured widely in Europe and made several recordings. The name comes from a legendary Russian Gypsy musician. CD: *The Fortune Teller* (1995).

LUBBOCK, Eric 1928–. England. Politician. A Liberal member of UK Parliament, he added a section on Gypsy sites to a bill he was introducing in Parliament to champion the rights of non-Gypsies living in mobile homes. This became the **Caravan Sites Act 1968**. As a result he became to some extent the guardian of Gypsy rights, a role that he has continued as Lord Avebury in the House of Lords.

LUGHA. Secret vocabulary of the Middle East probably developed by Arabic speaking Dervishes. Many of the words are found in languages spoken by Middle Eastern Gypsies. *Lugha* is the Arabic word for 'language'.

LULUDJI ENSEMBLE. Song and dance group from Moscow. Leading members are the singer and guitarist Slava Vasiyev and Vladimir Kutenkov who teaches the children's ensemble Gilori.

LUNDGREN, Gunilla 1942–. Sweden. Author. She writes mainly children's books, especially biographies written in collaboration with Romani children.

LUNIK IX. A housing project on the edge of the town of **Košice** in Slovakia. The population of Lunik IX is already 70 per cent Romani, and the city council of Košice has proposed moving the remaining Gypsy population of the city there.

LURE. Every summer Gypsies from across France and elsewhere in Europe travel to Lure in eastern France for an annual religious meeting.

LURI. Iran. (i) The name by which Firdausi called a group of musicians who were brought by Shah Bahram Gur from India in the fifth century.

(ii) A **clan** of singers and musicians living in Iran at the time of Hafiz and other poets.

(iii) A Gypsy clan in today's Iran, possibly of Indian origin. They are craftworkers and blacksmiths who move around, offering their services to the semi-nomadic tribes. They also prepare food for weddings and ceremoniously wash the groom. Their language is a variety of Beluchi with a jargon vocabulary.

The connection between these three groups is not clear.

LUTE. It is thought that some of the Gypsies of Europe are descended from **Luri** lute players brought from India to Persia. There are early records of a Gypsy lutanist in Dubrovnik. With the dying out of the lute as a popular instrument its players adopted the violin and other stringed instruments.

LUTHER, Martin 1483–1546. Germany. Religious leader. The reformer Luther was no friend of the Gypsies or the Jews, condemning both in his sermons.

LUXEMBOURG. Estimated Gypsy population: 150. The first Gypsies appeared during the sixteenth century. They struggled against newcomers from Germany and France to preserve their trading area. In 1603 a mercenary, Jean de la Fleur, was put on trial for entering the country contrary to a decree forbidding Gypsies to enter the Grand Duchy. During the Second World War, the Germans deported a handful of Gypsies from the country to camps in Poland. After 1945 immigration control has remained strict using a law against vagrancy.

LYULI. A **clan** of Gypsies living mainly in Uzbekistan and Tadjikistan, though some families have moved to Russia. The Lyuli (not to be confused with the **Luri** of Iran) probably left India later as they have not integrated with the local population as have other Gypsy groups.

M

MacCOLL, Ewan 1915–89. Scotland. Singer. The stage name of a twentieth century Scottish singer, born Jimmie Miller. He recorded the Gypsies' own stories of their life and composed the music for a popular documentary – a radio ballad, as it was called by the BBC – *The Travelling People*. Many of his songs have become part of the traditional repertoire of Gypsy singers such as *The Moving on Song* and *A Freeborn Man*.

MACE, Jem 1831–1910. England. Boxer. A bare-knuckle fighter known as the Father of Modern Boxing. At one time he also ran a fairground known as Strawberry Gardens in Liverpool. A memorial was recently erected by his grave at Anfield Cemetery, Liverpool. Nicknamed 'The Gypsy,' Jem was the bare-knuckle English boxing champion in 1861.

MACEDONIA, REPUBLIC OF. Estimated Gypsy population: 100,000. The 1994 census listed only 43,707, a decrease on the 55,575 recorded in 1991. This was in spite of the availability of census forms in the Romani language. This entry deals with Macedonia from 1941 onward. Previously it was part of the **Ottoman Empire** and the kingdom of Yugoslavia. Macedonia became independent through a peaceful process in 1992.

During the Second World War, Macedonia was handed over by the Germans to the Bulgarians and Italians. Most of the Romanies managed to persuade the occupiers that they were Turks or Muslim Albanians. Those who were identified as Romanies had to wear yellow armbands. Some were taken as forced labourers to Bulgaria and a small number to camps in Poland. Many joined the partisans, and it was said that Tito promised them their own state after the war. This promise – if it had been made – was not carried out as the Yugoslav government would have seen a smaller Macedonia as a prey for Greek and Bulgarian expansionist ambitions.

The largest Gypsy community in Europe developed in **Shuto (Šuto) Orizari** on the outskirts of Skopje in the aftermath of the earthquake of 1963. About 90 per cent of the inhabitants are Gypsies.

In May 1980 Naša Kniga, a publishing house in Skopje, produced the first Romani grammar to be written in the Romani language. The author was **Shaip Jusuf**. The **Pralipe** theatre operated until 1990 when the Communist party forced the company to vacate its premises and the actors emigrated to Germany.

In 1990, too, the Egyptian Association of Citizens was founded in Ohrid by Nazim Arifi, consisting of some 4,000 residents of Ohrid and neighboring Struga, who, although many scholars consider them to be of Romani origin, claim to be descendants of **Egyptians** brought to the Balkans during the Ottoman rule. The Association claimed 20,000–30,000 adherents, and Egyptian (*Gjupci*) was included as a separate identity in the 1994 census in Macedonia. The number returned was 3,000.

On 1 September 1990, the leaders of the Macedonian Romani community called on all Romanies to stop identifying themselves as Albanians simply on the basis of a common religion, Islam, and declared 11 October 1990, already a public holiday, to be a day of celebration of the cultural achievements of Romanies in Macedonia. Nevertheless, the census in 1994 recorded only 43,000 'Roma,' as many declared themselves to be Macedonians or, if they were Muslims, Albanians or Turks.

In 1991 Macedonia became *de facto* independent. President Kiro Gligorov publicly acknowledged the Romanies as "full and equal citizens of the Republic of Macedonia". They were recognised as a nationality in the new constitution. Romani language radio and television programs from Skopje joined those already being broadcast from Tetovo. A few bilingual (Macedonian and Romani) magazines are published.

A Romani educational programme in schools began in principle in September 1993 consisting of language classes for grades 1-8. A 40,000-word Macedonian-Romani dictionary and other teaching material are still being prepared. The main dialects are Arli (*Erlia*), the most widely spoken and the mother tongue of an estimated 80 per cent of Macedonia's Romanies, Burgudji, Djambazi and **Gurbet**. It has been agreed to use Arli as the basis for a standard language using the Latin alphabet for educational purposes. In addition to the planned introduction of the Romani language in primary education classes from the 1993–4 academic year, there are proposals for Skopje University to inaugurate a Department of Romani Studies for the study of, and research into, language, history and culture. Some hundred potential teachers of Romani attended a seminar convened by the Ministry of Education at Skopje University in October 1993. The full implementation of the Romani language programme has been slowed down by the lack of materials and qualified teachers.

The main political party for the Gypsies in Macedonia is PSERM (Party for the Complete Emancipation of Romanies in Macedonia), claiming a membership of 36,000. Its president, **Faik Abdi,** is also a member of the Macedonian parliament representing Shuto Orizari. PSERM has been the prime mover in securing Romani rights.

The association of Romani women known as Daja (Mothers) has its headquarters in Kumanova and branches elsewhere. It was set up with a grant from the Soros **Open Society** Institute but is still financially weak. Amongst the many other Romani non-governmental organisations should be mentioned Mesecina in Gostivar, which played an important role in helping Romani refugees from Kosovo.

Looking at the fragmented former Yugoslavia it can be said that, in spite of some discrimination and harassment, it is in Macedonia that Romani culture is most alive, both in the home and beyond with regular radio and TV broadcasts. In spite of the central government's encouragement of the political and cultural advancement of the Roma, there is much unemployment and poor housing. Some inter-ethnic conflict, mainly between Albanians and Roma, has been reported, as well as police brutality, often directed against street traders.

Recent violations of the human rights of Roma in Macedonia include instances of police violence against Roma and an outbreak of anti-Romani expression in the media. We cite one example of police behaviour.

On 7 February 2003 two police officers arrived at the house of Memet Dalipovski in Kumanovo and searched his house without warrant, looking for a safe stolen from a local church containing a substantial amount of money. The officers then took Mr Dalipovski to the house of Skender Sadikovic, also of Kumnovo, where they performed the same procedure and, reportedly, beat Mr Sadikovic. Both men were then taken to Kumanovo police station where they were subject to physical abuse. Mr Sadikovic was reportedly handcuffed and beaten with instruments including handles of axes, particularly on the lower part of his back, while Mr Dalipovski was punched in the head until he fell to the floor, at the which point, five police officers started kicking him mainly in his ribs. In the course of the abuse, the officers also cursed the men's ethnic origins. Under threat of further physical abuse, Mr Sadikovic was coerced into falsely confessing that the safe was at his house. The two Roma men were reportedly later brought together and forced to fight each other to make it seem as if the injuries caused by the officers had been inflicted by the men themselves. Mr Sadikovic was released after six hours when police apologised to him and explained that the real culprits had been identified. Mr Dalipovski was held for twenty-six hours and subject to further physical abuse, before being released with the same apology and explanation. He was, however, warned not to report his physical abuse. Following their release, the men underwent physical examinations and were found to be in need of hospital treatment for their injuries but were unable to afford this. Subsequently, the two were contacted by police officers who agreed to cover the medical expenses in exchange for an agreement that the men would not pursue complaints against them. When the men refused the offer, officers reportedly made unspecified threats. These officers have since been disciplined and made to pay paltry fines not, however, levied on the grounds of physical abuse, but for the inadequate conduct of the investigation. The Macedonian Ministry of the Interior is reportedly conducting an investigation into the case.

The Romani ethnicity of alleged perpetrators of crimes is increasingly emphasised by the Macedonian media, creating a link between Roma and crime. For example, on 22 February 2003, the Skopje dailies *Dnevnik* and *Vesti* reported that during a violent conflict between a group of teenagers in Skopje in which a young non-Romani man was killed, two of the minor perpetrators were Romani. Other accounts of physical assaults, drug dealing and the sale of children into prostitution, have been reported in a similar way. In the case of alleged child abuse in Štip on 13 February 2003, the daily *Vesti* published the full names of both the two-year-old

Romani victim and her mother, violating the privacy of the persons involved and also their right to the presumption of innocence guaranteed *inter alia* by the Macedonian Constitution.

MACEDONIAN ROMA UNION. An organisation in northern Greece whose President is Savas Georgiadis.

MACFIE, Robert Andrew Scott. England. Contemporary Scholar. Contributor to the *Journal of the **Gypsy Lore Society,*** he sometimes wrote under the Romani pseudonym Andreas Mui Shuko (Dry Face). His collection of books was donated to the Liverpool University Library.

MACHVAYA. A Gypsy **clan** originating in the Balkans.

MACPHEE, Willie 1910–. Scotland. A **Scottish Traveller** musician, tinsmith, basket-maker, piper and singer. He has been a regular performer at folk clubs and festivals.

MAGERIPEN. A **Sinti** term for the hygienic rules of the Romani community. Romani names in other dialects for the same concept are the adjectives mockerdi (in England) and mahrime (**Kalderash**). There is a broad set of concepts of cleanliness and a system of taboos maintaining the opposition of the socially or spiritually clean to persons or objects seen as unclean or dirty. Traditionally, Gypsies have placed much emphasis on the uncleanness of women at the time of their menses and after childbirth. Dogs are considered as having the potential to make things dirty and are excluded from the caravan or home. To preserve cleanliness a strict separation is observed when washing clothes, food and the human body. Similar rules are observed by the majority populations in the Balkans. Many Western European Gypsies consider non-Gypsies to be dirty by definition and reserve special cups for visitors.

MAGNETEN. A company of Gypsy dancers, musicians and singers from many countries, formed by Andre Heller, that toured Germany and elsewhere with great success in 1993. The ensemble included **Kalyi Jag, Kálmán Balogh, Loyko** and **Esma Redjepova.**

MAHRIME. See MAGERIPEN.

MAKHOTIN, Djura 1952–2004. USSR. Poet.

MALIKOV, Jashar 1922–94. Bulgaria. Composer and musician. He also collects folk music and tales. While at school he played the trumpet and accordion in a band at weddings. He learned to write music and took up composing light music, including the so-called town songs. In 1949 he was in charge of music at the **Teatr Roma** in Sofia. He was one of the first Gypsy musicians to be recorded by the company Balkanton. He also wrote the first Romani-Bulgarian dictionary.

MALTA. There are no Gypsies currently living on the island and no historical record of their presence in the past.

MANISCH. See JENISCH.

MANITAS DE PLATA. See BALIARDO, Ricardo.

MANOLESCU, Stella. Romania. Contemporary artist. She paints in oil and acrylic. A daughter of **Ion Cioaba**, she now lives in Austin Texas.

MANOUCHE. A **clan** of Gypsies living mainly in France and Belgium but whose ancestors spent many years in Germany. The word manouche means 'man' in Romani. Their dialect has many German loan words and is close to that of the **Sinti**.

MANUŠ, Leksa. See BELUGINS, Aleksandr.

MARCINKIEWICZ, Jan. Russia. Bear trainer. In 1778 he set up a school for bear trainers in Russia and held the title of Gypsy King. After the failure of the so-called Katyushka Revolt against the Czar he fled to Turkey.

MARIA THERESA 1717–80. Austria, Vienna. She was Empress of Austria-Hungary from 1740 to 1780. From 1758 she brought in a series of decrees with the intention of turning the Gypsies into *Ujmagyar* (New Hungarians). Government-built huts replaced tents while travel and horse-dealing were forbidden. Gypsy children were taken away,

often by force, to be fostered by Hungarians. Her eldest son **Joseph II** continued her policies.

MARKOVIĆ, Boban. Serbia. Contemporary musician and band leader. He is leader of Serbia's biggest brass band.

MARSHALL, Billy 1672–1792. Scotland. A **Traveller**. In 1724 he led an alliance of extreme Protestants and peasants against land enclosures and the imposition of the Presbyterian church. They were defeated after an initial success.

MAXIMOFF, Matéo 1917–99. Spain. Writer, translator and preacher. He was born in Barcelona but moved to France with his family as a child. As a young man he was involved in an interfamily dispute concerning an abducted girl and was sent to prison, where he met the lawyer Jacques Isorni. The latter suggested that he write about his life and thus he began his writing career. Matéo Maximoff has written many novels, including *The Ursitory* (1946). He has published ghost stories told to him by his mother and also translated the Bible into Romani after becoming a convert to **Pentecostalism**. Matéo Maximoff worked on his Old Testament translation for over nine years, finishing it in 1981. So far, only two parts have been published. His New Testament was finally produced in 1995.

MAYA, Pepe Heredia (José Heredia) 1947–. Spain. Teacher and dancer. He founded a **flamenco** company whose first production was the history of the Gypsies in Spain portrayed through a flamenco presentation – *Camelamos naquerar* (1976). This was made into the film *Let Us Be Heard* (1983).

McALISKEY, Bernadette (née DEVLIN) 1947–. Ireland. Political activist. Bernadette McAliskey is from an **Irish Traveller** family and is a nationalist politician in Northern Ireland. She was for a time a member of the British Parliament.

MEDZITLIJA. A town on the Greek-Macedonian border. In June 2003 some 700 Romanies from Kosovo whose refugee camp in Macedonia had been closed tried unsuccessfully to cross the border into Greece. They remained in poor conditions on the border for several weeks while negotiations took place as to their fate. Finally, with a partly kept promise of satisfactory accommodation they returned to Skopje in Macedonia.

MERCE, José. See SOTE, Jose.

MERCER, Peter, MBE. England. Contemporary community worker and civil rights activist. He was involved in the original **Gypsy Council** and the **National Gypsy Education Council** as well as setting up the **East Anglian Gypsy Council**. Peter Mercer is the British representative on the Praesidium of the **International Romani Union.**

MEREJAN, Mehmed. Bulgaria. Contemporary poet. He received a 2003 Roma Literary Award for his verse.

MERIMÉE, Prosper 1803-1870. France. Writer. He worked in the civil service and under Napoleon III was employed on unofficial missions. Among his literary activity he wrote the novel **Carmen** in 1846 after a visit to a tobacco factory in Spain. After his death, the novel served as the basis of the romantic scenario for Bizet's opera, first performed in 1855.

MESHARE, MESHARYAVA. An internal legal system, similar to the **Kris**, operated by the elders of the Bulgarian **Karderash**.

MESSING. UK. Essex. The village of Messing in Essex became infamous for evicting its Gypsy families. After rumours that the American President George Bush might want to visit his ancestral home there whenever he came to England it was thought he might be offended by the sight of Gypsies. This visit never actually occurred but the Romani families were still forced back onto the roadside and had to look for a new place to stop.

MÉSZÁROS, Gyorgy d. 1987. Hungary, Eger. Museum worker. An expert on Gypsies, he wrote numerous articles and a dictionary. The eyewitness accounts he collected from victims of the Nazi period were an invaluable record.

METECH, Juliette. France. Contemporary painter. She grew up as an artist in her father's circus until the age of nineteen when her father died. She then went into business selling carpets door to door and it was not until the age of fifty-two that Juliette Metech began to paint seriously. Many of her pieces can be seen in French galleries.

MICHALCZUK, Kazimierz d. 1996. Poland. Political activist. The vice president of the Roma Organisation of Poland. He was killed by an unknown assassin on 1 September 1996.

MINA (LA) A high-rise suburb of Barcelona, Spain where many Gypsies were resettled during the Franco period.

It was the setting for the documentary film *La Mina* by the British photographer Hannah Collins and local leader Manuel Fernández Cortés. The film is made to be shown on five TV screens simultaneously and was first shown at the Toulouse image festival in 2003.

MINORITY RIGHTS GROUP, Slovakia. Partners in a project with the **Minority Rights Group** in the United Kingdom. The Group is concerned with offering training to young Romanies in central and eastern Slovakia.

MINORITY RIGHTS GROUP. UK. Amongst its manifold activities the Group runs a project for Romani rights and education with partners in Bulgaria, Poland and Slovakia. These are the **Committee for the Defence of Minority Rights** (Bulgaria), the **Helsinki Foundation for Human Rights** (Poland) and the **Minority Rights Group**, Slovakia. It has also published two editions of a report on Romanies by **Grattan Puxon** and a new report by **Jean-Pierre Liegeois** and **Nicolae Gheorghe**.

MINORITY SELF-GOVERNMENT (HUNGARY). Hungarian law provides for the establishment of local minority self-governments as a necessary precondition for the enforcement of the rights of ethnic minorities. With some funding from the central budget local minority self-governments seek to influence matters affecting minorities, particularly in the fields of education and culture. Local minority self-government elections, in conjunction with local government elections, have been held since 1994. Any of the thirteen minorities can set up a minority self-government.

Since ethnicity is not registered officially, voting on minority self-governments is not limited to the minorities themselves. All voters received a minority ballot in addition to the local government ballot. Minority self-government has been criticised mainly on two grounds. First, several minority representatives have objected to the fact that members of the majority can vote for minority candidates and thus influence minority politics; secondly, critics called for an increase in the power of the minority self-governments and considerably more financial resources for them.

There were cases of candidates who did not belong to the ethnic minority being elected to minority self-governments in the 1992 elections. In Jaszladany, the votes of members of the Hungarian majority in the Roma minority self-government elections resulted in four non-Roma being elected to the five-member body. Roma rights observers viewed this move as a deliberate attempt to undermine the local Roma community. The Minister of Justice and the State Secretary for Roma Affairs criticised the election outcome, but there were no legal grounds to overturn it.

In October 2002 there were 1,004 Roma minority self-governments elected in the local minority elections, an increase over the 770 elected self-governments in the minority elections held in 1998. Of those elected in 1998 a number of self-governments had ceased functioning due to a lack of resources, knowledge and leadership. In contrast to other minorities for whom the preservation of their identity and culture is the basic goal, the elected Roma representatives also have to face the task of improving the lives of their constituents with no additional financial resources

MINORITY STUDIES SOCIETY. Bulgaria. The society was founded in 1992 as a centre for studying the minorities in Bulgaria. As the situation of the Gypsies is the most complicated, this topic has been the main focus of the group's work. Its aims include popularising Gypsy culture, stopping discrimination and researching the history and culture of the Gypsies of Bulgaria. The society publishes the journal *Studii Romani*. Members have taken part in a number of international projects such as the History Group previously based at the **Centre de Recherches Tsiganes** in Paris.

MINUNE, Ionica. Romania. Contemporary Musician. One of the leading accordion players in the world, his repertoire ranges from folk music to jazz in the style of **Django Reinhardt**.

MIRANDO, Tata JR and SR. See WEISS Kokalo and Meisel.

MISS ROMA INTERNATIONAL BEAUTY CONTEST. An annual contest, organised by TV BTR Natsional, a Roma TV Station located in Skopje, Macedonia.

MITTEILUNGEN ZUR ZIGEUNERKUNDE (Bulletins on Gypsy culture). At least two publications have had this title. (i) *Organ der Gesellschaft für Zigeunerforschung*, volume 1, January 1891. This is identical with volume 7 of the journal *Ethnologische Mitteilungen aus Ungarn* and contains a German translation of **Archduke Joseph's** Romani grammar.
(ii) Several issues of a journal with this title were published in Mainz, Germany, in the 1970s.

MLADENOV, Toma Nikolaev. Bulgaria. Contemporary civil rights activist. He set up the organisation Spasenie (Rescue) in Bulgaria. During a lengthy visit to England he co-operated with the **Trans-European Romani Federation**.

MLADENOV, Zlato. Bulgaria. Contemporary civil rights activist. He is President of the organisation **Kupate** (Together) and was elected Treasurer of the **International**

Romani Union in Prague, 2000.

MLAWA. Town in Poland that was the scene of an anti-Gypsy pogrom at the end of the communist period in 1991 during which many houses were burned down. Many of the town's Romanies fled to Sweden but were refused residence and returned to Poland.

MOCKERDI. An adjective used by English Gypsies for 'ritually unclean'. See MAGERIPEN.

MODON. Greece. Town with a Gypsy settlement of 300 huts in 1483–86, 200 in 1495, and dropping to 100 in 1497. By the time the Turks took Modon in 1500, most of the inhabitants had fled to escape their advance and in 1519 only thirty occupied huts remained. The Gypsies living there were shoemakers. Their fate is unknown. There is no trace of the arrival of any Gypsy shoemakers in the West, and the trade is generally considered unclean by today's Gypsies as it involves working with the skin of dead animals.

MOLDAVIA. A province of **Romania**.

MOLDAVIAN SOVIET SOCIALIST REPUBLIC (1945–91). See MOLDOVA.

MOLDOVA. Estimated Gypsy population: 22,500. The Soviet census of 1989 recorded 11,517 of whom 85 per cent had Romani as their mother tongue. It occupies part of Bessarabia, which belonged to Russia from 1812 to 1917 and to Romania from 1917 to 1940. From 1945 to 1991 the territory was the Moldavian SSR. In February 2001 the Government adopted Decree No.131 on certain support measures for Roma in Moldova, aiming to create the necessary conditions for their social and cultural development.

A collection of oral literature from the region made by **Georgi Kantea** was one of the few publications in Romani to appear in the Soviet Union between 1945 and 1991.

See also BESSARABIA.

MONDIALE OF GYPSY ART. The first Mondiale was held in Paris in 1985 and the second in Budapest from 31 August to 31 October 1995. Alongside the exhibition of paintings, the second Mondiale had a programme of music and dance.

MONTENEGRO. Estimated Gypsy population: 2,000. The 1971 census recorded 396 Romanies. Montenegro was independent or semi-independent from 1389 to 1918, when it became part of Yugoslavia. Up to 1940 the Gypsies in Montenegro were almost entirely nomadic, unlike elsewhere in the Balkans. During the 1930s police prevented them from entering the then capital Cetinje. During the Second World War Montenegro was occupied by the Italians. Some Gypsies organised an independent partisan unit in the mountains but eventually succumbed to the Italian army. Many Romanies from Montenegro emigrated as workers to Western Europe in the 1970s.

Roma in Montenegro have not escaped prejudice – a pogrom in Danoilovgrad when the Gypsy quarter was burnt down being the most visible manifestation of this feeling. The small Romani population has been augmented by refugees from Kosovo who may stay and bring their cultural heritage to build a larger and more vibrant community. For the period 1918 onward see YUGOSLAVIA.

MONTOYA, Antonio Nunez (El Chocolate) 1931–. Spain, Jerez. **Flamenco** singer. He is related to the Montoya family through his mother. Antonio Montoya made his debut at the age of nine in Seville.

MORELLI, BRUNO 1958–. Italy. Artist. As a self-educated painter, Morelli specialises in graphics and realistic portraiture and has had many exhibitions since his first in Avezzano in 1981. He exhibited at the first and second **Mondiale of Gypsy Art.**

MOTHER TERESA. See BOJAXHIU, Agnes.

MOVABLE DWELLINGS BILLS. These Bills were proposed as legislation in the British Parliament between 1885 to 1908, under the instigation of **George Smith**. In 1891, for the first time, English Gypsies went on delegations to Parliament. There were two delegations – one led by the non-Gypsy George Smith–and the other led by a Gypsy, George Lazzy Smith, to oppose the bill. The bills were never passed because the opposition of the owners of circuses and fairs persuaded members of Parliament to vote against them.

MUNTEANU, Boris 1949–. USSR. Doctor. A doctor by profession he was active in the Roma civil rights movement. He is now living in England.

MUSEUMS. Museums devoted to Gypsy culture operate in **Brno**, Czech Republic; Pecs, Hungary; **St Maries de la Mer**, France and the private **Boswell Museum** in Spalding, Lincolnshire. Sections are devoted to Gypsy history and culture in the district museum in Tarnów, Poland, the Lapp provincial museum in Rovaniemi, Finland, and Paultons Leisure Park in Hampshire. The Museum für Völkerkunde in Hamburg owns the Max Haferkorn Gypsy collection, but this is not on permanent display. Gypsy handicrafts and wagons are exhibited in a number of museums, including a small display as far afield as the National Museum of Ethnology in Osaka, Japan.

A museum illustrating Romani basket-making was opened in 1995 in Komotini in Thrace (Greece). An application by the **Romany Guild** for planning permission for a museum in Essex, England, was refused by the Planning Inspectorate. There is currently a proposal for a museum in Bedfordshire.

MUSIC. There is probably no such thing as Gypsy music – that is relics of the music brought from India – except, some would say, in Albania – but there is a Gypsy style of playing that is often improvised and always dramatic. A small selection of the many professional Gypsy musicians have individual entries in the dictionary. See also FLAMENCO.

MUSTAFOV, Ferus. Macedonia. Contemporary musician. He plays the clarinet, saxophone and most other instruments and currently leads a band in Skopje. He has toured widely and has recorded.

N

NA CHMELNICI. A theatre in Prague that has a Romani company attached to it.

NAFTANAILA, Lazar. Romania. Civil rights activist. A farmer from Calbor in Transylvania, he was the first to fight for Gypsy civil rights in Romania. In the 1920s he set up the society Infratirea Neorustica (The Brotherhood of New Farmers), which organised lectures and theatre events to raise the cultural level of the Romanies. In 1933 he founded the journal *Neamul Tiganesc.*

NAGY, Gusztav. Hungary. Contemporary translator. Winner of the 2003 Roma Literary Award for Translation.

NARI-KURAVAR. See VAGHRI

NATIONAL ANTHEM. The internationally recognised anthem for the Gypsies is **Gelem, Gelem**. In Hungary a second song is popular, sung to words by **Károly Bari.** See also GELEM, GELEM.

NATIONAL ASSOCIATION OF GYPSY WOMEN. UK. The Chair of the Association is Sylvia Dunn. Its aim is to give more voice to Gypsy women. It holds traditional rather than feminist values.

NATIONAL DAY. See ROMA NATIONAL DAY

NATIONAL EMBLEM. See FLAG.

NATIONAL GYPSY COUNCIL. UK. Formed in 1973 after a merger of the **Gypsy Council** and the **Romany Guild**. The *de facto* successor to the Gypsy Council. The president is Hughie Smith. The **Romany Guild** later withdrew and again became an independent body.

NATIONAL GYPSY EDUCATION COUNCIL.

UK. Founded in 1970 with a committee of Gypsy activists and educationalists. Lady Plowden, author of the **Plowden Report**, was invited to head this body, and it was able to obtain substantial grants from charitable funds. A programme of education by volunteers was set up that continued for several years until local authorities gradually took over the work of teaching Gypsy children, whether they were living on official sites or still travelling. In 1988 the council split, with some members forming the **Advisory Council for the Education of Romanies and Other Travellers** (ACERT). The National Gypsy Education Council changed its name recently to the **Gypsy Council for Education, Culture, Welfare and Civil Rights**.

NATIONAL ROMANY RIGHTS ASSOCIATION. UK. A civil rights organisation founded by the activist and poet **Eli Frankham**.

NATIONAL TRAVELLER ACTION GROUP. UK. The leading members are Clifford and Janie Codona.

NAWKIN. A name the Scottish Travellers use for themselves. Also spelled 'Noggin'. The word is possibly from Gaelic *an fheadhainn* – pronounced 'an nyogin' and meaning 'the people'.

NAWWAR, NURI. A clan of Gypsies living in Lebanon, Syria and elsewhere in the Middle East. They call themselves **Dom** and speak a language of Indian origin, related to Romani. The name may have originally meant 'blacksmith' – from the Arabic word *nar* (fire). In 1912 two Nuri women from Jaffa travelled through Germany with a circus troupe. Since about 1970 a number of individuals and families have come to Western Europe, including Britain.

For Nawwar (Dom) in Israel and Ghaza see those entries. See also DOMARI.

NEILNDS, Janis 1919. Latvia. Teacher and activist for Roma Rights. He became a consultant for the Romani people with the Latvian government and through his efforts the Romani school in Ventspils was opened in 1988. He was co-author of the *Romani-Latvian Dictionary* in 1997 and went on to supervise the ABC of Latvian Romani which was being compiled by **Alexandr Aledzunz-Belugins**. He has also been translating St Luke's Gospel into Romani.

NETHERLANDS, THE (HOLLAND). Estimated Gypsy population: 37,500 (including Dutch **Travellers**, the *Woonwagenbewoners*).

In 1420 the first Gypsies appeared in Deventer, in the shape of Andrew, Duke of Little Egypt, with a company of 100 persons and forty horses. In 1429 a similar group appeared in Nijmegen. In 1526 Gypsies were forbidden to travel through the country by the German Emperor Charles V who, at that time, had authority over much of the Netherlands. The punishment would be a whipping and their noses would be slit. In the sixteenth century placards begin to appear throughout the country warning the Gypsies of punishments if they remained in the district.

In 1609 the Netherlands became independent. With the emergence of a central government, it became more difficult for Gypsies to escape persecution in one province by fleeing to another. ''Gypsy hunts' (*Heidenjachten*) at the start of the eighteenth century were to be the means by which the Gypsies were finally driven out of the country. Soldiers and police combined to scour the woods for Gypsies. An edict of 1714 forbade citizens to harbour them. Ten Gypsies were executed at Zattbommel in 1725. It is likely that all Gypsies left the country by 1728, the year that saw the last of the hunts, and that there were none in the country for over a century until the 1830s when new **Sinti** Gypsy immigrants arrived from Germany.

From 1868 there are reports of the arrival of three groups of Gypsies: Hungarian coppersmiths (**Kalderash**), Bosnian bear leaders and Sinti with circuses from Piedmont. These immigrants had money and valid travel documents but were nevertheless put under strong control which made it difficult for them to earn their living. At the beginning of the twentieth century, **Lovari** horse dealers arrived from Germany. In 1918 the *Caravan and Houseboat Law* was instituted to control the indigenous Travellers and the newly arriving Gypsies. A few caravan sites were set up.

During the Second World War, the German-controlled government made all caravan dwellers live on fixed sites. Fearful of what might happen to them next, many of the Travellers and Gypsies abandoned their caravans to live in houses. The Germans deported all the Romanies they could lay their hands on to **Auschwitz**. The transport held 245 prisoners in all, of whom only thirty survived.

After the end of the Second World War, the Dutch government decided to tackle the problem of caravans. In 1957 local authorities were allowed to link up and build sites. The Government gave a grant per caravan and 50 per cent of the running costs. Then in 1968 it was made compulsory for all local authorities to take part in the programme. The aim was fifty large regional sites, on the scale of a village with a school, shop and church. Soon 7,000 Travellers were on the large sites and a similar number on smaller sites. Recent policy has been to close the larger sites and move the Travellers to smaller ones so that there is less competition for work in a particular area.

After 1945 there was a steady immigration of Romanies from Yugoslavia in particular. The newcomers were made unwelcome by the authorities and their caravans were moved on by the police. Some were pushed over the border into neighbouring countries. In 1978 the Dutch government decided to legalise those Gypsies who had come into the country from Eastern Europe after the Second World War. This followed adverse publicity in the media on the situation of these largely stateless aliens and lob-bying by the ROM Society. In 1977, Zeevalking, the Minister of Justice, legalised some 500 of these Gypsies. A separate civil servant with responsibility for Gypsies was appointed to the Department of Caravan Affairs which had, until then, mainly been concerned with the indigenous Dutch caravan dwellers. In fact, the majority of the immigrants have been settled in houses. The late **Koka Petalo** was recognised as a leader by many of the **Vlah** Romani families.

The Sinti in the Netherlands first organised themselves into an association, the Zigeunerorganisatie Sinti, in 1989. In 1991 the Stichting Sinti-werk was set up and currently the Landelijke Sinti Organisatie represents the Dutch Sinti. The **Lau Mazirel Association**, with its journal *Drom* (Way) and exhibitions, has been informing the public and fighting against discrimination.

A feature of the Romani and Sinti community is the large number of musicians amongst them, such as the Gipsy Swing Quintet, Hotclub de Gipsys, Het Koniklijk Zigeunerorkest Tata Mirando Jr.(**Meisel Weiss**), Zigeunerorkest Tata Mirando Sr. (**Kokalo Weiss**), the Rosenberg Trio and many others.

NETOTSI. The name given to a group of Romanies in the nineteenth century who, according to one account, escaped from slavery in Romania and lived in the forests, resisting all attempts to recapture them. An alternative explanation of their origin is that they fled from **Maria Theresa's** efforts to sedentarise them.

NETWORK OF CITIES. The Network of Cities interested in Roma/Gypsy issues was set up by the **Standing Conference Of Local And Regional Authorities** of Europe following its resolution 249 of 1993. It has held a series of hearings on human rights and legal issues. The second hearing took place in Košice (Slovakia) and the third in 1996 in Ploesti (Romania).

NEVIPENS ROMANI. A periodical in Barcelona published in Spanish by the **Instituto Romanó**. About once a year there is a special number in **Romanó-kaló**, which the Institute supports.

NEW TRAVELLERS. UK. From around 1960 a number of house-dwellers started living in caravans and buses. Some did this for economic reasons, others because of frustration at town life. By 1986 the numbers had grown to several hundred and they are mentioned in a report on Gypsies prepared in that year for the Secretary of State for the Environment by Professor Gerald Wibberley of London University. The government brought in the concept of trespassing on private property as being a crime, to deal with what it saw as a new problem. This was introduced into the *Criminal Justice Act* of that year and strengthened in the 1994 *Criminal Justice Act*. New Travellers are classed as 'Gypsies' in English law if they travel for an economic purpose. The term is sometimes loosely applied to people who do not travel at all but live in tents and grow food on organic principles.

NICULESCU, Gheorghe. Romania. Civil Rights Activist. A flower dealer from Bucharest, in 1934 he took over the presidency of the Uniunea Generala a Romilor din Romania (General Union of the Gypsies of Romania) from **Lazarescu Lazurica**. This organisation continued its activities until 1940.

NOMADISM. The Romanies were never cattle-raising nomads who moved from place to place with their herds. Many of them were, however, industrial nomads (sometimes termed peripatetics) who travelled from place to place practising their crafts, whether they were smiths, acrobats or fortune-tellers. The word Gypsy has become a synonym for nomad. However, it is not sure that all Gypsies were nomadic by choice in the past. The Gypsies of **Modon**, for example, lived in a settlement and worked as shoemakers for several generations until the Turkish occupation of the town. Often Gypsies moved because they were forced to do so. Nomadism was almost impossible during the Second World War

and, afterwards, many countries in Eastern Europe banned nomadism. In Western Europe it became more difficult to travel as land became scarce. At present it is doubtful whether as much as 10 per cent of Europe's Romanies are nomads.

NORDISKA ZIGENARRÅDET. Founded in 1973 to link Gypsy organisations in the Nordic countries.

NORTHERN GYPSY COUNCIL. Regional association formed in the north of England in 1992. The chairman was William Nicholson.

NORTHERN IRELAND. **Traveller** population: 1,100. Northern Ireland is from time to time ruled directly from London, depending on the political situation there. The first legislation concerning sites was contained in *the Local Government (Miscellaneous Provisions) Order* of 1985. This gave 100 per cent grants for site provision and councils the power (but not the duty) of providing sites. In 1986 an Advisory Committee on Travellers was set up to advise the Department of the Environment for Northern Ireland. About seven families out of ten live on authorised sites, including ten run by local authorities. Four districts have been 'designated' under the Order as areas where Travellers cannot stop except on official sites. In 1997 the *Race Relations (Northern Ireland) Order* was passed. The outlawing of discrimination on racial grounds in this order also applies to discrimination against Irish Travellers. As a result, it was proposed to repeal the designation paragraphs of the 1985 order. The Travellers in Northern Ireland have the same lifestyle as those in the Irish Republic. The Traveller Support Movement is a network of local groups that works for the civil rights of Travellers, in addition to the Belfast Travellers Education Development Group.

NORWAY. Estimated nomadic or semi-nomadic population: 400 Romanies and some 5,000 **Travellers**. Norway had become part of Denmark in 1380 and Danish laws applied. So, when the

Danish King Christian III expelled Gypsies from his kingdom in 1536, this action applied to Norway as well. It is thought that, because he and his people became Protestant in that year, his tolerance waned for immigrants claiming to be pilgrims. There may well have been no Romanies in Norway at the time. One group was deported from England to Norway in 1544, and others entered from Germany. In 1554 the king again ordered their banishment from his territories. If they then returned, the magistrates were to set them in irons to work for up to a year, after which they were to be expelled again. A further order from King Frederick II in 1589 became valid for Norway on August 1, when Gypsies were to be imprisoned, their possessions confiscated and the leaders executed without mercy. The followers would be killed if they did not leave. Mayors of towns would forfeit their property if they did not denounce Gypsies and anyone protecting or sheltering them for the night would be punished, as were ferrymen and captains of ships that brought Gypsies into the country.

Some Romanies then left – for Finland probably – and others went underground in the country, mixing and intermarrying with Norwegian nomads to form the group known as **Reisende** (**Norwegian Travellers**).

In 1814 Norway set up its own Parliament. In 1860 the immigration of Romanies from Romania and Hungary was helped by the relaxation of the *Passport Law* in 1860, and in 1884 the first Romani birth in the country for many years was recorded. In 1888 a new law stating that citizenship depended on descent, not birth, was introduced. That meant that Romanies born in Norway did not get Norwegian citizenship until 1914 when the law was changed, and between thirty and forty Romanies acquired Norwegian citizenship. However, between 1918 and 1939 the Norwegian government tried hard to keep Romanies out, specifically invoking the *Foreigners Law* of 1901, which meant they could not get permission to enter the country to work as nomadic craftspeople. A few who had relatives already in the country were allowed to come. In 1924 the Justice Department accused the Catholic Church of issuing false baptism certificates to Romanies. The following year the Justice Department said that all Norwegian passports held by Romanies were false and should be withdrawn. In 1927 all the Romanies left the country, precipitated by the *Aliens Law*, which stated that "Gypsies or other Travellers who cannot prove they have Norwegian citizenship shall be forbidden access to Norway."

An international incident occurred in 1933 when a group of Romanies, some with Norwegian passports, wanting to go to Norway were stopped on the frontier between Germany and Denmark. The Danish government would not allow them transit until the Norwegian government agreed to take them, which it refused to do. These Gypsies were held in an internment camp in Germany for some months then pushed over unmanned border crossings into Belgium. During the Nazi occupation of Belgium, some of these Gypsies with Norwegian nationality were to be arrested and sent to **Auschwitz**.

Between 1927 and 1954 there were no Romanies in Norway. After 1954 a number of Gypsy families came into the country from France but there has never been a large population. Some families were able to regain Norwegian citizenship. In 1955 Oslo social workers ordered a Romani family to move from their two tents to the workhouse at Svanvike. The parents refused because they had heard about the conditions there from Travellers. Their six children were then taken away by force, The press took up the story and the authorities then agreed to return the children to the parents. In 1956 a new *Foreigners Law* left out an earlier provision about Gypsies (Sigøiner) seen as racist and replaced it by a section on nomads: "foreigners shall be refused admittance at the border if it is thought that they will try and support themselves as nomads."

In 1956 some Romani families regained their Norwegian citizenship and permission to live in the country. Temporary camps were set up around Oslo. In 1961 the authorities in Oslo discussed the problem of Romani children not going to school. The Mission for the Homeless, set up for the Norwegian Travellers, was still involved and suggested sending families to work in a kind of labour camp. A Gypsy committee was set up by the Social Services Department in 1962 for a Romani population of about forty persons. A new Gypsy committee was set up in 1969, excluding the Mission for the Homeless. In fact, no Romanies were in Norway at this time. In 1970 and again in 1973 the government published reports and proposals for the Romanies. By this time some families had returned and in 1973 Parliament passed a decree on support for Gypsies. In 1975 all immigration was stopped, affecting newcomers but not the existing population of about 100.

Several initiatives of 1978 were aimed at Romanies in Oslo: the opening of the first nursery school, an agreement that all Romani children were to have mother tongue tuition and the appointment of a special employment adviser. Romanies were not, however, considered as immigrants but had a special status. In 1979 an ABC book in Romani was printed, *Me ginavav Romanes* (I Read Romani), and two years later a reader for primary-age children appeared. In the last years there has been renewed immigration from Eastern Europe.

NORWEGIAN TRAVELLERS. The 5,000 indigenous Travellers in Norway have many names but they prefer to be known by the non-pejorative name of *Reisende* (Travellers). They are traditionally divided into two groups by both themselves and outside experts – the *storvandringer* and the *småvandringer* (long-and short-distance Travellers). The long-distance Travellers are generally considered to be the descendants of Romanies who went underground to avoid deportation in the fifteenth and sixteenth centuries and intermarried with local nomads. On the other hand, the short-distance Travellers are thought to be of Norwegian origin, with some intermarriage with German **Jenisch**, who came to Norway to trade.

By the nineteenth century the existence of the Travellers was worrying the government and in 1841 a Commission of Enquiry was set up. Three years later the discussion of the problem of the 'Fanter' (another name for the Travellers) in the Norwegian Parliament resulted in a new *Poor Law (1845)*. Aimed specifically at the Travellers, it imposed a punishment of two years' imprisonment for any of them who nomadised in bands. The government voted in 1855 an annual sum of money to educate Travellers. This budget was later used for placing them in workhouses where they were forced to labour. The policy failed due to a lack of suitable institutions. In 1893 the Church Department, which had responsibility for Travellers, estimated that there were some 4,000 of them. In 1896 a law was passed permitting the state to remove children from parents to state institutions. In some cases the child could be detained until the age of twenty-one. This law was also invoked against some Romani families in the twentieth century.

In 1897 pastor Jacob Walnum followed **Eilert Sundt** as the official expert on Travellers. He became general secretary of the Association for the Fight against Nomadism, which, under the new name of Norwegian Mission for the Homeless, operated until 1986. In 1934 about 1,800 Travellers were said to still be living as nomads. Articles written by J. Scharffenberg appeared in the press recommending their sterilisation, and many Traveller women were operated on from 1935 until 1950 or even later. During the Second World War and the German occupation moves were made to intern the Travellers in work camps. A story is told that some Traveller families painted swastikas on their caravans to convince the Germans that they too were of Aryan origin, but this has not been substantiated. The proposal of the puppet Norwegian government was to submit the Travellers to tests to see to what extent they were of Romani origin and sterilise those who were. The government minister Jonas Lie compared the Traveller question with the Jewish question, while the Norwegian Mission for the Homeless offered its card index of Travellers to the police and recommended more stringent laws. Fortunately, the German occupation of Norway ended before these plans could be put into effect.

Two varieties of Norwegian are spoken by the Travellers, known as romani and rodi (or rotipa). The grammar of both is Norwegian but there are many loans of vocabulary from Romani as well as from Jenisch. Many Travellers played the violin and contributed to Norwegian folk music, including in the nineteenth century Karl Frederiksen and his pupil Fredrik Fredriksen. Another Traveller musician was Nils Gulbrand Frederiksen. The songs and melodies of the Travellers have been collected and form part of the repertoire of contemporary folk singers. A cultural centre is being established.

NORWOOD, Vera, Councillor. England. Political leader. For many years a member of the Stow Town (Parish) Council and later Mayor of Stow. Like all other Stow Councillors, Cllr Norwood stood for the Council as an independent. She was for many years an active member of the Conservative Party. Disillusioned by the Conservative stance on Romani and some other issues, Cllr Norwood (who anyway dislikes party politics taking too much prominence in local government) stood in 2001 for the District Council against the official candidate and won. Subsequently she resigned from the Conservative party. This is possibly the first time when someone refused an official candidacy for being too pro-Gypsy has gone on to win in such circumstances. She also joined the Gypsy Council and has campaigned for the retention of the **Stow-on-the-Wold Fair**.

NOVITCH, Miriam. 1908-1990. Germany. Writer. Novitch escaped death during the Second World War because she was arrested as a Resistance worker – not as a Jew – and therefore held in a prison rather than a camp. She was among the first to become interested in the fate of the Gypsies during the **Holocaust**. In 1961 she wrote her first article on the subject – 'Le second génocide' (The Second Genocide) – and followed this up in 1965 with a thirty-one page report on the killing of the Gypsies and a pamphlet supporting a campaign to get a monument erected for the Gypsies killed in **Auschwitz**. She addressed the second **World Romani Congress**. After emigrating to Israel, she established a section on Gypsies in the Museum of the Kibbutz Lohamei ha-Ghettaoth in Israel.

NUREMBERG LAWS. From 1933 to 1938 the German Nazi Party held rallies in the town of Nuremberg. During the 1935 rally three decrees were announced, including two on nationality and marriage. They made 'non-Aryans' second-class citizens and forbade marriage between the Aryan Germans and persons of 'foreign blood' (defined as Jews, Gypsies and Blacks).

NUREMBERG TRIBUNAL. After the end of the Second World War a series of trials of war criminals was held at Nuremberg from 1945. Former SS General Otto Ohlendorf told the court that in the campaigns of killing in the east "there was no difference between Gypsies and Jews". The accused at the first trial (1945–6) included Ernst Kaltenbrunner, who had been involved in the murder of Jews and Gypsies. He was sentenced to death and executed.

NUSSBAUMER-MOSER, Jeanette 1947–.
Switzerland. Author. A **Jenisch** nomad
living in Switzerland, she has published
an autobiography, *Die Kellerkinder von*

Nivagl (The cellar children of N.)
describing the life of her family, with a
winter base in a small village and travelling in the summer with her grandfather.

O

OCAL, Burhan. Turkey. Contemporary
musician. Born in Kirklareli, a town in
Thrace near Istanbul, he is a virtuoso on
a variety of Turkish percussion instruments, including the bendir, darbouka,
kos and kudum. He is also a skilled
player of Turkish string instruments and
a vocalist. He plays with the **Istanbul
Oriental Ensemble** and has made
numerous recordings, winning many
awards.

OCCUPATIONS. Certain occupations are
associated with Gypsies such as **fortune-telling**, music, metalwork and
trading with horses but Gypsies are to
be found in many fields. There are surgeons, lawyers and other professionals
especially in Eastern Europe, where
most Gypsies are sedentary and educational opportunities better. It is not
always easy to identify professionals
who are Gypsies (Romanies) as they
may hide their origin because of real or
imagined prejudice.

OFFICE FOR DEMOCRATIC INSTITU-
TIONS AND HUMAN RIGHTS (ODIHR).
Est. 1992. An institution of the **Organisation for Security and Co-operation in
Europe** (OSCE). Founded in 1992, its
aim is to promote human rights by
assisting participating states to build
democratic societies. Its field of work
includes the Romanies, and it organised
the first Human Dimension Seminar on
Roma in the OSCE region in Warsaw as
early as 1994. It also published for some
time a newsletter for the **Contact Point
for Roma and Sinti Issues** (CPRSI),
which works within ODIHR. In October

2003 ODIHR brought together 200 par-
ticipants in Vienna for a Supplementary
Meeting during its eighth Human
Dimension Implementation Seminar in
order to boost OSCE's Action Plan for
Roma and **Sinti**.

OLAH, Dezider. Slovakia. Contemporary
political activist. President of the
Demokraticky zvaz Romov na Slovensku
(Democratic Union of Romanies in Slo-
vakia) and the Strana Socialnej
Demokracie Romov (Romani Social
Democratic Party).

OLAH, Vlado 1947–. Slovakia. Teacher and
writer. Now living in the Czech Republic.
A collection of his poetry was published
in 1996 under the title *Khamori Lulud'i*
(Sunflower). He is a founder of Matice
Romska, a Christian-oriented educational organisation, and co-author of a
children's Bible in Romani. Vlado Olah is
now translating the *New Testament*.

OPEN MEDIA RESEARCH INSTITUTE
(OMRI). Prague. **Soros Foundation**-sup-
ported organisation whose field of interest includes Gypsies.

OPEN SOCIETY [INSTITUTE]. Budapest,
Hungary. Est. 1993. The Institute (OSI)
was created by the Jewish investor and
philanthropist **George Soros** to support
his foundations in Central and Eastern
Europe and the former Soviet Union.
Those foundations had been established from 1984 to help former communist countries in their transition to
democracy. OSI is a privately operating
and grant-making foundation that
implements a range of initiatives to
promote an open society by shaping

government policy and supporting education, media, public health, and human and women's rights, as well as social, legal and economic reform. To foster an open society on a global level, OSI aims to bring together a larger Open Society Network of other non-governmental organisations, international institutions and government agencies. OSI has expanded the activities of the Soros foundations' network to other areas of the world where the transition to democracy is of particular concern. The network encompasses more than fifty countries but Roma remain an important priority for funding.

OPERA NOMADI. Italy. Est.1963. Organisation concerned to promote the education of Gypsy children. It was founded at Bolzano by Bruno Nicolini.

OPRE (upwards). Switzerland, Zurich. Music producers whose aim is to preserve the authenticity of Romani music and further its development. They have issued several CDs to date.

ORGANISATION FOR SECURITY AND CO-OPERATION IN EUROPE (OSCE). The OSCE was set up at a meeting of the Great Powers in 1975 as the Conference on Security and Cooperation in Europe. Its present name and structure date from 1994. It has included Gypsy affairs in its meetings and other activities. In September 1995 it organised a hearing of twenty-three Gypsy women from all over Europe. During the meeting of the OSCE in Warsaw in October 1995, a workshop on networking was run for Romani associations.

In November 2003 its Permanent Council published a detailed Action Plan on improving the situation of Roma and **Sinti** within the OSCE area. In December the OSCE Ministerial Council adopted the Plan. It covers the police, mass media, housing, health, education and other issues. A working group to develop the Plan is chaired by Liviu Bota of Romania

See also CONTACT POINT FOR ROMA AND SINTI ISSUES and OFFICE FOR DEMOCRATIC INSTITUTIONS AND HUMAN RIGHTS.

ORHAN, Galyus 1958–. Yugoslavia. Journalist. He is currently living in Slovakia and is editor of *Patrin*, a bilingual Romani-English journal.

ORIGINS. The Romanies have their origins in northern India though they may have formed as a people after their emigration westwards. See INDIAN ORIGIN.

OSTIA CONFERENCE. Under the title 'East and West' the **Centro Studi Zingari** organised a conference for Gypsies and non-Gypsy experts at New Ostia near Rome in 1991. The arrangement of workshops by topics gave an opportunity for the members of the working parties elected at the fourth **World Romani Congress** to meet. The results of the conference were published in the journal *Lacio Drom*.

OSWIECIM (**AUSCHWITZ**) Town in Poland which was the site of the largest Nazi concentration camp. In the town of Oswiecim itself there was a small Gypsy population after 1945 but in 1981 local Poles organised a pogrom against them and most then left the town.

OTTOMAN EMPIRE. The Ottoman Turks conquered Constantinople (present-day Istanbul) in 1453. They were to expand and rule parts of Eastern Europe for many hundreds of years beginning in the sixteenth century. The Gypsies were generally treated like other minority ethnic groups with their own leaders often being responsible for tax collection. Gypsies of all faiths paid higher taxes than the Turkish Muslims but were exempt from most obligations to the state.

Under Ottoman rule many Gypsies in the Balkans became converts to Islam, while other Gypsies who were already Muslims came into Europe with the Turkish conquerors as soldiers, musicians and courtiers of various kinds. From time to time the Ottomans banned nomadism, probably because of the difficulty of collecting taxes from nomads rather than any special ill will toward nomadism as such.

P

PAINTING. See ART.

PAKISTAN. Although today there are no
direct commercial or family links
between European Gypsies and
nomadic artisan **clans** in Pakistan, it is
possible that some of these groups share
a common ancestry with European
Romanies. For the purposes of this
volume we confine ourselves to the
Paryātan communities –nomadic artisans
and entertainers –as it is these who
would have links to Europe's Romanies.

There are perhaps eight separate
communities of Paryātan living in
Pakistan, each with distinct occupations. First there are the Jogi. These communities, who are also found across
western and northern India, live mainly
in tents and are renowned as snake
charmers. Many of them are also peddlers and make potions for a living. Next
are the Kanjar who live in grass tents.
The Kanjar are most famous for the ter-
racotta toys they produce and are often
greeted warmly by the children in local
villages who know they have toys for
sale! The Kanjar are also nomadic entertainers and, along with families who
provide carnival rides, many of them are
particularly renowned for their dancing
and singing.

The Mirasi are another peripatetic
group known for their singers and
dancers. Living in bender tents, Mirasi
people travel from village to village
entertaining the locals with their
singing, dancing and impersonations.
Many families are also trained to be
genealogists for the majority population. Another group of peripatetic entertainers are the Qalandar. Like the Mirasi
and Jogi they live in tents similar to the
bender tent of Romanies in Britain—tar-
paulin thrown over a framework of
poles. The Qalandar make a living
through performing circus acts. As well
as being jugglers, acrobats and magicians they are famous as animal trainers.

The remaining four Paryātan communities are known for their specialist
skills as artisans. The Chungār are
basket- and broom-makers and live in
grass tents, like the Kanjar. The Chriga
are peddlers of bangles and jewellery
and live in bender tents. The Kowli are
groups of peddlers and tinkers who also
live in bender tents and lastly there are
the Lohārs, whose main occupation is
smithing.

Many of these communities speak
their own languages and can also be
found in areas of north-west India. As
with peripatetic groups in India,
Paryātan populations in Pakistan tend to
be excluded from the usual social rules
governing caste and class interaction,
which has enabled them to be flexible in
their economic activities and to supply
specialised services not offered by
sedentary clans.

PALESTINE. See GHAZA AND THE WEST
BANK

PALM, Kai and Pertti. Finland. Contemporary singers. These brothers in Finland
play rock music. They have lately begun
to introduce songs in **Romani** into their
repertoire.

PALM, Olli. Finland. Contemporary singer.
He combines the tradition of the Finnish
tango with the American folk-rock style.
Among his repertoire are jailhouse
blues.

PALM-READING. **Fortune-telling** was one
of the occupations mentioned in the
early reports of Gypsies, for example, in
1422 in Belgium and in the same year in
Italy. The first record of palmistry in
England is in 1530. The art probably
originated in India. Many **clans** have
continued the tradition though the

increasingly popular **Pentecostal** Church disapproves of any form of fortune-telling. It is predominantly women who read palms.

PALMROTH, Arvo Valte 1916–. Finland. Singer and songwriter. He began his music career in 1962 after his wife's death. He had been involved in music on a casual level for many years but was then inspired to record an eponymous record in 1973 that included Gypsy songs, romances and airs and some original compositions. Some of his family accompanied him. This record launched him on his singing career.

PANKOK, Otto 1893–1966. Germany. Artist. Otto Pankok drew many Gypsy subjects, his *Passion* was based on visits to a Gypsy camp in Heinefeld near Düsseldorf in 1933–4. In July 1937 came the opening of the National Socialist propaganda exhibition attacking Degenerate Art (Entartete Kunst). Amongst the works on display was Otto Pankok's lithography *Hoto II*, the portrait of a **Sinto**.

PANKOV, Nikolai 1895–1959. Russia. Journalist and writer. With only a primary education, he translated **Prosper Merimée's** *Carmen* and works by **Aleksandr Pushkin** into Romani. He worked as a journalist, first on a Russian newspaper and then on the Romani magazine *Romani Zorya*. He strove from 1924 onwards to persuade the Romanies to settle down and have an education. His writings include *Buti i Džinaiben* (Work and Knowledge) (1929) and *Džidi Buti* (Living Work) (1930). Nikolai Pankov taught in the Gypsy technical school in Moscow from 1933 to 1938. In 1942 he suffered from an illness brought on from working as a nightwatchman after which he wrote little. He was elected a member of the Union of Soviet Writers in 1944.

PANNA, Czinka 1711–72. Slovakia. Musician and composer. Coming from a musical family, she was encouraged to study music and later played the violin in her own band with her husband and broth-ers-in-law. Her repertoire included folk songs and her own compositions. Czinka Panna was honoured both during her life and after her death as a great musician. Since 1970 musical festivals in her honour have been organised in the Gemer, the county of her birth. She has appeared on an official postage stamp.

PAPP, Katalin. Slovakia. Contemporary artist. Katalin Papp is a Hungarian Rom from Slovakia presently residing in the US. Her work has been exhibited in several locations including New York City.

PAPUSZA. See WAJS, Bronislawa.

PARA-ROMANI. A name given by some linguists to varieties of non-Romani languages that have been influenced by Romani.

See also CANT.

PARIS CONGRESS. 1986. The Paris Conference, which some books wrongly call the fourth **World Romani Congress**, took place on 22–23 February. It has been called variously an open meeting of the Presidium of the **International Romani Union** (IRU) or a meeting of the **Comité International Tsigane.** The main purpose of the conference was to consider the campaign to get reparations from the German government for victims of the Nazi period. This meeting saw one of the last public appearances of **Vaida Voevod III**, the founder of the modern Gypsy civil rights movement. Some delegates regarded it as a prelude to holding a fourth congress of the IRU in Paris but efforts to obtain financial backing failed, and that congress was eventually held in Poland.

PARLIAMENT, ROMANI (Hungary). See ROMA PARLIAMENT.

PARLIAMENT (UK). See ALL-PARLIAMENTARY GROUP ON ROMA.

PASHOV, Shakir 1952–. Bulgaria. Editor, politician and political activist. In 1933 he was editor of *Terbie* (Education) but a year later the right-wing government banned all the minority and opposition magazines and organisations. Following the establishment of a Communist government in 1945 he became head of the new Gypsy organisation Ekhipen (Unity) and editor of a new magazine for Gypsies. He became a Member of Parliament but was interned at Belen prison camp during the later Communist clamp-down on Romani nationalism.

PATRIN. An international periodical in Romani and English. Two issues appeared. The current editorial office is in Prešov, Slovakia. The editor was **Galjus Orhan** and assistant editor, Erika Godlová.

PAVEE. A word used by Irish Travellers for self-ascription.

PAVEE POINT. (i) The name given to the headquarters of the Dublin Travellers' Education and Development Group. (ii) The new name of the Group. Its membership consists of settled people (non-Travellers) and **Irish Travellers** who are committed to the right of Travellers to equality in Irish society. It runs training courses, has publications and tries to influence local and national policy.

PAVEES, The. An Irish folk band from the 1980s that had mixed membership, including both **Travellers** and non-Travellers.

PEN. See ROMANI PEN.

PENTECOSTAL-ISM. The start of a Pentecostal revival among Gypsies came in 1952 when a French **Manouche**, Mandz Duvil, asked the Breton pastor **Clement Le Cossec** to baptise him and his partner. Mandz Duvil spread the news of his new faith among his family and friends. Two years later, the hundred or so converted Gypsies chose four of their number to be elders. In the same year the first large convention was held in Brest. From 1960 the movement spread outside France, to Germany, Spain and most countries in Europe, as well as the United States. Along with the Manouche who were the original converts, members of other Gypsy groups (**Kalderash** and **Gitanos**) also became converted. By 1982 it was estimated that 70,000 Gypsies had already been converted and baptised.

The first contact with England came when an English Gypsy visited a convention of the Pentecostals in Montpellier in 1954. The first convention in England was held in 1983 at Fox Hall Farm, Nottinghamshire, and the second – also in the Midlands – in 1984. *Vie et Lumière* is the organ of the movement. In 1995 the Romani speakers (Kalderash and others) decided to form their own organisation known as **Centre Missionaire Évangelique Rom International** (CMERI).

PERIPATETICS. Term used by some authors to describe industrial or commercial nomads, as opposed to traditional nomads who move around with cattle.

PERUMOS. A popular music troupe from the Czech Republic.

PETALO, Koka d. 1996. The Netherlands. Civil rights activist. He was a spokesman for Gypsies in the Netherlands in the first years after the Second World War.

PETROV, Mihail 1968–. Bulgaria. Poet. A collection of his poems, *Mo Vogi* (My Soul) was published in 1996.

PETROVA, Dimitrina. Bulgaria. Contemporary political activist. The former director of the **Human Rights Project** (Bulgaria), she is now director of the **European Roma Rights Center** in Budapest.

PETROVIC, Alexander 1890–1942. Russia. Medical practitioner. Alexander Petrovic aided victims of the dysentery epidemic in Smolensk, Russia. He was a military doctor in Corfu during the First World War and in Yugoslavia. Between 1920 and 1931, he was a medical assistant at the University of Odessa, after which he returned to Yugoslavia to the Central Institute of Hygiene. He was murdered by unknown assailants in September 1942.

PETULENGRO. The Romani word for a blacksmith and used by several authors named Smith as a penname. One of these, Xavier Petulengro, wrote *A Romani Life* (1935).

PHRALIPE (Brotherhood). (i) The name given to a number of Gypsy organisations, particularly in Yugoslavia after 1945.

(ii) A national organisation founded in Hungary in 1988.

(iii) A Hungarian Romani monthly literary magazine.

See also PRALIPE.

PIKEY. Originally a derogatory term for a Gypsy. It is probably derived from the word 'turnpike'—a tollgate on a road. It is also used in contemporary English slang for someone who is always looking for bargains and ways of saving small sums of money.

PISTA, Danka 1858–1903. Hungary. Composer. He specialised in urban folk songs in Hungary.

PITO, Jozko 1800–96. Slovakia. Musician. Born in south-west Slovakia, he was a popular violinist in the town of Liptovsky Mikulás. Jozko Pitko collected and played folk songs. His sons and grandsons have followed in his musical footsteps.

PLOWDEN REPORT. UK. Under the chairmanship of Lady Plowden, a report was published entitled *Children and their Primary Schools* (1967). It found that Gypsies were "probably the most severely deprived children in the country."

Lady Plowden was later to become President of the **National Gypsy Education Council**, set up to help Gypsy children obtain schooling.

PLYUNI, PLYUNIAKI. A sub-group of the Polish Roma.

POETRY. Romani poetry has developed from song. Some verse was written during the early years of the Soviet Union before the use of the Romani language was discouraged. **Aleksandr German** and O. Pankova were the outstanding names in a repertoire that followed the state policy in seeing nomadism as romantic but outdated. Poetry has become a common literary form only since 1945. Well-known poets include **Rajko Djurić, Aleksandr Belugins** (Leksa Manuš) and **Bronislawa Wajs**. A number of anthologies are listed in the bibliography.

Increased settlement and educational opportunity have also produced writers who use the language of the country where they live. They include **Dezider Banga** (Slovakia), **Károly Bari** (Hungary), **Slobodan Berberski** (Serbia), **Luminita Mihai Cioaba** (Romania), **Sandra Jayat** (France) and Jozsef Kovacs (Hungary), together with many in the CIS. Their themes often mirror those of non-Gypsy poets.

In former Yugoslavia, where radio and periodicals have fostered the language, there developed alongside a flourishing theatre in Romani, a circle of poets in **Skopje** and its satellite town of **Shuto (Šuto) Orizari.**

The lyric writers of Kosovo are better known. Characteristic of this school is the creation of neologisms from Romani roots rather than using loan words from Serbo-Croat or Albanian. From the score of writers in former Yugoslavia we can mention only three: Dzevad Gasi, Iliaz Saban and Ismet Jasarevic. The latter in his rhymed autobiographical poem *Te dzanel thaarako ternipe* (That Tomorrow's Youth Might Know) tells of his hard struggle against poverty and illness. On a lesser scale than in the 1920s and 1930s, the CIS has seen a small revival with, **Nikolai Satkievic** and **Djura Makhotin**. Gypsy poets in Hungary have seen their work appear in a number of anthologies and in magazines, one of the earliest being *Rom som* (I Am a Rom). **Jószef Choli Daróczi** takes his inspiration from Brecht and the Hungarian poet Joszef Attila. **Ervin Karsai**, on the other hand, is best known for his children's poems. Characteristic of Czech and Slovak writers was that they had often been manual workers with little formal schooling. Worthy of mention are **Bartolomej Daniel**, **Tera Fabianová**, Frantisek Demeter, **Elena Lacková**, Vojtech Fabian and Ondrej Pesta.

Vitorio Pasquale writes in the less-used **Sinti** dialect and, together with Rasim Sejdic, has been published in Italy. There are other occasional poets such as **Matéo Maximoff** (better known for his novels), **Dimiter Golemanov** (primarily a composer of songs) and **Rosa Taikon** (an artist in metal).

An outstanding achievement of post-1945 Romani poetry is the full-length verse ballad *Tari thaj Zerfi* (Tari and Zerfi) by the **Lovari** dialect writer **Wladyslaw Jakowicz** (1915–), recounting the story of two lovers. It has been published in Sweden with a glossary in **Kalderash**, thus making it accessible to a wider circle of readers. The poets writing in Romani are part of the wider European tradition and important figures in Gypsy cultural life.

POGADI CHIB/JIB (broken language). The name given to the variety of English spoken by Gypsies in England and South Wales that has a large vocabulary borrowed from Romani but with the grammar and syntax largely based on English. This form of speech spread during the nineteenth century, replacing the Romani language proper. There are conflicting theories about its origin.

An example of a sentence in Pogadi Chib is: The rakli jelled to lel some pani (The girl went to fetch some water). Similar varieties of the majority language have been developed in Ireland, Norway, Scotland, Spain (**Caló**) and Sweden.

POLAND. Estimated Gypsy population: 35,000. According to the last national census (2003) there are 12,900 Roma in Poland.

Romanies first arrived on the territory of present-day Poland during the fifteenth century. By the end of that century several places were named after the Gypsies (such as Cyhanowa Luka) where Gypsies had presumably settled. Following harassment in Germany and other countries, more Gypsies followed. In 1501 a Gypsy, Vasil, was appointed by Earl Alexander of Lithuania to govern the Romani clans in Poland, as well as Lithuania and Belarus. However, in 1557 the Polish Parliament ordered the expulsion of Gypsies from the country. This was not carried out, as is shown by the passing of similar laws five times between 1565 and 1618. From around 1650 Polish kings began to appoint Gypsies as heads of their own **clans**. Even when this role was given to non-Gypsies, the Romanies continued to have their own recognised leaders. The Polish Lowland Gypsies still acknowledge the **Shero Rom** (Gypsy chief) as their leader.

In the eighteenth century Gypsy families immigrated from Slovakia and settled in the Carpathians. These Gypsies settled in permanent communities and formed the group now known as **Bergitka Roma** (Mountain Gypsies) as opposed to the longer established Lowland or Polish Romanies. In 1791 the *Settlement Law* was passed, abolishing the previous decrees on expulsion but, again unsuccessfully, banning nomadism. By 1793 Poland ceased to exist as a separate nation, being partitioned between Russia and Prussia (Germany).

The first writings on the Gypsies in Polish were by Tadeusz Czacki at the end of the eighteenth century and, in 1824, by Ignacy Danilowicz. In the nineteenth century **Kalderash** and **Lovari** Gypsies from Romania arrived on Polish territory. Poland regained its independence in 1918. After the end of the First World War, the Kalderash elected their own kings, forming the **Kwiek** dynasty. These kings were recognised by the Polish government.

In 1939 Germany occupied part of Poland and in 1940 began to deport Gypsies and Jews there from Germany. These Gypsies were put in ghettoes and work camps. In 1941 Germany occupied the rest of Poland and the following year massacres began. At Karczew 200 Gypsies were killed, at Lohaczy 115, at Zahroczyma 104 and smaller numbers throughout the country. Hundreds were deported to the extermination camps at Belzec, Chelmno, Sobibor and Treblinka. These camps, as well as **Auschwitz** (Oswiecim), also witnessed the death of Romanies brought from outside Poland.

Probably some 13,000 Polish Romanies were killed during the Nazi occupation.

In the first years after 1945 the Polish authorities did not regard the Romanies as a problem, in contrast to the attitude of other countries of Eastern Europe. Romanies make up only one per cent of the population and many have been sedentary for generations. There was also little fear that the Polish Catholics would be outstripped in births by the Romanies and any racist feeling was directed toward the small Jewish population. After the election of a Communist government in 1947, Romanies were required to take up employment in factories and farms alongside the rest of the population and private trading was restricted. Many Lovari and Kalderash were allowed to leave for Sweden or West Germany and were provided with exit visas.

A Government resolution of 1952, the 'Resolution on Assistance to the Gypsy Population in Moving Toward a Settled Style of Life', aimed at integrating the Gypsy population but this had little effect at local level. Then in 1964 nomadism was completely stopped by strict interpretation of laws on schooling, camping and so on. Many young Gypsies subsequently moved into towns to work in factories. Until 1989 national minorities were supervised by the Ministry of Internal Affairs and Romanies were *de facto* classed as an ethnic minority.

In 1963 the first Romani cultural organisation in Poland was founded in Andrychów. However, all cultural associations were in those years controlled by the government. The only publishing in Romani in that period was the poems of **Bronislawa Wajs** (Papusza). There were also a small number of books in Polish about the Romanies by **Jerzy Ficowski**, Lech Mroz and others. Some musical ensembles were formed, including the Roma Ensemble in Kraków founded in 1948 which toured in Poland and abroad. A cultural club was established

and a Gypsy exhibition put on permanent display in Tarnów.

In the late Communist period (1981) there were pogroms in Konin and **Oswiecim**. Houses were broken into, plundered and set on fire.

As Poland moved toward democratic government, an annual Gypsy music festival was started in Gorzow Wielkopolski and the bilingual newspaper *Rrom p-o Drom* (Romanies on the Road) began in 1990 under the editorship of **Stanislaw Stankiewicz**. Since 1998 the Roma have been considered a national minority.

After the end of the Communist regime, surplus unskilled labourers were sacked from their work. These were mainly Gypsies. On the other hand, many Gypsies have established small businesses and attracted the envy of their poorer Polish neighbours. Since the break-up of the Communist state there has been one big pogrom in **Mlawa** where the houses of Gypsies were set on fire, following an incident in which a car driven by a Gypsy hit three pedestrians. This was in 1991. In the same year, three Gypsies were killed in a second incident elsewhere. In 1992 there was an attack on the house belonging to one of the only seven remaining Gypsies in Oswiecim, the majority having left after the 1981 pogrom. Windows were smashed, and anti-Gypsy slogans were painted on nearby walls. The political party Narodowy Front Polski (Polish National Front) circulated leaflets during 1993 complaining about the (exaggerated) number of 90,000 Gypsies and campaigning for them all to be expelled from the country. In March 1995 a Romani couple was killed in Pabianice, and in October of the same year a mob attacked a house in the Warsaw suburb of Marki. In July 1997 the police opened an inquiry into an incident in which a grenade was left by the door of a Romani family's flat on First of May Street.

The locally based **Helsinki Foundation**

for Human Rights report in September 1997 said that after 1989 the treatment of Roma by authorities in Poland changed markedly and that the situation was better than in other countries in Central and Eastern Europe. The problem of harassment is, however, widespread.

Incidents of skinheads clashing with Roma and racially motivated violence directed at Roma continue to be reported. In April 1998, there were five separate attacks in Zabrze including the beating of a five-year-old boy. In the same month, skinheads in Sporysz invaded a Romani settlement and set fire to a house inhabited by an elderly woman. Also in April, the residents' association of Tarnow's Krzys district opposed the decision to settle in their area a poor Romani family from a condemned cottage in the town centre. In November 1999, a group of Poles from Pilsudski Street, Limanowa, demanded that councillors evict their Romani neighbours. They also insisted that no flats be allocated to Roma in the future, and that they be accommodated in separate, walled-off quarters. In the event of local authorities refusing to meet their demands, protesting residents threatened to take matters into their own hands.

In September 1998 a nineteen-year-old skinhead attacked a Romani home in Bytom, throwing a petrol bomb into a room in which two girls were sleeping. The swift action of the girls' parents prevented lives being lost but as a result of the attack, twelve-year-old Pamela received second and third degree burns to 20 per cent of her body and was in a critical condition. In June 1999 the skinhead responsible for the attack was sentenced to five years' imprisonment. During the trial, the girl's family was repeatedly threatened by the defendant's associates who stoned their home and, shortly before the sentence was passed, attacked the girl's fourteen-year-old brother.

In September 1999 in Andrychow, fascist skinheads undertook a 'city-cleansing' exercise in the course of which they attacked a sixteen-year-old Romani girl, not only beating her but choking her with a chain. The girl, whose throat and neck were badly lacerated, was taken to a specialist hospital.

At the end of September 1999, UK Prime Minister Tony Blair sent Jerzy Buzek, the Polish Prime Minister at the time, a letter demanding better treatment of Roma in Poland, threatening to introduce entry visas for Polish citizens if this was not done. The request was a response to some 400 Polish Roma seeking political asylum in England, citing the racist persecution they continually suffered in Poland.

In the same month, in Krosnica, local racists burnt out three houses in the Gypsy settlement between Kroscienko and Nowy Targ, rendering about thirty people homeless.

In April 2000 anti-Semitic and anti-Roma graffiti was painted on the wall of the Jewish cemetery at Oswiecim. In August 2000, a Romani woman was attacked in her home with an axe by two men wearing masks whom she believed to be skinheads. She suffered serious injuries and had to be admitted to hospital. Police detained two suspects but were reportedly unable to proceed with the case for lack of evidence. In August 2001, a group of teenagers vandalised cars and other vehicles at a holiday camp where a Romani family were staying; police arrested three suspects but there were no developments in this case by the end of 2003.

Violent attacks against Roma have also been perpetrated by the police and include an incident in July 1998 where three Roma were beaten up in a spa park following a festival of Romani culture and song. Before seriously assaulting the men, the police called them 'blackies' and threatened to drown them in the river.

The law provides for the educational

rights of ethnic minorities, including the right to be taught in their own language but there is currently a shortage of qualified teachers with a knowledge of Roma languages. Most Roma children do not complete primary schooling; education for these children ends at twelve and many are illiterate. In the majority of cases, Roma are integrated in mainstream classes and some schools, recognising economic disadvantage, language barriers and parental illiteracy, have introduced special preparatory classes for Romany children. In July 2001 the Ombudsman called for the implementation of institutional and long-term solutions in Roma education which took account of the history, specific culture and traditions of the community. He expressed the opinion that the low level of education amongst Roma was not only the result of attitudes and lifestyle but was also caused by a lack of initiative in this area on the part of the Polish authorities.

The central government made several moves to improve the situation of the Roma prior to entry into the **European Union**. The school enrolment rate among Roma children increased from 30 per cent to 80 per cent and a number of new homes are being built specifically for Roma.

In 2000 the Interdepartmental Group for National Minorities discussed the issues of Bergitka Roma, who have been recognised as the poorest Roma group in Poland. As a result, the Pilot Government Programme for the Roma Community in the Malopolska Province for the years 2001–3 was prepared and launched in March 2001. The government's spending on the programme rose to 3 million PLN during 2003; the aim was to end the disparities between the Malopolska Roma and the rest of society. The programme covers education, employment, health and accommodation conditions. In addition, two plenipotentiaries for Roma issues were appointed in 2000 in two Malopolska

counties in which there are significant Roma populations.

Several hundred Romanian Gypsies emigrated to Poland. At the same time large numbers of Polish Romanies have sought to establish themselves in Western Europe – some as asylum seekers on the grounds of racial persecution.

The Gypsy population consists of a number of different groups speaking different dialects. Apart from those already mentioned (Lowland Gypsies, Bergitka, Kalderash and Lovari) there also Russian Gypsies who have immigrated since (and even in some cases before) 1945 and **Sinti** Gypsies.

Current organisations include the Central Council of Polish Roma (chairman: Stanislaw Stankiewicz) which has representatives of the five largest associations: the Fundacia Mniejszosci Roma w Polsce (Association of the Roma Minority in Poland), the Romanies Social and Cultural Association in Tarnow, the Friends of Romani Culture in Gorzow Wielkopolski, the Kraków/Nowa Huta Romani Association and the Solidarity Association for the Romani Minority in Kielce. There is also the independent Romani Association in Poland (chairman: Andrzej Mirga) with headquarters in Oswiecim. The association publishes a number of books under the title of the Polish Library of Gypsy Studies (Biblioteczka Cyganologii Polskiej). There is also a monthly television programme aimed at the Romani population. Reverend Edward Wesolek, a Jesuit, has been appointed the National Catholic Minister to the Romani community.

PONOMAREVA, Valentina. USSR. Contemporary singer and musician. She blends her vocals with electronic orchestral accompaniment. She toured internationally in the late 1990s with the Volgograd (Stalingrad) band Orkestrion which incorporates made-up instruments recycled from rubbish tips giving a unique performance of poetry and music.

POPES. Over the years a number of popes have interacted with the Gypsies – in a positive or negative way.

Martin: In 1423 Pope Martin possibly gave a safe conduct letter to Duke Andrew of **Little Egypt**. A copy of the presumed document has survived and there is a record of Andrew and his followers setting off for Rome but no record of a meeting.

Between 1550 and 1557 several edicts were passed in the Papal States. Gypsies had to leave the territory or the men would be sent to the galleys and the women whipped.

Pius XII: In his Christmas message of 1942 he spoke of the "hundreds of thousands of people who, solely because of their nation or their race, have been condemned to death or progressive extinction." He has been criticised for not opposing the Hitler regime more actively.

Paul VI: In September 1965 he addressed 2,000 Gypsies at Pomezia. He talked of his "dearest nomads – perpetual pilgrims who have found a home in the heart of the Catholic Church" and named Mary as queen of the Gypsies. This was followed by a mass and a concert in St Peter's Square, Rome.

John Paul II: He attended the **Ostia conference** organised by the **Centro Studi Zingari** in 1991 and addressed the delegates. He stressed the Gypsies' love of the family and the fact that they were not using weapons in their fight for their rights. Later, in 1993, he wrote a letter of solidarity to the Gypsy memorial gathering at **Auschwitz**. John Paul includes Romani as one of the languages of his regular greetings.

PORRAIMOS (Tearing apart). A term used to describe the genocide of the Gypsies under the Nazis, corresponding to the Hebrew term S*hoah*. See HOLOCAUST.

PORTUGAL. Estimated Gypsy population: 60,000. Although there are no reports of the first Gypsies to arrive in Portugal, references to them appear in literature in 1516 and 1521. The number in the country must have been significant since in 1525 a law on Gypsies was passed, followed by twenty-six subsequent edicts. A law of 1573 ordered Gypsies to be arrested and used as galley slaves. In 1579 the wearing of Gypsy dress was banned. Deportation to the colonies in Africa and South America was a common way of dealing with Gypsies in Portugal from the sixteenth century.

In 1920 a law defining the role of the National Guard contained special provisions concerning Gypsies. The members of this police force were told to "exercise strict vigilance over the Gypsy population to suppress their habitual stealing" and "to detain immediately any Gypsy accused of any crime." In 1980 after the political changes in the country, the provisions of the law of 1920 were declared unconstitutional because they conflicted with paragraph 13 (against racial discrimination) of the new Portuguese Constitution.

The majority of Portugal's Gypsies live in the poorer areas of towns or on the outskirts. There was some migration to Spain during the twentieth century. There is no active national Gypsy organisation in Portugal though the Catholic Church has a body working with Gypsies. Marcellino Cabeca is a leader within the community, and his son Inocencio has attended international meetings.

POSHA. See LOM

POVERTY 3. The third European anti-poverty programme 1990–4. This was a **European Community** programme to support experimental projects to eradicate local poverty. A number of Gypsy projects received funding through Poverty 3 as either 'Model Actions' or 'Innovatory Measures'.

PRALIPE. Macedonia/Germany. Est. 1970. Director: **Rahim Burhan**. A theatre company originally from **Skopje** performing in Romani. It moved to Mühlheim in Germany after the Yugoslav Communist party evicted it from its theatre building and its grants were stopped. It toured widely using the buildings of the Theater a.d. Ruhr in Mühlheim as a base but has recently moved to Cologne. Pralipe's repertoire includes **William Shakespeare**'s *Othello* and *Romeo and Juliet* and **Federico Garcia Lorca**'s *Blood Wedding*. The name of the group comes from the Romani word for 'brotherhood', generally spelled **Phralipe**.

PREMIO HIDALGO. Spain. Est.1979. A prize awarded by the Asociación Nacional **Presencia Gitana** in Madrid. It is awarded each year to two personalities, one Spanish and one international, who have contributed to the development of Gypsy culture or rights. Laureates include **Günther Grass**.

PRESENCIA GITANA. Spain, Madrid. An organisation with Gypsy and non-Gypsy members. It promotes education through projects and publications. It awards the annual award, **Premio Hidalgo.**

PRESLEY, Elvis 1935–77. US. Singer. The legendary singer Elvis Presley reportedly comes from a Romani background, with his mother Gladys Love Smith being an English Romani. His surname, common as Priestley among **Scottish Travellers**, may indicate that he also has Traveller blood from his father's side.

PRESS. Before 1939 a small number of short-lived journals for the Gypsy community were published.

Bulgaria: *Terbie* (Education) (1933–4)
Romania: *Glasul Romilor* (Voice of the Romanies) (1934–44) bilingual.
Neamul Tiganesc (Gypsy News) (1933–5) bilingual.
Timpul (The Time) (1933–8) bilingual.
Soviet Union: *Nevo Drom* (New Way) (1930–?) in Romani.
Romani Zorya (Romani Dawn) (1929) in Romani
Yugoslavia. *Romano Lil* (Romani Paper) (1935–?) bilingual.

The rise of fascism put a stop to these periodicals and it was not until around 1970 that new magazines began to appear. Since 1989 there has been a spate of publications in Eastern Europe, some short-lived and some that have lasted longer. Yet others have closed and then revived as money again became available. A selection is listed alphabetically at the end of the bibliography.

PRO JUVENTUTE. SWITZERLAND. Est. 1920s. A Swiss charitable organisation that in the period 1926–73 took many Gypsy and **Jenisch** children away from their parents and sent them for adoption.

PROJECT ON ETHNIC RELATIONS (PER). US. Est. 1991. A non-governmental organisation founded to encourage the peaceful resolution of ethnic conflicts in the new democracies of Central and Eastern Europe and the former USSR. It has organised a number of conferences in Europe on the position of Romanies. There is a council composed of Gypsies who advise PER, known as PERRAC (PER Romany Advisory Council).

PUSHKIN, Aleksandr 1799–1837. Russia. Writer. His lyric poem *The Gypsies* took three years to write and was completed in 1827, depicting the Romanies of **Bessarabia** as ideal representatives of a natural state of human society. While celebrating the freedom of the Gypsy way of life, the poem also describes a fateful union between a Gypsy and a non-Gypsy. This poem inspired Mikhail Lermontov's 1829 poem *The Gypsies* and was later turned into a play, with moderate success, by the Moscow **Teatr Romen**.

PUXON, Grattan 1939–. England. Journalist and political activist. He went to Ireland and there became involved with the campaign of the **Travellers** to get caravan sites. He returned to England and in 1966 helped set up the **Gypsy Council**, of which he was the first secretary. In 1971, he organised the first **World Romani Congress** and became secretary of the **International Romani Union**. He served as its secretary until the third World Romani Congress. He is currently the organiser of **Uštiben**.

Q

QUENITE. See KENITE.

QUINQUILLEROS, QUINQUIS. 'Tinkers' in Spanish. They were semi-nomadic in Spain until this century, trading from village to village. Some think the Quinquilleros are of German origin, as many are blond and blue-eyed. Another theory traces their origin to landless Castillian peasants. Until the 1950s they were completely nomadic but punitive laws barring nomadism – with the penalty of from six months to five years prison or forced settlement – have caused them to settle. Some 85 per cent now live in urban slums. They prefer to be called Mercheros (Traders).

QUITO CONFERENCE. March 2001. Alongside the Forum of the Americas for Diversity and Plurality the Roma organised their own meeting. Representatives attended from several Romami organisations including those of Argentina, Chile, Colombia, Ecuador as well as **Sa Roma** (US), The American Romani Union, *Romano Lil* (Canada) and the Western Canadian Romani Alliance. They issued a declaration on behalf of 4 million Roma in the Americas asking for recognition as a people with full rights rather than an ethnic minority.

R

RACZ, Aladar (JASZBARENY, Aladar). Hungary. Twentieth-century musician. A **cimbalom** player of international standing. Aladar Racz was well known for his interpretation of Bach, Beethoven and other classical composers by playing the technical equivalent on a reconstructed sounding board. He played in Budapest in a Gypsy band for sixteen years. His recitals in Europe included a 1910 performance in Paris, a 1926 recital at the Concert Hall, in Lausanne and a 1938 concert in Rome, after which he was invited to join the Academy of Music in Budapest.

RADIO. No broadcasts for Gypsies were aired until after 1945. Now a number of stations regularly broadcast programmes in Romani or aimed at Gypsy audiences. The earliest was perhaps in 1973 when a radio programme started at Tetovo (Yugoslavia/Macedonia).

There are stations currently broadcasting such programmes for Romani listeners in Belgrade, Budapest, Paris, Prague and Skopje. In addition, there are some religious radio programmes broadcast from stations, such as Trans World Radio. The proposed broadcasts from Peterborough, England (which are mentioned in some books and articles) were never started.

RADUCANU, Gheorghe 1960–. Romania. Political and civil rights activist, professor and politician. He is a professor of Ecomomics at the Academy of Science. As a member of the political party Partida Romilor (Romani party), he was the first Romani to be elected to the Romanian Parliament in 1990.

RADULESCU, Iulian. Romania. Contemporary political activist. A **Kalderash** head of family. He was crowned Emperor of 'All the Gypsies' in August 1993 in

Romania. His son is married to Lucia, the daughter of his one time rival, the late **Ion Cioaba**.

RAFTO FOUNDATION. Norway. Est. 1997. The Foundation in Norway awarded the Thorolf Rafto Memorial Prize to the Romani People. The prize was collected by Professor **Ian Hancock** on behalf of all Romani Gypsies.

RAJKO DJURIĆ FOUNDATION. Prague. Named after the writer **Rajko Djurić,** the Foundation carries out a number of charitable and civil rights activities. It organises a national festival, Romfest, each year in Moravia, and has produced a number of TV programmes for Czech television.

RAJKO SCHOOL. A school for gifted Romani children in Hungary where they specialise in music.

RAMÍREZ HEREDIA, Juan De Dios. Spain. Political leader and politician. Former teacher and community worker in Barcelona, he is now a politician. He was elected to the Spanish Parliament and then became a member of the European Parliament in Brussels. He is active in the **Unión Romani**, based in Barcelona, and writes for the journal *Nevipens Romani* (Romani News). He helped to organise the **European Congress** in Seville.

RANJIČIĆ, Gina 1830–91. Serbia. Singer. Her songs were recorded by Heinrich von Wlislocki and published in a book called *Vom Wandernden Zigeunervolke* (Of the Wandering Gypsy People) in 1890.

RAOUL WALLENBERG FOUNDATION. Budapest. Est. 1997. President: Baruj Tenembaum. A civil rights organisation in Budapest named after the famous Second World War figure. It has investigated cases of discrimination or harassment against Gypsies in Hungary.

RASUMNY, Mikhail 'King' 1890–1956. Actor. He played the Gypsy grandfather, Nino Koshetz, opposite Jane Russell and Cornel Wilde in the film *Hot Blood* (1955).

RAYA see BIELENBURG, Raya.

RAZVAN, Stefan d. 1595. Romania. Politi-

cian. The son of a slave and a free woman in Romania, he became ruler of Moldavia in April 1595. He was deposed four months later and murdered in December of the same year.

REDJEPOVA, Esma 1943–. Macedonia, Skopje. Singer. She has her own ensemble, originally set up with her late husband. They have made many recordings and have toured widely in Europe and North America. She sang the Romanies' national anthem, **Gelem Gelem**, to open the fourth **World Romani Congress** and performed at the grand concert for TV during that conference.

REINHARDT, Babik. France. Contemporary musician. Guitarist son of **Jean-Baptiste 'Django' Reinhardt**. He also organises the annual Django Festival in Samois-sur-Seine, France.

REINHARDT, Jean-Baptiste 'Django' 1910-1953. France. Musician.

Reinhardt was his mother's surname, while his father was, in fact, called Weiss. As a young Gypsy musician, Django Reinhardt began his career busking in Paris. In 1920 a French accordionist heard him playing his guitar and offered him a professional engagement in a dance hall from where he earned his first real money. Jack Hylton, the famous British band leader, travelled to Paris twice to find him to offer him a contract. The night of their meeting, tragedy struck when a candle set fire to Django Reinhardt's caravan and his left hand was burned. It was a year before he could play in public again. Yet because of this disability he spent hours working out how to play with the three fingers, usable on his left hand, whereby his technique was said to reinvent guitar playing. At this stage he discovered jazz and formed a quartet with his brother Joseph and two non-Gypsies, Louis Vola and Stefan Grappelli. A fifth player was added, and they formed the quintet which gained fame as the Hot Club de France.

In September 1939 the quintet was playing in London on the eve of the

Second World War which prompted the guitarist to return to France. Ultimately, that country was occupied by the Germans and jazz was condemned as 'Negro music.' Concerts were no longer advertised as 'jazz.' While playing later in occupied Belgium, at the Club Rythmique de Belgique, Django Reinhardt was asked to tour Germany. He knew Gypsies were being arrested there and sent to the death camps so he avoided this danger by requesting 120,000 francs per concert, knowing the Germans would not pay such an amount. Toward the end of the war, he sensed danger again and moved from Paris to near Thonon-les-Bains at the Swiss border, where he once dared to play *La Marseillaise* in front of German officers. From there he tried to slip across the border but was arrested and found to have a membership card of the British Society of Composers. The German officer who interrogated him was a jazz fan and let the musician go free.

His being cut off from the international world of jazz in occupied France led to a lukewarm reception in New York when later he did play there in 1946. Café society there no longer felt jazz was an art with mass appeal and the Reinhardt name was not enough to make up for his lack of professionalism. On his return to France he began to learn the electric guitar but died in Samois after refusing to call a doctor when suffering from a brain haemorrhage.

Contemporary performers of 'Gypsy Jazz' include Lollo Mejer, Andreas Oberg and Matcho Winterstein as well as others who are listed individually in this publication.

REINHARDT, Schukenack 1921–. Germany. Musician. Born in Weinsberg, a violinist playing jazz and swing, he leads a quintet. His recordings include *Musik deutscher Zig*euner in four volumes.

REISENDE (Traveller). See NORWEGIAN TRAVELLERS.

REIZNEROVÁ, Margita 1948–. Slovakia. Writer and political activist. President of the Organisation of Romani Authors, she translated Chekhov into Romani. Her work includes poetry and her most recent publication is *Kali*, a collection of stories about the goddess, in Romani with an introduction in Czech.

RELIGION. Gypsies have tended to adopt the religion of the country where they live or travel so there are Protestant, Catholic and Orthodox Christians, as well as Muslims. Recently there has been a move among many persons to adopt **Pentecostalism.**

REPARATIONS. After the end of the Second World War, the Bonn Convention said that persons who, during the Nazi period, were persecuted because of their race should be compensated. However, in 1950 the Interior Ministry in the German state of Württemberg told judges to remember that Gypsies were persecuted not because of their race but because they were antisocial. In 1953 a law on reparations (*Bundesergänzungserlass zur Entschädigung für Opfer des NS*) made reparations available but only to Gypsies who were of German nationality, stateless or refugees. The arrangement (from 1959) was that West Germany would pay global reparations to Western European countries which they would then use to pay their nationals who had suffered. In the case of Eastern European countries, a number of Gypsies who had been used for medical experiments have received reparations but otherwise very few others have been compensated for their sufferings in this period.

In 1956 there was an important decision of the Higher Court (Bundesgerichthof) that a Gypsy woman should not be compensated for the 1940 deportations to Poland as these, the Court said, were not for racial reasons but because of the fear of espionage. In 1962, however, the Higher Court accepted that persecution had started as early as 1939 (the Blum case). In 1965 a new law (*Bundesentschädigungsschlussgesetz*) confirmed that Gypsies did not have to prove that persecution from 1938 was racial. This was assumed. Finally, a new law provided for reparations to be paid for those victims who had not yet been compensated.

Requests have been made for block reparations to be paid to international Gypsy organisations, in particular for families where all the members perished and no one survived to claim reparations. Following the third **World Romani Congress**, the **International Romani Union** has been pursuing a claim for block reparations against first the West German and then the Federal German Government. The Indian government informally offered to be the trustee for such payments. The German government has given money to German **Sinti** organisations for cultural and educational purposes but these payments have not been seen by the government as being a form of global reparations. Since the fourth **World Romani Congress** no progress has been made on this question, though two international funds have now been set up to provide pensions for survivors. See also HOLOCAUST.

REPUBLICA SRPSKA. When Bosnia was partitioned, the political entity known as Republika Srpska was set up which is *de facto* under Serb rule. The current total Romani population figure is unknown but there are around 200 living in the area of Banja Luka and a similar number in Bijeljina. The Romani population is small because during the three years of fighting those Roma who were Muslims – the majority – were expelled from this area. Roma expelled from Bratunac, for example, now live in Virovitica in Croatia. Almost the entire pre-war populations of Banja Luka and Bijeljina, both numbered in thousands, have left. The Roma in Bijeljina were told: "Either leave or be killed" and the majority fled. The Romani settlements of Jasenje and Staro Selo have been destroyed. In 1994 the 200 Roma in the village of Klasnice in northern Bosnia, in Republika Srpska,

asked the UN High Commissioner for Refugees to arrange their evacuation. Several thousand Roma who formerly lived in the area now under Serb control are living as refugees in Western Europe, in particular Germany, Italy and the United Kingdom, and they, too, like those from Bosnia proper, are unlikely to be accepted as citizens if they return.

RESANDE/RESANDE-ROM (Travellers). See SWEDISH TRAVELLERS.

REYES, Antonio El Mono. Spain. Contemporary singer. He is the grandfather of **Joaquín Cortes**, and sings in the **Flamenco** style.

REYES, Jose 1930–. Spain. Singer. Metalworker, carpet-seller and amateur **flamenco** singer. Cousin of **Ricardo Baliardo**, Jose Reyes sings largely for his own pleasure.

REYES, Jose Antonio 1983–. Spain. International footballer. Sevilla's top-scoring player in 2002–3 who signed for Arsenal in January 2004. He wears a No. 9 shirt, and is a forward. He signed his first semi-professional contract with Sevilla at the age of fifteen and made his debut for the Spanish national squad at nineteen. He has been described as a 'play station footballer' who will take the ball as close to goal as he can at the fastest pace.

REYES, LOS. See GYPSY KINGS.

RIEFENSTAHL, Leni. 1902–2003. Germany. Film director. She made propaganda films for Hitler during the Nazi regime. For the film *Tiefland* (April 1942) she used Gypsies from two internment camps, sixty-eight Gypsy extras from Marzahn near Berlin and fifty from Salzburg.

RIPPLE (Roma influence on Policy and Practice in Localities in Eastern and Central Europe). Est. 2000 by **Minority Rights Group** International. A two-year project intended to progressively develop the knowledge and skills of national and regional themed networks of young Roma in seven countries in Eastern and Central Europe to enable them to influence public opinion, policy and practice.

RISHI, W.R. 1917-2002. India. Interpreter in the diplomatic service. He spent some time during his service in Europe studying the Romanies. He attended several congresses and conferences and was a strong link between the Romanies in Europe and their motherland India. After retiring and returning to the Punjab, he set up the Indian **Institute of Romani Studies**, edited the journal *Roma*, as well as organising the two **Chandigarh Festivals**. In the 1990s, he founded a Gypsy museum in Chandigarh, the Nehru Romano Kher (Gypsy house). His publications include two Romani dictionaries a Romani-Punjabi phrase book and a book, *Roma: the Punjabi Emigrants and India*. He was elected Honorary President of the **International Romani Union** in 1978.

RITTER, Robert. Graduated 1927. Germany. Psychologist and doctor. A German race scientist during the Nazi regime who in 1936 founded an institute which later became the Race Hygiene and Population Biology Research Centre of the Ministry of Health in Berlin. He took over existing records on Gypsies. His aim was to track down all Gypsies in the country and classify them as pure or part-Gypsy. By 1942 he claimed to have files on 30,000 persons living in Germany and Austria. The policy he proposed was to intern part-Gypsies in work camps and sterilise them. Pure Gypsies should be allowed to travel but kept apart from mixing with Germans.

ROBERTSON, Jeannie MBE 1908–75. Scotland. Singer. A **Scottish Traveller** and performer of folk songs, Jeannie Robertson's parents travelled principally in north-east Scotland. She first came to prominence in folk-song circles in 1953 when she was recorded by Peter Kennedy. Acknowledging her mother as the main source of her musical knowledge, she gained a reputation as one of the finest ballad singers in Western Europe. She made several records and videos and was honoured by Queen Eliz-

abeth II with the Medal of the British Empire. Her daughter Lizzie Higgins is also a singer and can be found on several recordings.

ROBERTSON, Stanley 1940–. Scotland. Musician and singer. A **Scottish Traveller** and the nephew of **Jeannie Robertson**, he is a piper and singer in the folk tradition as well as a storyteller. He joined the Mormon Church and with its encouragement became a professional entertainer. Stanley Robertson has toured in the US and Europe.

ROKYCANY. Town in Bohemia (Czech Republic) with a large Romani population which emigrated soon after 1945 from Slovakia. The community has a strong musical tradition, and the players include the Gina family, who formed a folk band first called Ginovci and later, playing more modern music, Rytmus 84.

ROM. The name used to describe themselves by the majority of ethnic Gypsies in their own language. The etymology is unclear but the term may come from an old Indian word *dom*, the original meaning of which was 'man.' Derivation from the God Rama is unlikely. The plural is Rom or Roma according to the dialect. Other Gypsy groups – for example the **Sinti** and **Manouche** – have the word 'rom' in their dialect but only in the sense of 'husband.' The term is commonly employed when UK media are writing about Romanies from Eastern Europe and we have adopted this usage alongside 'Romani'.

The primary unifying concepts of the Romani people are their awareness of a common history and destiny and of a language (even if no longer spoken). Gypsy culture preserves a spirit of nomadism, whether exercised or not, a preference for self-employment and – for most groups – laws of hygiene (**Mageripen**).

ROM-LEBEDEV, I. 1901–91. Russia. Author and songwriter. He was active in the 1930s. Some of his songs have been recorded by artists of the **Teatr Romen**.

ROMA CULTURAL SOCIETY. Poland. Est.

1966. Founded in Poland in 1966 and still active.

ROMA DAY. See ROMA NATIONAL DAY.

ROMA ENSEMBLE. Poland. Est. 1946. Founding Director: Michael Madziarowicz. This Romani song and dance ensemble was originally formed in Kraków in 1946 by some ex-members of the Moscow **Teatr Romen**. The first director of the ensemble was Michael Madziarowicz, followed by Wladyslaw Iszkiewicz in 1967. It toured abroad frequently and in 1970 came under the management of the state-owned Estrada Agency in Poznan. It made two recordings in Poland before some of the ensemble left for Sweden to form the group **Svarta Pärlor.**

ROMA INFORMATION CENTRE. Serbia. Est. 1999. Director: Rozaliza Ilic. This organisation was founded in January 1999. Its mission is to improve the Roma's life and to preserve their culture and traditions. The Centre is dedicated to the emancipation of Roma through education, and it runs several workshops for adults and children offering psychological support, numeracy and literacy projects and creative activities such as art and drama. It also runs cross-cultural projects and houses a library within its offices containing some 1,200 titles. RIC works alongside other NGO's and Roma support groups and is supported by **Open Society**.

ROMA LITERARY AWARDS. Established in 2002 by the **Open Society** Institute in Budapest to honour Roma artistic achievement in literature and first awarded in 2003. An international jury of Roma select finalists from four categories: fiction, non-fiction, poetry and translation.

ROMA NATION DAY/ROMANO DIVES. 8 April was chosen by the first **World Romani Congress** – the day it opened – to be celebrated by all Gypsy communities as a national day. It was at first sporadically honoured. For example, in 1993 the Cidinipe Roma (Gypsy Association) of Zagreb held a formal meeting in the Hotel Intercontinental. In recent years there has been a growth in celebrations including adopting the Indian custom of flowers into a river, first used in 2002 in London when the booking of a hall had to be cancelled as earmarked funds were diverted to helping victims of the floods in India.

ROMA OPRE. Belgium. Est. 1998 Chairperson: Wolf Bruggen. An NGO which offers a large number of activities and services. It promotes Romani culture, tradition and history and defends the interests of all groups within the larger Romani community in Belgium and Europe. Liberation and development, emancipation and equal participation are the key principles of the organisation.

ROMA PARLIAMENT (i) The Roma Parliament set up at the fifth **World Romani Congress** has met several times bringing forward proposals for the democratisation of the **International Romani Union's** statutes and for reconciliation with its main rival, the **Roma National Congress.**
(ii) A Hungarian institution that has been very dynamic in Romani politics since 1989, perhaps because it was built up by local organisations. It protects and promotes the interests of Roma through negotiations with the government during the development of new legislation for minorities.

ROMA PRESS AGENCY (RPA). Slovakia. Est. 1999. Director: Ivan Hriczko. This organisation began with the aim of improving the presentation of Roma in the Slovak media. The organisation was set up as an NGO on a voluntary basis but, since 2002, at the request of **Open Society** and with the support of the American Peace Corps, it is now more formally constituted. The Agency also provides training to young Roma for the profession of journalism.

ROMA RIGHTS and ACCESS TO JUSTICE IN EUROPE (RRaJE). UK. Est. 2001. President: **Peter Mercer**. A three-year programme supported by the UK Department for International Development, it aims to tackle the social exclusion of the Romanies in Central and Western Europe. In 2003 they produced a Background Report for the UK **All Party Parliamentary Group on Roma Affairs.**

ROMA SUPPORT GROUP. UK. Est. 1998. Previously known as the Romany Support Group, the Group is a community organisation committed to improving the quality of life of Roma asylum seekers and refugees from Eastern European countries especially Poland. The Group runs an advice/advocacy service as well as a football club, indoor sports activities, a summer programme, visual art workshops and a music and dance project (**Romani Rad**) in East and West London.

ROMA WOMEN'S ASSOCIATION IN ROMANIA (RWAR). Bucharest. Est. 1996. Coordinator: Violeta Dumitru. RWAR's mission is to defend the rights of Roma women and support the development and expression of the ethnic, cultural, linguistic and religious identity of its members.

ROMA WOMEN'S NETWORK (IRWN) Est. 2003. It was set up following a Conference on Romani women and access to public healthcare, organised by the **Council of Europe**, European Monitoring Centre and **OSCE/ODIHR**.

RomaDEX (Roma Development Equity Exchange). Europe. Est. 2003. Technical Director: Hector McNeil. Extensive fieldwork by **the European Committee on Romani Emancipation** (ECRE) and the Agricultural Development Foundation (ADF) led to the development of RomaDEX in 2003. RomaDEX has been designed to address the specific problems facing rural Roma. RomaDEX will provide market identification, the selection of appropriate technology, training and business development and thereby help jump start, in the short to medium term, a substantial rise in the real incomes of those involved.

ROMAN. The name given by its speakers to the Romani dialect of **Burgenland**,

spoken by some 2,000 persons.

ROMANE DYVESA (Romani Days). An annual international meeting of Gypsy musician groups held in Gorzow, Poland, and organised by a local committee. The first gathering was in 1989.

ROMANES. An adverb in the Romani language meaning 'in the Romani manner.' So we find the usage 'to speak Romanes.'

ROMANESTAN (The Land of the Romanies). The name given to a planned Gypsy homeland in the 1930s on the lines of the Zionist movement's vision at that time to create a Jewish state. The idea was first proposed by the kings of the **Kwiek** Dynasty in Poland. The Second World War put an end to these dreams. The idea of a Gypsy state was revived after 1945 by **Vaida Voevod III** but nowadays most Gypsies would perhaps follow the thoughts of the Canadian Gypsy writer **Ronald Lee** who has said: " Romanestan is where my two feet stand".

ROMANEZ, Esmeralda. Writer. Her mother was a Romani from Andalusia and her father a French **Manouche**. She has published numerous books.

ROMANI. (i) Originally a feminine adjective formed from Rom, the term most Gypsies use for themselves. It is replacing the old English spelling 'Romany'. See the entry for ROM.
(ii) See ROMANI LANGUAGE below. Check also for entries listed under ROMANY.

ROMANI ASSOCIATION OF AUSTRALIA (RAA). Est. 1990. President: Jimmy Storey. The RAA is affiliated to the **International Romani Union**.

ROMANI BAXT FOUNDATION. (Baxt = Good fortune). Sofia, Bulgaria. Est. 1996. Chairperson: Michali Georgiev. The organisation focuses on legal and social programmes designed to promote the Roma people's inclusion in society and to promote human rights and equal treatment. Within this framework the team monitors and reports on the situation in Bulgaria and provides educational as well as legal and social services. It offers free legal advice to Roma as well as working alongside the Sofia Municipality to develop a strategy for improving education. In 2002 the Foundation was selected from fifty nominees to win a **Body Shop** Human Rights Award. It also receives the support of **Open Society** Institute.

ROMANI CHEL. See ROMANY CHAL.

ROMANI CIVIC INITIATIVE (ROI). Czech Republic. Est. 1981. Chairperson: **Emil Sčuka**. A political party that fields candidates in local and national elections in the Czech Republic.

ROMANI DEMOCRATIC CONGRESS. Czech Republic. Est. 1992. A nationwide forum in the Czech Republic to which many leading Romani figures contribute. It has no activities as such.

ROMANI LANGUAGE The Romani language belongs to the north Indian group and is close to Punjabi and Hindi. It was brought to Europe by the Gypsies and has retained more of its earlier structure than the modern Indian languages. The sound system includes up to four aspirated consonants. There are five or six cases, and the verb has a number of tenses. Words are inflected to show changes of tense, person, gender and case. There is a masculine and feminine gender.

Romani is taught at INALCO (Paris University V), Charles University in Prague, Bucharest University, Manchester University and some other colleges and schools. It remained largely a spoken language until the nineteenth century when it began to be written.

In accordance with the European Charter for Regional or Minority Languages, Finland, Germany, the Netherlands, Slovenia and Sweden officially recognise Romani as a minority language

See LITERATURE, GYPSY.

ROMANI LANGUAGE – DIALECTS. At the time of their arrival in Europe there were perhaps two main dialects (Romani and **Sinti**) but since then different **clans** have developed separate features that may have been present in the speech of some speakers of the two original dialects. Sedentary Gypsies have also been affected by the language of the majority population where they live. Now there are many dialects of which the main living ones can be grouped in the following five clusters:

I. **VLAH**

II. BALKAN

III. NORTHERN

IV. CENTRAL

V. The Romani of Calabria and Abruzzi, Italy.

With recent migration, speakers of the Balkan dialects can now be found in most countries of Western Europe.

ROMANI LANGUAGE – ORIGINS. During the 1700s, a Hungarian pastor called Vályi, when at the University of Leiden in Holland, met some fellow students from west India's Malabar coast. They made a list of over 1,000 Sanskrit words for him which the pastor took back to Hungary. Comparing them with words Romanies used in his region, he found some similarities. An article about this study was published in Vienna in 1776 and was noticed by the German linguists **Heinrich Grellmann** and Jakob Rüdiger who each compiled a table of Romani words and compared these with a number of languages. The latter saw the similarities between Romani and Hindustani (Urdu) and in 1781 first recorded his discovery. A further publication of his, a year later, demonstrating a scientific comparison between the two languages, aroused more attention. Another student of languages, Christian Büttner, then found similarities between Romani and the Pashto language. Heinrich Grellman saw the young man's work and went on to publish in 1783 his book *Die Zigeuner. Ein historischer Versuch* (published in English as *A Dissertation on the History of the Gypsies*) which included a section on the Indian origin of Romani.

Meanwhile in England, independently of all this, Jacob Bryant, an amateur coin collector and historian, compared Romani words with a printed vocabulary of Hindustani around 1780. He revealed the similarities between words such as Romani rup (silver) and Hindustani *rupee*, but he also identified Greek words that Gypsies had borrowed on their journey across Europe to England. However, some of his links were unlikely and more important discoveries were made by William Marsden, famous for his work on the Malay language. He made the Romani/Hindustani link in 1783, compiling a paper that was presented to the London Society of Antiquaries on 3 February 1785. The Society then published his findings.

The news of the relationship between the two languages (Romani and Hindustani) spread across Europe and with it the forgotten truth as to the north Indian origin of Europe's Gypsies. The Russian Academician Petr Pallas mentioned this in his collection of comparative dictionaries published in St Petersburg in 1787.

ROMANI NATIONAL CONGRESS. Germany. An organisation based in Hamburg and largely supported by Romanies from Eastern Europe. It has links with individuals and groups in other countries and publishes the bulletin *Romnews*. It is organised the **Lodz Congress**. The leading figure is **Rudko Kawczynski**.

ROMANI PEN. President: **Rajko Djurić.** Secretary: Johano Strasses. The Centre is a member of international PEN and has its official base in Berlin. Membership is open to writers in Romani and to those writing about Romanies. A newsletter *Stimme des Romani PEN* first appeared in 1996. After the death of Reimar Gilsenbach, **Rajko Djurić** took over the running of the organisation. In 2003 it ran an international competition for literary work on the **Holocaust**. See also INTERNATIONAL ROMANI WRITERS ASSOCIATION.

ROMANI RAD. England, London. Band and dance ensemble, they are run by and for Polish Romanies in London. They have performed with Terry Hall and Mushtaq.

ROMANI STUDIES. There are courses in Romani Studies at Greenwich University, the University of Texas and elsewhere.

ROMANI UNION. See INTERNATIONAL ROMANI UNION.

ROMANI WRITERS ASSOCIATION. See INTERNATIONAL ROMANI WRITERS ASSOCIATION.

ROMANIA. Estimated Gypsy population: 1,000,000. According to the 2002 census, the Roma population numbered 535,25. The majority belong to **Vlah** clans but there are also **Ursari** and Muslims. Gypsies may have arrived with the invading **Tartars** in the thirteenth century. By the end of the next century they were already treated as slaves. They had even fewer rights than the native serfs, as families could be split up and the members sold or given away as gifts. The first recorded transfer of Romani slaves took place in 1385. The Gypsies may have been brought to Romania as slaves by the Tartars and remained in the country with this status when the Tartars were driven out. Alternatively, they may have been forced to sell themselves into slavery through debt. They had no rights and could be beaten by their masters. The slaves included both farm workers and craftspeople.

The Gypsy slaves have a place in Romanian literature. Bogdan Hasdeu wrote the play *Razvan si Vidra* (Razvan and Vidra) in which he tells the true story of a slave (**Stefan Razvan**) who was liberated in the sixteenth century and became a local leader in Moldavia. *Istoria unui galban* (The Story of a Gold Coin) was written by Vasile Alecsandri in the nineteenth century. The heroine is Zamfria who is bought by a cruel owner. A Gypsy kills him and saves her but he is executed while Zamfria is gripped by insanity. The ruler of the Wallachia region of Romania, Vlad IV (Dracula), is said to have brought back 11,000–12,000 Gypsies to his capital to be tortured or executed for his entertainment.

In Transylvania slavery was not widespread. In Moldavia it was, however, not to be abolished until 1855 and in Wallachia (Muntenia) one year later. Liberty did not mean equality. A trickle of emigration then became a flood and hundreds, if not thousands, of liberated slaves left Romania for other countries. Many Gypsies of the Vlah clans went as far as Australia and America.

A census in 1930, which counted only sedentary Gypsies, recorded 262,000, but this figure was recognised as too low. In the period between the wars Gypsies began to organise themselves and demand social equality. In 1933 the journal *Glasul Romilor* (The Voice of the Romanies) was started and continued to appear until 1939. It was followed by other newspapers, such as *Neamul Tiganesc* (The Gypsy Nation), and associations were set up in different parts of the country. In 1926 the first local Gypsy organisation was founded in Calbor. In 1933 the Asociatia Generala a Tiganilor din Romania (General Association of Gypsies in Romania) was formed. It soon split into two organisations but later was reunited. **Lazarescu Lazurica**, **Gheorghe Niculescu** and **Popp Serboianu** were amongst the leaders at this time.

In 1934 the General Union arranged an international meeting, the **Bucharest Conference,** although there were few, if any, foreign participants. A number of resolutions were passed on education, employment and civil rights, but little was done to put these into practice.

At the same time, as fascist ideas spread through the country, racist commentators such as Ioan Facaoru put forward a policy of preventing contact between the Gypsy and the Romanian peoples to avoid contaminating Romanian blood. This meant in theory that the nomadic clans who did not intermarry should be allowed to continue their traditional life.

Romania allied itself with Germany during the Second World War. It began a policy of deporting Gypsies to land in the east captured from the Soviet Union. During 1942 the government removed 25,000 Romanies to this land, known as **Transdniestria**, where some 19,000 died.

When the Communists came to power after the Second World War the lot of the Gypsies changed again. The nomads were forced to settle down and abandon the nomadic life. The sedentary Gypsies found themselves placed in high-rise flats in the mini-towns created later by Communist leader Nicolae Ceausescu's policy of destroying villages and resettling the population. At an official level the Romanies did not exist during this period. There were no books about them and in contrast to, say Bulgaria, Romani musicians were not advertised as such even for the tourist trade. Only one scholar, Olga Nagy, was able to publish work on Romany culture. For an idea of the treasures that were being lost through neglect, consider the fact that she alone produced eight volumes of tales and folk tales, all gleaned from Romanies.

During the Communist period, Gypsies were given jobs on state farms and in state factories. Prejudice against Gypsies continued, however. It was alleged that often police would raid their houses and steal their gold jewellery, claiming that it was the result of black market dealing. Visits from Romani leaders from the West were not made easy by the law that imposed a heavy fine on anyone allowing a non-member of the household to stay in their accommodation after darkness. Leaving Romania was also difficult and costly. Only two Romanian Gypsies were able to attend the third **World Romani Congress**. **Pentecostal** missionaries worked underground and in 1979 St John's gospel was translated into Romani and printed in Holland by Open Doors for smuggling into Romania. During this period, **Ioan Cioaba** was an intermediary between his people and the government. The census of 1979 counted 225,000 (less than had been recorded in 1930) because many Gypsies registered themselves as Romanian or Hungarian.

The fall of Communism in 1989 brought both good and bad results for the Gypsies. In the first place, they were free again to form associations and publish magazines. On the other hand, the new governments and many Romanians often blamed the Gypsies for the economic difficulties that the change to a free market brought. There were to be many pogroms in the following years. The worst attack was in Bucharest in 1990 when the then Prime Minister Petre Roman brought in miners to help him to retain power. After beating up opposition students and others in the centre of Bucharest, the miners, together with secret police, then attacked the Gypsy quarter causing much damage and injuries. In March 1993 a report in a Bucharest newspaper concerned the Ion Antonescu Command, a vigilante organisation with a national network and considerable financial capital whose proclaimed aim was to "kill Gypsies who commit crimes against society". A representative of the Command stated that its members were not concerned about European public opinion and that the Gypsies were not a minority but a "curse on the Romanian nation". Romanies have formed paramilitary self-defence groups in response to the authorities' failure to protect them.

Since 1990, some fifty villages in Romania have experienced ethnic conflict where Romanians and/or Hungarians have come together to burn Gypsies out of their homes. More than 300 houses belonging to Romanies have been burned down and ten persons killed by mobs. No one has yet been convicted of arson or murder. In January 1995 houses were set on fire in Bacu and Botosani. In the same year there were heavy-handed police raids in Akos Bontida, Sectorul Agricol Ilfov and Tandarei. In the town of Curtea de Arges twenty-one houses were burned down in June 1996. The majority of those who lost their homes have been unable to return to them. Many now live in very poor circumstances as 'illegal residents' in other towns.

There are many examples of Roma being forced to leave their places of residence. In May 2002, city hall representatives pulled down the tents of twenty families who had been living in the Vacaresti Lake area of Bucharest, after the families failed to obey a notice to leave. In July of the same year, Roma were forcibly removed from public land in Sector 6 of the city of Bucharest and made to return to their counties of origin. In 2003,the same thing happened to Roma living on the outskirts of Bucharest's Militari district.

In August 1997 Cioc Liviu was beaten by four police officers and a civilian then taken in a car and left in a forest in a critical condition, only because he had been confused with another person who had robbed the civilian. The Rom required twenty-four days of hospital treatment as a result of this incident but his complaint to the Mures Military Prosecutor's Office was not even considered. In 1999 after two years' investigation, the Office finally ruled that the police officers had only made a mistake by allowing the civilian to beat Cioc Liviu and the police involved were absolved of any criminal responsibility.

Also in 1997 four persons were finally arrested for trial in connection with events in 1993 in Hadareni where three Romani men were killed. These are the first arrests of anyone for this series of attacks. The four who were convicted were released in 2000, after serving their sentences, and the victims appealed to the **European Court of Justice** arguing that the sentences were too light. The attacks in Hadareni had led to a second exodus; Romanian Gypsies can be found in Poland as well as many Western countries where they are usually tolerated for a short time and then sent back to their birthplace.

Instances of police brutality towards Roma continue in the twenty-first century with numerous reports of police torture and mistreatment which fail to result in due punishment of the officers concerned. In 2002 the Supreme Court acquitted a police officer indicted in 1999 for illegal use of a weapon in the 1996 killing of Mircea Muresul Mosor, a Rom from Cemani who was shot in the back while in police custody. Another court ruling held that a police officer was justified in his use of lethal force against Radu Marian, an unarmed Rom, killed during a police raid. In June 2002 eighteen year old Nelu Balasoiu died in detention in Jilava prison near Bucharest. Witnesses claimed he was beaten every day by the police during his three months in prison. The prosecutor's office decided not to begin a criminal investigation of the police officers involved in the case, ruling that according to medical investigation, Balsoiu died because of health reasons and not as the result of the officers' behaviour. His family maintain that he was healthy before he entered prison and allege that his death resulted from his detention. In December 2002 fifty-two policemen and gendarmes from the County of Bacau and Nemt who were involved in a search for several wanted criminals, ended up shooting dead a Romani father and son, and wounding three others, including a fourteen-year-old Romani boy. In April 2003 Leonard Drugu and Aurel Gandac were shot by police officers in civilian clothing in a street in Iasi in north-eastern Romania.

In June 2003 Mihai Dumitru was also the victim of a police officer in civilian clothes who was involved in a raid in Tulcea. Dumitru suffered a severe beating and was subsequently hospitalised. Although the Ministry of Administration and Interior acknowledged the officer's guilt, his punishment had not been determined by the year's end and although the case had been referred to court for criminal prosecution, it had

still not been decided. Other cases under investigation at the end of 2003 included that of a married Roma couple in Simleul Silvaniei, Salaj County, who were beaten after the wife refused to sign a report concerning a fine and the husband went to the police to ask about her. Another incident was in April 2003 when a drunken police officer in Parancea, Buzau County, beat Lucia Lacatusu, a nineteen-year-old Rom, and a third incident from June of the same year when police allegedly beat four Roma from one family.

Roma children have also been subjected to police brutality. In February 2002 fourteen-year-old Calin Sterica was beaten in a Galati schoolyard by gendarmes using fists and clubs. They were there to investigate a disturbance in which she was not involved. Calin's mother, who arrived to see what was happening, was fined four million lei (120 dollars) for "disturbance of the public order." The Roma County Bureau subsequently discouraged the mother from filing a complaint. The *Police Organisation Law*, which took effect in May 2002, allows the use of firearms against persons fleeing arrest, contrary to the widely accepted principle in other countries that such measures may be used only against individuals who represent and imminent threat of death, or of grievous injury to others.

On a more positive note, an emergency ordinance passed in January 2002 prohibited discrimination based on a number of factors, including ethnicity, and established the ability to sue on the grounds of discrimination. The National Council on Combating Discrimination, the agency enforcing the ordinance, fined two private companies for denying access to Roma.

At the end of November 2003, the ruling PSD signed an agreement of cooperation with the Roma Party. It called for the continued monitoring of the Roma situation, the hiring of Roma to work in state institutions, and programmes to educate the public about racism and discrimination. A partnership protocol that sets out co-operative measures to ensure that Roma have access to health care continued during the year.

In June 2003 the Department for Interethnic Relations and the National Office for Roma were placed under the General Secretariat of the Government. While the government reported that 60 per cent of the goals of the 2001 National Strategy for the Improvement of the Situation of Roma were achieved. Under this National Strategy some 400 Roma experts and councillors were appointed in ministries, prefects' offices and some mayoral offices. Ministerial Committees for Roma were subordinated to a joint committee to monitor the implementation of the strategy, and joint working groups at the local level have been set up. Roma NGOs asserted that, with the exception of the establishment of bodies to implement the strategy, there were few practical achievements.

The situation today is that, while in some parts of Romania Gypsies live in fear of attack by their neighbours and police, elsewhere the community has been able to develop associations and magazines. The Bible is being translated and published legally and the Romani language is taught in several schools and colleges. There was a move to replace the pejorative term *Tigan* by the word 'Rom' but in 1995 the government changed it back officially to *Tigan* on the grounds that there was confusion with the word *Roman* (a Romanian). Some schools continue to segregate children but the situation is being addressed. Romani organisations currently operating include the Ethnic Federation of Roma, the Young Generation of Roma, the United Association of Roma, **Aven Amentza** Foundation and **Rromani CRISS**. There is a national body linking Gypsy associations, and one Gypsy is in the Upper House of Parliament. In 2003 there were two Romani Members of the Lower House (Chamber of Deputies). The former Romani minority representative joined the PSD and sat in the Chamber, while the Constitution and electoral legislation allowed an extra seat for the Roma.

After being discouraged under Ceausescu, Romani musicians are active. Apart from **Taraf de Haiduks**, Taraf din Baiai and Mahala Rai Banda are popular groups.

ROMANO CENTRO. Vienna. Est. 1991. President: Dragan Jevremovic. A cultural and welfare centre which publishes a regular magazine.

ROMANO CHAVO. (Romani youth). A term used by some groups in Eastern Europe as a self-denomination.

ROMANO DIVES. See RROMANO DIVES.

ROMANO DROM. Hungarian group, some of whose members were previously in the band Ando Drom. They play **Vlah** music in a popular style. Antal Kovacs is their leader. CD: *Ande Lindri* (In a Dream).

ROMANO DROM SCHOOLS. The Romano Drom (Romani Way) schools were established in England and Wales by the **Gypsy Council** around 1970 to provide education in caravans for nomadic Gypsies.

ROMANO-KALO. A development of **Caló** in Spain. Its aim is to reintroduce the lost grammar of Romani with the preserved vocabulary of Caló. The magazine *Nevipens Romani* (Romani News) sometimes publishes in this form of speech. **Juan de Dios Ramírez Heredia** is one of the leading proponents of this programme.
See CALO (i).

ROMANO ROM. A **clan** of **Vlah** Gypsies in Hungary.

ROMANO THEM. A literary competition organised annually by the magazine of the same name.

ROMANO VODI. This magazine, financially supported by the Czech Republic Ministry of Culture and based in Prague, was first published in February 2003.

ROMANOV, Manush. See MUSTAFA ALIEV.

ROMANY. An older spelling of Romani.

ROMANY GYPSY COUNCIL. UK. Chairwoman: Mrs Bendell-Smith.

Local organisation in south-west England which supports and advises Gypsies and **Travellers** in the fields of accommodation and welfare.

ROMANY INSTITUTE. UK. Est. 1968. Set up in Britain after the first **World Romany Congress** with the support of **Slobodan Berberski**. It carried on the work of the Cultural Commission of the Congress until the third Congress.

ROMANY AND TRAVELLER FAMILY HISTORY SOCIETY. UK. Co-ordinator: Janet Keet-Black. A non-profit making self-help group for those interested in research on Gypsy and **Traveller** family history, particularly in the UK. The Society has published a number of booklets.

ROMANY CHAL (Romani tribe). The name of a **clan** and sometimes used as self-ascription by Gypsies in England and Scandinavia. In France – in the form *romanichel* – it has become a pejorative term.

ROMANY GUILD. UK. Est. 1972. Founded in 1972 by Gypsies, this group was led by the late **Tom Lee**, who felt the non-Gypsy members of the **Gypsy Council** were too influential. Later it reunited for a short time with the **Gypsy Council** under the name **National Gypsy Council.** After the death of Tom Lee its activities waned but members of the Lee family are re-establishing it as a cultural non-political organisation.

ROMANY TOWER. UK. Est. 2003. An organisation in London, founded in 2003, running English language, drama and dance classes, mainly for Polish Romanies.

ROMATHAN. Slovakia. Est. 1992. A theatre in **Košice** using the Romani language.

ROMEN THEATRE, MOSCOW. See TEATR ROMEN.

ROMERÍA. The name given to Gypsy festivals in Spain.

ROMINTERPRESS. Yugoslavia. Est.1995 Initiator: **Dragoljub Acković**. RomInterpress is a cultural organisation in Yugoslavia with the main aim of publishing films, books and periodicals. It intends to co-ordinate the activities of the Gypsy élite in Yugoslavia, and other plans include establishing a Gypsy news agency and arranging cultural events, including film shows, of Romany interest.

ROMNET. A news group on the Internet.

ROMNEWS. A fax and e-mail news service from the **Romani National Congress** in Hamburg.

R.O.S. KUPATE. See KUPATE

ROSE, Romani. Germany. Contemporary civil rights activist. A **Sinto**, he is Secretary of the **Verband der Deutschen Sinti**. He has written extensively on Gypsy rights, in particular those of the Sinti as a long-standing minority living in Germany.

ROSTÁS-FARKAS, György. Hungary. Contemporary writer and political activist. He is president of the cultural association Cigány Tudományos és Müvészeti Társaság (Gypsy Scientific and Art Society) and organiser of the international Gypsy conferences held in Budapest since 1993.

ROTARU, Ionel, See VAIDA VOEVOD III.

ROTWELSCH. A variety of German and the speech of the **Jenisch**, non-Romani nomads in Germany. It was used before the arrival of the Gypsies but has since borrowed words from Romani.

ROUDA, Vanko. Algeria. Contemporary civil rights activist. He worked for Romani rights in post-1945 Europe together with his brother Leulea. In the early 1950s, whilst living in North Africa, he read a newspaper report of a speech by **Vaida Voevod III**. He then worked with Vaida in the **Communauté Mondiale Gitane** in Paris and later set up the **Comité International Tzigane**.

For names beginning with RRomani or RRomano, see also entries for Romani and Romano.

RROM. In the standard alphabet adopted by the fourth **World Romani Congress**, Rom is spelt Rrom. There are two r sounds in most Romani dialects. The one that is retroflex or guttural (depending on the dialect) is written rr in the standard alphabet and the trilled r is written with a single r.

RROMANI BAXT. (Romany good fortune). Poland. Est. 1991. Chairperson: **Marcel Cortiade**. An international organisation developing educational and cultural projects in Albania and elsewhere.

RROMANI CEXRAIN. (Romani star). Spain. A contemporary cultural and social action organisation.

RROMANI CRISS. Romania. Est. 1993. Director: **Nicolae Gheorghe**. The Rroma Centre for Social Intervention and Studies is based in Bucharest. The centre is currently engaged in human rights activities including local social action, mainly in Romania, the documentation of violence and training for mediators.

RROMANO DIVES (Gypsy Day). Albania. Band, founded in 1991, which has toured to other countries. The lead female singer is Astrit Qerimi (Titi). CD: *Chaj Zibede*.

RUDJEVICS, Karlis (RUDEVITCH, Karlo). Latvia. Contemporary writer.

RUMANIA. See ROMANIA.

RUSSIA. The 2002 Census for the Russian Republic recorded 183,000 Gypsies which may be closer to the real figure than earlier estimates of 400,000. There are two main dialects of Romani spoken in Russia: North Russian Romani, the dialect which was to be used in the education programme of the 1930s in the Soviet Union and South Russian Romani. A contemporary poet writing under the name Sandor uses this latter dialect. In the area around St Petersburg, a third dialect, Livonska, is spoken. Toward the end of the nineteenth century there was an influx of **Vlah** Romanies whose dialect was much influenced by Romanian. The overwhelming majority of Roma in Russia are Orthodox and a small group of Crimean Roma are Muslims.

The first record of Gypsies in Russia dates from around 1500. They entered from Wallachia but are distinct from the later arrivals of Vlah Gypsies. On the whole there was less persecution under the tzars compared with Western Europe. In 1759 a law promulgated by Empress Elizabeth prohibited Gypsies from entering St Petersburg. The prohibition was not repealed until 1917 although musicians were exempted in practice and played in many cafés and restaurants. Passports were imposed in an attempt to stop nomadism in 1775. In 1783 Gypsies were encouraged to 'settle.' In 1800 Tzar Nicolas I exempted sedentary Romani farmers from military service though this decision was rescinded in 1856. In 1809 and 1839 the obligation to settle was re-enacted.

Many musicians were adopted by nobles and made a good living as Gypsy music and songs were much appreciated. Count Orlov set up one of many Gypsy choirs formed from families living and working on the large estates, at the beginning of the nineteenth century, and the Tolstoy family, among others, patronised these choirs. Lev Tolstoy's brother and son (Sergei) both married Gypsies. Aleksei N. Aputkin wrote *The Old Gypsies* in 1870 to commemorate the growing love between Sergei Tolstoy and Maria Shishkin. In 1919 when the tzarist government collapsed, some Gypsy singers accompanied their patrons to the west. One of these was V. Dimitrova. (A record of hers was pessimistically, though not realistically, entitled *La dernière des voix tsiganes*.)

After the Revolution of 1917 and the subsequent civil war, Russia became part of the Union of Soviet Socialist Republics until 1991.

Following the political changes in 1991 and the break-up of the USSR, the situation slowly became worse for Gypsies in Russia as the curbs on open expression of racial hatred disappeared. Under Gorbachev, right-wing and nationalist groups were still kept under control, but after the succession of Boris Yeltsin, the hatred toward minorities came into the open, most potently in the shape of Vladimir Zhirinovsky, leader of the so-called Liberal Democratic Party.

Anti-Gypsy pogroms have been reported from Nyevil, Ostrov, Safornovo, Yeroslavni, in the Urals and near Moscow. Gradually, the situation improved and in 1999 the Russian government granted the Romani Association (Romano Kher) full cultural autonomy. The president of the Association is Professor George Demeter. There are currently sixteen branches of this Romani cultural association in different regions and cities of Russia, headed by Alexander Bariyev. There is also an influential Romani council of elders once headed by the Romani General Yan Rechetnikov. It deals with disputes between Roma and the authorities and operates throughout the CIS countries and Baltic states. Moscow runs annual international festivals of Romani music and dancing headed by Y. Mauer and Georgi Tsvetkov, as well as numerous local competitions, concerts, festivals and fairs. Russia is part of the **Union of Roma of the CIS countries and Baltic states** which was set up in Smolensk in 2002.

Some cultural activity has taken place in Russia since the political changes. For example, a dictionary of the **Kalderash** dialect has been published.

See also UNION OF SOVIET SOCIALIST REPUBLICS for the period 1917–91.

S

SA E ROMA. Organisation in Tuzla, Bosnia. Not to be confused with Sa Roma, a body in the US.

SAARTO, Tuula. Finland. Contemporary writer. She has written a biography of her father–in-law, Kalle Hagert, a well-known figure in Gypsy circles, and a book for young people *Suljetut Ovet* (Closed Doors) which aims to dispel the prejudice against Gypsies.

SAINTES MARIES DE LA MER. A town in France where a pilgrimage of Gypsies occurs in May every year. The two saints of the town's name are Mary Magdalen and Mary the mother of Jesus who, according to legend, arrived by boat at the town after fleeing from Palestine after the crucifixion. They were accompanied by their Gypsy maid, Sarah, whose statue is in the church.

SAMPSON, John 1862–1931. England. Librarian and scholar. He worked at Liverpool University from 1892 until 1928. With the help of **Dora Yates** he compiled the comprehensive study *The Dialect of the Gypsies of Wales* (1926), the result of his collaboration with the **Wood clan**. In 1894 he had met Edward Wood, a harpist who spoke Romani fluently, and he extended his research during a stay at Abergynolwyn. Together with Dora Yates he recorded folk tales and songs of the language and spent many hours with the descendants of **Abraham Wood**, specifically in the company of the violinist Matthew Wood. He translated some fifty verses of the Rubaiyat of Omar Khayyam (who may have been a Romani tentmaker) into Welsh Romani, with the aid of D. Macalister. Many of his articles were published in the *Journal of the Gypsy Lore Society*.

SANDFORD, Jeremy 1934–2003. England. Writer and amateur musician. He became well known for his play *Cathy Come Home* dealing with the issue of the homeless. He had many friends among the Gypsy and **New Traveller** communities and was for some time editor of the periodical *Romano Drom*. His books include *The Gypsies,* reissued as *Rokkering to the Gorgios* (2002), *Songs of the Road* and in addition the video *Spirit of the Gypsies.*

SAPERA. See KALBELIA.

SARAJEVO. Bosnia. In the years leading up

to the Second World War there were a
few Muslim Gypsies living on the outskirts of the town, some assimilated
Muslim Gypsies living among non-
Gypsies in the town itself, a **clan** of non-
Romani-speaking Christian Gypsies and
some **Vlah** peripatetics nomadising in
the region. The situation was probably
similar at the outbreak of the recent war
in Bosnia. A small number still remain in
the town.

See also BOSNIA-HERZEGOVINA.

SARAJEVO CONFERENCE. 1986. A scientific conference of Gypsy and non-Gypsy
experts was held in what was then the
peaceful town of Sarajevo. Speakers
included the veteran scholar **Rade Uhlik**,
who was living nearby. The conference
was particularly remarkable in that
Romani was used as a major language,
either as the language of papers or for
translation. The papers of the conference were edited by Milan Šipka and
have been published.

SARAJEVO PEACE CONFERENCES. The
International Romani Union decided in
1994 to sponsor a conference for peace
in the Balkans. At the time it was
thought that this conference could be
held in **Sarajevo**. In the end, however, it
was decided to hold it in May 1995 in
Budapest. The programme covered
issues pertaining to the Romanies and to
international relations in general.
Because of the success of this conference, a second one was held in 1996.
Again it was felt premature to hold the
conference in Sarajevo and so instead it
was held in the town of Vittoria in the
Basque country.

SARAY, Jozsi. Hungary. A nineteenth century Gypsy boy adopted by the composer
Franz Liszt. Liszt talks of him in his
book *Des Bohémiens et de Leur Musique
en Hongrie* (1859).

SARDINIA. The first record of Gypsies
stems from the records of the Sardinian
Parliament in the middle of the sixteenth century (1553–4) discussing the
problem they are causing.

SARI, Anneli. Finland. Contemporary

singer. She is the sister of Feija and
Taisto from the band **Hortto Kaalo**. Her
repertoire is mainly light music by
Finnish composers. She has performed
in France and was one of the stars at the
concert that took place in Geneva
during the third **World Romani
Congress**.

SASTIPEN NETWORK. Spain. European
network for drug abuse and HIV/AIDS
prevention in the Rom community.

SATKIEVICH, Nikolai 1917–91. USSR. Poet
and civil rights activist. He was enthusi-
astic about education and went to great
lengths to get Siberian Roma children to
attend school, including using the
police.

SATTLER, Jaja d. 1944. Germany. Missionary. While his family was living in a caravan in Berlin, he was sent by
missionaries to study at a convent in
Marburg. After this he took up missionary activities himself. Jaja Sattler translated *St John's Gospel* and some of the
Psalms into the **Lovari** dialect of
Romani. In 1944, he was deported to the
concentration camp at **Auschwitz**,
where he was killed.

SAVCHEV, Slavcho. Bulgaria. Contemporary
journalist. He is the editor of *Andral*
(Outwards), a literary periodical in
Romani (Sliven dialect) and Bulgarian.

SCHNUCKENACH, Reinhardt 1921–. Ger-
many. Musician. His musical studies at
Mainz Conservatoire were stopped
when the Nazis deported him to Poland.
With Reinhardt Daweli, he formed the
Schnuckenach-Reinhardt Quintet,
which plays Gypsy jazz in the style of
Django Reinhardt.

SCOTLAND. Estimated population of
Romanies, **Scottish Travellers** and **Irish
Travellers**: 4,000. On the basis of the
2003 census, it appears that some 560
families live all the year round in caravans. In 1491 there is a record of
'Spaniards' dancing before the Scottish
king on the pavement at Edinburgh,
although these may not have been
Romanies. In 1505 a small party of Gypsies arrived – probably also from Spain –

saying they were pilgrims and being given money by James IV. They were then sent to Denmark with a letter of recommendation. A second group of dancers from Spain in 1529 undoubtedly were Romanies. This group danced for King James V. There is a record in 1540 of the King granting the Gypsies their right to their own laws and customs under John **Faa**, Duke of **Little Egypt**, in 1540. A year later this decree was repealed and all Gypsies were ordered to leave Scotland, allegedly because James V – who had the custom of travelling in disguise around the country – had been in a fight with three Gypsies. He died in the following year and so this law was not carried out. In 1553 John Faa was again confirmed as officially in charge of the Scottish Gypsies.

In 1573, however, a law was passed that Gypsies should either leave the country or settle down in paid work. If not, they would be imprisoned, publicly scourged and removed from the realm. A year later the law was strengthened. Gypsies were to be scourged and branded. Those who remained and did not settle down would be executed. In 1597 forced labour or banishment for life were added as punishments. The seventeenth century brought in heavy pressures against Gypsies and anyone who aided them. In 1608 two Scots, David Gray and Alexander Aberdere, were fined for selling food and drink to Gypsies. Noblemen who protected Gypsies on their estates were fined. In 1611 three Gypsies were brought to trial and hanged. In 1624 eight more Gypsy men were hanged at Burgh Muir. Further executions took place then banishment became a regular treatment for Gypsies. In 1665 a Scottish company received permission to send Gypsies to Jamaica and Barbados.

In 1707 the Scottish Parliament was dissolved and all future legislation was made in Westminster (see ENGLAND) until devolution late in the twentieth century. After 1707 the existing Acts

against Gypsies of England (1530, 1554 and 1562) were applied in Scotland. In 1714 two female Gypsies were executed under the provisions of an English Act from 1554 and ten Gypsies were deported in 1715 from Scotland to Virginia in accordance with the English 1598 *Act for the Punishment of Rogues, Vagabonds and Sturdy Beggars*. The heavy pressure on Romanies in Scotland led to their virtual disappearance until the twentieth century. They either moved to England or hid themselves among bands of native Scottish Travellers to escape arrest and punishment.

The *Trespass (Scotland) Act* of 1865 was introduced to control the indigenous Scottish Travellers and has been used up to the present day to move Travellers and Gypsies on from stopping places. The British ***Caravan Sites Act 1968*** did not apply to Scotland, although the 1994 *Criminal Justice and Public Order Act* – which further criminalises trespass – does. An **Advisory Committee on Scotland's Travelling People** was set up in 1971 and has produced several reports. Scottish local authorities have been encouraged to build caravan sites for the Scottish Travellers and the small numbers of Irish Travellers and Romanies from England who visit the country. A target of 941 pitches was set of which 742 had been provided by 1996. Authorities with insufficient pitches are asked to apply a toleration policy to illegally parked caravans. The scheme by which the government gives grants was due to end in 1998 but was continued by the autonomous Scottish Parliament.

In 2001 the Scottish Parliament's Equal Opportunities Committee made a number of recommendations concerning Travellers but these have not been put into practice.

The Scottish Travellers were, however, given the status of a 'racial group.' See also SCOTTISH TRAVELLERS.
SCOTTISH GYPSY/TRAVELLER ASSOCIATION. Scotland. Est. 1993. Set up to

unite Gypsies and Scottish Travellers to campaign for their rights. It has organised two conferences and published a magazine.

SCOTTISH TRAVELLERS. For the population figures, see SCOTLAND. It is likely that there were travelling nomads in Scotland before the arrival of the Romanies. Therefore, we cannot be sure whether records in the Middle Ages refer to indigenous Scottish Travellers or Romanies. Over the centuries the two groups have mingled and intermarried and the present-day population of Scottish Travellers is of mixed descent. They call themselves **Nawkins**. The Scottish Travellers have a rich tradition of singing and have preserved many ballads. Singers include **the Stewart** family, while contemporary folk storytellers include Jimmy McBeath and Duncan Williamson. Most Travellers speak a variety of English known as **cant**, with an 'exotic' vocabulary of words from a number of sources. In the north-east of Scotland the cant is based on a Gaelic framework.

SCOTTISH TRAVELLERS' ACTION GROUP (STAG). Scotland.
  A civil rights group operating around 1970 and cooperating with the **Gypsy Council** in England.

SCOTTISH TRAVELLERS' COUNCIL. Scotland. Active around 1985. Founder: Belle Stewart. A civil rights group initiated by the singers **Belle Stewart** and **Sheila MacGregor**.

SČUKA, Emil. Czechoslovakia. Contemporary political and cultural activist. He was elected secretary of the **International Romani Union** at the fourth **World Romani Congress**, and President at the fifth Congress. He is also president of the **Rajko Djurić Foundation**.

SEFEROV, Suli (Samuil) 1943–. Bulgaria. Artist. He is a painter who was brought up in a district of Sofia inhabited by many Gypsies and who painted Romanies among other subjects. He has exhibited in many countries.

SEJDIČ, Rasim (1943–80). Yugoslavia. Poet.

He was also a collector of folk tales from Yugoslavia. His poem *Gazisarde Romengi Violina* (They smashed the Romanies' violin) commemorates the concentration camp at **Jasenovac**.

SEPEDJI. Basket-maker (Turkish). The Basket-makers of the Shumen area in Bulgaria and those of Turkey and Greece speak different dialects of Romani and are not related.

SERBEZOVSKI, Muharem 1950–. Macedonia. Musician. He was one of the first Roma musicians to be a commercial success in Yugoslavia in the 1970s. As a professional vocalist, he sung in Macedonian, Serbian and Romani. As well as being a musician, he is also known for writing short stories and poems and in 1983 he published his first book *Shareni Dijamanti* in Serbo-Croatian.

SERBIA. Estimated population (including Voivodina but excluding Kosovo and Montenegro): 600,000. It is likely that the first Gypsies to reach Serbia were shoemakers who lived in Prizren some time around 1348. Under the **Ottoman Empire** (from 1459) the Gypsies were classed as one of the many ethnic groups in the country. No overall census figures are available for the Gypsy population at that time. The Viennese Gypsiologist Franz Miklosich reported that there were some 25,000 Gypsies in Serbia in the 1860s. At one time the Turkish rulers of the country attempted to ban nomadism but they were not successful. Many **Vlah** Gypsies came after the emancipation of the slaves in Romania, joining earlier immigrants from across the Danube who had by the end of the eighteenth century already become sedentary.

From 1878 Serbia was independent. In 1879 and 1884 the new state passed laws to prohibit Gypsies from nomadising and in 1891 there was an order that Gypsies who were not settled and without an occupation should be reported to the authorities. Foreign Gypsies were to be expelled. The censuses at the end of the nineteenth century showed around

50,000 Gypsies in Serbia. About half claimed Romani as the mother tongue and 25 per cent were Muslim.

In 1918 Serbia became part of Yugoslavia, until 1941 when it came under military rule by the German army. Soon after the German conquest of Yugoslavia regulations forbade Gypsies in Serbia to use public transport or cafés. They had to wear an armband with the sign Z on it. At first the Germans took Gypsy men to act as hostages and then shot them in reprisal for the deaths of German soldiers at the hands of partisans. The women and children were placed in a concentration camp at Zemun (Semlin). Many were killed in gassing vans. Harald Turner, head of the German military administration, reported to Berlin that the "Gypsy problem had been solved" as he wanted to concentrate on the fight against the partisans. However, large numbers were still living outside Belgrade. The German occupying forces began to round up Gypsies in Niš in eastern Serbia and imprison them at a concentration camp at Crveni Krst. Again, many were shot in reprisals for attacks on German soldiers. During the German occupation of Serbia, some 30,000 Gypsies were killed.

In 1944 Yugoslavia was re-established as a republic. The 1971 census recorded 49,894 Romanies for Serbia (including Voivodina and Kosovo) and 396 for Montenegro, an unbelievably low figure, even allowing for the losses during the Nazi period.

In 1991–2 Yugoslavia was split again. Only Serbia (including Voivodina and Kosovo) and Montenegro remained in the Yugoslav Republic. After 1993 the Serbian government made some efforts to get its Gypsy population to support the government. Government officials attended an official church service in Romani and subsidies were given to newspapers. The poet **Trifun Dimić** was able to publish the New Testament in Romani as well as a first reader for schools. One cloud in the picture was

the harassment of **Rajko Djurić** who was forced to flee the country because of his opposition to Serbia's support for the Bosnian Serbs.

The 1991 census gave a figure of 70,126 Roma in Serbia (excluding Kosovo and Voivodina). The figures were rising steadily which reflected not merely the high birth rate of the population but also increasing self-confidence and willingness to be recognised as Roma at the start of the 1990s. However, there still remains some way to go before the recorded population reaches the estimated real figure of 600,000. Roma in Yugoslavia can be classified by religion (Orthodox, Catholic or Muslim) or language (Arlia, the speech of the long-settled urban populations, or a range of dialects used by previously nomadic groups, such as the Gurbet). This applies equally to Serbia-Montenegro.

Before the break up of the federal state the Roma in Serbia had made attempts to get their status raised to that of a national minority, a desire that was voiced at academic conferences in Belgrade in 1976 as well as Novi Sad (Voivodina) in 1990 and 1997. In the terms of the 1991 Constitution of Serbia, the Roma had the lowest status – the third rank, as an 'ethnic group.'

The Romani Congress Party (RKSD) was founded at a meeting in Belgrade in 1997 on the symbolic date of 8 April (declared as Romani National Day at the First **World Romani Congress)** and soon had a membership of 2,000. One of its aims is for Roma to attain the status of a national minority. Its president, **Dragoljub Acković**, is editor of the magazine *Romano Lil.*

Yet, in spite of more overt Belgrade government support for Roma, police harassment is common and street-traders are a prime target. There have been reports of isolated cases of racist attacks on Roma though Romani leaders have said they hear of such attacks in Belgrade every two or three days. Skinheads are active and in one reported incident in September 1996 they assaulted Roma in Kraljevo. Mostly, the skinheads choose as their targets individual Roma in isolated streets. Graffiti saying 'Death to Roma' have appeared in Kragujevac while houses have been set on fire in some places. Prejudice is widespread and some villages will not allow the Roma to bury their dead in Orthodox cemeteries while there have cases of been discrimination in bars in Raska. In October 1997 the Serbian daily *Nedeljini Telegraf* published an article entitled 'We shall expel the Roma, Negroes, Gays and Junkies and create a Great White Serbia' quoting the words of skinheads from Novi Sad. In April 2001 the Roma cemetery in Niš was brutally violated and the grave belonging to Sait Balić, a prominent Roma activist, was particularly badly damaged. In March 2003 a Romani man and his friend were beaten by police officers at the police station in Vozdovac.

Even before the current economic depression, living conditions for Roma were inadequate and in some parts of Serbia Romani life expectancy for Roma is only 29–33 years. Unemployment is high and such work as the Roma have is usually of low status such as day labourers, herdsmen, skinners, street-sweepers or in cemetery workers. Meat is rarely on the menu in the Romani home and clothing is poor. Child allowances have not always being paid to Roma and Albanians.

The majority of Romani children do not complete primary education and even the cultural association, Matica Romska, accepts that more than 80 per cent of the Romani population is illiterate. One reason is that 30 per cent of Romani children arrive at primary school with no knowledge of Serbian because of the isolation of their communities and there is little pre-school provision by which they could learn the language of the education system. Less than one per cent of Roma have com-

pleted higher education. There is, however, a Romani Cultural Federation, whose members must have at least a college degree. Members of the Federation were active in founding the Romani Congress Party (see above). As elsewhere in Eastern Europe a number of Romani children are placed in special schools, not because of lack of intelligence but after failing tests designed for those living in a different culture.

Organisations having a brief other than culture and political activity are the [Romani] Committee for the Protection of Human Rights in Yugoslavia, founded in 1997 and based in Kragujevac, and the Society for the Improvement of Romani Settlements, established under the leadership of the architect Vladmirt Macura and the sociologist Aleksandrea Mitrovic.

For the periods 1918–41 and 1944–91 see YUGOSLAVIA.

Serbia includes the previously autonomous regions of Voivodina and Kosovo, all three of which of which have separate entries.

SERBIA-MONTENEGRO. See separate entries for SERBIA and MONTENEGRO. Also YUGOSLAVIA

SERBOIANU, Popp. Romania. Priest. He set up a nationwide Gypsy organisation in 1933, the Asociatia Generala a Tiganilor din Romania (General Association of the Gypsies of Romania). One of his committee, **Lazarescu Lazurica**, broke away and set up the rival General Union of the Gypsies of Romania. Serboianu Popp continued to be active in the Oltenia region, together with the poet Marin Simion. In 1933 he also set up a Chimney Sweeps Guild that acted as a front for Gypsy civil rights activities. A conference was planned for the Romanies of Oltenia for late 1934 but before this took place there was a further split, this time between Serboianu Popp and Marin Simion. The former's influence then waned. In 1934 **Lazarescu Lazurica** resigned from the presidency of the General Union and **Gheorghe**

Niculescu, a flower dealer from Bucharest became president. Marin Simion joined the Union and helped to set up their magazine *O Rom*. Lazarescu Lazurica then allied himself once more with Serboianu Popp but Gheorghe Niculescu remained the most powerful Gypsy leader and his association continued work until 1940. The nomadic Gypsies did not take part in either of the two organisations but recognised as their leader the **Kalderash** Bulibasa Gheorghe Mihutescu.

SETTELA. 1935–44. Netherlands. A Gypsy girl whose picture, peering through the door of a cattle wagon, has symbolised in many books the deportations to concentration camps during the Nazi period. Originally thought to be Jewish, she has recently been identified as a Romani. She was taken to **Auschwitz** on 19 May 1944 and gassed two months later. A Dutch TV film has been made about her short life.

SEVILLE CONGRESS. See EUROPEAN CONGRESS.

SHAKESPEARE, William 1564–1616. England. Playwright. By Shakespeare's time Gypsies were well known throughout England and the playwright could make references to them in his plays. He sometimes calls them **Egyptians** and sometimes Gypsies. In *Othello*, (first performed in 1604) Desdemona talks of a handkerchief that "an Egyptian gave to my mother." It has been suggested that the name of the character Caliban in *The Tempest* comes from a Romani word (Kaliben) meaning 'blackness'.

SHELTA. (i) The name used by scholars for **Irish Travellers' Cant**.
(ii) A secret vocabulary from the Middle Ages formed by changing the first consonant of a word. An example is the word *feen* (man) from Irish *duine*. According to some scholars, it is one of the sources of vocabulary for Travellers' Cant. The name Shelta itself is probably formed from the Irish word *béarla*, which originally meant 'language.'

SHERO ROM, SZERO ROM. Romani chief.

The leader of the Lowland Gypsies in Poland. In 1890 Baso was elected to this office. He founded a hereditary dynasty that continued at least until 1976. During 1946 his grandson, Felus, was deposed for breaking the **Mageripen** Code and was purified in 1950 to take up leadership again, until 1975 when he was succeeded by his second cousin.

SHUTO (ŠUTO) ORIZARI (popularly called Shutka). Shutka is a satellite town outside **Skopje** in Macedonia. It grew rapidly after the Skopje earthquake of 1963 when large numbers of Gypsies from the town were resettled there in houses donated by foreign governments. Numbers increased further as the result of a decision by Gypsies themselves to leave the old Gypsy quarter of Topana and move into the new town. By the mid-1970s Shuto Orizari had its own district council, offices, a cinema and a football ground. Some 5,000 more houses were subsequently built, assisted by the granting of free building land and flexible town planning regulations, and it became the only place in Europe where Gypsies were not a minority. The estimated population in 1977 was 40,000 and is now perhaps double this. The inhabitants are 90 per cent Romani. However, facilities in Shutka are poor. There is one ambulance and specialist medical care is lacking while the standard of education in the two primary schools is low.

SICILY. The earliest positive reference to Gypsies on the island dates from 1485 and refers to a horse dealer named Michele Petta. The first Gypsies had probably arrived some years earlier and from the Balkans by sea rather than from the mainland of Italy. In 1521 Duke Giovanni came with a group of followers and a safe conduct from Charles V. This party had previously been in Spain and passed down through Italy. For some time the nomadic Gypsies enjoyed a limited form of self-government under their leaders. During the Mussolini period, some Gypsy families from Italy were deported to Sicily. The island also has a population of non-Romani **Travellers** known as **Camminanti**.

SIM. A secret vocabulary based on Arabic used by the Helebi Gypsies of Egypt.

SIMFEROPOL. A town in the Ukraine where Gypsies settled from 1874. During the 1930s there was a strong cultural life with a Gypsy Club – Ugolka Demirdji (Ironworkers Circle) – and a football team. However, the Romani population of some 800 were all massacred by the German occupiers in December 1941.

SINTO (singular), Sinti/Sinte (plural). The term may originate with the Indian province of Sindh or it may be an old Indian word meaning 'community'. It is a **clan** living mainly in Germany but with some families now established in Belgium, Holland, northern Italy, Poland and Russia. It is likely that the Sinti came to German-speaking lands during the sixteenth century and nomadised there until the nineteenth century when some families moved into other countries. The dialect contains a large number of loan words from German. The Sinti suffered large losses during the Nazi period. The German organisation **Verband der Deutschen Sinti und Roma** in Heidelberg (led by **Romani Rose**) is their main civil rights organisation. Sinti organisations also operate in Holland.

The term Sinti is additionally used by the Sinti for some Gypsy clans who are not linguistically Sinti, e.g. the Istriani Sinti from the Trieste region and the **Lalore Sinti** from Bohemia and Moravia.

SINTE UNION. Germany, Freiburg. Under the leadership of Oskar Bierkenfelder it operated independently of the **Verband der Deutschen Sinti und Roma**. The Union took part in the 1981 **World Romani Congress.**

SKOPJE. The capital of the Macedonian Republic with a large Gypsy population. The Folklore Institute in Skopje has set up a Romani section under the direction of Trajko Petrovski. Radio and TV broadcasts are aired in Romani.
See also SHUTO (SUTO) ORIZARI.

SKOU, Mathiassen. Norway. Author. He was of mixed Norwegian and **Traveller** descent and wrote a book about the travelling life, *Paa Fantestien* (On the Gypsy Trail), published in 1893. He then married a **Norwegian Traveller** and returned with her to become a nomad himself.

SLOVAKIA. Slovakia became an independent state in 1993. Estimated Gypsy population: 400,000. According to the 2001 census, Roma number only 90,000 but experts estimate the population to be higher. In 1989 figures held locally gave the number as 253,943 but these excluded many who were not in receipt of any welfare support.

Apart from a group passing through Spis in 1423, the earliest record of Gypsies on the territory of present-day Slovakia is of an execution in Levoca in 1534. They were accused of starting fires in Levoca and other towns. Slovakia was part of the Austro-Hungarian Empire until 1918. **Maria Theresa** tried her assimilationist policy of settling the Gypsies, with some success. By the end of the nineteenth century it was estimated that around 90 per cent of Slovak Romanies were settled. There were also several thousand nomadic **Vlah** Gypsies who had emigrated from Romania. The settled Gypsies in general lived in isolated settlements and pursued a range of trades from blacksmiths and bricklayers to musicians.

In 1918 Slovakia became part of an independent Czechoslovakia. From the 1920s a strong nationalistic movement arose in Slovakia and there was a pogrom in Pobedim in which six Gypsies were killed in 1928. The anti-Semitic Slovenska Narodná Strana (Slovak People's Party) saw Gypsies as "an ulcer which must be cured in a radical way". This party gained 25-40 per cent of the votes in elections in the years after 1918 and paved the way for the establishment of a puppet Slovak state following the German invasion of Czechoslovakia in 1938.

In 1940 the fascist government

imposed compulsory labour on Gypsies and they were forbidden to enter parks, cafés or use public transport. The following year all Gypsies living among Slovaks were ordered to move and build themselves new isolated settlements. From many areas male adults were sent to labour camps. In 1944, after the failure of a popular uprising against the fascist regime, Gypsies were accused – in some cases unjustly – of helping the Resistance movement. Massacres of men, women and children took place in Cierny Balog, Ilija, Kriz nad Hronom, Slatina, Tisovec and elsewhere. Anton Facuna and Tomas Farkas had been active in the partisan movement and were decorated after the war.

In Slovakia more Gypsies survived the war than did in the Czech lands (Bohemia and Moravia) but discrimination continued after 1945. They are still referred to as 'blacks' (*cierny*) by the Slovaks. The Communist National Front government tried to eliminate the shanty towns (with little success) and force the Gypsies into paid employment. There was some voluntary movement in the first years of peace after 1945 to the Czech lands, where they took the place of ethnic Germans who had been expelled. In 1958 the *Act for the Permanent Settlement of Nomadic Persons* prohibited nomadism and ordered local councils to help the integration of the ex-nomads. The Czechoslovak government tried to introduce compulsory resettlement of Gypsies from Slovakia to the Czech lands to eliminate the high concentrations of Romanies in some areas. Sterilisation was also introduced as a means of controlling the Gypsies' population growth. Reports say that sterilisation without the woman's consent was still being carried out in some hospitals as late as 2003.

Romanies are classed as a national minority. As well as their own cultural organisations there are consultative bodies such as the Council for the Affairs of Minorities and specialised advisory bodies concerned with education and other fields. The central control of solutions to 'Romani problems' was abolished by the new state and the responsibility given to local councils. Nevertheless, the national Ministry of Labour, Social Affairs and the Family issued a resolution in April l996 'Citizens in Need of Special Care'. This saw Romanies as a problem and a burden to the state.

Discrimination and prejudice continue. Slogans can be seen on the walls proclaiming 'White Slovakia' or 'Gypsies to the gas chambers.' The Slovak National Party is openly anti-Gypsy. The sometime Prime Minister Vladimir Meciar said that social welfare payments should be cut to stop the Gypsies having so many children and the Minister of Labour accused them of not wanting to work. In 2003 authorities closed with no criminal charges the investigation of Vitazoslav Moric, former deputy of the nationalist political party SNS, who stated at a press conference in August 2000 that the Roma should be rounded up and put on reservations the way Native Americans were. His immunity was lifted and he was due to be prosecuted for incitement to racial hatred. Another controversial former leader of the SNS party, Jan Slota, publicly stated that the government should offer Roma money to undergo sterilisation. He also said in 2000 that what was required to deal with Slovakia's Roma population was "a small courtyard and a whip". In the same year Michael Drobny of the Movement for Democratic Slovakia compared Roma to 'locusts' and said that they "must be isolated because co-existence is impossible."

In this atmosphere it is not surprising that racist attacks, mainly but not always by skinheads, have been reported regularly. In July 1995 Mario Goral was killed by skinheads in Ziar nad Hronom. In the same month masked policemen beat up Gypsies in Jarovnice. In 1996 a group of skinheads armed with chains attacked Romani children from a special school after the children had attended a hockey match. In the same year Jozef Miklos died when villagers burned down his house in Hontianske Nemce. In December 1996 a skinhead murdered Gustav Balaz and wounded his son at Handlova. Twenty skinheads attacked and killed a Romani in Prievidza in 1997. Skinhead violence against Roma continues to be a serious problem in the twenty-first century, and police remain reluctant to take action. The skinhead movement has grown and become more organised; there are an estimated 500–800 skinheads and 3,000–5,000 skinhead sympathisers.

In August 2000 Anastazia Balazova, a Romani mother of eight, died from injuries sustained in a brutal attack on her family in Zilina, north-west Slovakia. Later in the same month, a second Romani family was attacked in Zilina. Six men were arrested. In September of the same year, sixty young Roma left **Košice** for Norway where they intended to ask for asylum because of the continued attacks. The Scandinavian countries had cancelled visa requirements for Slovaks in August. This marked the start of an influx of Slovak Romany asylum seekers to Sweden which was continuing in October of that year. None of the requests were approved.

In August 2001, eighteen-year old Milan Daniel suffered permanent brain damage after a beating by three fascist skinheads, during which his assailants used baseball bats and iron bars. When the police asked them for a motive, they replied that he was a 'Rom'.

In October 2001 six young Romani men were attacked by a group of fifteen skinheads in Prievidza, central Slovakia. One of the Romani men was hospitalised after being struck on the head with a stick. Also in 2001 a group of farmers with baseball bats attacked Gypsies in the village of Klacany, near Hlohovec. Four Gypsies were taken to hospital.

Mario Bango was imprisoned in

2001, awaiting trial after intervening to help his brother Edo who was being attacked by a skinhead. The skinhead was wounded in the fight and died a few weeks later. Despite waiting on the spot after the fight and calling an ambulance, Mario was arrested and taken to prison. Reports in the Slovak press stated that Mario and his brother were thieves who had been stopped by the skinhead who was a "brave citizen." Parliament held one minute's silence for the dead skinhead. The case has been largely ignored except by left-wing groups. A final verdict had not been reached at the time of going to press. However, in December 2002, the regional court of Bratislava did sentence a skinhead to four years in jail in connection with the murder of Ignac Mezei who had been killed in April 2001.

In 2002 three skinheads were prosecuted for causing serious bodily harm with racial motivation and given sentences ranging from four and a half years down to four months for one passive observer of the attack. In 2002 a Roma family fled the country after repeated physical and verbal attacks by skinheads, including a serious assault on the father at Zilina railway station. The family, which had been attacked in their home by skinheads who killed their mother in 2000, continued to be targeted even after the original assailants had been convicted. This family was given asylum abroad.

In 2003 an investigation was closed and no perpetrators were charged for a February 2002 attack by fifteen unknown men on residents in the village of Ganovce during which numerous Roma were injured. The case was taken to the **European Court of Human Rights**. In September 2003 seven masked men reportedly beat several Roma in Zahorske Ves on their property. In December there were reports of another attack on several more victims in which three homes were set on fire.

Although the Constitution prohibits such practices, there are many examples of police beating Roma. They reportedly used threats and pressure to discourage Roma from pressing charges of police brutality. In January 1999 two police officers in the eastern Slovak city of Košice conducted a raid on Roma households at one o'clock in the morning. The officers harassed families in fourteen flats in the apartment block, shouting racial slurs and pointing revolvers at them. The three Berkova sisters, aged between thirteen and fifteen, were made to strip to the waist.

In August 1999 twenty-one-year-old Lubomir Sarissky was shot in the stomach whilst in police custody and subsequently died. In October 1999 during a raid on a Romani community in Zehra, police used excessive force, resulting in the hospitalisation of a Romani boy who was shot with a plastic bullet. In July 2001 the police beat Karol Sedrei in the police station at Revuca in the presence of the mayor who did not intervene. Karol Sedrei died. His two sons were also injured and had to be taken to hospital. The seven officers were charged with inhuman and degrading treatment and were dismissed from the force. Investigation of the case was completed in September 2002; the four defendants remained in detention and their case was returned to the prosecutors for further investigation. The prosecutor appealed the decision to the Supreme Court and the remaining four officers were released from pre-trial detention, while an investigation into the alleged involvement of the mayor of Magnezitovce was reopened after a judgement from the Supreme Court. A complaint filed by the **European Roma Rights Center** in the case of a Rom killed during an interrogation in 1999 remained pending before the **European Court of Human Rights** at the end of 2003. Additionally, police have often been found to be unwilling to investigate thoroughly crimes against Roma. Lawyers too, are often reluctant to represent Roma for fear it will have a negative

effect on their legal practices. In February 2002 a new Police Code of Conduct was introduced. Also in 2002 a special police unit to monitor extremist activities began operating at the Police Praesidium. The most frequent targets of racially motivated crime have been Roma.

Public perception of Roma remains very negative. According to a newspaper survey, 50 per cent of those questioned did not want to have a Romani neighbour. A 2001 study by the Institute for Public Questions and UNDP reported that 71per cent of the majority Slovak population believed that relations with Roma were to some degree conflict-ridden or unpleasant, while only 31.5 per cent of Roma held the same view.

In 2003 the national unemployment rate dropped to less than 15 per cent but approached 30 per cent in some regions. However, it was 95 per cent in Roma settlements in eastern Slovakia.

Roma continue to face discrimination in housing. Although the law requires state administrators to register all citizens, some local officials refused to give registration stamps to Roma citizens which, in turn, prevented them from receiving social benefits and housing. However, in October 2001 the majority of eighty-eight flats built in Prešov with funding from the **European Union** were allocated to Romani families.

In 1989, members of seven Romani families who were permanent residents in the towns of Nagov and Rokytovce in Medzilaborce County, north-east Slovakia, were forced from their homes when their employer, an agricultural co-operative ceased operations. No village in the county would allow these Roma to settle within their territory. In 1993 temporary dwellings built by some of the Roma were torn down, forcing them to flee. Their return to Medzilaborce in 1997 sparked a series of meetings by local political leaders, culminating in the banning of Roma from settlement in two municipalities. The Rokytovce resolution stated that those who settled would "with the help of the village inhabitants, be expelled", and the N'agov municipal council resolved not to allow the Roma citizens to enter the village. The resolutions were revoked in April 1999 but the municipalities did not acknowledge that the resolutions were illegal or provide any form of compensation to the victims. The Slovak government admitted that the resolutions were unlawful but argued that they had never been enforced against anyone. The Roma from these two villages were, however, still living at the time on the bank of a river in the town of Cabiny.

Roma are discriminated against in the healthcare system and have unequal access to public services. The mortality rate for children is three times that of the majority population and the life expectancy for Roma was lower by almost seventeen years. At the end of 2003 the government reduced welfare payments to families with childen, a move which had a disproportionate effect on Roma families.

In December 1998 a Romani named Marian Billy was elected as mayor of the northern Slovakian town of Petrova, which has a 50 per cent Romani population. His election was contested by non-Romani residents of Petrova and the Slovak parliament subsequently annulled the election. In September 1999 a fresh election returned a non-Romani named Jan Borecky as mayor. The Slovak government later stated that the annulment had taken place not as an issue of racism but due to the low educational achievement of Marian Billy, although no provisions exist in national law which would justify annulling a local election result on grounds of educational attainment.

In February 1999 Parliament created a special Parliamentary Advisory Committee for Roma Issues. Many political parties promised to place Roma on their candidate lists, however, only five received positions on a total of three lists and none was elected to parliament. Some ethnic Romani parties were successful at winning representation at local level.

In 2003 the village of Bystrany in the Spisska Nova Ves district has elected a Roma mayor, František Pacan. Nine other Roma were also elected to the local board which for the first time consists entirely of Roma deputies.

The Government's special programme for Roma has a budget of 50 million SKK (one and a half million dollars). In May 2003 the Government approved the creation of a twenty-four-member government advisory council for national minorities and ethnic groups which includes three Roma members. Further, the Government evolved a ten-year strategy for the development of Roma which included elements of positive discrimination or affirmative action.

In 2001 the country ratified the European Charter on the Use of Minority Languages to protect minority rights. The law provides that in municipalities with a minority that constitutes at least 20 per cent of the population, the minority language is an official language. In 2003 Romani was an official language in fifty-three towns. There is little use of Romani in educational establishments.

Many Romani children are born into poor families where the parents are unemployed, and as a result, large numbers of them are abandoned, either at the hospital, immediately after birth, or during infancy. These children become wards of state and are sent to orphanages. Roma make up the majority of the population in state institutions for children.

A high percentage of Romani children do not attend school regularly. Some efforts have been made to establish a pre-school year where the Romani children can improve their knowledge of Slovak or Hungarian (where the local language is Hungarian). In 1992–3, some primary schools in Košice opened bilingual classes in Slovak and Romani. On the whole, however, little attention is paid to the fact that the Romani children come to school not knowing the language of instruction. Low attendance by Roma children at pre-school kindergartens means their knowledge of the Slovak or Hungarian language is minimal by time they enrol at primary school. In 1999 kindergarten attendance among Romani children was only 15 per cent, lower than previously. Parents often do not have the money to cover expenses of kindergarten or extra-curricular activities in schools. Many continue to be placed in special schools or in schools and classes where the majority of the pupils are Roma. Once placed in a special school, their future prospects are very limited as they are not given the possibility of completing the primary education course required for entrance to secondary schools and university. The best they can hope for is to find themselves a place at a training school for blue-collar workers. In 2003 there were only three Romani students enrolled in colleges of further education in eastern Slovakia.

In 2003 the principal of one elementary school in Svinia, eastern Slovakia, stated that if the school placed Romani and non-Romani pupils in the same class during their first year, non-Romani parents would pull their children out of the school. Romani children are segregated at the school: they attend classes in a separate building, and eat their lunches in a separate room on dishes marked to indicate that they are for Romani students only. They are also forced to eat with cutlery made of aluminium although this type of cutlery was banned elsewhere long ago.

The *Act on Public Service* was amended in June 2002 to introduce assistant teachers for primary and nursery schools. This step is intended to facilitate the integration of Roma children into the standard educational system. Educational specialists have shown that a preparatory programme for five-year-olds has shown that they can make it, without the need for special schools.

Klara Orgovanova, Government Commissioner for Romani Issues, said that Roma should be allowed the chance to be educated in their mother tongue, in addition to the Slovak language. She said that for this purpose the Romani language needs textbooks in Slovak as the standard dictionary and grammar book put out in 1971 uses Czech-Romani translations. She also said that she would promote creating a secondary school that would primarily prepare Romani students for working in state administration.

The major associations that exist have received grants since the new state was formed. They include the Cultural Society of Citizens of Romani Origin, Romani Culture, the Association of Romani Intelligentsia and the Cultural Union of the Romani Community. Seventeen Romani associations met in 1993 and formed the Council of Romanies in Slovakia (ARSS). After an initial impetus, the council has not been very active. In 1995, therefore, six Romani parties formed a new umbrella organisation, the Union of Roma Political Parties in the Slovak Republic (URPSDR). The **Roma Civic Initiative** (ROI) had had one seat in the regional Slovak Parliament from 1990 but it was unsuccessful in the elections of 1992 and 1995 that followed independence.

A new Romani organisation has been set up in Slovakia. The Council of Slovak Roma (RRS) which held its first conference in **Košice** in January 2003, is chaired by Frantisek Gulas and has 15,000 members. The RRS will co-operate with other Romani organisations and work with the Slovak government to improve the situation for the country's Roma population. At the time of writing, the RRS envisage that an Office for Romani Affairs in Košice will be set up in 2004, focusing on training social workers, as well as on fund-raising and project design. In 1991, a Department of Romani Culture had been established at the Pedagogical Faculty in Nitra. A Romani professional theatre, **Romathan**, exists since 1992 at Košice and a specialist music school is based in the town. There is some broadcasting in Romani – within the Hungarian service – and six bilingual publications.

See also CZECHOSLOVAKIA.

SLOVENIA. Estimated Gypsy population: 10,000. The 2002 census puts the figure at 3,246. The 1971 Yugoslav census recorded 977 Romanies while in the 1991 census (the last in the Yugoslav Federation) 2,293 had declared themselves as Roma and, inexplicably, a larger number – 2,847 – said Romani was their mother tongue. A report from the Institute for Nationality Questions in Ljubljana gave the figure of 5,300 for the Gypsy population for the year 1997.

The first report of Gypsies on the territory of present-day Slovenia dates from 1453 and refers to a smith. During the Second World War part of Slovenia was annexed to Germany and the Gypsies living there were taken to concentration camps.

Gypsies live in three regions: Prekmurje and near the borders of Austria and Hungary, Dolnesjska (south-east of Lubljana) and Gorenjska-Alta Carniola near Bled. Slovenia became an independent state in 1991 after a brief skirmish with the Yugoslav Federation. Speaking of Roma, Article 65 of the Constitution of the new republic runs: "The legal situation and particular rights of the Romani population living in Slovenia will be settled by the law". This vague statement has never been fully defined. The national law on local self-government stipulates that in areas where minorities live they should have members on councils but in 1998 there was only one such Romani representative.

Although the Roma in Slovenia have escaped the miseries of the wars in the neighbouring countries, their situation is unenviable. Most live in segregated settlements, are unemployed and subsist on welfare payments, while the percentage in prison is much higher than for the Slovenian population as a whole. Only 509 were registered as having work and only 25 per cent of the children were at school. Roma children, as elsewhere in central and Eastern Europe, have problems when they come to school because they do not know the majority language and lack social skills, while many schools try to avoid registering Romani children. Their lack of education leads the majority of Roma to depend on unskilled work and they are the first to go when factory personnel are reduced. Such employment as there is includes cleaning, farmwork, road construction, stonemasonry and dealing in horses. Even qualified Roma find it difficult to get work because of discrimination. The rate of mortality is higher than for the Slovenian population.

There have been some examples of extreme prejudice in housing as in 1997 when the Slovene inhabitants of Malina prevented a Romani family from moving into a house in their village – a move designed as part of an integration programme. Local authorities refuse planning permission for Roma to build houses, refuse to find accommodation for them and then blame them for building houses illegally or for living in poor conditions.

The central government of Slovenia has set up an Inter-Departmental Commission for Roma Matters which, apart from representatives of ministries, also has members of the local authorities in areas where Roma live and from the Romani organisations. Twenty distinct Romani communities, each designated 'autochthonous', are entitled to a seat on their local municipal councils and all but one council (Grosuplje) has complied.

In 1995 the Government started a programme to improve the lot of the

Roma. Its aims included improving the living conditions in Romani settlements and increasing the educational opportunities for Romani children from nursery school to university. However, such official initiatives for Roma depend on local goodwill to carry them out. The Roma in Prekmurje are best organised and generally co-operate with the authorities. But, in 1998 they organised a demonstration – blocking a highway – to press for the building of a road to the Romani village of Beltinci.

In the first seven years of the new state seven Romani organisations were founded and they have now come together in one union, Zveza Romskih drustev Slovenije (The Association of Romani Organisations in Slovenia), whose president is the author Jozuek Horvat-Muc. These organisations are involved in the fields of culture, education, information and sport but not politics. Radio broadcasts in Romani come from Murska Sobota and Novo Mesto. In Murska Sobota there is also a theatre group which has been functioning since 1992. A magazine, *Romano Them* (Romani World), is published by a non-governmental organisation, while the Romani organisation in Murska Sobota produces its own bilingual paper, *Romske novice*.

SMITH, Charles 1956. England. Poet (in English and Romani English) and civil rights worker. He is currently chairman of the **Gypsy Council** for Education, Culture, Welfare and Civil Rights. He recently premiered a film he directed for the Gypsy Council, *Footprints in the Sand*.

SMITH, Cornelius 1831–1922. England. Craftsman and evangelist. His parents were caners and basket-makers. He is the father of **Rodney Smith** and grandfather of **Reverend George Bramwell Evens**. He was converted to being an active Christian at a revivalist meeting in Notting Hill, London. He wrote a short autobiography, entitled *The Life Story of Cornelius Smith*, during the 1890s.

SMITH, Lady Eleanor Smith 1845–1914.

England. Writer and a champion of the Gypsy cause. Her writings include *Red Wagon, Tzigane, Caravan* and her autobiography, *Life's a Circus*. She supported the right of the Gypsies to come to Epsom for the Derby race week.

SMITH, George. England. Nineteenth century preacher. He wanted to settle the Gypsies. He saw the Gypsy way of life as requiring reform through education and improved sanitary conditions. His books on the subject were *Gipsy Life: Being an Account of Our Gipsies and Their Children, with Suggestions for Their Improvement* (1880), and the anti-romantic view of Gypsy life in *I've Been a Gipsying*. The *Movable Dwellings Bills*, which he tried to promote in Parliament, failed to be adopted.

SMITH, Jasper Derby 1921–2003. England. Singer. He was born in a caravan at Epsom as was his father, born on **Derby** Day. Jasper Smith was a well-known folk singer who made recordings and sang on radio and TV. He was a founding member of the **Gypsy Council** in the 1960s and campaigned for caravan sites in Kent and Surrey. After a ten-year battle he persuaded Epsom to re-open in 1983, the Cox's Lane site, of which he became the first warden. He is featured on the CD, *My Father is King of the Gypsies* (1999) and two *Topic* records: *Songs of the Open Road* (1975) and *The Travelling Songster* (1977). He also contributed to BBC's *Folkweave: Acoustic Roots*.

SMITH, Phoebe. England. Contemporary singer. She is from the south of England, and has a large repertoire of English folk songs that were recorded by several collectors.

SMITH, Rodney 1860–1947. England. Evangelist. The son of **Cornelius Smith**. Born in East Anglia and known as Gypsy Smith, he was a Methodist preacher who could stir a crowd of 10,000 by his speechmaking and attracted popularity with his vocal recordings of hymns. He wrote many religious pamphlets and received the Medal of the British Empire. His brother, Ezekiel, worked with the

Railway Mission for many years and wrote hymns, and his son, Hanley, was a Methodist minister at Sutton Coldfield. His autobiography, written in 1902, *Gipsy Smith: His Life and Work*, was published by the Religious Tract Society (1902).

SOCIETY FOR THE IMPROVEMENT OF LOCAL ROMA COMMUNITIES Yugoslavia. Est. 1997. President: Aleksandra Mitrović. The Society is a non-governmental organisation which brings together experts, scientists, and social activists to aid the development of Roma communities and improve their living conditions.

SOFIA CONGRESS. 1905. This was not an international congress, as stated in some books, but a national gathering aimed at winning the vote for Bulgarian Gypsies.

SOLARIO, Antonio 1382–1455. Italy. Artist. The son of a nomadic smith who seems to have come to Italy as an individual, he became a painter at the court of Naples.

SOLER, Antonio Ruíz (El Bailarín, Antonio) 1921–96. Spain. Dancer. Seville. He was known as Spain's most famous and charismatic traditional dancer, who possessed the quality of **duende**, the spirit of **flamenco**. He also included in his repertoire the stamping of feet, known as *taconeado*. Antonio Ruiz Soler showed early promise by dancing publicly at the age of four and, by the age of six, he had joined a dancing school. Already, when eight years old, he had started a partnership with another pupil and in 1937 they left for a tour of North and South America, performing as Antonio and Rosario. They performed in films with **Rita Hayworth** and Judy Garland, before returning to Madrid, where Antonio made his debut in 1949. The duo danced together for twenty-two years before splitting in 1952. Antonio Soler also performed at Pablo Picasso's eightieth birthday party in 1961 when the painter joined him in a rumba. He was director of the Spanish National

Ballet 1980–3 and again for a short period in 1989.

SOROS FOUNDATION (ROMA SOROS FOUNDATION). USA. Est. 1993 by **George Soros**. It has set up a number of cultural programmes in Eastern Europe in particular. See also OPEN SOCIETY.

SOROS, George 1930–. Hungary. Philanthropist. A financier of Jewish-Hungarian origin who has donated money to many Romani causes. See OPEN SOCIETY.

SOTE, JOSE (Jose Merce) 1955–. Spain. **Flamenco** Singer. His professional career as a singer began at the age of fifteen. He has worked with **Antonio Gades'** company and took part in the film *Bodas de sangre*.

SOUZA, John Philips 1894–1932. US. Composer. The composer of the song *Stars and Stripes Forever* and several well-known marches, Souza is a descendant of **Calo** Portuguese Gypsies

SOVIET UNION. See UNION OF SOVIET SOCIALIST REPUBLICS.

SPAIN. Estimated Gypsy population (excluding the non-Romani **Quincalleros**) :700,000. The first records of Gypsies in Spain date from the fifteenth century and refer to companies who crossed the border from France. However, some scholars think that Gypsies had entered Spain much earlier, accompanying the Arabs when they invaded from the south. The Egyptian writer Abd-ul-Mulk, writing around 1200, advised Arabic poets in Spain (then under Arab rule) not to be "garrulous in the manner of the Zott" (the Arab term for Gypsies). Firmer evidence of their presence comes in 1425 when Don Johan of **Little Egypt** and Duke Thomas obtained letters of protection from King Alfonso V of Aragon. These leaders had certainly come via France.

From 1492 Spain was united under one government which in 1499 ordered Gypsies to stop nomadising, settle down and find a trade within sixty days and to cease travelling. If they continued to nomadise, they would be whipped, have a cut made in their ears (as an identification mark) and be forcibly bound to a master. Many did take up trades, replacing the expelled Moors as masons and bakers, for example. From 1539 Gypsies who continued to nomadise in groups were arrested and males were used as galley slaves.

In 1633 Philip IV's government decreed that the Gypsies did not exist. They were not an ethnic group, he said, but Spanish people who had disguised themselves and made up a language. They were forbidden to speak any language other than Spanish or wear distinctive clothes. In 1695 they were, ineffectively, forbidden to have any employment other than farming. By 1746 a list of seventy-five towns had been drawn up, and Gypsies were – in theory – allowed to live only in the named towns.

Persecution continued. A round-up of all Gypsies was ordered in 1749. The aim was to eliminate the population completely by locking up the men and women separately and setting them to forced labour. Several hundred Gypsies were arrested and imprisoned in this campaign. Most of them were gradually released and allowed to return to their previous homes as it was realised that they performed useful services in the villages which found themselves suddenly without a blacksmith or a baker. The last of the arrested Gypsies were finally released in 1765, after sixteen years of confinement. Repression finally ceased and was replaced by a firmer policy of assimilation with the enactment of the decree of Charles III in 1783, under which the Gypsies were granted equal citizenship. The use of the word *Gitano* (Gypsy) was to be banned. The Gypsies were again forbidden to speak Romani or wear distinctive dress. Many took the opportunity of free movement to migrate to the south of France. Largely, as a result of the past penalties for speaking Romani in public, the language has died out and Spanish Gypsies now speak a variety of Spanish with a few Romani words, known as **Caló**.

The Gypsies have continued to live in Spain on the edge of society, looked down upon by the majority population unless they are musicians or bullfighters. The Catholic Church took an interest in the Gypsies during the twentieth century by organising local missions and pilgrimages. Many Spanish Gypsies are, however, now turning to **Pentecostalism**.

With the fall of the Franco dictatorship in 1975, the Gypsies have been free to organise and publish magazines. However, latent anti-Gypsy racism has surfaced on many occasions. In one incident in 1984 a crowd of several hundred in Zaragoza demonstrated against the occupation of thirty-six prefabricated houses built for Gypsies in the Actur district. Slogans included 'Fight for your rights against Gypsies'. In 1986 there were attacks on the Gypsy quarter of Martos; thirty houses were set on fire and the inhabitants fled to the nearby village of Torredonjimeno. The villagers there did not allow them to stop and drove them out. The local authorities then tried to settle the evacuees in a third place, Monte Lope Alvárez, but the local population protested and the Gypsies had to sleep in tents provided by the Red Cross, protected by the police, until alternative accommodation was found. In the district of Otxarkoaga in Bilbao in 1996 Gypsy children were denied entry to the local school and a special school was set up for them in a disused secondary school building. Some of the Gypsy parents then boycotted the new school, in a protest against segregation.

Gypsies are among the best musicians and singers in Spain, and several of them have individual entries in this book, such as **Joaquín Cortes**, as does the footballer **Jose Antonio Reyes**. The economic situation has led to some young unemployed Gypsies trafficking in drugs and even beginning to experiment with the wares they sell. It is probably the only country in Europe where a serious drugs problem exists among Gypsies. On the other hand, a significant number of Romanies are going to college. **Juan de Dios Ramirez Heredia** was a lecturer then member of parliament for the Socialist Party in the Spanish and European parliaments. The Spanish royal family supported the **European Congress** in Seville. Other positive features are the great interest in the revival of the Romani language and links with Gypsy organisations in other countries. The **Presencia Gitana** association in Madrid has a wide programme of educational and cultural work. Many of the local organisations are united in a network, the **Union Romani**, and their activities are reported in the journal *Nevipens Romani* (Romani News).

SPECIALIST GROUP ON ROMA/GYPSIES (MG-S-ROM). In 1995 the Committee of Ministers of the **Council of Europe** decided to set up the Group to advise the Council. The seven original members of the group were Outi Ojala (Finland), Carmen Santiago Reyes (Spain), Josephine Verspaget (Netherlands), Catalin Zamfir (Romania), Milcho Dimitrov (Bulgaria), Claudio Marta (Italy) and Andrzej Mirga (Poland). The first meeting of the Group was held in Strasbourg in March 1996. The second meeting, in October 1996, considered human rights among other topics. Two members of the Group took part in a fact-finding mission to Bosnia under the auspices of the Council of Europe. The Group met for the sixteenth time in Strasbourg in November 2003 with housing, caravan sites and health high on the agenda.

SPINELLI, Santino 1964–. Italy. Singer and cultural worker. He is editor of the journal *Them Romano* and organiser of an annual arts competition.

SPITTA, Melanie 1946–. Germany. Civil rights activist and film-maker. A **Sinti,** who together with Katryn Seybold, has made several documentary films about Sinti, including *Wir Sind Sintikinder und*

Keine Zigeuner (We Are Sinti Children and Not Gypsies) and *Das Falsche Wort* (The False Word). The latter deals with the question of **reparations** for Nazi crimes.

ST GEORGE'S DAY. This day is celebrated by both Christian and Muslim Gypsies on 5/6 May according to the Orthodox calendar. Scholars have seen relics of the Indian Baisakhi (New Year's Day) rituals in the celebrations, for example, the custom in **Skopje** (Macedonia) of going to a river and bringing back from it bottles of water.

ST SARAH. See SAINTES MARIES DE LA MER.

STANDING CONFERENCE FOR CO-OPERATION AND CO-ORDINATION OF ROMANI ASSOCIATIONS IN EUROPE. This body was founded in July 1994, in Strasbourg and brings together representatives from some forty Gypsy organisations. Meetings have been held at various locations, including Warsaw (19–20 January 1996), Strasbourg (19–23 March 1996), Brussels (July 1996) and Vienna (November 1996). The Strasbourg meeting sent representatives to a parallel meeting of the **Specialist Group on Roma/Gypsies** of the **Council of Europe**. The November meeting in 1996 took place in the **Romano Centro**, Vienna.

STANDING CONFERENCE OF LOCAL AND REGIONAL AUTHORITIES. See CONGRESS OF LOCAL AND REGIONAL AUTHORITIES OF EUROPE.

STANKIEWICZ, Stanislaw 1942–. Poland. Television producer and publisher. He is the editor of the journal *Rrom p-o Drom* (Romanies on the Road). He was elected in 1990 as a vice-president of the **International Romani Union**.

STARKIE, Walter 1894–1976. England. Author. He was an authority on Gypsy lore and music. He travelled widely in Europe between the two World Wars with his violin and has described the Gypsies he met in several books.

STENCL, A.N. 1897–1983. England. Poet. In 1962 he wrote a series of sonnets in

Yiddish dedicated to the Gypsies that he published in the magazine he edited, *Loshn un Lebn* (Language and Life).

STENEGRY, Archange. France. Contemporary musician and political leader. A Resistance leader during the Second World War, he later became the president of the Communauté Tzigane de France which replaced the Organisation Nationale Gitane.

STEREOTYPES. We find in literature and in the popular mind many stereotypes of Gypsies. Cervantes was one of the first to introduce the theme of Gypsies stealing a child in his novel *La Gitanilla*. They teach her to dance and sing but in her heart she remains a Spaniard. At the end of the novel she is restored to her family and married to her Spanish lover. Beautiful and handsome Gypsies appear in plays, novels and operas. We may think of Bizet's *Carmen* and D. H. Lawrence's *The Virgin and the Gypsy*.

STEWART, Belle 1906–97. Scotland. Singer. She is a **Scottish Traveller**. Herself, her husband Alex (singer and piper) and her daughters **Sheila MacGregor** and **Cathie Higgins** have become famous in folk clubs and concert halls throughout Scotland and England. Their many recordings include the CDs *The Travelling Stewarts* and *Festival at Blairgowrie*.

STEWART, Davie 1901–72. Scotland. Scottish Traveller, singer and musician. Davie served as an under-age soldier in the First World War and became a piper with the Gordon Highlanders. He earned his living as a street busker in Scotland and Ireland, playing the accordion and the pipes. After his return to Scotland, he was a well-known figure in folk clubs and made several recordings.

STEWART FAMILY. Most of the musical **Scottish Travellers** named Stewart are descended from the singer Jimmy Stewart of Struan. See STEWART, BELLE; STEWART, DAVIE.

STOJKA, Ceija 1933–. Austria. A **Lovari** writer and singer. She has followed in her brother **Karl Stojka's** footsteps and taken up painting.

STOJKA, Harri 1957–. Austria. Musician. The son of **Mongo Stojka** and nephew of **Ceija** and **Karl Stojka**. Harri is a guitarist in the rock, reggae and heavy metal styles. His first LP record was *Off the Bone* and since then he has made about a dozen records. He has played in various rock bands such as Gipsy Love and Harri-Stojka Express. His song, *I Am So in Love with You*, made the Austrian Hit Parade. Together with his father he made one CD, *Amari Luma* (Our World) (1994), which is traditional and in quite a different style from his other recordings.

STOJKA, HOJDA. See AMENZA KETANE.

STOJKA, Karl 1931–. Austria. Artist. A brother of **Ceija Stojka**, he has had paintings exhibited in the US and Europe.

STOJKA, Mongo. Austria. Contemporary musician. Based in Vienna, he produced the CD *Amari Luma* (Our World) in 1994 with his son **Harri Stojka**. The music is modern but the lyrics are all in Romani. The original CD had five songs but the second edition (1996) contains ten songs.

STOW-ON-THE-WOLD FAIR. England, Cotswolds region. A popular gathering for Gypsies. In 1476 a royal charter was granted by Edward IV for the fair. Gypsies have been attending it since about 1890. The fair takes place in May and October and trading is on a Thursday. The Gypsies arrive in caravans on the preceding Sunday or Monday and leave on the Friday. In May 1996, at its peak, there were some 400 caravans; in October, about 100. Numbers are slightly lower now. From 1990 the local authorities have been trying without success to stop Gypsies attending the fair in their caravans. Councillor **Vera Norwood** has been instrumental in securing the continuation of the Fair though the lack of a field where the visiting caravans can stop has been a problem.

SUCURI, Ljatif 1915–45. Yugoslavia. Civil rights activist. He was a prominent Gypsy in Kosovska-Mitrovica in Kosovo, at the time of the occupation of the country by Albanian fascist forces during the Second World War. On several occasions Ljatif Sucuri intervened with the Albanian police chief to stop Gypsies from being killed. The police chief was to tell the German authorities in Yugoslavia that there were no Gypsies in the town, only Muslims. At the end of the war, collaborators, trying to cover up their own activities, denounced him to the partisans who took him away, without checking the allegations, and shot him.

ŠUKAR. A Group based in Slovenia playing music in a Gypsy style. They appeared at the **Baxt** festival in Trondheim. CD: *Prvo Iv* (First snow).

SUMMER SCHOOLS. (i) The Romani language summer school (Nilajesqi Škola) organised by **Marcel Cortiade** and the **Rromani Baxt** organisation. The first was held in Belgrade in 1989. They bring together young and not-so-young Romanies from different countries who wish to advance their knowledge of the language and dialects.
(ii) Other language summer schools have been held in Scandinavia and the Balkans, principally for younger Romanies.

SUNDT, Eilert. Norway. Pastor and reformer. A Norwegian pastor who in 1848 obtained a government grant to study the problem of **Travellers**. His religious beliefs led him to think that they would be better off in workhouses than travelling the roads. In 1863 he reported that out of 425 Travellers who had been 'reformed' (i.e. settled), approximately 100 had gone back to nomadism. In 1869 the work was taken from Eilert Sundt and given to a department of the church. See also NORWAY and NORWEGIAN TRAVELLERS.

SVARTA PÄRLOR (Black Pearls). A musical group formed by members of the Roma Ensemble of Poland, which emigrated to Sweden around the 1970s.

SVARTA SAFIRER (Black sapphires). Now based in Sweden, this band is originally

from Yugoslavia.

SVETSKY. In spite of occasional references found in books on Gypsies, these are circus families, not Gypsies or **Travellers**, in the Czech and Slovak Republics.

SWANN REPORT. The 1985 report of a British committee investigating education chaired by Professor Swann. It found that, although more Gypsy children were attending school, they were suffering discrimination and bullying from other pupils.

SWEDEN. Estimated Gypsy (Romani) population: 16,500 (not including **Travellers**). In 1512 Gypsies crossed from Denmark to Sweden, even though at the time Swedish nationalists were fighting to free the country from Denmark. In 1515 there were more immigrants, this time from Estonia. In 1523 Gustav Vasa became king of an independent Sweden and two years later he wrote to the Gypsies, telling them to leave the country. During the second half of the sixteenth century a number of Gypsies did leave and migrated to Finland. In 1560 the Lutheran Archbishop Petri told the priests not to baptise or bury Gypsies. This was changed in 1586 when priests were told they should baptise children, teach parents the Christian faith and encourage them to settle down. However, eight years later the Synod of Linköping reversed this, and the previous policy was re-adopted.

In 1637 a new law was passed saying all Gypsies must leave the country, otherwise the men would be executed and the women expelled by force. In this law the word *Zigenare* was used for the first time for Gypsies. Previously they had been called *Tattare* (in various spellings). In 1642 and 1662 the law was strengthened. However, no cases are known of Gypsies being executed in Sweden under these laws. Finally, in 1748 a new decree was published banishing Gypsies who had not been born in Sweden. It is thought that a substantial number of Romanies stayed in Sweden and merged with the local nomadic population, forming the group now called *Tattare* or *Resande* (Travellers).

In 1860 entry restrictions in Sweden were lifted resulting in a new immigration, principally of **Vlah** Gypsies. Under the 1914 *Deportation Act*, Gypsies could be deported or refused entry. In fact, those already in the country were allowed to stay. The 1922 census in Sweden recorded 250 Gypsies and 1,500 Tattare. The wartime 1943 census listed 453 Gypsies. The government repealed the 1914 *Deportation Act* in 1954 and limited immigration began. In 1960 the state took responsibility for housing Gypsies, and nomadism for practical purposes ended. At the time there were about 100 sedentary and 125 nomadic families. By 1965 only five families remained in caravans.

In 1963 **Katerina Taikon** published her first book, *Zigenarska*, the story of her childhood. She later took up the campaign for the admission of **Kalderash** Gypsies from France and Spain. The government decided to set up a policy of 'organised importation' of Gypsies – a form of quota. In recent years considerable numbers of Gypsies have arrived from Eastern Europe and Yugoslavia, outnumbering the descendants of those Vlah Romanies who arrived at the end of the nineteenth century. Many hundreds of Finnish Gypsies have also immigrated to Sweden. The education authorities have introduced mother-tongue teaching in Romani and special classes for adults to improve their education. A number of Gypsies take part in these programmes as teachers or assistants.

Both the Romanies and the Travellers have set up self-help organizations: Romernas Riksforbund and Resanderomernas Riksforbund. Finnish Gypsies in Sweden are represented by the Finska Zigenarrådet, the oldest body, founded (as Stockholms Finska Zigenarförening)

in 1972. An advisory council of Romanies was set up in 2003 to work with the government. The Gypsy **Pentecostal** church is also active.

SWEDISH TRAVELLERS. The 1922 census in Sweden recorded 1,500 Tattare since when there has not been an official count. It is thought by some experts that a substantial number of Romanies stayed in Sweden after the expulsion order of 1748 and merged with the local nomadic population, forming the group now called *Tattare* (a pejorative term) or *Resande* (Travellers). The Swedish Travellers today speak a language with Swedish grammar and many words borrowed from Romani. They call this language chivi or rommani. In recent years they have set up a self-help organisation and many now call themselves 'resande Romer' (travelling Romanies).

SWITZERLAND. Estimated Gypsy population (mainly **Jenisch**): 32,500. Between 1418 and 1422 Gypsies came to Basle, Bern and Zurich as pilgrims with letters of recommendation. They were given food and wine and then escorted out of the towns. In 1471, however, the parliament of the Swiss Confederation, meeting in Lucerne, expelled Gypsies from the land. In 1510 the penalty of hanging was introduced for any Gypsies found in Switzerland. This edict was repeated six times in the years up to 1530. In 1532, however, a company of 300 Gypsies appeared on the outskirts of Geneva. It evidently took some years before all the Gypsies were finally expelled, as is indicated by a decree in Graubünden in 1571 ordering any Gypsies who were captured to be sent to be galley slaves. One wonders whose galleys these would be. During the following centuries, very few Romanies came to Switzerland and as late as the middle of the twentieth century they were still being turned back at the borders – even Romanies in cars intending to pass through the country in transit. The second **World Romani Congress** was, nonetheless, held in Geneva.

For many years no Romanies lived in Switzerland and there are very few even today. However, Switzerland has a large population of indigenous Jenisch nomads and semi-nomads. Early this century the authorities began to take away the children of Jenisch families and bring them up in orphanages or give them to Swiss foster parents. Often the children were told their parents were dead and vice versa. When news of this programme became public there was great indignation. Many of the children who were taken away – now grown up – have rediscovered their Jenisch identity. An organisation known as Scharotl (Car-avan) publishes a magazine of the same name.

SZÁSZCÁSVÁS BAND. Romania, Transylvania. They play in the Gypsy, Hungarian, Romanian and Saxon (German) styles and have made several recordings from their Hungarian village of Kiskükülló. Their singer, István 'Dumnezu' Jámbor, leads the band. CD: *Folk Music from Transylvania: Szászcsávás Band*

SZEGÖ, László. Hungary. Contemporary translator, teacher and poet.

SZTOJKA, Ferencz C19th. Hungary. Writer. He was one of the first Gypsies to write literature in Romani, toward the end of the nineteenth century.

T

TABOR. Romani word for **clan** or camp. It is of Slav origin.

TAIKON, Fred 1945–. Sweden. Political activist and editor. President of the Romani Culture Centre in Stockholm, he is also the editor of the bilingual journal *Romani Glinda.*

TAIKON, Johan Dimitr C19th. Sweden. Coppersmith and storyteller. He travelled in Russia and Scandinavia. Taikon's stories were recorded by the Gypsiologist Carl Herman Tillhagen and published as *Taikon berättar*. These and other material he produced were the basis for the study of the Coppersmith (**Kalderash**) dialect of Romani by Olof Gjerdman and Erik Ljungberg.

TAIKON, Katarina 1932–95. Sweden. Writer and civil rights activist. Katarina Taikon's involvement in politics began when a group of Gypsies coming from France were interned at the border and refused entry to Sweden. After pressure, they were let in, and the Swedish government agreed to a programme of organised immigration. Katerina Taikon edited the magazine *Zigenaren* together with her husband Björn Langhammer. She also became well known as a chil-dren's writer with her semi-autobiographical books about a Gypsy girl, **Katitzi**.

TAIKON, Rosa 1926–. Sweden. Artist. The sister of **Katerina Taikon**, her jewellery is typically crafted in metal. Both she and her sister have written poetry.

TARAF. Name, of Arabic origin, given to village bands in Romania. Many of the tarafs are Gypsies, such as Taraful Soporu de Cimple, Taraf de Carancebes (from Banat) and **Taraf de Haidouks.**

TARAF DE HAIDOUKS (Band of brigands). A Romanian Gypsy band, from the village of Clejani who have toured widely across Western Europe. After the fall of Ceausecu in 1991, the band members were discovered by two Belgians who were in Romania searching for folk musicians. They found over 200 during their trip and it was out of these that the band developed. The ages of the players range from the youngest at twenty to their talented lead-violinist Nicolae Neacu who died recently aged seventy-seven. Taraf de Haidouks also appeared in the film *The Man Who Cried* (starring their number one fan **Johnny Depp**) and have modelled on the catwalks of

Paris for designer Yohji Yamamoto. CD: *Taraf de Haidouks, Musiques des Tsiganes de Roumanie, Dumbala Dumba*.

TARNÓW. A town in Poland where the museum has a strong Gypsy section, originating from an exhibition of 1979. It has been built up by the curator Adam Bartosz. Nevertheless, there are right-wing elements in the town and the twenty-first century has seen a serious attack on a Romani family and daubing of anti-Gypsy graffiti.

TAROT CARDS. The tarot cards were invented in Italy in the fifteenth century and used as a game. In the eighteenth century they became popular for fortune-telling and have been adopted by some Gypsy fortune-tellers.

TARTARS/TATARS. A Turkic people. Until the sixteenth century a large independent Tartar state existed in west Asia that at one time reached into Europe as far as Romania. Some historians think that the Tartars had Gypsy slaves and brought them to Romania around the thirteenth century, where both they and some of their captors – after the defeat of the Tartars – became slaves of the Romanians.

TATERE. A pejorative term used for Norwegian **Travellers** who prefer to be called *Reisende* (Travellers). The name Tatere was first used for both indigenous Travellers and Romanies in Norway and Denmark because of confusion with the **Tartars**, who made incursions into Europe in the Middle Ages. See DANISH TRAVELLERS, NORWEGIAN TRAVELLERS.

TATTARE. A pejorative term used for **Swedish Travellers**, who prefer to be called *Resande* (Travellers). The name was first used for indigenous Travellers and Romanies because of confusion with the **Tartars**, who made incursions into Europe in the Middle Ages. See SWEDISH TRAVELLERS

TCHATCHIPEN (Truth). An organisation based in Toulon, working for the promotion of Romani culture. The president is Michel Zanko and the secretary,

Bernadette Pennes.

TEATR ROMA. A theatre in Sofia from 1947 to 1951 when it was closed by the government. The director was **Mustafa Aliev** (Manush Romanov).

TEATR ROMEN. USSR, Moscow. The theatre was founded in 1931 during the encouragement of Romani culture by Joseph Stalin. Its aim was to replace the stereotypical romantic Gypsy figure by a new image of Gypsies taking part in the building of socialism. The theatre was meant to help the sedentarisation of the Gypsies. It officially opened in April 1931 and was assisted by the Moscow Jewish Theatre and the actor Moshe I. Goldblatt who became its director. Popular songs and sketches were presented for censorship to the Commissariat of Enlightenment (Ministry of Culture), to convince them that Gypsies were following an appropriate political direction. The theatre was also to fight the popular stereotype of Gypsies. Three Gypsy writers worked with the company, Michael Bezliudsky, **Aleksandr German** and **I. Rom-Lebedev**. In 1933 a performance of **Carmen** was in the repertoire.

The Teatr Romen toured Siberia and the Soviet Far East after much of the western USSR was taken over by the Germans early in the Second World War. It returned later with the advancing Soviet army across the Caspian Sea and, with the Luftwaffe above, performed to soldiers at Rostov, showing its commitment to the combat. Two actors joined the war effort and were decorated for bravery. The Theatre encountered accusations of 'nationalistic deviation' but survived the later suppression of Gypsy culture.

The current repertoire of the theatre varies from world classics to political plays still encouraging Gypsies to give up the nomadic life and settle. Plays with songs and dance have always been a feature of the repertoire, and the artists have included many popular singers.

TEKAMELI (a message of love). Roussillon,

France. A band who play the music of the **Gitanos** of Southern France. CD: *Ida y Vuelta.*

TELEPHONE LEGAL ADVICE SERVICE FOR TRAVELLERS (T-LAST). Wales. Est. 1995. Operated by the Cardiff Law School as a three-year project. T-LAST aimed to provide not only a telephone legal advice service for Britain, as the name suggests, but also to develop a network of legal practitioners and to publish research about the needs of **Travellers** and Gypsies. Its first conference took place in March 1997. It began to publish a newsletter called *Travellers' Times* which has outlasted the telephone service. There are currently phone advice lines in Birmingham and Brighton.

TELEVISION. The first regular TV broadcasts in Romani were from Priština (in Kosovo) from around 1985 and other Yugoslav stations (Novi Sad and Prizren) followed later. In recent years a number of TV stations have broadcast regularly in Romani or in the national language but for Gypsy viewers. They include Bratislava, Bucharest, Budapest and **Skopje**.

TERESA, Blessed Mother. See BOJAXHIU, Agnes.

THEATER ROMANCE. Ukraine, Kiev. The company performs in Russian and Romani. In November 1996 it made a guest visit to Vienna.

THEATRE. Apart from the long-established **Teatr Romen** in Moscow, Romani drama companies are a phenomenon of the post-1945 years. Three major professional theatre groups are now playing in or largely in the Romani language: **Pralipe**, **Romathan** and **Teatr Romen**. For original plays in Romani, see DRAMA.

THEM ROMANO. See ROMANO THEM.

THESLEFF, Arthur. Finland. Diplomat and writer. He wrote a comprehensive survey of the situation of the Gypsies in Europe at the end of the nineteenth century. It was printed in 1901 and much of it was later reproduced in the *Journal of the Gypsy Lore Society*. Arthur Thesleff also compiled a Romani dictionary based on an earlier word-list.

TINKER. (i) A worker with tin, often nomadic. The profession goes back many centuries in Europe. There are references to persons with the surname or trade of tinker in England from around 1175. In 1551–52 the *Act for Tinkers and Pedlars* was passed in England. It is likely that the travelling tinkers in England were absorbed by the Romanies when they arrived in the country. **William Shakespeare** refers to Henry V being able to speak with every tinker in his tongue; some have seen this as a reference to the **cant** of **Irish Travellers**. (ii) A pejorative name for **Travellers** in Ireland and Scotland.

TIPLER, Derek 1940–90. England. Radio and TV journalist. While working for Radio Vatican he decided that his mission was to translate the Bible for his own people. He then travelled with Italian Gypsies and set to work on the translation, earning money by playing in restaurants. He died of a heart attack after completing only one gospel (St Mark) which has been published. He was an occasional contributor to the *Journal of the **Gypsy Lore Society**.*

TRANSDNIESTRIA. During the Second World War, the German and Romanian armies conquered the Ukraine as far as the River Bug. Romanian troops were responsible for security up to the River Dnieper, and a new name was invented for the territory between the Dniester and Dnieper – Transdniestria.

Some of this newly occupied area in the East was used by the Romanians as a dumping ground for Gypsies and Jews, as the Germans had used Poland. In the years 1941-1942 some 25,000 Gypsies were to be transported across to the other side of the Dniester. The government policy was to expel the Gypsies from the Romanian homeland to stop them mixing with the majority population and intermarrying. For those to whom the policy was applied, it brought disruption of family life, suffering, hardship, hunger and death.

Between June and August 1942, over 11,000 nomads were evacuated to the east. Although less danger to Romanian blood than the settled Roma – since they lived isolated socially from the townsfolk – their expulsion could be carried out with little effort. They had their own horses and wagons and just needed guards to accompany them on the journey east. In a few towns in Transylvania, the German-speaking villagers resisted attempts to deport 'their' Gypsies. Clinic (Kelling) and Ungurei (Gergeschdorf) were amongst the villages where the Romanies remained unharmed. Policemen on horseback forced the Gypsy chiefs from Profa, Tirgu Jiu and elsewhere to set off with their extended families eastward. Mihai Tonu and Stanescu Zdrelea each led forty families. A few leaders set off willingly, not knowing what awaited them. On arrival they had to build huts for themselves. Some dug holes to sleep in and broke up the wagons to use as a roof and protection against the weather. The rest of the wagon was gradually burned as fuel to keep warm. The horses were eaten. Conditions were hard that first winter. At night the temperature dropped and every morning frozen bodies were to be found. It is said that 1,500 died after one freezing night. The nomads had been able to take their gold with them. At night they would creep out of the camp to exchange gold for food in the neighbouring villages. Those who had no gold had to beg. Although some were surrounded with barbed wire, the camps were guarded ghettoes rather than labour camps, and for much of the time the inmates could leave not only to shop but also to celebrate weddings and baptisms in Russian Orthodox churches nearby.

The deportation of settled Gypsies followed. In May 1942 the Ministry of Internal Affairs ordered that 12,500 settled Gypsies "dangerous to public order" should be deported across the Dniestr and this measure was carried out in September of that year. General Constantin Vasiliu was in charge of the operation, with nine trains at his disposal. Dispatched from Bucharest in cattle trucks with only the possessions they could hold, the journey took some weeks with stops and starts, and because of the cold nights, lack of blankets and inadequate food supply, many died of hunger and exposure before arriving at the River Bug in the Ukraine. Those who had survived were lodged in huts and (later) made to work digging trenches. Those found with gold teeth had them pulled out. Anyone caught returning from Transdniestria to Romania was sent back and interned at Tiraspol.

The policy of transporting the Gypsies into the Ukraine aroused opposition among the local German officials. The Nazi governor of the Ukraine wrote on the subject to the Minister for Occupied Eastern Territories in Berlin in August 1942. After this a letter was sent from the minister to the Foreign Office in Berlin, dated 11 September 1942, pointing out the danger that these Gypsies would try to settle on the east bank of the Bug and would then be a bad influence on the Ukrainian population. The minister said the area set aside for Gypsies was populated by ethnic Germans and asked the Foreign Office to persuade Romania to change its policy. During 1943 the deportations decreased in number. After this, the Gypsies in Romania remained comparatively free. As far as we know, no further large-scale activity against them took place and many served in the army.

Toward the end of 1943, after the Germans had been driven back over the Bug with their Romanian allies, the guards fled, and Gypsies took the opportunity to try to return to Romania. Weakened by months of hunger and cold many children and old people did not survive this return journey. The survivors eventually reached Dabuleni, Profa, Tirgu Jiu and the other towns from which they had been driven.

After the war when the Romanian People's Court appointed an investigation committee to look into war crimes, it took a very unfavourable view of the treatment of the deportees. Ion Antonescu, the fascist dictator, said at his trial that the Gypsies had been deported because they had robbed people during the curfew and because the Governor of Transdniestria needed workers. The dictator was executed for war crimes. It is thought that 19,000 Romanian Gypsies had perished in the east.

TRANS-EUROPEAN ROMA FEDERATION (TERF). Est. 2002 Chairperson: Ladislav Balaz. London-based umbrella organisation for Roma refugee groups in the UK. TERF has campaigned for an end to the detention and deportation of Roma asylum seekers in Britain.

TRANSPORTATION. Many European countries transported Gypsies to their colonies as one way of removing them from their territory. In 1648 Sweden proposed to deport the Gypsies to its colony in America, Delaware. This plan was not carried out. Gypsies were, however, transported from England and Scotland to North America and Australia, and from Portugal to Africa and South America. A magistrate is still sometimes called a bitcherin' mush in Romani English from the phrase bitcherdi pawdal (sent overseas)

TRAVELLER. A term used in this dictionary and elsewhere for industrial nomadic groups (peripatetics) who are not of Indian origin.

In many countries there are indigenous nomadic or semi-nomadic groups. In Europe they include the **Camminanti** of Sicily, the **Jenisch** of France, Germany and Switzerland, the **Karrner** of Austria the **Quincalleros** (or Mercheros) of Spain, the Resande (or Reisende) of Sweden and Norway, and the **Woonwa-genbewoners** of the Netherlands. They live very similar lives to the nomadic Romanies, and some intermarriage has occurred over the years.

In Ireland and Scotland they have been called **Tinkers**, but they themselves prefer the name Travellers. The term quinquis or quinquilleros of Spain is the equivalent of 'Tinkers' and there they prefer the name Mercheros. Norwegian and Swedish Travellers became known as **Tattare** and now prefer the terms Reisande and Resande.
See also IRISH TRAVELLERS; NEW TRAVELLERS; NORWEGIAN TRAVELLERS; SCOTTISH TRAVELLERS; SWEDISH TRAVELLERS.

TRAVELLER LAW REFORM BILL. UK. A Bill based on a draft prepared by **TWIG** which was sponsored in the House of Commons during 2003 by David Atkinson MP.

TRAVELLER LAW REFORM COALITION. UK. Est. 2002. Co-ordinator: Andrew Ryder. A pressure group comprising Gypsies, **Irish Travellers** and **New Travellers**, its primary aim is to get the government to address Gypsy and Traveller accommodation needs principally by placing on local authorities a duty to provide or facilitate site provision. It campaigns for Parliament to pass the proposals in the **Traveller Law Reform Bill**.

TRAVELLERS' ADVICE TEAM (TAT). UK. Est. 1996. Founder: Chris Johnson. Linked to the Community Law Partnership firm of solicitors this team is dedicated to helping Gypsies and **Travellers** with legal problems, in particular relating to stopping places.

TRAVELLERS' AID TRUST. UK. Est. 1988. Coordinator: Susan Alexander. The Trust was founded in 1988 and has recently been revived. It is a charity and its objectives include the relief of hardship among **Travellers** and the advancement of the education of their children.
The Trust has launched a grants programme, including the Small Grants Programme for Travellers which offers grants to a maximum of £250 for a wide range of purposes that are of benefit to individual Travellers or the Traveller

community.

TRAVELLERS' SCHOOL CHARITY. UK. Est.
1997. Founder: Alan Dearling. A charity
which supports education on site for
New Travellers' children.

TRENT, COUNCIL OF. This conference of
the Catholic Church, which ended in
1563, decreed that persons without a
fixed address could not become Catholic
priests.

TROLLMANN, Johann 'Ruckelle' d. 1943.
Germany. Boxer. He was the light-heavyweight boxing champion of Germany. In
March 1933 the reigning champion
Erich Seeling was deprived of his title
because he was Jewish. On 9 June the
same year, Johann Trollmann fought
Adolf Wilt for the title and won on
points. On 17 June he in turn was
deprived of his title for racial reasons. In
1942 he was arrested and sent to
Neuengamme concentration camp,
where he was shot in February 1943.

TROSTANIETS. A concentration camp in
the occupied Soviet Union during the
Second World War, in which many Gypsies died.

TSIGAN, TSIGANE, TZIGANE. The Slav and
French terms for Gypsy, derived (like the
German *Zigeuner* and Italian *Zingaro*)
from the Greek **athingani** (heretics).

TURKEY. Estimated Gypsy population:
350,000. An estimate for the years
1960–70 gave a figure of 10,633 nomads.
When the Turks captured the land that
forms present-day Turkey from the
Byzantine Greeks, they found a substantial Gypsy population already there.
Sultan Bayezid drove many Romanies
out of the parts of Anatolia under his
control and they came into Thracia and
Serbia. Only those who were or became
Muslim were allowed to stay in Turkey.
Later records show the Gypsies to have
had an important role in the Turkish
state as musicians, smiths and entertainers. The report of a celebration
organised by Sultan Murad III in Istanbul in honour of his newly born son
talks of a procession including sixty
Gypsy smiths, pulling a cart in which
three smiths were working. In a second
procession in the following month, 400
Romani smiths took part, as well as
broom-makers, bear trainers, chimney-
sweeps, musicians, acrobats and
dancers. In the Turkish **Ottoman
Empire,** the Gypsies were generally
treated as a slightly lower rank of Muslims. They paid higher taxes and were
exempt from military service. In 1874
Muslim Gypsies gained equality with
other Muslims in the Ottoman Empire.
They were called up for military service
and ceased paying the special tax.

After the Second World War many
Muslim Gypsies moved from Greece to
Turkey. Gypsies are referred to in Turkish
by the pejorative term *Cingene* and also
Kipti. Apart from the Romanies, there
are also **Lom** (Bosha) and Dom
(**Nawwar**) **clans**, in particular in the
eastern regions. The nomads are
fortune-tellers, sell crafts or work with
metals. The trades of the settled Gypsies
include musicians, flower sellers or
porters.

During the twentieth century the
Gypsies played a substantial role in creating music in the regions of Edirne,
Istanbul and Izmir, since strict Islam forbade the playing of music. Greek, Jewish
and Gypsy music filled this gap. The
most important instruments they play
are the darabuka (drum), tambourine,
the qanun (zither), the oud (lute), the
clarinet and the kemam (violin).
Kibariye is a well-known singer of popular melodies.

There is much prejudice against Gypsies and there have been some incidents
of conflict with the local population. In
1995 Zehala Baysal died in police custody in Istanbul. In 1996 five thousand
Gypsies were evicted from the Selamsiz
quarter of Istanbul. Ali Celikbilek was
Turkey's representative on the **Comité
International Tsigane** until his death in
2001. One of his ideas was for Imrali
Island to become a home for all the Gypsies in Turkey. An academic conference
held in Istanbul in 2003 has awakened

local interest in the history and culture of the Gypsies.

TWIG. UK. Est. 2002. Working party of Gypsies and non-Gypsy planning and legal experts which produced the first draft of the **Traveller Law Reform Bill**. TWIG also organised a series of public meetings where this and related topics were explored.

TZIGANE. (i) A composition for piano and violin by the twentieth century French composer Ravel.

(ii) See TSIGANE

U

UHLIK, Rade 1899–1991. Yugoslavia. Scholar. He published a number of articles on Romani and compiled a dictionary. Many of the folktales he collected are printed in the *Journal of the **Gypsy Lore Society**.*

UKRAINE. Estimated Gypsy population: 75,000. Since 1991 the Ukraine has been an independent state. The first Gypsies arrived in what is now the territory of Ukraine in the sixteenth century and a substantial Gypsy population has lived there ever since.

During the Second World War, the Ukraine was occupied by the Germans and many Gypsies were killed by Task Force (**Einsatzgruppe**) D in Duma-Eli, Krasnye Yerchi, Staryi Krum, Ungut and elsewhere. A delegation of three older Crimean **Tartars** in the village of Asan-Bey asked the German commander to spare the Gypsies there but the officer said he would only free them if the Tartars were willing to die in their place. The Gypsies were locked in a storehouse and shot.

There have been some anti-Gypsy pogroms since the political changes in 1991. In March 1996 a Gypsy woman was raped in Mukačevo during a police raid and in October 2002 an entire Romany family was burnt to death after an arson attack on their home in the village of Malaya Kahnivka, in the Kremenchuk area of Central Ukraine. According to a relative who witnessed the attack, one of the three men responsible for setting the house on fire, was a Police Major in the Kryukov area Police Department. There have also been other reports of Roma being harassed by the police.

The Ukrainian Association of Roma, formed in 2002, is based in Kiev. In June 2003, a conference entitled 'Roma Women: Double Discrimination' took place in Kiev, organised by the Chirikli Romani Women Charity Foundation and the International Renaissance Foundation, Roma of Ukraine Programme.

In the Ukraine three dialects of Romani are spoken: Carpathian, Ukrainian (or Servi) and **haladitko**. The poet Kazimierenka writes in the haladitko dialect as did **Djura Makhotin**. In addition, the Crimean Gypsies speak their own (Krimitka) dialect, which is close to Balkan Romani, or a dialect known as **Ursari** (which is not the same as the Ursari of Romania).

For legislation in the period before 199, see RUSSIA and UNION OF SOCIALIST SOCIALIST REPUBLICS.

UNION OF POETS AND WRITERS. USSR. An élite literary organisation, based in the former Soviet Union. Several Roma belonged to the Union including **Alexander Germano, Nikolai Pankov, Ivan Rom-Lebedev, Nikolai Satkevich**, Ivan Romano and **Valdemar Kalinin**.

UNION OF SOVIET SOCIALIST REPUBLICS (USSR) 1919–91. Estimated Gypsy population in 1991: over 500,000.

For a short time after the success of the 1917 Revolution, the Gypsies in the newly formed Soviet Union were given rights as an ethnic group in exchange for supporting communism. Nomadism was discouraged. In 1926 the Soviet Communist Party's Central Executive Committee issued a decree 'On Measures for Aiding the Transition of Nomadic Gypsies to a Working and Settled Way of Life'. This encouraged Gypsies to adopt a settled life and accept land in each Union Republic. Gypsies who had supplied the Red Army with horses during the Revolution farmed 4,700 acres at a collective farm called Hutor Krikunovo, near Rostov. There were fifty-one Romani collective farms (kolhozi) where all the clerical work was done in the Romani language. However, many Gypsies resisted land settlement, initiating a further settlement decree in 1928. The main factor in the resistance was the change from the tradition of working in extended family groups and inexperience in farming. The estimate for 'settlers' stood at 5,000 between 1926 and 1928 out of the official census of 61,229 Gypsies.

In 1925 the All-Russian Union of Gypsies had been formed, headed by Aleksandr Taranov from Siberia, with **I. Rom-Lebedev** as its secretary. It pressed for Gypsies to be classed as a nation and achieved this status the same year. The journal *Nevo Drom* (New road) began publishing at this time. The authorities later took advantage of some irregularities in the accounts of the Union to dissolve it. The haladitko dialect of Romani was approved as a language for official use within the USSR in the following year. In 1927 the influential journal *Romani Zorya* (Romani Dawn) published its first issue. Wall posters in Romani were seen that year and the All-Russian Union recorded 640 members. In 1929 a popular library series began publication, Biblioteka Vase Skoli Nabut Siklyakirde Manusenge (Library for Schools for People with Little Educa-

tion). The series included *Nevo Džiben* (New Life) (ed. **Aleksandr German**) and **Nikolai Pankov's** *Buti i džinaiben* (Work and Knowledge). The Romengiro Lav (Romani Word) writer's circle in Moscow had among its members I. Rom-Lebedev, the teacher Nina Dudarova, the poet N.I. Pankov and G. Lebedev. Cultural clubs were set up in **Simferopol** and elsewhere. A first reader for schools *Džidi Buti* (Living Things) by Pankov and Dudarova was published the following year, as was a story *Baxt* (Fortune) by Rom-Lebedev and *Nevo Gav* (New Village), an agricultural magazine edited by Alexandr Taranov. The first four schools were opened using the Romani language.

In 1928 the first Romani Congress for the Soviet Union took place. In 1931 the Soviet policy promoted drama in the languages of national minorities, but the theatres were not intended to promote separate national identity. A specially commissioned play with a message of integration, *Romano Drom* (Romani Way), was a success that led eventually to the creation of the Gypsy **Teatr Romen** in that year.

In the period 1928–38 an educational programme flourished and in due course eighty-six Gypsy schools were opened and teacher-training colleges and courses established. There were over forty Gypsy medical students at Smolensk. Alongside these educational developments were more publications, for example, Maksim Sergievski's *Grammar of Romani*, which replaced the earlier grammar by Kerope Patkanov which had been based on the Ukrainian (Carpathian) dialect. Maksim Sergievski and the linguist Aleksei Barannikov later published a Romani-Russian Dictionary.

In 1931 the first issue of a second journal, *Nevo Drom* (New Way) appeared with a 1,000-copy run and some twenty-eight pages in size. Publication continued until issue 6 in June 1932 with political, literary, children's and chess sections. N.I. Pankov translated a treatise on agricultural problems. In 1935

Aleksander German published a number of short stories and plays, *Ganka Chyamba i vavre rosphenibena* (Ganka Chyamba and Other Stories). Leo Tolstoy's children's stories about animals were translated into Romani as *Rosphenibena vas Zivotnonenge.*

All this cultural activity came abruptly to a halt when, in 1938, Joseph Stalin decided that the Gypsies were not a nation as they had no territory and ordered an end to all cultural activity in Romani. The schools were closed and a number of intellectuals, such as **Averian Voitiehovski**, were executed. Others were sent to labour camps in Siberia. Only the Teatr Romen was to survive. The Second World War and the **Holocaust** followed and not until 1970 did any further publication appear in Romani in the USSR.

Soon after the invasion of the Soviet Union in 1941 by Nazi Germany, the Task Forces (**Einsatzgruppen**) and other units set about killing Jews and Gypsies. Task Force B shot and buried alive 1,000 Gypsies at Rodnya near Smolensk, while Task Force D murdered over 800 Gypsies in Simferopol in the Crimea in December 1941. Ivan Tokmakov, who had been in charge of the Communist Party's Gypsy programme and who looked after the Gypsy collective farms, was executed by the Germans. Many Gypsies served in the Soviet armed forces, such as naval hero Ivan Kozlovski, while others joined the partisans. Over 30,000 Gypsies were murdered, representing about half of the population of the occupied territories.

After 1945 Stalin's rule became even more despotic. The remaining Romani collective farms were abandoned, forcing Gypsies to move to non-Gypsy farms. A number of **Sinti** Gypsies were deported by Stalin to the east alongside the Volga Germans who were accused of collaborating with the German invaders. After Stalin's death in 1953, Nikita Krushchev, his successor, was to adopt policies in 1956 that aimed at finally destroying the nomadic traditions of the Romanies. In 1956 nomadism was forbidden by the law *On Reconciling Wandering Gypsies to Work.* Some Gypsies resisted sedentarisation by travelling round farms for seasonal labour or working as herdsmen moving from pasture to pasture.

The Gypsy Writers' Club was set up for writers in the Russian language but writing in Romani was still discouraged. The first census after the Second World War registered 130,000 Gypsies in the whole of the Soviet Union (including the Asian republics) but many Gypsies put themselves down as belonging to another nationality. Under Leonid Brezhnev (from 1964) some liberalisation occurred in the USSR. In 1970 the first publication in Romani since 1938 appeared when **Georgi Kantea** published in the Moldavian SSR a collection of poems, proverbs and tales in the Ursari dialect. Prominent Gypsy writers in the Russian language included Kantea himself, **K. Rudevics** in Latvia, **Aleksandr Belugins** (Leksa Manush) in Moscow and Vano Romano in the Altai region. **N. Satkievich** published some of his poetry and re-opened Gypsy schools in Siberia.

Romanies began to outstrip the average of population growth in the 1980s when the census recorded 210,000 Gypsies, with 74 per cent claiming Romani as their mother tongue. With the advent in 1985 of yet a new national leader, Mihail Gorbachev, a new freedom was in the air with *glasnost* (openness) and *perestroika* (restructuring). Gypsy culture thrived but was, until 1990, prevented from international contact. Then, government officials in 1990 allowed Gypsies to attend the fourth **World Romani Congress** near Warsaw (8–12 April) which heralded a growth in Soviet Romanies' participation in international Gypsy affairs.

For this area in the period before 1919 and after 1991 see ARMENIA; BELARUS; ESTONIA; GEORGIA; LATVIA; LITHUANIA; MOLDOVA; RUSSIA; UKRAINE.

UNIÓN ROMANI. Spain. Est. 1986 President: **Juan de Dios Ramirez-Heredia**. An organisation linking the majority of the local and national associations.

UNITE (UNIFIED NOMADIC AND INDEPENDENT TRANSNATIONAL EDUCATION) UK. Co-ordinator: Barrie Taylor. The aim of the organisation is to build a centre that will provide supplementary education and advice to Gypsies. A site in Essex has been found to develop a **Holocaust** and Cultural Heritage Centre.

UNITED KINGDOM. See ENGLAND, NORTHERN IRELAND, SCOTLAND and WALES. Legislation passed by the London Parliament will generally apply in Wales.

UNITED NATIONS (UN). The first time the UN paid attention to Gypsies was in 1977. Then the Sub-commission on the Prevention of Discrimination and Protection of Minorities of the Economic and Social Council's Commission on Human Rights adopted a resolution on the protection of the Gypsies. This asked all states to accord equal rights to Roma (Gypsies). In 1991 the same sub-commission noted that there was still discrimination against Gypsies and so, in 1992, the main Commission on Human Rights passed Resolution 65 on the Protection of Roma (Gypsies). This measure "invites States to adopt all appropriate measures in order to eliminate any form of discrimination against Roma (Gypsies)."

Following the publication of its report *Avoiding the Dependency Trap* (2003), the UN has launched a new development programme, under the directorship of Kalman Miszei, which aims to empower Roma in central and Eastern Europe. The report underlined the fact that unemployment amongst Roma in Eastern Europe averaged 40 per cent, and 90 per cent was not unusual in some areas.

URSARI. Bear trainers. The word is derived from Romanian *urs*. It is the name of several clans of Gypsies who train bears and of at least two distinct dialects of Romani.

URSITORY. (i) In **Kalderash** tradition, female spirits who appear at the birth of a child to name the child.

(ii) A novel by **Matéo Maximoff** in which the Ursitory appear.

USTI INITIATIVE (arise). A programme supported by George Soros.

USTI NAD LABEM. In October 1999, a wall measuring 2 metres high and 65 metres long was erected on Matićni Street in the northern Czech town of Usti Nad Labem to separate Gypsies from their non-Gypsy neighbours. Romani activists from around the Czech Republic went to Usti Nad Labem to try to prevent the wall's construction, and it was finally built under police guard. Dubbed 'the wall of shame', it was erected at the request of non-Gypsy home-owners who complained of noise and disorder from nearby Gypsy flats. Although legally empowered to do so, central Czech authorities failed to prevent the wall's construction and only annulled the municipal resolution to build the wall after it had been completed. The wall has been removed.

UŠTIBEN (Rising up). UK. Est. 2001. President: Ladislav Balaz. Created to coordinate political activity on behalf of the Roma.

V

VAGHRI. It has been suggested that – at the same time as the ancestors of the European Gypsies moved west – a small group of nomads migrated south, the Narikuravar or Vaghri. They speak a north Indian language and their traditional occupation is catching birds – which is the meaning of their name in Tamil. They call themselves Vaghri. Since the enforcement of the *Wild Life Protection Act* 1972 many have switched to selling beads and other trinkets.

In 1961 a Tamil named K. Raghupathi gave up his work with a bus company and started a day school in Trichi. Six years later he set up a meeting of sixty-seven leaders of the community to form the Nadodi Nalvazue Sangam. K. Raghupathi married a woman from the **clan**, Jnasundari, which made him more accepted by the people he was working with. In 1972 he set up a boarding school in Madras against much initial opposition from the parents of the children, since when further school projects have been initiated.

The Vaghri have not reached the political maturity of the **Banjara** and links between them and European Romanies have been solely through **Pentecostal** missionaries.

VAIDA VOEVOD III (IONEL ROTARU). France. Political activist. In 1959 he was elected to the title Voevod by members of the Romanian **Ursari** tribe. In 1960 he founded the **Communauté Mondiale Gitane** (CMG). His aims included setting up an independent state, **Romanestan**. After the French government banned the CMG, he became less active.

VANNER. Britain. A breed of horse developed by the Romanies of Britain to pull their traditional caravans, whence the name. They are a combination of Friesian, Shire, Clydesdale and Dales pony. They are considered to be docile and intelligent. The first Vanner horse was imported to the United States in 1996 by Dennis and Cindy Thompson.

VERBAND DER DEUTSCHEN SINTI. Germany. The main organisation of **Sinti**, based in Heidelberg and run by **Romani Rose**. It represents the Sinti in consultations with the German government, has a documentation centre and intervenes on behalf of the rights of the Sinti.

VERBUNKOS. A dance used by recruiting units in Hungary in the eighteenth and nineteenth centuries. It was adopted and adapted by Gypsies and then by the composer **Franz Liszt**.

VIG, Rudolf 1929–83. Hungary. Musicologist. He collected over 3,000 Gypsy songs. Some have been issued as recordings, for example, those from Szabolcs-Szatmar County.

VLAH/VLACH/VLAX/OLAH. The 'ch' (or 'x') represents the sound in Scottish 'loch' or Yiddish *chutzpah*. The description Vlah would strictly be applied to Gypsy **clans** and dialects of Romani that originate from Wallachia but it is used more generally in Gypsy studies for those clans that come from, or are still on, Romanian-speaking territory (parts of Banat, Transylvania, Wallachia and Moldavia). These include **Kalderash** and **Lovari**.

The Vlah dialects are now divided by linguists into two groups. Those of the earliest clans to leave Romania have not palatalised the sounds ch and sh.

VOICE OF ROMA (VOR). US. President: Sani Rifati. The organisation promotes educational and charitable projects for and about Roma. In recent years, VOR has conducted humanitarian aid projects for Roma in and from Kosovo. In addition to these humanitarian aid projects, it has acted as an advocate for Romani refugees from Kosovo.

VOITIEHOVSKI, Averiand d. 1938. USSR. Teacher. He was headmaster of the Gypsy school in Leningrad during the period when Romani culture was encouraged by the Soviet authorities. In 1938 he was executed for 'anti-government activities.'

VOIVODINA. Estimated Roma population: 65,000. The official returns in the 1971 census showed 7,760 Roma but by 1991 the figure reached the more realistic total of 24,895. The estimated Romani population was 55,000 before the recent immigration from Kosovo. A province formerly of Yugoslavia and now of Serbia-Montenegro. It remains part of Serbia, its autonomy having been suspended in 1990 at the same time as a similar proclamation in the province of Kosovo. During the Second World War it was occupied by Hungary which tried to deport many of the Romani population into Serbia proper. Nevertheless, many Roma remained there throughout the wartime period. When Voivodina was re-occupied by Yugoslav forces after the Second World War the population was manipulated in various ways until the ethnic Hungarian majority became a minority.

A number of dialects are spoken, in particular **Vlah** and **Gurbet**, though many Roma have Hungarian or Romanian as their mother tongue. The frontier town of Sremska Mitrovica saw an influx of Muslim refugees from Bosnia after 1992 bringing its Romani population up to some 8,000. Further refugees have arrived from Kosovo in later years.

In Voivodina, the Roma are not integrated and most still live in settlements on the outskirts of towns and villages. Anti-Roma graffiti have appeared here and instances of police brutality have been reported. Just after midnight on 22 September 2001 two policemen approached a group of Roma children who were collecting waste paper outside a restaurant in Novi Sad. The officers asked the children what they were doing and then one of them suddenly struck E.M. on the head. The officer went up to the boy and knocked him to the ground by kicking him in the legs. The other officer ran up and both began kicking E.M. The boy tried to protect his head with his hands but one of his arms was fractured by a kick. The policemen then ordered the children to go home and cursed their "Shiptar [= Albanian] mothers."

Educational levels for Roma are low, as elsewhere in Yugoslavia. In 1996 the cultural organization Matrica Romska was set up in Novi Sad but with a remit to cover all Serbia. Its first President was the writer **Trifun Dimić**. The following year a round table on the Standardisation of the Romani Language in Yugoslavia was organised in Novi Sad by the Matrica Romska and the Voivodina Society for the Romani Language, one of many attempts in recent years to standardise Romani. The organisation Drustvo Voivodina (Voivodina Association) is also working for the advancement of the Romani language, while optional instruction in Romani has been introduced in primary schools in Obrovac and Tovarisevo.

VRANCKX, Agnes (Bibi Anisha). France. Contemporary political activist. She became secretary of a Gypsy organisation in Belgium. She then helped to set up the Common Market Gypsy Committee of the **International Romani Union** and, later, the **West European Gypsy Council**. She is currently living in Rajasthan.

W

WAJS, Bronislawa (Papusza) 1910–87. Poland. Poet. During the Second World War she survived by hiding in the forests, an experience described in her lyrics, written in Romani, such as *Ratvale jasva* (Tears of Blood). In those days her family were against the publication of her verse, which was published by **Jerzy Ficowski**.

WALES. Estimated Gypsy population: 3,000. In 1996, the date of the last formal count, there were 489 caravans recorded (a fall from earlier figures), of which thirty-six were on unauthorised encampments. For most legislative purposes, Wales is part of the United Kingdom while the Assembly has only limited powers.

Gypsies probably arrived in Wales for the first time during the sixteenth century. The first use of the Welsh term *Sipsiwn* for Gypsy can be found in a poem, composed by Morris Kyffin at the end of the sixteenth century. The first official record of Gypsies recorded in Wales dates from 1579 and refers to the arrest of Gypsies in the then county of Radnor. A Gypsy named Abraham Wood arrived in Wales around 1730 and founded the **Wood clan**. He is said to have brought the violin to Wales and his descendants included many well-known musicians. Other families who came to Wales and spent a long time there are the Ingrams and some of the Prices and Lees. They are classed as Welsh Gypsies.

Gypsies from Europe arrived in Wales in 1906 but they were kept under strict police supervision before being escorted back into England and deported from Hull.

The last named speaker of Romani (Manfri Wood) died around 1968. **Derek Tipler** met a group of Romani-speaking Welsh Gypsies in Caernarvonshire in 1950 but it is not known whether any of them are still alive. Many of the Welsh Gypsies have moved into houses. Others continue to travel in caravans and visit England and Scotland. The caravan-dwelling population of Wales today includes **Irish Travellers** and, in South Wales, descendants of marriages between English and Welsh Gypsies.

The Welsh Assembly commissioned a Review of Service Provision for Gypsies which was published in April 2003. It made fifty-two recommendations including re-establishing the twice yearly counts and putting a duty on local authorities to provide or facilitate sites. For legislation, see ENGLAND.

WALLACHIA. A province of Romania. The first record of Gypsies in Wallachia dates from around 1360 when a document records the transfer of slaves. Gypsies were among those who later suffered the cruelties of Vlad IV, Prince of Wallachia (known as Dracula). It is said that he had many of them boiled alive, burned and hanged. Slavery was abolished in Wallachia in 1856. See also ROMANIA.

WARD, Bernie. Ireland. Boxer. Known in Ireland as the 'King of **Travellers**', he was crowned at the Connemara pony fair. It is said that he beat a number of Travellers from the Sweeney clan in a bare-knuckle fistfight in a bid to settle an ongoing feud.

WASO. Belgium A group that plays Gypsy music from many countries. **Fapy Lafertin** can be heard on some of their recordings.

WEISS, Hänsche. Germany. Contemporary musician. Though leader of a jazz sextet, it was with a quintet that he recorded volumes 5 and 6 of the compilation *Musik Deutscher Zigeuner* (Music of German Gypsies).

WEISS, Kokalo and Meisel. Netherlands.

Two brothers who, performing as Tata Mirando, senior and junior, are the leaders of two contemporary bands playing Balkan-style music.

WEISS, Kussi. Germany. Contemporary musician. A guitarist and nephew of **Hänsche Weiss**, he plays Gypsy style and popular jazz.

WEISS, Lalla. The Netherlands. Contemporary civil rights activist. She is a spokesperson for the **Sinti**.

WELT-ZIGLER, Sterna. France. Contemporary poet. She writes in French and **Sinti** dialect.

WEST EUROPEAN GYPSY COUNCIL. 1981. A re-launch of the earlier Common Market Gypsy Council. **Agnes Vranckx** and **Giles Eynard** were the first secretaries. No longer active.

WIESENTHAL, Simon. 1908–. Jewish 'Nazi hunter' He has been active in seeing that the fate of the Gypsies during the **Holocaust** is not forgotten.

WILLIAMSON, DUNCAN 1928–. Scotland. **Scottish Traveller**, storyteller and singer. His tales have been published in many books. He has also recorded a cassette, *Put Another Log on the Fire*, on which he recites, sings and plays the mouth organ and jaw's harp. He is now settled in a house in Fife but tours widely in Britain, entertaining in schools and at festivals.

WINTERSTEIN, Titi. Germany. Contemporary musician and singer. A **Sinti** violinist. Since 1978, his quintet has played a variety of jazz and Gypsy music in the Hungarian style. His recordings include *Djinee tu Kowa Ziro* (Do You Know This Time), *Saitenstrassen* (String Streets—a pun on *Seitenstrassen*, side streets) and the compilation *Best of Titi Winterstein.*

WLISLOCKI, Henrich. Transylvania. Scholar. He studied the Gypsies in the nineteenth century and published a number of important books: *Vom wanderenden Zigeunervolke* (About the Roaming Gypsy People, 1890) and *Die Sprache der Transilvanischen Zigeuner* (The Language of the Transylvanian Gypsies, 1884).

WOOD, Abraham (Abram). England. Musician. He came to Wales from the west of England around 1730 with his wife Sarah and three children and set up a family base near Monmouth. He was a violinist and is said to have been the first person to play the violin in Wales. Abraham Wood had four children: Valentine (John), William, Solomon and Damaris. They married into other Gypsy clans, the Stanleys, Ingrams and Boswells and the eldest son, Valentine, was the grandfather of the famous harpist John Wood Jones (born 1800). John Wood Jones was also a teacher of the harp to blind and lame children in a school at Carmarthen. In 1843, a year before his death, he accompanied Thomas Gruffydd to Buckingham Palace to perform on the harp before the Prince of Wales, Prince Albert, and her Majesty Queen Victoria, to their apparent satisfaction.

Other harpist descendants of Abraham Wood included John Roberts and William Lewis. The former performed before the Grand Duke Constantine of Russia at Aberystwyth in 1847 and the King of the Belgians in the following year while William Lewis was to play at the Royal Command concert in London in 1932 and later gave performances at the *Phoenix* Theatre.

The great scholar of the **Romani language**, **John Sampson**, recorded the dialect, folktales and songs of the Wood clan and identified their dialect as distinct from that of the English Gypsies recorded by Leland Smart and Crofton during the nineteenth century. He learned Romani from the harpist Edward Wood, a descendant of Abraham Wood, and other members of the family.

WOOD, Fred (Manfri). England. Contemporary political activist. First President of the **Gypsy Council** in December 1966. A skilled woodcarver and performer on the jaw's harp, his biography is called *In the Life of a Romany Gypsy.*

WOONWAGENBEWONERS. (Caravan dwellers). Indigenous caravan dwellers in Holland. They number some 20,000 and form a separate community with their own customs. Some speak a variety of Dutch known as **Bargoens**. After 1945 the official policy was to build caravan camps and get them to stop travelling. These camps were at first very large, with a school, shop and church. It soon became evident that these large camps caused problems, for example, there was too much competition for the same sort of work. Policy then switched to building smaller camps and breaking up the large ones.

WORLD BANK. As the countries of Eastern Europe were moving towards accession to the **European Union**, the World Bank organised a conference in Budapest in 2003 under the title *Roma in an Expanding Europe: Challenges for the Future*. A report *Breaking the Poverty Cycle for the Roma* was presented at the Conference. James Wolfensohn, President of the Bank, said: "Europe must not leave the Roma behind."

WORLD ROMANI CONGRESS. There have been five congresses organised by the **International Romani Union** (IRU) and its predecessors in the years since the end of the Second World War.

The first World Romani Congress in 1971, with delegates attending from fourteen countries, was held near London under the auspices of the **Comité International Tzigane**. It was originally intended to be a preparatory meeting to plan the first congress. However, because of the number of delegates coming and the number of countries represented, it was decided to make this meeting the first congress itself. **Grattan Puxon** was elected secretary and **Slobodan Berberski**, from Belgrade, president. During the Congress work was divided between five specialised commissions dealing with education, social problems, war crimes reparations, culture and language. It was agreed to struggle against illiteracy and that the use of Romani in schools should be officially recognised. The language commission agreed that there should be a move toward unifying the language. The open-

ing day of the conference, 8 April, was proclaimed the national day (**Roma Nation Day**) to be celebrated every year. A **national anthem** and a **flag** were adopted.

The second World Romani Congress was held in April 1978 in Geneva, Switzerland, and was attended by 120 delegates from twenty-six countries. The **United Nations**, the Human Rights Commission of that organisation and **UNESCO** had representatives at the Congress who put the case for future co-operation. **Jan Cibula** was elected president replacing Slobodan Berberski and **Shaip Jusuf** was elected vice president. **Yul Brynner** was chosen as the honorary president and took part in the final press conference. During the Congress the **International Romani Union** (IRU) was established.

The work of organising further congresses was carried out by the IRU. The third World Romani Congress was in Göttingen, Germany, in May 1981, with 300 representatives from twenty-two countries and the support of the **Gesellschaft für Bedrohte Völker**. The history of the Gypsy people under the Nazis was confronted on the first day. **Simon Wiesenthal** and **Miriam Novitch** were among the speakers. At this Congress, Grattan Puxon was replaced as secretary by **Rajko Djurić**, and **Sait Balić** replaced Jan Cibula as president.

The fourth World Romani Congress organised by the International Romani Union was held in April 1990 near Warsaw. Over 200 delegates from eighteen countries were present. After a formal opening on 8 April, the next day was devoted to reports from different countries. It was preceded by a Language Conference on the Standardisation of the **Romani Language**. Language was an important point on the agenda as the Congress agreed to the proposal for a new common alphabet. This Congress had a higher number of delegates from Eastern Europe than any of the previous three. A highlight of the

Congress was a televised concert in which many well-known groups, took part including **Esma Redjepova's** ensemble. Rajko Djurić replaced Sait Balić as president and **Emil Sčuka** was elected general secretary. The membership of the commissions was fixed by elections. The following commissions were set up: Cultural, Encyclopaedia, Language, Holocaust/Reparations, Education and Information. Because of lack of funds these commissions were not particularly active.

The Fifth World Romani Congress, again organised by the IRU, was held in Prague in July 2000, in the headquarters of Radio Free Europe and 122 delegates from thirty-eight different countries attended in order to approve a new programme, statutes, and elect a new leadership of the IRU.

The first day was spent electing a committee to oversee the Congress and forming working groups. On the following day topics were agreed for the agenda, including the situation of Roma in Kosovo, restitution for Romani **Holocaust** victims, the migration of Roma from central and Eastern Europe, and the standardisation of the Romani language. Out of these discussions in the working groups, it was agreed that a new statute for the IRU be created, declaring that the Roma want to be recognised as a nation. There were also calls for Germany to apologise for what has become known as the Roma **Holocaust** in which up to half a million Roma were killed by the Nazis during the Second World War.

The culmination of the Congress was the election of a new president for the IRU. The successful candidate was **Emil Sčuka**, from the Czech Republic, previously the general secretary. **Hristo Kyuchukov** from Bulgaria was elected as the new General Secretary.

For other international gatherings see INTERNATIONAL MEETINGS and LODZ CONGRESS.

XY

X. In the international phonetic alphabet and in most systems of writing Romani the letter 'x' represents the sound in Scottish 'loch' or German *doch*.

YATES, *Dora* 1879–1974. England. Scholar. From a Jewish background she was for many years Secretary of the **Gypsy Lore Society** and editor of its journal.

YETHOLM. See KIRK YETHOLM.

YUGOSLAVIA. Estimated Gypsy population of Yugoslavia in 1992 (before the break-up of the republic): one million. In 1981 a census gave the figure of 850,000 Gypsies for the whole of Yugoslavia. This showed a rise throughout the country as Gypsies felt encouraged to declare their ethnicity. Only in Macedonia and Kosovo was there pressure on them to declare themselves as Albanians by that community. The reduced Yugoslav state after 1992 (Serbia and Montenegro) has a population of some 150,000–200,000 Gypsies.

The first Gypsies appeared on the territory of modern Yugoslavia in the fourteenth century. Yugoslavia existed as an independent country from 1918 to 1941 and again from 1945 to 1992, as well as from 1992 to the present day in a reduced form consisting of Serbia (with Voivodina and Kosovo) and Montenegro only.

In the Yugoslav state set up in 1918, there was a Gypsy population of some 200,000. These were for the most part settled or semi-nomadic and belonged to all three religions (Catholic, Muslim and Orthodox Christian). Only in Montenegro was there a large nomadic population. Some cultural activity took place in Belgrade where there was a settled community, mostly living in separate Gypsy quarters. Three issues of a bilingual magazine *Romano Lil* (Romani Paper), edited by Svetozar Simić, were published in 1935.

In 1941 the German army invaded Yugoslavia which was split into separate parts. After the liberation in 1945 the Yugoslav Federation was re-established, as a republic. It is said that Marshal Tito (the partisan leader and president of the new republic) had promised the Gypsies who fought with the partisans that they would have their own state after the war. It was likely that this would have been carved out of Macedonia. However, this plan was dropped probably because Tito did not wish to reduce Macedonia in size in case it became the object of territorial demands by Greece and Albania. Nevertheless, in communist Yugoslavia the Gypsies were declared a national minority though their exact status varied from state to state.

Over 50,000 Yugoslav Gypsies had perished during the Nazi **holocaust**, leaving a population of perhaps 600,000 in 1945. It was to be the Romanies of Macedonia who developed the largest Gypsy community called **Shuto (Šuto) Orizari** on the outskirts of **Skopje**. The economic restructuring of Yugoslavia during the 1960s also saw a wave of mass migration of many Gypsies to the west as the restrictions on emigration were eased. Predominantly from Bosnia-Herzegovina, Montenegro and Kosovo, the migrants moved to Germany, France and other countries. Many took jobs in factories, others nomadised in caravans.

The antagonisms among nationalities in the country intensified which led Tito and the Yugoslav government to hold back the official recognition of Gypsies as a nationality (as opposed to the lower status of an ethnic group)

across Yugoslavia. In 1971, however, **Faik Abdi**, the representative from Shuto Orizari in the Macedonian Parliament, was able to upgrade the status of Romanies to an officially recognised nationality in Macedonia. This allowed the use of the Romani **flag** and language as well as time on radio and television. In 1981 Roma were recognised as a National Minority across Yugoslavia.

The press began to refer to Roma instead of the pejorative *Tsigani*. Publications in Romani included local periodicals and a standard biography of Tito translated into Romani in 1978 by **Šaip Jusuf**. In 1981 Radio Tetovo began a half-hour programme in Romani. Eighty local Romani associations also sprang up during this period, many focusing on cultural activities and calling themselves **Phralipe** (Brotherhood).

In 1986 Muslim Gypsies were prevented from burying their dead in a Muslim cemetery in Bosnia and officials in Slovenia tried to stop Gypsies voting in local elections. In Kuršumlija a Gypsy woman was doused with gasoline and burned. The greatest barrier for the Gypsies remained illiteracy as most children did not complete secondary education.

Two bilingual magazines still appear irregularly, *Romano Lil* (Romani Paper) for adults and *Čhavrikano Lil* (Children's Paper). The editor of the former, **Dragomir Asković**, is also active in the radio broadcasts in Romani from Radio Belgrade. The government has made some attempt to gain the allegiance of the Gypsies, for example, by holding a ceremonial orthodox service with prayers in Romani and attended by government figures. See also BANAT; BOSNIA-HERZEGOVINA; CROATIA; KOSOVO; MACEDONIA; MONTENEGRO; SERBIA; SLOVENIA; VOIVODINA.

Z

ZAMOLY ROMA. In July 2000 twelve Roma families from the Hungarian village of Zamoly travelled to Strasbourg where they demanded political asylum and protection from racial persecution. They fled to France after their houses had been destroyed. In 2001 thirty-seven out of the original forty-six Roma were granted refugee status by the **European Court of Human Rights** in Strasbourg. It has been suggested that the Roma had been manipulated by the Russian secret service as part of a master plan to darken Hungary's human rights record and keep the EU from expanding east.

ZANKO. France. Twentieth-century political activist. A chief of the **Kalderash** of southern France. His stories were recorded by Père Chatard.

ZIGENARE See ZIGEUNER

ZIGEUNER. The old German word for Gypsies. Derived from Greek *athinganos* as are the Scandinavian equivalents (*Zigenare*, etc). Because of the association of the term *Zigeuner* with the Nazi period, books and the press in Germany now often use the term '*Rom und Sinti*' to refer to all Gypsies, regardless of whether they are in fact Roma or **Sinti.**

ZIGEUNERBARON (Unternehmen Zige-unerbaron). This was the code name for a German army operation in Yugoslavia in 1943, with no Gypsy connection. The name came from Johann Strauss's operetta of the same name.

ZIGEUNERLEBEN (Gypsy Life). The title of the writers' conference Biennale Kleinerer Sprachen (Biennial for Minor Languages) held in Berlin, October 1991, which was devoted to Gypsy writers. Amongst those taking part were **Rajko Djurić**, **Margita Reiznerová**, and **Philomena Franz** as well as Jovan Nicolić from Belgrad.

ZINGARI. The common Italian name for Gypsies, derived from Greek **athingani**. **Gitano** is also used.

ZOLTAN, Florina 1964–. Romania. Civil rights activist. She is now living in England.

ZOTT. An old Arabic word used for all Indians, not just the Jats. It was used to refer to the many people of Indian origin in the Middle East in the times of the great Arab Caliphate and is still used as another name for the **Nawwar**, a Gypsy clan.

ZSIGO, Jeno 1951–2000. Hungary. Youth leader and musician. He played with the band **Ando Drom**.

Bibliography

The bibliography is arranged by classes and subclasses. With very few exceptions, only works published after 1945 in western European languages have been included in this edition. For historical works, one should consult George Black's *A Gypsy Bibliography* (Edinburgh: Gypsy Lore Society, 1914). A supplementary list was published in 1940 in the *Journal of the Gypsy Lore Society* (3rd series) 19 nos. 1-2, 20-33. Translations are given for titles in Russian and less common languages. Books are entered only once. A book dealing with the history or present-day situation of one country only will be found under that country's heading, not under 'History'. However, many other titles are listed by subject (e.g. health, music). Books and articles dealing with more than one of the countries that make up the United Kingdom will be found under that heading. There are separate headings, however, for England, Scotland and Wales where titles deal only with one of the countries making up the United Kingdom. Northern Ireland will be found under Ireland

Apart from Black for the classical literature, Diane Tong's *Gypsies: A Multidisciplinary Annotated Bibliography* (New York: Garland, 1995) gives good coverage of material in English though it is not comprehensive on works in other languages.

A good overall introduction to the subject is Angus Fraser's *The Gypsies* (Oxford: Blackwell, 1992). For the modern period the various works by Jean-Pierre Liégeois should be consulted.

Nearly all works written up to 1939 are by outsiders and treat Gypsies as an exotic race. An exception was the substantial number of books written in Romani in the early years of the Soviet Union. After 1945 there is a wider coverage of themes and an increase in books written by Romanies themselves.

Until the end of the Second World War the *Journal of the Gypsy Lore Society* (*JGLS*) was the only serious publication and is still a rich source of information. Anyone embarking on a study of Gypsies should first leaf through the *JGLS* to see what has been written on the themes that interest them. There have been five series, the second being known as the New Series. The third series was the longest with 52 volumes. The fifth series is published from the United States under the title *Romani Studies*.

After 1945 more learned journals appear, in particular *Études Tsiganes* and (the discontinued) *Lacio Drom*. They, too, are a valuable source of information on a variety of topics. Some recent articles from all three journals have been included in the bibliography. As regards the different clans, the Kalderash and Manouche are those that have been described the most often. In fact, many books and articles purporting to be about Gypsies only write about the Kalderash.

The section on the Nazi genocide contains many titles and is one of the largest. Although in the first years after 1945 very little was written about the fate of the Gypsies, this lapse has been remedied in recent years, particularly with books dealing with the history of individual towns in Germany. The only overall picture of the period will be found in Donald Kenrick and Grattan Puxon's *Destiny of Europe's Gypsies* (London: Heinemann, 1972). This has an index and detailed references. The updated edition under the title *Gypsies under the Swastika* (Hatfield: University of Hertfordshire Press, 1995) is more for the general reader and has no references. A three-volume work on the Holocaust entitled *The Gypsies during the Second World War* was being prepared in Paris by the now-closed Centre de Recherches Tsiganes. Two parts have been published and a third volume is in preparation (University of Hertfordshire Press, 1997–). Michael Zimmermann's scholarly tome in German (*Rassenutopie und Genozid: Die nationalsozialistische 'Lösung der Zigeunerfrage.'* Hamburg: Christiansverlag, 1996) is due to be published in English. Both it and the more controversial book by Guenter Lewy (*The Nazi Persecution of the Gypsies.* Oxford: OUP, 2000) deal only with Germany and the lands occupied by its army and omit the satellite Axis countries.

There is only one comprehensive work dealing with literature written by Gypsies, whether in Romani or other languages (Djurić, Rajko, *Die Literatur der Roma und Sinti.* Berlin: Parabolis, 2002) but some articles are listed in the relevant section.

Currently, a large number of bilingual periodicals are being published in Eastern Europe. However, many of them are irregular and financial difficulties have sometimes led to gaps in their appearance. Addresses are provided below for a small number of publications that are informative, rather than literary, and that have a track record of reliability.

Table of contents

I. General

II.History

IX. Press

X. Websites   231

XI. Discographies   231

I. General

l. Overall Studies

Acton, T. A., ed. *Gypsy Politics and Traveller Identity.* Hatfield: University of Hertfordshire Press, 1997 (Proceedings of the ESRC Romany Studies Seminar Series vol. l)

— (ed.) *Scholarship and the Gypsy Struggle: Commitment in Romani Studies.* Hatfield: University of Hertfordshire Press, 2000

— and Gary Mundy, eds. *Romani Culture and Gypsy Identity.* Hatfield. University of Hertfordshire Press, 1997 (Proceedings of the ESRC Romany Studies Seminar Series vol. 2)

Andersen, Kirsten. *Sigojnere.* Copenhagen: Munksgaard, 1971

Asséo, Henriette. *Les Tsiganes, une destinée européenne.* Paris: Gallimard, 1994

Barany, Zoltan. *The East European Gypsies.* Cambridge: CUP, 2002

Block, Martin. *Die Zigeuner: Ihr Leben und ihre Seele.* Frankfurt am Main: Lang, 1997 (new edition.)

Bodi. Zsuzsanna, ed. *Readings of the 1st International Conference on Gypsy Ethnography* (Budapest, 1993*).* Studies in Roma (Gypsy) Ethnography. vol. 2. Budapest: Mikszáth Kiadó, 1994. In English and Hungarian

Bogaart, Nico, et al. *Zigeuners.* Amsterdam: El Sevier, 1980

Djurić, Rajko. *Seobe Roma* (Romany Migrations). Belgrade: BIGZ, 1987

Earle, Fiona, et al. *A Time to Travel? An introduction to Britain's newest Travellers.* Lyme Regis, UK: Enabler, 1994

Gronemeyer, Reimer, and Georgia Rakelmann. *Die Zigeuner, Reisende in Europa.* Cologne: Dumont, 1988

Guy, Will (ed.) *Between past and future: the Roma of Central and Eastern Europe.* Hatfield: University of Hertfordshire Press, 2001

Hancock, Ian. *We are the Romani people.* Hatfield: University of Hertford-shire Press, 2002

Hemetek, Ursula and Mozes Heinschink, eds. *Roma. Das unbekannte Volk.* Munich: Boehlau, 1994

Hohmann, Joachim, ed. *Handbuch zur Tsiganologie.* Frankfurt am Main: Lang, 1996

—. *Zigeuner und Zigeunerwissenschaft.* Marburg: Guttandin Hope, 1980

—. *Zigeuner: zehn in der Nacht sind neun: Geschichte und Geschichten der Zigeuner.* Darmstadt: Luchterhand. 1982

Hundsalz, Andreas. *Stand der Forschung über Zigeuner und Landfahrer.* Stuttgart: Kohlhammer, 1978

Karpati, Mirella, ed. *Zingari ieri e oggi.* Rome: Centro Studi Zingari, n.d. (Also in German as *Sinti und Roma: Heute und Gestern*)

Klein, N.*Sinti und Roma* Institut für Auslandsbeziehungen, Stuttgart 1981

Klopcic, Vera and Miroslav Polzer eds. *Wege zur Verbesserung der Lage der Roma in Mittel und Osteuropa.* Vienna: Braumüller. Special number (54) of *Ethnos,* 1999 (Papers from the Murdka-Sobota Conference,1997)

Liégeois, Jean-Pierre. *Roma, Gypsies and Travellers.* Rev.ed. Strasbourg:

Council of Europe Press, 1994 (Also in French as *Roma, Tsiganes, Voyageurs*)

Lo-Johansson, Ivar. *Zigenare.* Stockholm: Prisma, 1963

Lucassen, Leo et al. eds. *Gypsies and other Itinerant Groups.* Basingstoke: Macmillan, 1998

Maur, Wolf in der. *Die Zigeuner: Wanderer zwischen den Welten.* Vienna: Molden, 1969

Mayall, David, ed. 'Gypsies: The Forming of Identities and Official Responses'. *Immigrants and Minorities.* 2, no.1 (March 1992) (special edition)

Mercier, Denis. *Latcho Drom: Un film de Tony Gatlif.* Paris: K.G. Productions,1993

Mroz, Lech. *Cyganie.* Warsaw: Ksiazka i Wiedza, 1971

Nordström-Holm, Gunni and Armas Lind. *Om zigenare.* Stockholm: SI Pocket, 1982

Nordström-Holm, Gunni and Björn Myrman. *Vi kallar dem Zigenare.* Stockholm: Alfabeta, 1991

Osella, Carla. *Zingari, storie di un popolo sconosciuto.* Turin: 1985

Rehfisch, F. ed. *Gypsies, Tinkers and Other Travellers.* London: Academic Press, 1975

Rostás-Farkas, György. *Cigánységom vállalom.* Budapest: TIT, 1992 (Essays on Romani culture in Hungarian.)

Salo, Matt, ed. *100 Years of Gypsy Studies.* Cheverly, Md.: Gypsy Lore Society, 1990 (Papers from the 10th Annual Meeting of the GLS, 1988)

Šipka, Milan, ed. *International Symposium: Romani Language and Culture.* Sarajevo: Institut za Proučavanje Nacionalnih Odnosa, 1989 (Papers of the 1986 Sarajevo Seminar.)

Thesleff, Arthur. *Report on the Gypsy Question.* 1901 (reprinted in *JGLS* new series.)

Tong, Diana. *Gypsies: an Interdisciplinary Reader.* New York: Garland, 1998

Vossen, Rüdiger, ed. *Zigeuner.* Frankfurt am Main: Ullstein, 1983

Willems, Wim. *Op zoek naar de ware Zigeuner.* Utrecht: van Arkel, 1995

—*In Search of the True Gypsy.* London: Cass, 1997 (English translation of the above title.)

Wiliams, Patrick, ed. *Tsiganes: identité, évolution.* Paris: Etudes Tsiganes, 1989 (Papers of the 1986 Etudes Tsiganes seminar.)

Wedeck, H. E., and Wade Baskin. *Dictionary of Gipsy Life and Lore.* London: Owen, 1973

Zatta, Jane. *Gli Zingari i Roma: Una cultura ai confini.* Padua: Centro di Initiativa Democratica degli Insegnanti, 1988

2. Bibliography

Binns, Dennis. *A Gypsy Bibliography.* Manchester: Dennis Binns, 1982 (with later supplements)

Black, G. F. *A Gypsy Bibliography.* London: Constable, 1913

Collie, Michael, and Angus Fraser. *George Borrow: A Bibliographical Study.* Winchester: St Paul's Bibliographies, 1984 da Costa, Elisa Maria Lopes. *Os Ciganos: Fontes bibliograficas em Portugal.* Madrid: Presencia Gitana, 1995

Franzese, Sergio. 'Internet e gli Zingari'. In *Lacio Drom 33* (1997) nos.3-4, 40–5

Gmelch, G., and S.B. 'Ireland's Travelling People: A Comprehensive Bibliography.' *JGLS* (3rd series) 3 (1978): 159–69

Gronemeyer, Reimer. *Zigeuner in Osteuropa: eine Bibliographie zu den Ländern Polen, Tschechoslowakei und Ungarn: mit einem Anhang über ältere Sowjetische Literatur.* Munich: Saur, 1983

Hohmann, Joachim S. *Neue deutsche Zigeunerbibliographie: Unter Berücksichtigung aller Jahrgänge des 'Journal of the Gypsy Lore Society.'* Frankfurt am Main: Lang, 1992

Hovens, Pieter, and Jeanne Hovens. *Zigeuners, Woonwagenbewoners en reizenden: een bibliografie* (Gypsies, Caravan-dwellers and travellers: A Bibliography). Rijswijk: Ministry of Cultural Affairs, Recreation and Social Welfare, 1982

Leeds University. *Catalogue of the Romany Collection.* Edinburgh: Nelson, 1962

Lockwood, William and Sheila Salo. *Gypsies and Travelers in North America: an annotated bibliography.* Cheverly: Gypsy Lore Society, 1994

Neacsu, Dana. *Roma and Forced Migration: an annotated bibliography.* New York: Open Society Institute, 1997

Ortega, José. *Los Gitanos: Guia bibliográfica y estudio preliminar.* Manchester: Binns, 1987

Streck, Bernhard, ed. *Zigeuner des Schwarzmeergebiets: Eine Bibliographie.* Halle-Wittenberg: Martin Luther University, 2003

Tong, Diane. *Gypsies: A Multidisciplinary Annotated Bibliography.* New York: Garland, 1995

Tyrnauer, Gabrielle. *Gypsies and the Holocaust: A Bibliography and Introductory Essay.* 2nd ed. Montreal: Institute for Genocide Studies, 1989 (A version of this work appears in *Genocide, A Critical Bibliographic Review.* ed. Israel Charney.*3, The Widening Circle of Genocide.* [New Brunswick N.J.: Transaction, 1994])

University of Liverpool. *A Catalogue of the Gypsy Books Collected by the Late Robert Andrews Scott Macfie, Sometime Editor and Secretary of the Gypsy Lore Society.* Liverpool: University of Liverpool Press,1936

3. Demography

Arnold, Hermann. *Fahrendes Volk.* Neustadt: Pfälzische Verlaganstalt, 1980 (Revised edition of his *Randgruppen des Zigeunervolkes,* 1975.)

Brown, Marilyn R. *Gypsies and Other Bohemians: The Myths of the Artist in Nineteenth-Century France.* Ann Arbor, Mi: UMI Research Press, 1985

Charlemagne, Jacqueline. *Populations Nomades et Pauvreté.* Paris: Presses Universitaires de France, 1983

Liégeois, Jean-Pierre, and Nicolae Gheorghe. *Roma/Gypsies: A European Minority.* London: Minority Rights Group, 1995

Vaux de Foletier, François de. *Le monde des Tsiganes.* Paris: Berger-Levrault, 1983

Webb, G. E. C. *Gypsies: The Secret People.* London: Barrie Jenkins, 1960 (Reprinted Greenwood Press, 1974)

Wilson, Nerissa. *'Gypsies and Tinkers,' Gypsies and Gentlemen: The Life and Times of the Leisure Caravan.* London: Columbus Books, 1986

4. Travel and Description

Croft-Cooke, Rupert. *Moon in My Pocket.* London: Sampson, Low Marston, 1984

Fonseca, Isabel. *Bury me Standing.* London: Chatto Windus, 1995 (Also in German as *Begrabt mich Aufrecht.*)

Harvey, Denis. *The Gypsies: Waggon-time and After.* London: Batsford, 1979

McDowell, Bart. *Gypsies, Wanderers of the World.* Washington, DC: National Geographic Society, 1970

Tomasević, Nebojša, and Rajko Djurić. *Gypsies of the World.* London: Flint River Press, 1988

Ward-Jackson C., and D. Harvey. *English Gypsy Caravan.* Rev.ed. Newton Abbot, UK: David Charles, 1986

II. HISTORY

1. General

Asséo, Henriette et al. *La chiesa cattolica e gli Zingari.* Rome: Anicia, 2000

Bartolomej, Daniel. *Dejiny Romu* (History of the Gypsies). Olomouc, Czech Republic: Univerzita Palackéhou, 1994

Crowe, David. *A History of the Gypsies of Eastern Europe and Russia.* New York: St Martin's, 1994

Crowe, David, and John Kolsti, eds. *The Gypsies of Eastern Europe.* Armonk, NY: Sharpe, 1991

Djurić, Rajko. *Seobe Roma* (History of the Romanies). Belgrade: BIGZ, 1985

Fraser, Angus. *The Gypsies.* Oxford: Blackwell, 1992

Gilsenbach Reimar. *Weltchronik der Zigeuner.* Pt. 1 and 4 only. Frankfurt am Main: Lang, 1994 and 1998

Liégeois, Jean-Pierre. *Gypsies. An Illustrated History,* trans. Tony Berrett. London: Al Saqi Books, 1985 (Translation in part of Liégeois, *Tsiganes.*)

—. *Tsiganes.* Paris: La Découverte, 1983

Nicolini, Bruno. 'La chiesa cattolica e gli Zingari.' In M. Karpati, ed. *Zingari ieri e oggi.* ed. M.Karpati. Rome: Centro Studi Zingari, n.d

Vaux de Foletier, François de. *Mille ans d'histoire des Tsiganes.* Paris: Fayard, 1970

2. Early Migration and Indian Origins

Hancock I. *The Indian Origins and Westward Migration of the Roma.* Manchaca, Tx: Romany Union, 1997

Kenrick, Donald. *Gypsies, from India to the Mediterranean*. Toulouse: CDRP, 1993 (Also available in other languages.)
— *Gypsies: from the Ganges to the Thames*. (Expanded edition of the above title). Hatfield: University of Hertfordshire Press, 2004
Marushiakova, Elena and Veselin Popov. *Gypsies in the Ottoman Empire*. Hatfield: University of Hertfordshire Press, 2001
Rishi, W. R. *Roma: The Panjabi Emigrants in Europe*. Patiala, India: Punjabi University, 1976
Singhal, D. P. *Gypsies: Indians in Exile*. Meerut, India: Archana, 1982
Soulis, G. 'The Gypsies in the Byzantine Empire and the Balkans in the late Middle Ages.' *Dumbarton Oaks Papers* 15 (1961)

3. History to 1939 (excluding the Holocaust)

Alfaro, A.Gómez et al. *Deportaciones de Gitanos*. Madrid: Presencia Gitana,1999
Daniel, Bartolomej. *Geschichte der Roma in Böhmen, Mähren and der Slowakei*. Frankfurt am Main: Lang, 1998
Gilsenbach, Reimar. *Von Tschudemann zu Seemann*. Berlin: Parabolis, 2002
Haley W. 'The Gypsy Conference at Bucharest.' *JGLS* (3rd series) 13 (1934)
Opfermann, Ulrich. *Dass sie den Zigeuner-Habit ablegen: Die Geschichte der Zigeuner-Kolonien*. Frankfurt am Main: Lang, 1996

4. Genocide (1933–45)

Acković, Dragoljub. *Stradanja Roma u Jasenovcu*. Belgrade: NIGP 'ABC GLAS' DD, 1994
—. *Roma Suffering in Jasenovac Camp* (Translation of previous title). Belgrade: Stručna Kniga, 1995
Alt, Betty and Silvia Folts. *Weeping Violins*. Kirksville, Mo: Thomas Jefferson University Press, 1996
Auzias, Claire. *Samudaripen: le génocide des Tsiganes*. Paris: Esprit Frappeur, 1999
Ayass W., et al. *Feinderklärung und Prävention* Berlin: Rotbuch, 1988
Beckers, Jan, ed. *Me hum Sinthu. Ik ben Zigeuner* (I am a Gypsy). The Hague: Horus, 1980
Berenbaum, M., ed. *A Mosaic of Victims*. New York: New York University Press, 1989; London: Tauris, 1990
Bernadac, Christian. *L'Holocauste oublié: le massacre des Tsiganes*. Paris: France-Empire, 1979
Bulajić, Milan. *Ustaški zlocini genocida* (Ustashe Criminal Genocide). Belgrade: RAD, 1988
Dlugoborski, Waclaw, ed. *50-lecie zaglady Romów w KL Auschwitz-Birkenau* (50th Anniversary of the Massacre in Auschwitz-Birkenau Concentration Camp). Oswiecim: Stowarzyszenie Romów w Polsce, 1994 (In Polish and German.)
Dokumentationzentrum Deutscher Sinti und Roma. *Kinder und*

Jugendliche als Opfer des Holocausts. Heidelberg: Dokumentationzentrum, 1995

Duna, Williams A. *Gypsies: A Persecuted Race.* Minneapolis: Duna Studios, 1984

Fings, Karola, and Frank Sparing. *'z.Zt.Zigeunerlager': die Verfolgung der Düsseldorfer Sinti und Roma im Nationalsozialismus.* Cologne: Volksblatt, 1992

Fings, Karola, et al. *Einziges Land, in dem Judenfrage und Zigeunerfrage gelöst: Die Verfolgung der Roma im faschistisch besetzten Jugoslawien 1941–5.* Cologne: Rom, n.d.

Friedman, Ina. 'Bubili: A Young Gypsy's Fight for Survival.' In *The Other Victims: First-Person Stories of Non-Jews Persecuted by the Nazis.* Boston: Houghton Mifflin, 1990

Gilsenbach, Reimar. *Oh Django, sing deinen Zorn.* Berlin: BasisDruck, 1993

Günther, Wolfgang. *Ach Schwester, ich kann nicht mehr tanzen: Sinti und Roma im KZ Bergen Belsen.* Hanover: SOAK, 1990

—. *Zur preussischen Zigeunerpolitik seit 1871.* Hanover: ANS, 1985

Hackl, Erich. *Abschied von Sidonie.* Zurich: Diogenes, 1989 and 1991

Hancock, Ian. *The Pariah Syndrome.* Ann Arbor, Mi: Karoma, 1987

— 'Uniqueness, Gypies and Jews'. In *Remembering for the Future.* Theme II. Oxford: Pergamon Press, 1988. p. 2017–25

Heuss, Herbert. *Darmstadt, Auschwitz: Die Verfolgung der Sinti in Darmstadt.* Darmstadt: Verband deutscher Sinti und Roma, 1995

Heuss, Herbert, Karola Fings and Frank Sparing. *The Gypsies during the Second World War—1: From Race Science to the Camps.* Hatfield: University of Hertfordshire Press, 1997 (Also in French and German.)

Hohmann, Joachim. *Robert Ritter und die Erbe der Kriminalbiologie.* Frankfurt am Main: Lang, 1991

—. *Zigeuner und Zigeunerwissenschaft: ein Beitrag zur Grundlagenforschung und Dokumentation des Völkermords im 'Dritten Reich.'* Marburg: Guttandin Hoppe, 1980

Holy, Dušan and Ctibor Nečas. *Zalujici pišen.* Straznica: Ustav Lidové Kultury, 1993

Johansen, Jahn Otto. *Sigöynernes Holocaust.* Oslo: Cappelen. 1989 (Original Norwegian edition.)

—. *Zigenarnas Holocaust.* Stockholm: Symposion, 1990 (Swedish edition.)

Kenrick, Donald (ed.) *The Gypsies during the Second World War: In the Shadow of the Swastika.* Hatfield: University of Hertfordshire Press, 1999 (Also in other languages)

— and Gratton Puxon. *The Destiny of Europe's Gypsies.* London: Heinemann Educational, 1972 (Also in other languages)

—. *Gypsies under the Swastika.* Hatfield: University of Hertfordshire Press, 1995 (A popular edition of *Destiny of Europe's Gypsies,* also in other languages.)

Kladivová, V. *Konečná Stanice Auschwitz-Birkenau.* Olomouc, Czech Republic: Univerzita Palackého, 1994

Krausnick, M. *Wo sind sie hingekommen?* Stuttgart: Bleicher, 1995

Lessing, A. *Mein Leben in Versteck*. Düsseldorf: Zebulon, 1993

Lewy, Guenter. *The Nazi Persecution of the Gypsies*. Oxford: OUP, 2000

Lipa, Jiri. 'The Fate of Gypsies in Czechoslovakia under Nazi Domination'. In M. Berenbaum. *A Mosaic of Victims*, ed. M. Berenbaum. New York: New York University Press, 1990

Müller, Josef Muscha. *Und weinen darf ich auch nicht: Ausgrenzung, Sterilisation, Deportation*. Berlin: Parabolis, 2002

Müller-Hill, Benno. *Murderous Science: Elimination by Scientific Selection of Jews, Gypsies, et al., Germany 1933–1945*, trans. George R. Fraser. New York: Oxford University Press, 1988

Nazi Genocide in Poland Seminar (1983). Papers by Ciechanowski, Galinski, Wilczur and Zabierowski, translated and reprinted in *Lacio Drom* 20 (May, June 1984) nos. 2 and 3

Nečas, Ctibor. *Ceskoslovenstí Romové v letech 1939–1945* (Czechoslovak Gypsies in the Years 1939–45). Brno: Masaryková Univerzita, 1994

—. *Nad osudem českých Cikánu a slovenskych cikánu v letech 1939–45* (On the fate of the Czech and Slovak Gypsies). Brno: Univerzita J. S. Purkyne, 1981

—. *Nemužeme zapomenout: našti bisteras* (We cannot forget). Olomouc, Czech Republic: Univerzita Palackého, 1994

Pape, Marcus. *A Nikdo vám Nebude Verit: dokument o koncentracním tábore Lety u Písku* (Nobody will believe you: Documents about the Lety Concentration Camp). Prague: GplusG, 1997

Parcer J., ed. *Los Cyganów w KL Auschwitz-Birkenau: Das Schicksal der Sinti und Roma im KL Auschwitz-Birkenau*. Oswiecim: Stowarzyszenie Romów w Polsce,1994

—. ed. *Memorial Book. The Gypsies at Auschwitz-Birkenau*. Munich: Saur, 1993

Pedersen, F. *Skyd Zigeunerne*. Copenhagen: Carnet, 1990

Peschanski, Denis. *Les Tsiganes en France 1939–1946*. Paris: CNRS, 1994

Puxon, Grattan, and Donald Kenrick. *Bibahtale berša* (Unhappy Years). London: Romanestan, 1990 (New edition, Madrid: Presencia Gitana, 1996)

Rose, Romani, and Walter Weiss. *Sinti und Roma im 'Dritten Reich': Das Programm der Vernichtung durch Arbeit*. Göttingen: Lamuv, 1991

Sigot, Jacques. *Ces Barbelés oubliés par l'histoire*. Bordeaux: Wallada, 1994

Sijes, B. A. *Vervolging van Zigeuners in Nederland. 1940–1945*. The Hague: Martinus Nijhoff, 1979

Sonnemann, Toby. *Shared Sorrows: a Gypsy family remembers the Holocaust*. Hatfield: University of Hertfordshire Press, 2002

Thurner, E. *Nationalsozialismus und Zigeuner in Osterreich*. Vienna: Geyer, 1983

— National Socialism and Gypsies in Austria. Tuscaloosa: University of Alabama Press, 1998 (translation of above title)

Tyrnauer, G. 'A Sinto Survivor Speaks.' In *Papers from the 6th and 7th Annual Meetings of the Gypsy Lore Society*. New York: Gypsy Lore Society, 1986 (Also in *Social Education* 55 2 Feb. 1991.)

Vexler, Y. 'J'étais médecin des Tsiganes à Auschwitz.' *Monde Gitan*, 27, 1973. pp.1–10

Wagenbaar, Aad. *Settela*. Amsterdam: Arbeiderpres, 1996

Winter, Walter. *Winter Time*. Translated from German by Struan Robertson. Hatfield: University of Hertfordshire Press, 2004

Wippermann, W. *Das Leben in Frankfurt zur NS Zeit*. Frankfurt am Main: Kramer, 1986

Yoors, Jan. *Crossing*. New York: Simon Schuster, 1971

Zimmermann, M. *Rassenutopie und Genozid: Die nationalsozialistische 'Lösung der Zigeunerfrage.'* Hamburg: Christiansverlag, 1996

—. *Verfolgt, vertrieben, vernichtet: Die nationalsozialistische Vernichtung gegen Sinti und Roma*. Essen: Klartext, 1989

5. History from 1945: General

Auzias, Claire (ed.). *Les familles Rom d'Europe de l'Est*. Paris: ALIZE, n.d.

Braham, Mark. *The Untouchables: A survey of the Roma people of Central and Eastern Europe*. Geneva: United Nations High Commissioner for Refugees, 1993

Brearley, Margaret. *The Roma/Gypsies of Europe: A Persecuted People*. London: Institute for Jewish Policy Research, 1996

Engbring-Roman, Ludo and Daniel Strauss. *Aufklärung und Antiziganismus*. Seeheim: I-Verb-de, 2003

Kocze, Angela. *The Roma of Central and Eastern Europe: Legal Remedies or Invisibility*. Warsaw: OSCE, 1996

Schenk, Michael. *Rassismus gegen Sinti und Roma*. Frankfurt am Main: Lang, 1994

Svanberg, Frederik Folkeryd-Ingvar. *Gypsies (Roma) in the Post-totalitarian States*. Stockholm: Olof Palme International Center, 1995

6. History 1945–90: Eastern Europe under Communism

Anon. *Destroying Ethnic Identity. The Gypsies of Bulgaria*. New York: Human Rights Watch, 1991

McCagg, W. 'Gypsy Policy in Socialist Hungary and Czechoslovakia 1945–1989.' *Nationalities Papers* 19 no. 3 1991. 313–36

Silverman, Carol. 'Bulgarian Gypsies: Adaptation in a Socialist Context.' *Nomadic Peoples* (1987)

Sus, Jaroslav. *Cikánská otázka v CSSR*. Prague: 1961

7. History 1990: Eastern Europe after Communism

Folkeryd, Frederik, and Ingvar Svanberg. *Gypsies (Roma) in the Post-totalitarian States*. Stockholm: Olof Palme International Center, 1995

Gedlu, Mesfin (ed.) *The Roma and Europe*. Prague: Institue of International Relations, 1998 (Papers from the Stirin Conference)

Johansen, Jahn Otto. *Folket som ingen vil ha*. Oslo. Aschehoug, 1995

Mihok, Brigitte. *Vergleichende Studie zur Situation der Minderheiten in Ungarn und Rumänien (1989–1996) unter besonderer Berückuchtsichtigung der Roma*. Frankfurt am Main: Peter Lang, 1999

III. Politics

1. General

Acton, Thomas. *Gypsy Politics and Social Change: The Development of Ethnic Ideology and Pressure Politics among British Gypsies from Victorian Reformism to Romany Nationalism*. London: Routledge Kegan Paul, 1974

Adams, Barbara, Judith Okely, David Morgan, and David Smith. *Gypsies and Government Policy in England: A Study of the Travellers' Way of Life in Relation to the Policies and Practices of Central and Local Government*. London: Heinemann, 1975

Bauer, Rudolph, Josef Bura and Klaus Lang, eds. *Sinti in der Bundesrepublik: Beiträge zur sozialen Lage einer verfolgten Minderheit*. Bremen: Universität Bremen, 1984

Fienborg, Gunoula, et al. *Die Roma: Hoffen auf ein Leben ohne Angst*. Hamburg: Rowohlt, 1992

Geigges, Anita, and Bernhard W. Wette. *Zigeuner Heute: Verfolgung und Diskriminierung in der BRD*. Bornheim-Merten: Lamuv, 1979

Liégeois, Jean-Pierre, et al. *Gypsies and Travellers: Socio-Cultural Data, Socio-Political Data*. Strasbourg: Council for Cultural Co-operation, 1987

Soest, George von. *Zigeuner zwischen Verfolgung und Integration: Geschichte, Lebensbedingungen und Eingliederungsversuche*. Weinheim: Beltz, 1979

Zürcher-Berther, Maria-Luisa. *Nomades Parmi les Sédentaires: Problèmes Posés par un autre Mode de Vie*. Basel: Helbing Lichtenhahn, 1989

2. Civil Rights Movements

Acton, Thomas. 'IV Congresso Mondiale dei Rom.' In *Lacio Drom* 26 (1990) no.5

Gesellschaft für bedrohte Völker. *III. Welt-Roma-Kongress 1981*. Special double number of *Pogrom* nos. 80, 81 (1981)

Liégeois, Jean-Pierre. *Mutation Tsigane*. Brussels: Complexe, 1976

López, Sergio Rodríguez ed. *I Congreso Gitano de la Unión Europea*. Barcelona: Instituto Romanó, 1995

Puxon, Grattan. 'The First World Romani Congress.' *Race Today* (June 1971)

Rishi, W. R. ed. 'IV World Romani Congress.' Special issue of *Roma* nos. 33, 34 (July 1990/January 1991)

3. Law

American Journal of Comparative Law. 46, 2. Spring 1997 (special issue on Gypsy law)

Bergen-Schuijt, Ada van. 'Buitenlandse zigeuners en de Nederlandse wetgeving in 1977 en 1978.' *Zigeuners in Nederland* ed. Peter Hovens and Rob Dahler. pp.229–56. Nijmegen: Instituut voor Culturele en Sociale Antropologie, 1988

Danbakli, Marielle, ed. *On Gypsies: Texts issued by International Institutions.* Toulouse: CRDP. 1994 and 2001

Doering, Hans-Joachim. *Die Zigeuner im Nationalsozialistischen Staat.* Hamburg: Kriminalistik, 1964

Forrester, Bill. *The Travellers' Handbook: A Guide to the Law affecting Gypsies.* London: InterChange, 1985

Helsinki Foundation for Human Rights. *Try to Use it. It is Your Right! A practical guide on the rights of Romanies.* Warsaw: Helsinki Foundation, 1997

Morris, Rachel and Luke Clements. *Gaining Ground: Law Reform for Gypsies and Travellers.* Hatfield: University of Hertfordshire Press, 1998

Mroz, Lech. 'Gypsies and the Law.' In *Ethnologia Polona* 3 (1977): 175–83

Wolfrum, Rüdiger. 'The Legal Status of Sinti and Roma in Europe: A Case Study Concerning the Shortcomings of the Protection of Minorities.' *Annuaire Européen/European Yearbook* 33 (1986), 75–91

IV. Economy

Chignard, Louis. 'Le système économique du voyage.' *Hommes et Migrations* (June/July 1995)

Webster, Lyn and Jane Miller. *Making a Living [New Travellers].* Bristol: Policy Press, 2001

V. Society

1. Anthropology/Ethnology

Acton, Thomas and David Gallant. *Romanichal Gypsies.* UK, Hove: Wayland, 1997

Clébert, Jean-Paul. *The Gypsies,* trans. Charles Duff. London: Vista, 1963

Csaba, Pronai. *Ciganykutatas es Kulturalis Antropologia.* Budapest: Kaposvar, 1995

Dollé, Marie-Paul. *Les Tsiganes Manouches.* Sand: Dollé, 1980

Graham-Yooll, Andrew. 'In Search of Saint George.' *London Magazine* (August/September 1990): 754–88

Okely, Judith. 'Some Political Consequences of Theories of Gypsy Ethnicity', in *After Writing Culture,* ed. Alison James et al. ASA Monographs 34. London: Routledge, 1997

Rao, Aparna, ed. *The Other Nomads.* Cologne: Böhlau, 1987

Stewart, Michael. *The Time of the Gypsies.* Oxford: Westview, 1997

University of Gothenburg. *The State of Ambiguity: Studies of Gypsy Refugees.* Gothenburg. University of Gothenburg Anthropological Research Series, n.d.

Williams, Patrick. *Mariage Tsigane.* Paris: L'Harmattan, 1984

—. *Nous, on n'en parle pas: les vivants et les morts chez les Manouches.* Paris: Maison des Sciences de l'Homme, 1993

—.ed. *Tsiganes: identité, évolution.* Paris: Syros Alternatives, 1989 (Papers of the Etudes Tsiganes conference.)

Wilson, N. *Gypsies and Gentlemen: The Life and Times of the Leisure Cara-van*. London: Columbus, 1986

2. Children

Réger, Zita. 'Bilingual Gypsy Children in Hungary: Explorations in 'Natural' Second-Language Acquisition at an Early Age'. In *International Journal of the Sociology of Language* 19, 1979 (Special number on Romani Sociolinguistics)

3. Education

Acton, Thomas, and Donald Kenrick. 'From Summer Voluntary Schemes to European Community Bureaucracy: The Development of Special Provisions for Traveller Education in the United Kingdom since 1967.' *European Journal of Intercultural Studies*, 1, no. 3 (March) 1991, 47–62

Anon. *Denied a Future: The right to education of Roma/Gypsy and Traveller children in Europe*. London: Save the Children, 2001 (4 vols)

—*Education of Travelling Children*. London: Office for Standards in Education, 1996

— *School Provision for Gypsy and Traveller Children*. Brussels: European Communities, 1996.(Not the same as Liégeois et al.'s study with the same title.)

Bhopal, Kalwant. 'Gypsy Travellers and Education: Changing Needs and Changing Perceptions'. *British Journal of Educational Studies*. 52 no.1 (March 2004): 47–64

Binns, Dennis. 'History and Growth of Traveller Education'. *British Journal of Educational Studies* 38 no.3 (August 1990): 251–258

Conway, Laura. *On the Status of Romani Education in the Czech Republic*. Prague: HOST, 1996 (Also available in Czech.)

Csapo, Marg. 'Concerns Related to the Education of Romany Students in Hungary, Austria and Finland.' *Comparative Education*. 18 no. 2 (1982): 205–19.

Donzello, G. and Mirella Karpati. Un ragazzo zingaro nella mia classe. Rome: ANICIA, 1998

Dowber, Hilary. *Travellers and School: Travellers in Lewisham Talk of Their Experiences of School*. London: Lewisham Bridge, 1991

Gustafsson, Inga. *Studies of a Minority Group's Efforts to Preserve Its Cultural Autonomy*. Stockholm: IMFO-GROUP, Institute of Education, University of Stockholm, 1973

Hermann Dyba. 'The Gandhi School: Seeds of Cross-cultural Conflict'. *JGLS* (5) viii, 2. August 1998. pp.133–44

Krause, Mareile. *Verfolgung durch Erziehung: Eine Untersuchung über die jahrhundertelange Kontinuität staatlicher Erziehungsmassnahmen im Dienste der Vernichtung kultureller Identität von Roma und Sinti*. Hamburg: An der Lottbek, 1989

Kyuchukov, Hristo. *Romany Children and Their Preparation for Literacy: A Case Study*. Tilburg: University Press, 1995

Lee, Ken, and Warren, W. 'Alternative Education: Lessons from Gypsy

Thought and Practice.' In *British Journal of Educational Studies,* 1991

Liégeois, Jean-Pierre. *Minorité et scolarité: le parcours tsigane.* Toulouse: CRDP. *1998.* French version of the title below.

—. *School Provision for Ethnic Minorities: The Gypsy Paradigm.* Hatfield, University of Hertfordshire Press, 1998 (An updated version of the title below)

— S*chool Provision for Gypsy and Traveller Children: A Synthesis Report.* Luxembourg: Commission of the European Communities, 1987

Reiss, Christopher. *Education of Travelling Children.* London: Macmillan, 1975

Sangan, Jean-Claude. *Une École chez les Tziganes.* Paris: Droit et Liberté, 1974

4. Religion

Ridholls, Joe. *Travelling Home: God's Work of Revival Among Gypsy Folk.* Basingstoke, England: Marshall Pickering, 1986

Trigg, E. B. *Gypsy Demons and Divinities: The Magical and Supernatural Practices of Gypsies.* Secaucus, NJ: Citadel, 1973

5. Sociology

Falque, Edith. *Voyage et tradition: Approche Sociologique d'un sous-groupe Tsigane: les Manouches.* Paris: Payot, 1971

Giere, Jacqueline (Ed.) *Die gesellschaftliche Konstruktion des Zigeuners.* Frankfurt/Main: Campus, 1996

Lucassen, Leo. 'Under the Cloak of Begging? Gypsy occupations in Western Europe in the 19th and 20th century.' *Ethnologia Europaea* 23 (1993): 75–94

—et al. *Gypsies and other itinerant groups.* London: Macmillan, 1998

Rakelmann, Georgia. *Interethnik. Beziehungen von Zigeunern und Nichtzigeunern.* Münster: Literatur, 1988

Reyniers, Alain. 'Le rôle de la parenté dans la formation d'une communauté manouche'. In *Etudes Tsiganes* (new series) 6 (1994) no.2

San Roman, Teresa. *La diferencia inquietante: viejas y nuevas estrategias culturales de los gitanos.* Madrid: Siglo XXI, 1997

Tauber, E. 'Studi sugli Zingari: recensione critica secondo la teoria di Gerarchia di Dumont.' *Lacio Drom* 30 no. 5 (Sept-Oct. 1994): 4–55

Ward-Jackson, C., and D. Harvey. *The English Gypsy Caravan.* Newton Abbott: Charles. 1972, 1986

Wippermann, Wolfgang. *Wie die Zigeuner: Antisemitismus und Antiziganismus im Vergleich.* Berlin: Elefantenpress, 1997

Zoon, Ina. *On the Margins: Roma and Public Services in Romania, Bulgaria and Macedonia.* NY: Open Society Institute, 2001

6. Women

Chaderat, Sarge. *Variations Gitanes.* Paris: Flammarion, 1992

Cipollini, Roberta, Franca Faccioli and Tamar Pitch. 'Gypsy Girls in an Italian Juvenile Court.' In *Growing Up Good: Policing the Behaviour of Girls in Europe,* ed. Maureen Cain London: Sage, 1989

Fernández, Maria Dolores, and Carmen Bajo. *Jornadas sobre la situación de la Mujer Gitana.* Granada: Asociación de Mujeres Gitanas de Granada 'Romi,' 1990

Mossa. *La Gitane et son destin: Témoignages d'une jeune Gitane sur la condition féminine et l'évolution du monde gitan.* Textes présentés par Bernard Leblon. Paris: L'Harmattan, 1992

Okely, Judith. 'Gypsy Women: Models in Conflict.' In *Perceiving Women,* ed. Shirley Ardener. London: Malaby, 1975

Wang, Kirsten, ed. *Mujeres Gitanas ante el Futuro.* Madrid: Editorial Presencia Gitana, 1990

VI. Cultural

1. Dance

Balázs, Gusztáv. *A nagyecsedi oláh cigányok tánchagyománya* (The Dance Tradition of Vlach Gypsies in Nagyecsed). Studies in Roma (Gypsy) Ethnography, vol.3. Budapest: Magyar Néprajzi Társaság, 1995

Dunin, Elsie. 'Dance change in the Context of the Gypsy St George's Day, Skopje. Yugoslavia 1967–77.' *Papers from the 4th and 5th Annual Meetings of the Gypsy Lore Society,* ed Joanne Grumet. pp.110–20. New York: Gypsy Lore Society, 1982

2. Folk Arts

Dummett, Michael. 'The Gypsies and the Tarot.' In *Traveller Education* 17 (1982) (Reprinted from M. Dummett, *The Game of Tarot from Ferrara to Salt Lake City.* London: Duckworth, 1980)

3. Linguistics

a. General

Bakker Peter, and Cortiade, M., eds. *In the Margin of Romani: Gypsy Languages in Contact.* Holland, Amsterdam: Institute for General Linguistics, 1991

Bakker, Peter and Kyuchukov, Hristo, eds. *What is the Romani language?* Hatfield: University of Hertrfordshire Press, 2000

Boretzky, Norbert. *Burgudži.* Wiesbaden: Harrasowitz, 1993

—Romani: *Grammatik des Kalderaš-Dialekts.*Wiesbaden: Hrrasowitz, 1994

—.'Sind Zigeunersprachen Kreols?' *Akten des 1. Essener Kolloqiums über Kreolsprachen und Sprachkontakte (1985),* ed. Boretzky, Enninger and Stolz. pp. 43–70. Bochum: Brockmeyer, 1985

— and Birgit Igla. 'Romani Mixed Dialects' in Peter Baker and Maarten Mous (Eds) *Mixed Languages.* Amsterdam: IFOTT, 1994

Halwachs, Dieter and Florian Menz (Eds). *Die Sprache der Roma* (Papers from the 1997 Vienna Symposium), Klagenfurt: Drava, 1999

Hancock, Ian. 'The Development of Romani Linguistics.' In *Languages and Cultures: Studies in Honor of Edgar C. Polomé.* ed. M. Jazayery and W. Winter. Holland, Amsterdam: Mouton, 1988

—*Handbook of Vlax Romani.* Columbus: Slavica, 1995

—'Standardisation and Ethnic Defence in Emergent Non-Literate Societies: The Gypsy and Caribbean Cases'. In T. Acton and M. Dalphinis (eds). *Language, Blacks and Gypsies.* London: Whiting and Birch, 2000

Hübschmannová, Milena. 'Bilingualism among the Slovak Rom.' In *International Journal of the Sociology of Language,* 19, 1979

Kenrick, D. S. 'Report on the Warsaw Linguistics Conference.' *Roma* 33/34

Kirk, John and Baoill, Dónall P O, eds. *Travellers and their Language.* Belfast: Queen's University, 2002

Matras, Yaron. *Untersuchungen zur Grammatik und Diskurs des Romanes.* Wiesbaden: Harrassowitz, 1994

— *Romani. A Linguistic Introduction.* Cambridge: CUP, 2002

— ed. *Romani in Contact.* Amsterdam: Benjamin, 1995

— et al (eds). *The Typology and Dialectology of Romani.* Amsterdam: Benjamin, 1997

McLane, M. 'The Calo of Guadix.' In *Anthropological Linguistics* 19, 1997

Wexler, Paul. 'The case for the Relexification Hypothesis in Romani.' In Julia Horvath and Paul Wexler (eds). *Reflexification in Creole and Non-Creole Languages.* Wiesbaden: Harrassowitz, 1997

b. Grammars and description

Acton, Thomas and Kenrick, Donald, eds. *Romani Rokkeripen To-Divvus* (The contemporary English Romani dialect). London: Romanestan, 1984 (In English)

Bakker, Peter. 'Basque Romani: A Preliminary Grammatical Sketch of a Mixed Language'. In Bakker and Cortiade, *In the Margin of Romani: Gypsy Languages in Contact.* pp. 56–90. Amsterdam: Institute for General Linguistics, 1991

Boretzky, Norbert. *Romani: Grammatik des Kalderas-Dialekts mit Texten und Glossar.* Wiesbaden: Harrassowitz, 1994

Borrow, George. *Romano Lavo Lil* (Romani Wordbook). London: Murray, 1874 (Many reprints since.)

Cech, Petra, and Mozes Heinschink. *Sepečides Romani.* Munich, Unterschleissheim: Lincom Europa, 1996

Daroczi, József Choli and Feyer Levente. *Zhanes Romanes?* (Do you Know Romani?) Budapest: Cigany Nielkónvy, 1988

Friedman, Victor. 'Problems in the codification of a standard Romani literary language.' In *Papers from the 4th and 5th Annual Meetings of the Gypsy Lore Society* ed. Joanne Grumet. New York: GLS, 1985

Gjerdman, Olof and Erik Ljungberg. *The Language of the Swedish Coppersmith Gipsy Johan Dimitri Taikon.* Uppsala: Lundequist, 1963

Haarmann, Harald. *Spracherhaltung und Sprachwechsel als Probleme der interlingualen Soziolinguistik: Studien zur Gruppenmehrsprachigkeit der Zigeuner in der Sowjetunion.* Hamburg: Busje, 1980

Halwachs, Dieter. *Amaro vakeripe Roman hi: Unsere Sprache ist Roman.* Klagenfurt: Drava, 1998

— et al. *Roman: The Dialect of the Burgenland Romanies.* Munich, Unterschleissheim: Lincom Europa, 1997

Hancock, Ian. *Grammar and Dictionary of the Hungarian-Slovak Romani Language*. Manchaca, Tx: Romany Union, 1990

—.*Handbook of Vlax-Romani*. Columbus, Ohio: Slavica, 1985

Holzinger, Daniel. *Romanes (Sinti)*. Munich, Unterschleissheim: Lincom Europa, 1997

Igla, Birgit. *Das Romani von Ajia Varvara*. Wiesbaden: Harrassowitz, 1996

Iversen, R. *Secret Languages in Norway*. Pts. 1 and 2. Oslo: Norske Viden-skapsakademi, 1944, 1945

Kepeski, Krume, and Šaip Jusuf. *Romani Gramatika-Romska Gramatika*. Skopje: Naša Kniga, 1980 (Bilingual, Macedonian and Romani.)

Kochanowski, Jan. *Gypsy Studies*. 2 vols. New Delhi: International Academy of Indian Culture, 1963

Kochanowski, Vanya (Jan). *Parlons Romanes*. Bordeaux: Wallada, 1995

Macalister, R.A.S. *The Secret Languages of Ireland*. Cambridge: Cambridge University Press, 1937

Pobozniak, T. *Grammar of the Lovari Dialect*. Krakow: Polska Akademia Nauk, 1964

Russell, A. 'Scoto-Romani and Tinklers' Cant.' *JGLS* (New series) 8 (1914–15): pp.11–79

Sampson, John. *The Dialect of the Gypsies in Wales: Being the Older Form of British Romani Preserved in the Speech of the Clan of Abram Wood*. Oxford: Clarendon, 1992 (Reprint.)

Sarau, Gheorghe. *Limba Romani*. Bucharest: Ministerul Invatamantului, 1992

Smart, Bath Charles, and Henry Thomas Crofton. *The Dialect of the English Gypsies*. London: Asher, 1875

Soravia, Giulio. *Dialetti degli Zingari Italiani*. Pisa: Pacini, 1977

Tcherenkow (Cherenkov), Lev and Mozes Heinschink. *Kalderas*. Munich, Unterschleissheim: Lincom Europa, 1996

Toro, Rita Paola. 'Il Gergo dei Camminanti.' *Lacio Drom*. 27 (1991) nos 3/4

Ventzel, T. V. *The Gypsy Language*, trans. S. S. Gitman. Moscow: Nauka, 1983. (Also available in German as *Die Zigeunersprache*. [Leipzig: Enzyk-lopädie, 1980])

c. Dictionaries

Barthelemy, André. *Dictionnaire du Tsigane Kalderash*. Paris: Barthelemy, n.d.

Boretzky, Norbert and Birgit Igla. *Wörterbuch Romani-Deutsch-Englisch*. Wiesbaden: Harrassowitz, 1994

Calvet, Georges. *Dictionnaire Tsigane-Français, dialecte kalderash*. Paris: L'Asiathèque, 1993

Demeter, R. S. and P. S. *Gypsy-Russian and Russian-Gypsy Dictionary. (Kalderash dialect)*. Moscow: Russky Yazyk, 1990

Endt, Enno. *Een taal van horen zeggen: Bargoens*. Amsterdam: Scheltema Holkema, 1969

Hübschmannová, Milena et al. *Romsko-Česky a Česko-Romsky kapesní slovník*. (Czech-Romani Pocket Dictionary). Prague: Státní Pedagogické Nakladatelství, 1991

Koivisto, Viljo. *Romano-Finitiko-Angliko laavesko liin.* (Finnish-Romani-English dictionary). Helsinki: Painatuskeskus, 1994

Manush, Leksa et al. *Ciganu-Latviesu-Anglu un Latviesu-Ciganu Etimologiska Vardnica.* Riga: ABC, 1997

Messing, G. *A Glossary of Greek-Romani as spoken in Agia Varvara.* NY: Slavica, 1988

Mija, J. *Romčina do vrecka* (Slovak-Romani pocket dictionary). Košice: 1995

Rishi, W. R. *Multilingual Romani Dictionary.* Chandigarh: Roma, 1974

—. *Romani-Punjabi-English Dictionary.* Patiala: Language Department, 1981

Rostás-Farkas, György and Ervin Karsai. *Cigány-magyar, magyar-cigány szótár* (Hungarian-Romani Dictionary). Budapest: Kossuth Könyvkiadó, 1991

Sarau, Gheorghe. *Mic dictionar Rom-Roman* (Small Romani-Romanian dictionary). Bucharest: Kriterion, 1992

Uhlik, Rade. *Srpskohrvatsko-Romsko-Engleski rjecnik* (Serbocroat-Romani-English dictionary). Sarajevo: Svjetlost, 1983

Valtone, Pertti. *Suomen Mustalaiskielen etymologinen sanakirja* (Romani-Finnish-English Etymological Dictionary). Helsinki: Suomalaisen Kirjallisuuden Seura, 1972

Wolf, S. *Grosses Wörterbuch der Zigeunersprache.* Hamburg: Helmut Buske, (reprint) 1993

4. Literary Criticism

Acković D. 'Le journal Romano Lil.' *Études Tsiganes.* (new series) 7 (1995) no.1. 123–32

Binns, Dennis. *Children's Literature and the Role of the Gypsy.* Manchester: Travellers' School, 1984

Courthiade, M. 'Jeunes poètes roms de Cassove'. In *Etudes Tsiganes.* 28 (1982) no. 3 and 29 (1983) no. 1

Djurić, Rajko. 'Gli Inizi di una nuova Letteratura.' In *Zingari ieri e oggi* (Also available in German). ed. Mirella Karpati, Rome: Centro Studi Zingari, n.d. 175–9.

— *Die Literatur der Roma und Sinti.* Berlin: Parabolis, 2002

— *Roma und Sinti im Spiegel der deutschen Literatur.* Frankfurt am Main: Lang, 1995

Eder, Beate. *Geboren bin ich vor Jahrtausenden.* Klagenfurt, 1993

Kenrick, Donald and Gillian Taylor. 'The Portrayal of the Gypsy in English Schoolbooks'. In *Internazionale Schulbuchforschung.* 6 no. 1, 38–47

Kommers, Jean. *Kinderroof of Zigeunerroof* (Stealing Children or Stealing Gypsies). Amsterdam: Van Arkel, 1993

Leblon, Bernard. *Les Gitans dans la littérature espagnole.* Toulouse: France-Ibérie Recherche, 1982

Niemandt, Hans-Dieter. *Die Zigeunerin in den Romanischen Literaturen.* Frankfurt am Main: Lang, 1992

Panebianco, Candido. *Lorca e i Gitani.* Rome: Bulzoni, 1984

Reyniers A. 'Quelques élements pour une histoire des médias Tsiganes'. In
    Etudes Tsiganes (new series) 7 (1995) no.1, 141–6

5. Literature

a. Anthologies

Balić, Sait, et al. *Jaga. Vatre* (Fires). Leskovac: Napredak, 1984 (Poetry in
    Romani and Serbian)
Bari, Karoly, ed. *Tüzpiros Kígyócska/Feurige kleine rote Schlange.* Debrecen:
    Gondolat, 1985 (Romani and German editions)
—, ed. *Le vešeski dej* (The Forest Mother).
Budapest: Országos Közmövelödési Központ, 1990 (Folktales and poetry in
    Romani and Hungarian)
Binns, Dennis, ed. *Gavvered All Around* (Anthology of Poetry). Manchester:
    Manchester Travellers' Education Service, 1987
Daróczi, József Choli. *Romane Poetongi Antologia.* Budapest: Ariadne Foun-
    dation, 1995 (Poetry in Romani, English and Hungarian)
Daróczi, József Choli. *Mashkar Le Shiba Dukhades.* Roma Módszertani
    Kiadványok 1. 1994
Djurić, Rajko. *Märchen und Lieder europäischer Sinti und Roma.* Frankfurt
    am Main: Lang, 1997
Hancock, Ian et al. *The Roads of the Roma.* Hatfield: University of Hertford-
    shire Press, 1998
Lundgren, Gunilla. *Svarta rosor.* (Black roses) Stockholm: Tranen, 2003
Rostás-Farkas, György, ed. *Maladyipe. Találkozás* (Meeting). Budapest:
    Müfordítások, 1993 (Poetry in Romani and Hungarian)

b. Autobiography and Biography

Boswell, Silvester Gordon. *The Book of Boswell: Autobiography of a Gypsy,*
    ed. John Seymour. London: Gollancz, 1970
Caldaras, Hans. *I betraktarens ögon.* (In the eye of the beholder). Stockholm:
    Prisma, 2002
Cannon, Jon, and the Travellers of Thistlebrook. *Travellers: An Introduction.*
    London: Emergency Exit Arts/Interchange Books, 1989
Dawson, Robert (ed.) *Henry Dry-Bread* (Henry Sherriff). Alfreton:
    Derbyshire Gypsy Liaison Group, 1988
Delaunay, C. *Django Reinhardt.* London: Cassell, 1961
Dybing, Svein, and Terje Gammelsrud. *Raya.* Oslo: Tiden, 1983
Franz, Philomena. *Zwischen Liebe und Hass: Ein Zigeunerleben.* Freiburg:
    Herder, 1985
Joyce, Nan. *Traveller: An Autobiography,* ed. Anna Farmar. Dublin: Gill
    Macmillan, 1985
Lacková, Elena. *A false dawn.* Hatfield: University of Hertfordshire Press,
    2000 (translation of the title below)
—*Narodila jsem pod stasnou hvezdou.* (I was born under a lucky star).
    Prague: Triada, 1997
Lowe, Richard, and William Shaw, eds. *Travellers: Voices of the New Age
    Nomads.* London: Fourth Estate, 1993

Loveridge, Guy. *Biography of Bramwell 'Romany' Evens*. Huddersfield: Loveridge, 1995

Lundgren, Gunilla and Aljosha Taikon. *O Aljoša, o šiav le birevosko*. Stockholm: Podium, 1998 (Romani translation of the title below)

— *Aljosha: zigernarhövdingens pojke*. Stockholm: Bonnier Carlsen, 1998

— *From coppersmith to nurse: Alyosha, the son of a Gypsy chief*. (Bilingual edition English/Romani of the above title). Hatfield: University of Hertfordshire Press, 2003

Maximoff, Matéo. *Ce Monde qui n'est pas le mien*. Paris: Concordia, 1992

—. *Dites-le avec des Pleurs*. Paris: Concordia, 1990

—. *Routes sans Roulottes*. Paris: Maximoff, 1993

Nikolic, Miso. *Und dann Zogen wir weiter*. Klagenfurt: Drava, 1997

Nussbaumer-Moser, Jeanette. *Die Kellerkinder von Nivagl*. Basel: Friedrich-Reinhardt, 1995

Reeve, Dominic. *Smoke in the Lanes*. London: Constable, 1958 and Hatfield: University of Hertfordshire Press, 2003

—. *No Place Like Home*. London: Phoenix House, 1960

Rosenberg, Otto. *Das Brennglas*, Berlin: Eichhorn, 1998

Sampson, Anthony. *The Scholar Gypsy*. London: Murray, 1997

Sandford, Jeremy. *Gypsies*. London: Secker and Warburg, 1973

— *Rokkering to the Gorjios*. Hatfield: University of Hertfordshire Press, 2000 (new edition of the above title)

Sebková, Hana, Edita Zlanayová and Milena Hübschmannová. *Fragments Tsiganes: Comme en Haut, ainsi en Bas*. Paris: Lierre Coudrier, 1991

Skogholt, P. and K. Lilleholt. *En for hverandre: Sigoynere Milos Karol og Frans Josef forteller* (One for all. Gypsies Milos Karol and Frans Josef Relate). Oslo: Gyldendal, 1978

Stojka, C. *Reisende auf dieser Welt*. Vienna: Picus, 1992

—. *Wir leben im Verborgenen*. Vienna: Picus, 1988

Tremlett, G. *The David Essex Story*. London, 1974

Tschawo, Latscho. *Die Befreiung des Latscho Tschawo: Ein Sinto-Leben in Deutschland*. Bornheim-Merten: Lamuv, 1984

Wang, Kirsten. *The Story of Tio Carlos*. Frankfurt am Main: Lang, 1996

Whyte, Betsy. *The Yellow on the Broom: The Early Days of a Traveller Woman*. Edinburgh: Chambers, 1979

Williamson, Duncan. *The Horsieman: Memories of a Traveller 1928–1958*. Edinburgh: Canongate, 1994

Winterstein, Adolf Boko. *Zigeunerleben: Der Lebensbericht des Sinti-Musikers und Geigenbauers*, ed. Erich Renner. Frankfurt am Main: Büchergilde Gutenberg, 1988

Wood, Manfri Frederick. *In the Life of a Romany Gypsy*. London: Routledge Kegan Paul, 1979

Yates, Dora. *My Gypsy Days: Recollections of a Romany Rawnie*. London: Phoenix House, 1953

Yoors, Jan. *Crossing: A Journal of Survival and Resistance in World War II*. New York: Simon Schuster, 1971 *c. Folk Tales and Folk Poetry*

Berki, János. *Tales of János Berki Told in Gypsy and Hungarian*, ed. Veronika Görög-Karády. Budapest: MTA Néprajzi Kutató Csoport, 1985

Copoiu, Petre. *Povesti Tiganesti. Rromane Paramica* (Romany tales), ed. Gheorghe Sarau. Bucharest: Kriterion, 1996

Court, Artelia. *Puck of the Droms: The Lives and Literature of the Irish Tinkers*. Los Angeles: University of California Press. 1986

Demeter, R. *Obrazoy Folklora Cygan-Kelderarej* (Collection of the Folklore of the Kalderash Gypsies). Moscow: Nauka, 1981

Gila, Vania de. *Le Roi des Serpentes: Contes Tsiganes*. Bordeaux: Wallada, 1996

Gjerde, Lars and Knut Kristiansen. *'The Orange of Love' and Other Stories: The Rom-Gypsy language in Norway*. Oslo: Scandinavian University Press, 1994

Grabócz, Gábor, and Katalin Kovalcsik. *A Mesemondo Rostás Mihály/ Mihály Rostás: A Gypsy Story Teller*. Budapest: MTA Néprajzi Kutató Csoport, 1988

Groome, Thomas E. *Gypsy Folk-tales*. London: Hurst Blackett, 1899

Hübschmannová, Milena, ed. *Romske Pohádky* (Romany Tales). Prague: Odeon, 1973

Jagendorf, M. A., and C. H. Tillhagen. *The Gypsies' Fiddle and Other Gypsy Tales*. New York: Vanguard, 1956

MacColl, Ewan, and Peggy Seeger. *Till Doomsday in the Afternoon: The Folklore of a Family of Scots Travellers, the Stewarts of Blairgowrie*. Manchester: Manchester University Press, 1986

—. *Travellers' Songs from England and Scotland*. London: Routledge Kegan Paul, 1977

Mode, Heinz, and Milena Hübschmannová, eds. *Zigeunermärchen aus Aller Welt*. Leipzig: Insel, 1983

Nagy, Olga. *A havasi sátaro: David Gyula mesel*. (The ten [fingers] of a Gypsy of the Alps. Tales Told by Gyula David). Budapest: MTA Néprajzi Kutató Csoport, 1988

—. *Barangolásaim varázslatos tájban*. Székeludvarhely, Hungary: Erdélyi Gondolat Könyvkiadó, 1994

Osella, Carla. *Racconti Zingari*. Turin: 1978

Sampson, John, ed. *Gypsy Folk Tales*. London: Robinson, 1984 (Reprint from 1933 ed.)

Serra, Maria Joao Pavao. *Filhos da Estrada e do vento: contos e fotografias de ciganos Portugueses*. Lisbon: Assirio Alvim, 1986

Solet, Bertrand. *Mille ans de contes tsiganes*. (A thousand years of Gypsy tales) Milan: Editions Milan, 1998

Szegö, László. *Cigány bölcsödal* (Gypsy Lullaby). Budapest: Móra, 1980 (Songs in Romani with Hungarian translations)

—. *Csikóink kényesek*. Budapest: Europa Könyvkiadó, 1977 (Songs in Romani with Hungarian translations)

Taikon, Katerina, ed. *Zigenerdikter* (Gypsy Poems). Stockholm: FIB's Lyrikklubb, 1964

Tillhagen, Carl Herman. *Taikon erzählt Zigeunermärchen*. Zurich, Artemis, 1948 (Translation of *Taikon Berättar*. Stockholm: Norstedt, 1946)

Tong, Diane. *Gypsy Folk Tales*. San Diego, California: Harcourt Brace Jovanovich, 1989

Valet, Joseph. *Contes Manouches*. 2 vols. Paris: Etudes Tsiganes. 1988, 1991

Williamson, Duncan. *May the Devil Walk Behind Ye*. Edinburgh: Canongate, 1989

Williamson, Duncan and Linda. *A Thorn in the King's Foot*. London: Penguin, 1987

d. Literature in Romani

Balić, Sait, ed. *Po Tito* (About Tito). Niš, Yugoslavia: Prosveta, 1980 (Essays)

Cioaba, Luminita Mihai. *O Manuši kai Bitinel Brišind. (The Rain Merchant)*. Sibiu: Neo Drom, 1997

Dimić, Trifun, trans. *Nevo Sovlahardo Cidipe*. (New Testament). Novi Sad, Yugoslavia: Dobri Vest, 1990

Djurić, Rajko. *A i U. A thaj U*. Belgrade: Narodna Knjiga, 1982 (Poems in Romani and Serbian)

—. *Bi kheresko bi limoresko: Bez doma bez groba*. (Without a House, without a Grave). Belgrade: Nolit, 1979 (Poems in Romani and Serbian); also in French as *Sans maison sans tombe*. [Paris: L'Harmattan, 1990])

—. *Les disciples d'Héphaistos*. Troyes: Librairie Bleue, 1994 (Selected poems in French)

—. *Zigeunerische Elegien*. Hamburg: Helmut Buske, 1989 (Poems in German and Romani)

Fazli, Serbez. *Dzenetesere Bahce*. (Islamic texts) (2nd edition). Skopje: 2002

Gjunler Abdula. *Bizoagor/Eindeloos* (Without End). Oss, Holland: Gjunler, 1995 (Bilingual Dutch/Romani)

Jusuf, Šaip, trans. *Amen sam e Titoske: O Tito si Amaro. (We Are Tito's. Tito Is Ours)*. Ljubljana: Univerzum, 1978. Translation from Slovenian original *Mi smo Titoske: Tito je naš*. Ljubljana: Partizanska knjiga, 1995

Manuš, Leksa (Aleksis Belugins), trans. 'Ramayana.' In special double number of *Roma*, nos. 31–32 (July 1989/January 1990)

Maximoff, Matéo, trans. *E Nevi Vastia* (New Testament). Paris: Societé Biblique Française, 1995

— *E Nevi Viasta ai O Psalmo* (sic.) Paris: Societé Biblique Française, 2002 (new edition of the above bound in with the Psalms)

Metkov, Sulyo, trans. *Neevo Zakon* (New Testament). Sofia: Adventist, 1995

Olah, Vlado. *Khamori luludi: slunecnice* (Sunflower). Prague: MMM, 1996 (Bilingual Romani/Czech)

Papusza (Bronislawa Weiss). *Piesni Papuszy* (Songs of Papusza). (In Romani and Polish.) Wroclaw: Ossolinski, 1956

Wlislocky H., ed. *Volksdichtungen der siebenbürgischen und südungarischen Zigeuner*. Vienna: Graeser, 1890 (Romani and German) *e. Literature in Other Languages (by Gypsy Authors)*

Baltzar, Veijo. *Brännande väg* (Burning Road). Borgå: Norstedt, 1969
  (Swedish translation of the Finnish original *Polttava tie*)
Doughty, Louise. *Fires in the Dark*. London: Simon and Schuster, 2003
Jayat, Sandra. *Nomad Moons*, trans. Ruth Partington). St Albans: Brentham
  Press, 1995 (A selection from *Lunes nomades* and other collections)
Lakatos, Menyhért. *Bitterer Rauch*. Stuttgart: Deutsche Verlags-Anstalt, 1979
  (German translation of *Füstös Képek* [Budapest: Könyvkiadó])
Maximoff, Matéo. *Condamné à survivre*. Paris: Concordia, 1984
—. *La poupée de mamaliga*. Paris: Concordia, 1986
—. *Prix de la Liberté*. Paris: Concordia, 1981
—. *Savina*. Bordeaux: Wallada, 1986
—. *Septième Fille*. Paris: Concordia. 1982 (new edition)
—. *The Ursitory*. London: Chapman Hall, 1949 (Translated by Brian Vesey-
  FitzGerald from the French original *Les Ursitory*.)
—. *Vinguerka*. Paris: Concordia, 1987
Smith, Charles (Charlie). *Not All Wagons and Lanes*. Aveley: Smith, 1996
  (Poems)
—. *The Spirit of the Flame*. Manchester: Manchester Travellers Education
  Service, 1990
Spinelli, Santino, ed. *Baxtalo Drom: Felice Cammino* (Happy Road).
  Lanciano, Italy: Them Romano/ Tracce, 1995 (Anthology in Italian and
  Romani)

f. The Holocaust in Fiction

De Lint, Charles. *Mulengro: a Romany Novel*. New York: Ace Fantasy, 1985
Florence, Ronald. *The Gypsy Man*. New York: Villard, 1985
Kanfer, Stefan. *The Eighth Sin*. New York: Random House, 1978
Kosinski, Jerzy. *The Painted Bird*. New York: Bantam, 1965
Ramati, Alexander. *And the Violins Stopped Playing*. New York: Franklin
  Watts, 1986
Sagan, Françoise. (trans. Anthea Bell). *Painting in Blood*. Henley-on
  Thames: Aidan Ellis, 1988
Stancu, Zaharia. *The Gypsy Tribe*, trans. Roy MacGregor-Hastie. London:
  Abelard-Schuman, 1973

g. The Gypsy in World Literature

Cervantes, Miguel de. *The Gipsy Maid: Six Exemplary Novels*, trans. Harriet
  de Onis. Woodbury, NY: Barron's Educational, 1961
Christie, Agatha. *Endless Night*. New York: Pocket Books, 1969
Eliot, George. 'The Spanish Gypsy.' In *The Writings of George Eliot*, vol. 18.
  Boston: Houghton Mifflin, 1908 (Reprinted NY: AMS Press n.d.)
Florence, Ronald. *The Gypsy Man*. New York: Villard, 1985
Freud, Jonathan. *Uppbrott*. Stockholm: Carlssons. 1993
García Lorca, Federico. *Gypsy Ballads*, trans. Langston Hughes. *The Beloit
  Poetry Journal*, Chapbook No. 1 (Fall 1951). Beloit, WSC: Beloit College, 1951

Hugo, Victor, *Notre-Dame de Paris* (The Hunchback of Notre Dame). Various editions

Kaygili, Osman. *Cingeneler*. Istanbul: Etiman Kitabevi, 1939

Lawrence, D. H. *The Virgin and the Gipsy*. New York: Bantam, 1970 (Reprint from 1925)

Márquez, Gabriel García. *One Hundred Years of Solitude*. New York: Avon, 1971

Mérimée, Prosper. *Carmen, and other stories*, trans. Nicholas Jotcham. Oxford: Oxford University Press, 1989

Podgorets, Vidoe. *Beloto Tsiganche* (The White Gypsy). Skopje: Naša Kniga, 1988

Pushkin, Alexander. 'Gypsies.' In *The Bronze horseman: Selected Poems of Alexander Pushkin*, trans. D. M. Thomas. New York: Viking, 1982. Also in *Selected Verse*, trans. John Fennell. London: Penguin. 1994 (Reprint Bristol: Classical Press, 1991) and *Selected Works in Two Volumes*. Vol. 1. Poetry. Moscow: Progress Publishers, n.d. (The poem 'The Gypsies,' trans. by I. Zheleznova)

Scott, Walter. *Guy Mannering or the Astrologer*. London: Soho, 1987 (Reprint from 1815 ed.)

h. Music and Theatre

Acton, Thomas, Rosy Denaro and Bernard Hurley, eds. *The Romano Drom Song Book*. Oxford: Romanestan, 1971

Barrios, Manuel. *Gitanos, Moriscos y cante flamenco*. Seville: Rodríguez Castillejo, 1989

Beissinger, Margaret. *The Art of the Lautar; The Epic Tradition of Romania*. New York: Garland, 1991

Billard, Francois and Alain Antonietto. *Django Reinhardt: un géant sur son nuage*. Paris: Lieu Commun, 1993

Bobri, Vladimir. 'Gypsies and Gypsy Choruses of Old Russia.' *JGLS*. (3rd series). 40, nos. 3–4 (1961): 112–20

Brune, John. 'Songs of the Travelling People'. In *Folksongs of Britain and Ireland*, ed. Peter Kennedy. London: Cassell, 1975

Coughlan, Tim. *Now Shoon the Romano Gillie: Traditional Verse*. Cardiff: University of Wales Press, 2001

Davanellos, Nick. 'Les Tsiganes et la musique démotique grècque.' In *Tsiganes: Identité, Evolution*. Paris: Etudes Tsiganes, 1989

Davidová, Eva and Jan Zizka. *Folk Music of the Sedentary Gypsies of Czechoslovakia*. Budapest. Magyar Tudományos Akadémia, 1991

Equipo, Alfredo. *El Flamenco y los Gitanos: una aproximación cultural*. Granada: Universidad de Granada, 1978

Framework. Vol. 44 (2) Fall 2003. New York. Special edition on Gypsy Cinema.

Gillington, Alice E., and Dowsett Sellars. *Songs of the Open Road: Didakei Ditties and Gypsy Dances*. Norwood, Pa: Norward, 1973 (Reprint of 1911 ed.)

Haederli, Freddy. *Django Reinhardt. Discography*. Geneva: Haederli, 1996

Hemetek, Ursula, et al. *Romane Gila: Lieder und Tänze der Roma in Österre-*

ich. Vienna: Institut für Volksmusikforschung an der Hochschule für Musik und darstellende Kunst, 1992

Kertész-Wilkinson. *The Fair is ahead of me: The performances of a Hungarian Gypsy Slow Song.* Budapest: Hungarian Academy for Sciences, 1997

Kovalcsik, Katalin, ed. *Ernö Király's Collection of Gypsy Folk Music from Voivodina.* Budapest: Magyar Tudományos Akadémia, 1992

—. *Vlach Gypsy Folk Songs in Slovakia.* Budapest: Magyar Tudományos Akadémia, 1985

Lajtha, Lázsló. *Instrumental Music from Western Hungary: From the Repertoire of an Urban Gipsy Band,* ed. Bálint Sárosi, trans. Katalin Halácsy). Budapest: Akadémiai Kiadó, 1988

Leblon, Bernard. *El cante flamenco, entre las musicas gitanas y las tradiciones andaluzas.* Madrid: Cinterco, 1991

—. *Gypsies and Flamenco.* Hatfield: University of Hertfordshire Press, 1995 (Also available in French, German and Italian) (new edition) 2003

— *Musiques tsiganes et flamenco.* Paris: L'Harmattan, 1990

Lemon, Alaina. *Between Two Fires: Gypsy Performance and Memory from Pushkin to Postsocialism.* Durham: Duke University Press, 2000.

—'Roma (Gypsies) in the USSR and the Moscow Teatr Romen.' In *Nationalities Papers* 14, no.3, 1991. Also in Diane Tong, *Gypsies: an Interdisciplinary Reader.* New York: Garland, 1998

Leranc, Pierre. *Le Cante Jondo.* Nice: Faculté des Lettres, 1998

Liszt, Franz. *The Gypsy in Music.* (English translation of *A cziganyokrol és a czigány zenérol Magyarországon,* Pest: Heckenast, 1861). 1926

Mitchell, T. *Flamenco Deep Song.* New Haven, Ct: Yale University Press, 1995

Rasmussen, Ljerka Vidic. 'Gypsy Music in Yugoslavia: Inside the Popular Culture Tradition.' *JGLS* (5th series) 1, no. 2 (August 1991)

Sandford, Jeremy. *Songs from the Roadside: 100 Years of Gypsy Music.* Clun: Redlake, 1995

Sárosi, Bálint. *Cigányzene.* Budapest: Gondolat, 1971 (German translation, Zurich: Musikbuch, 1977: English translation, *Gypsy Music.* Budapest: Corvina, 1978)

—. 'Gypsy music.' In *The New Grove Dictionary of Music and Musicians,* ed. S. Sadie. London: Macmillan, 1980

Seton, Marie. 'The evolution of the Gypsy theatre in the USSR'. In *JGLS* (3rd series) 14: 66–72

Stanley, Denise and Rosy Burke. *The Romano Drom Song Book.* Warley, England: Romanestan, 1986

Uffreduzzi, Marcella, ed. *Canti Zigani* (2nd ed.) Genoa: Sabatelli Editore, 1973

van de Port, Mattijs. *Gypsies, Wars and other Instances of the Wild.* Amsterdam: University Press, 1998

Williams, Patrick. *Django.* Paris: Parentheses, 1998

i. Painting

Balázs, János. *A Hungarian Gipsy Artist.* Budapest: Corvina, 1977

Dzurko, Ruda. *Ich bin wieder Mensch geworden,* ed. Milena Hübschman-nová. Leipzig: Stiepenheuer, 1990

Stojka, Karl. *Ein Kind in Birkenau.* Vienna: Stojka, 1990

—. *The Story of Karl Stojka: A Childhood in Birkenau,* ed. Sybil Milton. Washington, DC: US Holocaust Memorial Council, 1992 (English edition of the previous title)

j. Photography

Carret, Marie-Jose, and Claude Carret. *Les Anges du destin.* Trézélan, France: Filigranes, 1996

Koudelka, J. *Gypsies.* London: Hale, 1975

Kuznetsova, Ljalja. *Gypsies: Free Spirits of the Open Steppe.* London: Thames Hudson, 1998

—. *Shaking the Dust of Ages. Gypsies and Wanderers of the Central Asian Steppe.* NY: Aperture, *n.d.*

Szuhay, Péter, and Antónia Barati. *Pictures of the History of the Gipsies in Hungary in the 20th century.* Budapest: Néprajzi Museum, 1993

VII. Health

Anon. *Breaking the Barriers, Romani Women and Access to Public Health Care.* Luxembourg: European Community, 2003

Hawes, Derek. *Gypsies, Travellers and the Health Service.* Bristol: Policy Press, 1997

Smith, Tracy. 'Romani (Gypsy) Women and Mainstream Health Services' in *European Journal of Women's Studies.* 4, 2 May 1997 pp.183–96.

Takman, John. *The Gypsies in Sweden: A Socio-Medical Study.* Stockholm: LiberFörlag, 1976

VIII. Country By Country Listing

Albania

Anon. *No Record of the Case: Roma in Albania.* Budapest: European Roma Rights Center, 1997

Hasluck, Margaret. 'The Gypsies of Albania' In *JGLS* (3rd series) 17 (1938) nos. 2,3,4

Austria

Cahn, Claude. *Divide and Deport: Roma and Sinti in Austria.* Budapest: European Roma Rights Center, 1996

Fennesz-Juhasz, Christiane et al. 'Sprache und Musik der Osterreichischen Roma und Sinti.' *Grazer Linguistische Studien* 46 (1996): 61–110

Mayerhofer, Claudia. *Dorfzigeuner* (2nd ed.) Vienna: Picus, 1988

—. 'Gli Ungrika Roma del Burgenland', *Lacio Drom* 21 (1985). no.6

Belgium

Cuijle, J. H. *Zigeuners in Vlaanderen.* Antwerp: Ecclesiola, n.d.

Mijs, J. 'Een bank vooruit. Onderwijs in Belgie.' *Drom* 10, no.4 (December 1995)

Tambour L. 'Roma in Belgium: Past and Present.' *Roma,* 3 no. 1 (January 1977)

Bosnia

Anon. *The Non-Constituents, Rights Deprivation of Roma in Post-Genocide Bosnia and Herzegovina.* Budapest: ERRC, 2004

Bulgaria

Anon. *Children of Bulgaria: Police Violence and Arbitrary Confinement.* New York: Human Rights Watch, 1996

—. *Increasing Violence against Roma in Bulgaria. (*pamphlet) New York: Human Rights Watch, 1994

—. *Police violence against Gypsies. (*pamphlet). New York: Human Rights Watch, 1993

Marushiakova, Elena and Veselin Popov. *Tsiganite v Balgaria.* Sofia: Klub 90, 1993 (Translated into English as *Gypsies (Roma) in Bulgaria.* Frankfurt am Main: Lang, 1997)

Silverman, Carol. 'Bulgarian Gypsies: Adaptation in a Socialist Context.' *Nomadic Peoples,* 21–2 (1986): 51–62

Tomova, Ilona. *The Gypsies in the Transition Period.* Sofia: International Center for Minority Studies, 1995

Croatia

Hrvatić, N., ed. 'Education and Upbringing of Romany Children in Croatia.' Special edition of the journal *Romano Akharipe* (1994)

Cyprus

Kenrick, Donald, and Gillian Taylor. 'Gypsies of Cyprus'. *Roma* 24 (January 1986)

Mene, Asik. 'Interview'. Translation from *Kibris* in *Drom* 10 (1995) no. 4

Czech Republic

Anon. *Roma in the Czech Republic: Foreigners in Their Own Land.* New York: Human Rights Watch, 1996

Conway, Laura. *Report on the Status of Romani Education in the Czech Republic.* Prague: HOST, 1996

Czechoslovakia

Anon. *A Special Remedy* (Roma in Schools). Budapest: ERRC, 1999

—*Struggling for Ethnic Identity: Czechoslovakia's endangered Gypsies.* New York: Human Rights Watch, 1992

Davidová, Eva. 'The Gypsies in Czechoslovakia.' *JGLS* (3rd series). 69 nos. 3–4 (1970): 84–97 and 70 nos. 1–2, (1971): 39-54

Guy, Will. 'Ways of Looking at Roma: The Case of Czechoslovakia'. In Diane Tong, *Gypsies: an Interdisciplinary Reader*. New York: Garland, 1998

Hübschmannová, M. 'Birth of Romani Literature in Czechoslovakia'.*Cahiers de Littérature Orale*, 30 (1991): 91–98

Kostelancik, David. 'The Gypsies of Czechoslovakia: Political and Ideological Considerations in the Development of Policy.'*Studies in Comparative Communism* 22 no.4 (1989): 307–21

Ulc, Otto. 'Communist National Minority Policy: The Case of the Gypsies in Czechoslovakia.' In *Soviet Studies* 20 no.4 April 1969. pp.421–43

—. 'Integration of the Gypsies in Czechoslovakia'. *Ethnic Groups* 9, no. 2 (1991): 107–17

Denmark

Albert, Jorn. *Sigøjnere er et folk.* (Gypsies are a People). Copenhagen: Forum, 1983

Anderson, K.*Sigøjnere* Beta Bog Munksgaard, 1971

Bartels E. and B. Brun. *Gypsies in Denmark.* Copenhagen: Munksgaard, 1943

Enevig, Anders. *Sigøjnere i Danmark.* Copenhagen: Fremad, 1969

—. *Tatere og rejsende* (Nomads and Travellers). Copenhagen: Fremad, 1965

Egypt

Hanna, Nabil Sohbi. *Die Ghajar: Zigeuner am Nil.* Munich: Trickster, 1993

England

Birtill, Angie. *Rights for Travellers.* London: Irish Women's Centre, 1995

Crawley, Heaven. *Moving Forward: the provision of accommodation for Travellers and Gypsies.* London: IPPR, 2004

Dodds, Norman N. *Gypsies, Didikois and Other Travellers.* London: Johnson, 1966

Kenrick, Donald, and Sian Blakewell. *On the Verge: The Gypsies of England.* London: Runnymede Trust, 1990. (For new edition entitled *Moving On* see under United Kingdom below)

Mayall, David. *English Gypsies and State Policies.* Hatfield: University of Hertfordshire, 1996

—. *Gypsies-Travellers in Nineteenth-Century Society.* Cambridge: Cambridge University Press, 1988

Morris, Rachel and Luke Clements. *At what Cost? The economics of Gypsy and Traveller encampments.* Bristol: Policy Press, 2002

Sibley, David. *Outsiders in Urban Society.* Oxford: Blackwell, 1981

Finland

Grönfors, Martti. *Blood Feuding among Finnish Gypsies.* Helsinki: University of Helsinki Department of Sociology, 1977

France

Vaux de Foletier, François. *Les bohémiens en France au 19e siècle*. Paris: Lattès, 1981
— *Les Tsiganes dans l'Ancienne France*. Paris: Connaissance du Monde, 1981

Germany

Geigges, A., and Wette, B. *Zigeuner heute*. Bornheim-Merten: Lamuv, 1979
Hohmann, Joachim, ed. *Sinti und Roma in Deutschland*. Frankfurt am Main: Lang, 1995
Hohmann, Joachim. *Verfolgte ohne Heimat. Geschichte der Zigeuner in Deutschland*. Frankfurt am Main: Lang, 1990
Lucassen, Leo. *Die Zigeuner: die Geschichte eines polizeilichen Ordnungsbegriff in Deutschland 1700–1945*. Cologne-Weimar-Vienna: Böhlau, 1996
Margalit, Gilad. *Antigypsyism in the Political Culture of the Federal Republic of Germany*. Jerusalem: Hebrew University Vidal Sassoon Centre for the Study of Antisemitism, 1996
Martins-Heuss, Kirsten. *Zur mythischen Figur des Zigeuners in der Deutschen Zigeunerforschung*. Frankfurt am Main: Hagg Herchen, 1983
Opfermann, Ulrich. *Dass sie den Zigeuner-Habit ablegen*. Frankfurt am Main: Lang, 1996
Rinser, Luise. *Wer Wirft den Stein? Zigeuner sein in Deutschland: eine Anklage*. Stuttgart: Weitbrecht, 1985
Schenk, Michael. *Rassismus gegen Sinti und Roma*. Frankfurt am Main: Lang, 1994
Tebbutt, Susan (Ed.). *Gypsies in German-speaking Society and Literature*. New York: Berghahn Books, 1998

Greece

Anon. *Cleaning Operations: Excluding Roma in Greece*. Budapest: ERRC, 2003
Bereris, Petros. 'Information File. Greece.' *Interface*, 13 (February, 1994)

Hungary

Anon. *Rights Denied: The Roma of Hungary*. New York: Human Rights Watch, 1966
—. *Struggling for Ethnic Identity. The Gypsies of Hungary*. New York: Human Rights Watch, 1993
Hajdu, Mihaly. 'Gypsies, 1980'. *Hungarian Digest* 6 (1980): 28–34
Kállai, Emo. *The situation of the Roma in Hungary*. (brochure). Budapest: Ministry of Foreign Affairs, 2000
Karsai, László. *A Cigánykérdés Magyarorzágon 1919–1945: út a Cigány holocausthoz*. Budapest: Scientia Hungariae, 1992
Kovats, Martin. 'The Roma and Minority Self-Governments in Hungary'. *Immigrants and Minorities*. 15, no. 1 (March 1996)
Pradka, Peter. *Self-Government in Hungary: The Gypsy/Romani Experience*. Princeton, NJ: PER, 1998

Stewart, Michael et al. *Roma Migration*. Budapest: Hungarian Academy of Sciences, 2002

Szabó, György. *Die Roma in Ungarn*. Frankfurt am Main: Lang, 1991

Vekerdi, Jozef. 'The Gypsies and the Gypsy Problem in Hungary.' *Hungarian Studies Review*. 15, no.2 (1988): 13–26

Wagner, Francis 'The Gypsy Problem in Postwar Hungary'. *Hungarian Studies Review* 14, no.1 (1987): 33–43

India

Olsson, Torvald and Lukas Werth. *Sjakalerna: Nomader i kastsamhällets utkant*. (Jackals: Nomads on the edge of caste society). Stockholm: Fjärde Världen, 1990

Robertson, Miriam. *Snake Charmers*. Jaipur: Illustrated Book Publishers, 1998

Ireland

Gmelch, George. *The Irish Tinkers: The Urbanization of an Itinerant People*. Menlo Park, Ca: Cummings, 1977

McCann May, et al., eds. *Irish Travellers, Culture and Ethnicity*. Belfast: Institute of Irish Studies, 1994 (Papers from a conference in 1991)

Paris, C., et al. *A Review of Policies affecting Travellers in Northern Ireland*. Coleraine: Magee College, 1995

Israel

Williams, Allen (ed.) *The Dom of Jerusalem*. Cyprus: Dom Research Center, 2001

Italy

Luciani, A. 'Zingari a Roma nel 1700.' *Lacio Drom*, 31, no. 6 (November–December, 1995)

Martelli, Vladimyr. 'Gli Zingari a Roma dal 1525 al 1680.' *Lacio Drom*, 32, nos. 4–5 (August–October, 1996)

Piasere, Leonardo, ed. *Italia Romaní*. Rome: CISU di Colamartini Enzo, (parts 1 and 2) 1996 and 1999

Viaggio, Giorgio. *Storia degli Zingari in Italia*. Rome: Anicia, 1998

Luxembourg

Reynier, Alain. 'Luxembourg. The presence of an invisible population'. In *Interface* 29, February 1998

Macedonian Republic

Anon. A Pleasant Fiction: *The Human Rights Situation of Roma in Macedonia*. Budapest: European Roma Rights Center, 1998

Barany, Zoltan. 'The Romas in Macedonia.' *Ethnic and Racial Studies* 18 (1995): 515–31

Friedman, Victor. 'Language Policy and Language Behavior in Macedonia:

Background and Current Events'. In *Language Contact: Language Conflict*, ed. Eran Fraenkel and Christina Kremer. New York: Peter Lang, 1993. pp.73–99

Netherlands

Buis, Hans. 'Zigeuners gezien? Haal dan de was binnen! (Seen Gypsies? Then take the washing inside!) In Jan Dubleman et al. *Vreemd Gespuis*. Amsterdam: Anne Frank Stichting, 1987

Cottaar, Annemarie. *Kooplui, Kermisklanten en ander Woonwagenbewoners*. Amsterdam: Het Spinhuis, 1996

Cottaar, Annemarie, et al. 'The Image of Holland: Caravan Dwellers and Other Minorities in Dutch Society'. *Immigrants and Minorities* 2, no. 1 (March 1992)

—. *Mensen van de Reis, Woonwagenbewoners en Zigeuners in Nederland 1868–1995*. Zwolle: Waanders, 1995

Hovens P., and R. Dahler eds. *Zigeuners in Nederland*. Nijmegen: Instituut voor Culturele en Sociale Antropologie, 1988

Lucassen, Leo. *En Men noemde hen Zigeuners*. Amsterdam: Stichting IISG/SDU, 1990

Schaap, Dick and Wim Bont. *Het volk van Koka Petalo*. Amsterdam: ABC, 1965

Tanja, Jaap. 'Een zeldzaam volk geneegen om te dwaalen'. In Jan Dubleman et al. *Vreemd Gespuis*. Amsterdam: Anne Frank Stichting, 1987

Van Kappen, O. *Geschiedenis der Zigeuner in Nederland*. Assen: Van Gorcum. 1965

Willems, Wim and Leo Lucassen. 'A Silent War: Foreign Gypsies and Dutch Government Policy, 1969–89'. *Immigrants and Minorities* 2, no. 1 (March 1992)

Norway

Flekstad, K. *Omstreifere og sigøynere* (Travellers and Gypsies). Oslo: Aschehoug, 1949

Hanisch, Ted. *Om sigøynersporsmalet* (On the Gypsy Question). Oslo: Institutt for Samfunnsforskning, 1973

Midboe, O. *Eilert Sundt og fantesaken* (Eilert Sundt and the Nomad Question). Oslo: Universitets Forlaget, 1968

Rydberg, Roger. *Uten Livets Rett*. (Without rights). Asen. Dokumentarforlaget, 1994

Schlüter, Ragnhild. *De Reisende* (The Travellers). Oslo: Gyldendal, 1993

Poland

Anon. *The Limits of Solidarity*. Budapest: ERRC, 2002

Ficowski, Jerzy. *Cyganie na polskich drogach*. Krakow: Wydawnictwo Literackie, 1985

—. *Gypsies in Poland: History and Customs*. Warsaw: Interpress, 1991 (Also in German and Polish)

—. *Wieviel Trauer und Wege*. Frankfurt am Main: Lang, 1992

Postolle, Angele. 'Who are the Romanian Roma Living in Poland?' *CPRSI Newsletter*, 3 no. 3 (1997)

Portugal

Coelho, Francis Adolpho. *Os Ciganos de Portugal: com um estudo sobre o calao*. Lisbon Imprensa Nacional, 1892 (reprinted 1995)

Nunes, Olimpio. *O Povo Cigano*. Porto: Livrari Apostolado da Imprensa, 1981

Serra, Joao Pavao. *Filhos da Estrada e do Vento: contos e fotografias de Ciganos Portugeses*. Lisbon: Assirio Alvim' 1986

Romania

Achim, V. *Tiganii in istoreia Romaniei*. Bucharest: Editura Enciclopedica, 1998

Anon. *Destroying Ethnic Identity: The Persecution of the Gypsies in Romania*. New York: Human Rights Watch, 1991

—. *Lynch Law: Violence against Roma in Romania*. New York: Human Rights Watch, 1994

—. *Sudden Rage at Dawn: Violence against Roma in Romania*. Budapest: European Roma Rights Center, 1996

Beck, Sam. 'Ethnicity, Class and Public Policy: Tiganii/Gypsies in Socialist Romania.' In *Papers from the Vth Congress of Southeastern European Studies. Belgrade*, ed. K. K. Shangriladze and E. Townsend. pp. 19–38. Columbus, Ohio: Slavica, 1984

—. 'The Origins of Gypsy Slavery in Romania'. In *Dialectical Anthropology*, no. 14 (April 1989): 53–61

—. 'Racism and the Formation of a Romani Ethnic Leader (Gheorghe Nicolae).' In *Perilous States*, ed. G. Marcus. pp.165–91. Chicago: University Press, 1993

Block, Martin. *Die materielle Kultur der rumänischen Zigeuner*. Revised J. Hohmann. Frankfurt am Main: Lang, 1991

Nicolae, Gheorghe. 'Origin of Roma's Slavery in the Romanian Principalities.' *Roma* 7, no. 1 (1983): 12–27

Potra, George. *Contribiuni la istoricul tiganilor din Romania*. Bucharest, Fundatia Regele Carol I, 1939

Remmel, Franz. *Die Roma Rumäniens*. Vienna: Picus, 1993

Russia

Demeter, Nadezhda and others. *Istoria Tsigan*. Voronezh: Russian Academy of Science, 2000

Gilsenbach, Reimar. 'Roma in Russia: A Community Divided.' *Transition. Open Media Research Institute Reports* 1, no. 4. Prague: OMRI, (March 1995)

Gilsenbach, Reimar, with Ljalja Kuznetsova. *Russlands Zigeuner*. Berlin: BasisDruck, 1994

Scotland

Duncan, Tom. *Neighbours' views on official sites for travelling people.* Glasgow: Planning Exchange, 1996

Gentleman, Hugh, and Smith, Susan. *Scotland's Travelling People: Problems and Solutions.* Edinburgh: HMSO, 1971

MacRitchie, D. *Scottish Gypsies under the Stewarts.* Edinburgh: Douglas, 1894

Neat, Timothy. *The Summer-Walkers: Travelling People and Pearl Fishers of the Highlands of Scotland.* Edinburgh: Canongate, 1996

Secretary of State's Advisory Committee. *Scotland's Travelling People: Reports.* Edinburgh: HMSO/Scottish Office, 1974 onwards

Serbia

Vojvodanska Muzej. *Etnoloska Grada o Romima: Ciganima i Vojvodine.* Novi Sad: Vojvodanska Muzej, 1979

Slovakia

Anon. *Time of the Skinheads: Denial and Exclusion of Roma in Slovakia.* Budapest: European Roma Rights Center, 1997

Horváthová, Emilia. *Cigáni na Slovensku.* (Gypsies in Slovakia). Bratislava: Vydavatelstvo Slovenskej Akadémie Vied, 1964

Mann, Arne. *Neznami Romovia* (The Unknown Romany Story). Bratislava: Ister Science Press, 1992

Slovenia

Strukelj, Paula. *Romi na Slovenskem.* Ljubljana: Cankarjeva Zalozba, 1980

Spain

Alfaro, Antonio. *The Great Gypsy Round-Up.* Madrid: Presencia Gitana, 1993 (Also available in French, Italian, Romanian and Spanish.)

Calvo Buezas, Tomás. *España racista? Voces payas sobre los Gitanos.* Barcelona: Anthropos, 1990

Garcia, José Manuel Fresno. 'La situation sociale de la communauté gitane d'Espagne.' *Ethnies* 8 (1993), no.15

Leblon, Bernard. *Les Gitans d'Espagne: prix de la différence.* Paris: Presses Universitaires de France, 1985

—. *Los gitanos de España: el precio y el valor de la diferencia.* Barcelona: Gedisa, 1987 (Spanish translation of previous title)

Leon-Ignacio. *Los Quinquis.* Barcelona: Ediciones 29, 1974

Lopez de Menses, A. *La inmigración gitana en España en el siglo XV.* Madrid: Martínez Ferrandi Archivero, 1968

Luna, José Carlos de. *Gitanos de la Bética.* Madrid: EPESA, 1951

McLane, M. *Proud Outcasts.* Cabin John, MD: Carderock, 1987

—. *Los Gitanos españoles.* Madrid: Castellote, 1977

—. *La Inquisición y los Gitanos.* Madrid: 1988

Ramírez Heredia, Juan de Dios. *En Defensa de los Míos: Qué sabe Vd. de los*

Gitanos? Barcelona: Ediciones 29, 1985

—. *Nosotros los Gitanos.* Barcelona: Ediciones 29, 1972

—. *Vida Gitana.* Barcelona: Ediciones 29. 1985

Sánchez Ortega, Maria Helena. *Dieser wichtige Zweig der Landesordnung: Zur Geschichte der Zigeuner in Spanien.* Frankfurt am Main: Lang, 1998

Yoors, Jan. *The Gypsies of Spain.* New York: Macmillan, 1974

Sweden

Heymowski, A. *Swedish Travellers and Their Ancestry.* Uppsala: Almquist Wiksell, 1969

Marta, C. *A Group of Lovara Gypsies Settle Down in Sweden.* Stockholm: INFO-Gruppen, 1979

Taikon, Katerina. *Förlat att vi stör.* (Excuse the Disturbance). Stockholm: 1970

Tillhagen, Carl-Hermann. *Zigenarna i Sverige.* Stockholm: Natur Kultur, 1965

Trankell. A. *Kvarteret Flisan* (The Flisan district). Stockholm: Nordstedt Soner, 1973

Switzerland

Thodé-Studer, Sylvia. *Les Tsiganes suisses: la marche vers la reconnaissance.* Lausanne: Réalités Sociales, 1987

Turkey

Rooker, Marcia. 'Field Report from Turkey'. *Roma Rights* (Spring 1997): 33–5

Ukraine

Anon. *The Misery of Law: The Rights of Roma in the Transcarpathian Region of Ukraine.* Budapest: European Roma Rights Center 1997

United Kingdom

Acton, Thomas, and David Gallant. *Romanichal Gypsies.* Hove: Wayland, 1997

Hawes, Derek, and Barbara Pérez. *The Gypsy and the State* (2nd ed.) Bristol: Policy Press, 1996

Kenrick, Donald and Colin Clark. *Moving On: The Gypsies and Travellers of Britain.* Hatfield: University of Hertfordshire Press, 1998

Ministry of Housing and Local Government. *Gypsies and Other Travellers.* London: HMSO, 1967

Okely, Judith. *The Traveller-Gypsies.* Cambridge: Cambridge University Press, 1983

Vesey-Fitzgerald, Brian. *The Gypsies of Britain.* Newton Abbott: David Charles, 1973

Wales

Davies, J. Glyn. 'Welsh sources for Gypsy History. *JGLS* (3rd series) 9, 64–86

Jarman A.O.H., and Eldra. *Y Sipsiwn Cymreig* . Cardiff: University of Wales Press, 1979

— *The Welsh Gypsies*. Cardiff: University of Wales Press, 1991 (Rev. English ed. of previous title.)

Yugoslavia

Vukanović, Tatomir. *Romi (Tsigani) u Jugoslaviji*. Vranje, Yugoslavia: Nova Jugoslavia, 1983

IX. Press

These lists should not be seen as reflecting in any way the quality of those for which no address is given. Some of the latter may have ceased publication.

1. Learned Journals and Newsletters

Études Tsiganes. 59 rue de l'Ourcq, Paris 75019 France. (French)
Journal of the Gypsy Lore Society (JGLS). The fifth series is published as
    Romani Studies from the United States. 5607 Greenleaf Road, Cheverly,
    Md 20785. (English)
Roma. 3290/15–D, Chandigarh 160 015, India. (English)
Roma Rights. European Roma Rights Center. PO Box 906/93, Budapest
    1386, Hungary. (English and Romani)

2. Periodical Press

This list includes only magazines appearing since 1945. Pre-1939 magazines are mentioned in the dictionary under the respective countries and 'PRESS.' Most of the titles below are bilingual, in the majority language of the country and Romani.

Amaro Dives/Ditet Tona – Albania
Amaro Drom – Budapest, Hungary, journal of Pralipe
Amaro Gao – Valencia, Spain
Amaro Lav – Czech Republic
Asul de Trefla – Romania; organ of the Democratic Union of the Gypsies
Aven Amentza – Bucharest, Romania; organ of the Cultural Association
    Aven Amentza
CPRSI Newsletter – Warsaw; English and Romani
Cigányfurö – Budapest, Hungary; edited by Attila Balogh
Diálogo Gitano – Madrid, Spain; Catholic
Divano Romano – Romania
Gazeta Romilor – Romania
Drom Dromendar – Sliven, Bulgaria
Glaso el Romengo – Romania; first issue numbered 15
(The) Hub – UK. Gypsy Council
Informaciaqo Lil – published by Romani Baxt for the Romani Union
    (Romani and English)
Jekhetane – Spolu (Together) – Slovakia
Kethano Drom (Common Road) – Budapest, Hungary
Khamutne Dive Suncani Dani (Sunny Days) – Železnik, Yugoslavia

Krlo e Romengo (*Voice of the Romanies*) – Yugoslavia

Lacho Lav – Czech Republic. Ministry of Social Welfare

Loli Phabai – UK and Greece (three numbers only)

Lungo Drom – Szolnok, Hungary

Nachin News – Scotland

Neo Drom – Romania

Nevi Yag – Belgium. Comité international catholique pour les Tsiganes

Nevipe – Slovakia

Nevipens Romani – Barcelona. Union Romani of Spain. Spanish; occasional numbers in Romano-Caló

Nevo Drom. Novi Put – Croatia. Romapastorat

Nicovala – Romania

Nov Put (previously *Romano Esi* and *Nevo Drom)* – Bulgaria

Ocicat Romengo – Romania

Opre Roma – Australia

Patrin – Holland/Slovakia. Romani/English

Phralipe – Budapest

Pomezia – Barcelona; Secretariado Gitano

Roma – Slovakia

Romano Barvalipen – Sofia, Bulgaria

Romano Boodos – Finland, religious magazine

Romano Centro – Vienna. Romani and German

Romano Drom – UK, organ of the Gypsy Council then independent (under the editorship of Jeremy Sandford), finally organ of the National Gypsy Council

Romano Džaniben – Prague (Czech and Romani)

Romano Glendalos – Czech Republic

Romano Ilo – Sofia, Bulgaria

Romano Kurko – Brno, Czech Republic

Romano Lil- Romske Novine – Belgrade, Yugoslavia

Romano Lil – Berlin

Romano Lil – Slovakia

Romano Nevijpe – Murska Subota, Yugoslavia

Romipen – Bratislava, Slovakia

Romnews – Hamburg. Roma National Congress

Romologija – Voivodina, Serbia

Romska Revue – Bratislava, Slovakia

Rrom p-o Drom – Bialystok, Poland

Šatra (Tent) – Romania

Šatra libera – Romania

Scharotl (Caravan) – Organ of the Swiss Travellers

Studii Romani – Sofia (Bulgarian/English)

Tchatchipen – Barcelona

Te aves bahtalo – Romania

Thèm Romanó – Lanciano, Italy

Traveller Education – National Gypsy Education Council, UK

Tsiganologische Studien. Giessen. (German); successor to *Giessener Hefte*

für Tsiganologie 1984–1960.)
Vie et Lumière – Paris, organ of the Gypsy Pentecostal Church
Voix mondiale tzigane. Paris. Comité International Tsigane
Zigenaren – Sweden
Zirickli – Finland

X. Websites

Association of Gypsies/Romani International
http://www.niia.net/~rom/
http://www.gypsies.net

European Roma Rights Center
http://www.errc.com

Gypsy Lore Society
http://gypsynet/gls/
Gypsynet (Rroma Yekhipe)
http://www.rroma.com/

Indian Institute of Romani Studies
http://www.aloha.net/-bohem/rishroma.html

Patrin
http://www.geocities.com/Paris/5121/

Roma National Congress
htttp://www.romnews.com

RRPP
http://www.osi.hu/roma

Unión Romaní (Spain). http://www.unionromani.org
http://www.qsystems.es/gipsy/

XI. Discographies

A first step into the rich world of recorded Gypsy music can be made by consulting the review pages of the British magazines *Folk Roots* and *Songlines* as well as the book *World Music: The Rough Guide* (London: Rough Guides, 1994). Discographies have also appeared in *Journal of the Gypsy Lore Society* and *Études Tsiganes* (1994 no.1)

About the Authors

Donald Kenrick has retired from a career as an organiser of adult education during which he pioneered basic education courses for Gypsies and training for those working with them. He was at one time Honorary Secretary of the UK Gypsy Council and has been an official interpreter for the Romani language at many international meetings. He has written extensively on the history, languages and social situation of the Gypsies/Romanies. His latest book is *Gypsies: From the Ganges to the Thames* (University of Hertfordshire Press 2004). Honours include the Premio Hidalgo and awards from the Hiroshima Foundation and Bulgarian Romani Baxt.

Clare Paul is a native Londoner and a registered Blue Badge guide. She has a degree in Art History from the University of Manchester. She has worked in many fields including education and research, most recently contributing to the publications *Moving On* and *Gypsies: From the Ganges to the Thames.* Clare Paul will be curating an exhibition of international Roma Art for the University of Hertfordshire.